# FROM CRISIS TO CRISIS

# FROM
# CRISIS TO CRISIS

*American College Government*
1636–1819

JURGEN HERBST

Harvard University Press
*Cambridge, Massachusetts
and London, England*
1982

*Library of Congress Cataloging in Publication Data*

Herbst, Jurgen.
    From crisis to crisis.

    Includes bibliographical references and index.
    1. Universities and colleges—United States—History.
2. Degrees, Academic—United States—History.  I.  Title.
LA226.H386       378.73       81-4152
ISBN 0-674-32345-9           AACR2

*For Susan*

# CONTENTS

Preface   ix
Acknowledgments   xv

I. SCHOOLS OF THE REFORMATION IN THE NEW WORLD                    1

   1. A Provincial School in the Wilderness   5
   2. Harvard College: The New World's Oldest Corporation   17
   3. The College of William and Mary   29
   4. Connecticut's Collegiate School   38
   5. The Triumph of External Government   48

II. CULTURAL PLURALISM AND THE GREAT AWAKENING                   63

   6. Yale College and the Awakening   66
   7. College Founding in the Middle Colonies   82
   8. A College for New York   97
   9. Autocracy in Connecticut and Pluralism in Rhode Island   114
  10. The American Provincial College   128

III. FROM THE REVOLUTION TO THE DARTMOUTH COLLEGE CASE           143

  11. War and Revolution   148
  12. The Birth of the American University   159
  13. The People versus the Colleges   174
  14. The Private Colleges   189
  15. State Colleges and Universities   206
  16. Novus Ordo Collegiorum   219
  17. Dartmouth College: The Supreme Court Speaks   232

  *Appendix A:* The Fifty-Two Degree-Granting Institutions of
    Higher Learning Chartered between 1636 and 1820   244
  *Appendix B:* Number of Earned First Degrees Awarded by
    American Colleges and Universities, 1642-1820   254
  Notes   255
  Index   295

# PREFACE

This book had its inception in the days and months of unrest and up-heaval during the Vietnam war. While students were battling police on campus, questions of student and faculty rights and the nature of our academic institutions were debated in faculty meetings, legislative assemblies, and courts of law. Late in 1967, I prepared a statement for use in court on the relationship between civil and academic jurisdic-tion. I then asked whether what was traditionally known as the autonomy of the university protected an administration or faculty from judicial interference, and whether, conversely, it denied the protection of the courts to students subject to disciplinary action. These questions provided the starting point for my investigation of the legal and governmental history of the American college and university. In the pages that follow I present the results of my search as they relate to the first period in the history of American higher education, from the founding of Harvard College to the decision of the United States Supreme Court in the Dartmouth College case.

Little has been written on institutional, governmental, and legal developments in the history of American higher education. The literature in the field does not compare in quantity or quality with the writings on the social and intellectual history of our colleges. Worse yet, there are many serious misconceptions.

Frequently authors write from a partisan point of view. They protest government by external boards of trustees in order to promote, in the name of academic freedom, a concept of faculty self-government that, they claim, governed universities in the past. They foster the notion that academic government by boards of nonacademics was an American invention, a notion based on the mistaken assumption that

ix

the governmental roots of the American college grew solely in English soil. There is little understanding of the differences in law, structure, and government between colleges and universities in England and those on the continent. These differences are ignored or defined as merely semantic. The European concept of the public realm as the joint sphere and responsibility of secular and ecclesiastic authority, with the college as an instrument of that joint authority to foster the commonweal through the education of future governors, is not sufficiently understood. In not acknowledging the continuing viability of the European concept of the unity of *regnum*, *sacerdotium*, and *studium* in the colonies as the unity of established state, church, and college, writers on college historiography have fostered the erroneous impression — repeated again and again in textbooks — that American colleges from their beginnings in 1636 were similar to the English and continental colleges founded by private bequests.

Studies of individual institutions provide what little is known of the legal and institutional development of American colleges, and few attempts at comparative analysis or detailed probing of European antecedents exist. The general assumption has been that institutional growth and legal developments were shaped primarily by English tradition and by conditions peculiar to the American colonies and states.

This prevailing view of American colonial colleges as private and primarily religious institutions has obscured their status as civil corporations. It has made it difficult to see the importance of the Great Awakening and the growing religious heterogeneity of the colonial population in strengthening public supervision of the colleges during the eighteenth century. It has also made it difficult to appreciate the meaning of occasional rebellions against joint secular-ecclesiastic government, such as those of Increase Mather in the 1690s at Harvard and of Thomas Clap in the 1750s and 1760s at Yale. It has led to such perverse interpretations as that celebrating Clap's argument for ministerial rule at Yale as an early instance of the defense of academic freedom. Similarly, the assumption of the legal status of American colonial colleges as eleemosynary corporations has prevented an appreciation of just how radical an innovation the American private college was when it first emerged at the end of the eighteenth century in reaction to the early moves for state universities during the Revolution.

This book also seeks to describe and explain the genesis of the contemporary configuration of American higher education, in which public and private institutions exist side by side. This pattern emerged first in the four decades before 1820, when private collegiate foundations supplemented provincial and state colleges and universities. If the older, public institutions had fulfilled the traditional task of training the sons of a social elite for professional and governmental leadership, the newer, private schools appealed to a different clientele. In New England, they catered to impecunious young men in villages and small towns aspiring to middle-class professions. On the western and southern frontier, Presbyterian and community colleges did their part to supply teachers, preachers, lawyers, and business leaders for a flourishing population. The Dartmouth decision extended to them the same protection courts afforded business corporations. It thus confirmed their equal legal standing with the older, public colleges and universities. By 1820 the Supreme Court had constructed the legal foundation on which the structure of higher education has rested ever since.

A history of American higher education also permits insights into the country's social structure and its political ethos. Studying in depth the partisan arguments advanced in the many college quarrels analyzed in these pages, I have been struck by the aristocratic temper that made our earliest colonial colleges resemble the continental European territorial universities as much as the colleges in the English universities. Characteristic of the sponsors and governors of colonial colleges was a deeply felt responsibility for the public welfare shared by a leadership class of secular magistrates, clerical professionals, land-owning gentry, and commercial entrepreneurs.

However, a sense of corporate responsibility was hard to sustain in a society progressively more heterogeneous in its religious and ethnic composition and more socially pluralistic in its aspirations. The struggles in the colleges in the mid-eighteenth century demonstrate this development, and the founding of Queen's College in 1766 as the first nonprovincial institution marks the beginning of a new era in the history of American higher education that was well under way by the turn of the century. The American private college had become the institutional response to particularism and the embodiment of *laissez-nous-faire* in higher education. The college founders in the decades after 1780 ranged from land developers to Christian missionaries, from medical professionals to civic promoters, from responsible educators to shiftless charlatans. No longer could it be taken for granted that a college's main mission was the education of society's future leaders; instead, it might be the promotion of municipal growth, the spread of denominational influence, or the encouragement of land speculation. Education was often merely an incidental concern.

I have deliberately avoided the curricular and social history of American colleges. My focus has been on the conflicts that erupted among participants in college life and government, and on the relationships between colleges and state, society, and churches. I did not exclude curricular and social concerns from my purview, but I held fast to an insight that, I believe, is fundamental to understanding the prenineteenth-century college: for an institution of an unashamedly, even proudly, elitist character, designed to educate a governing class, its own relationship to external government and its own practice of internal government were more important than the specific content of its curriculum. What was taught was seen as a means to an end; the circumstances under which instruction was offered came as close to being the end itself as anything within the college possibly could. Seen in this light, the private colleges reveal more about the transformation of American society from a tradition-bound colonial past to a period of individualistic and acquisitive capitalist expansion than any discussion of curricular change could. The founding of private colleges marks the dispersal of social authority undertaken by the postrevolutionary generation from a few centers of decision-making to many private and semipublic associations all across the country. In short, I approach colleges and universities as expressions of the political, social, and economic realities of their society, not as institutions whose significance is circumscribed by discussions of curricular practice and pedagogical theory.

This approach, too, explains why I make no reference to "the great retrogression," the phrase used to describe the opening decades of the nineteenth century as a period of growing parochialism in American college education. This retrogression, during which the colleges lost much of their intellectual vigor, is seen as part of a national reaction to the Enlightenment and to the multiplying and scattering of denominational and sectarian schools. I have no quarrel with the definition of the phenomenon, but I wish to qualify the significance ascribed to it. Although the programs of many of the new colleges did indeed resemble those of academies and grammar schools, their significance as social institutions promoting economic growth was quite another matter. The contemporary role of American colleges and universities as stimulators of settlement is more suggestive than the changes in their academic programs.

Similarly, in this book I do not refer to academic freedom. While participants in American academic life in the period 1636-1819 frequently objected to infringement of academic autonomy by governing boards and legislatures, while they chafed under strict rules of attendance at religious services and occasionally learned of state censorship of academic publications in Europe, they did not define academic freedom as the freedom to teach and to learn. The very real battles fought by and in the colleges over autonomy and against oppressive government of one sort or another account for most of the material in this book, but they were not battles over academic freedom as we know it today.

Beyond the outlines of this history of the institutional, governmental, and legal development of American higher education before 1820, I hope the reader will perceive the changes that took place in the social and political life and beliefs of the American people. Colleges and universities were created as the most expedient means for translating into reality their vision of a well-regulated body politic. This study portrays the early history of American higher education as the transformation of European institutions by American conditions; it views the old as coexisting and also competing with the new; it perceives institutional policies as expressions of social purpose and economic interest; and it points to the tremendously innovative impact of early capitalist expansion after the Revolution. A beckoning continent with its apparently inexhaustible resources, an economic system freed from European mercantilist restrictions, an aggressive, acquisitive population — these were the elements that created a new configuration of colleges for a new land.

# ACKNOWLEDGMENTS

My thanks go to all who through their letters and conversations have encouraged me and urged me on when spirits flagged. I want to pay tribute to the late Carl J. Friedrich and Howard Mumford Jones for the inspiration and example they provided and to thank Bernard Bailyn, Lawrence A. Cremin, Merle Curti, Edward T. Gargan, and J. Willard Hurst for their counsel and never-failing willingness to lend a hand in support of my research. I am deeply appreciative of my colleagues on the Madison campus of the University of Wisconsin, especially in the Department of Educational Policy Studies and in the Department of History, who never ceased to provide a hospitable and supportive environment, and I want to acknowledge the superb contributions of my research assistants, Edward A. Gargan and Anne Topham. Much credit is due them all, while I accept full responsibility for the shortcomings of this volume.

As I pursued my research over the years I accumulated debts to archivists and librarians whose patient and efficient work deserves recognition. In Madison I have been aided by the staffs of the university's Memorial Library, the State Historical Society, the Wisconsin State Law Library, and the libraries of the Law School and the Medical School. Other institutions on whose services I relied were the Harvard University Archives, the Widener Library of Harvard University, and the library of the Harvard University Law School; the Massachusetts Historical Society and the Massachusetts State Archives; the Swem Library at the College of William and Mary and the Colonial Williamsburg Foundation; the Lambeth Palace Library in London; the University Archives and the Beinecke Library of Yale University, and the Connecticut State Library; the Rutgers University

Library, the Princeton University Library, and the New Jersey State Archives in Trenton; the Columbia University Libraries; the New-York Historical Society; the Archives of the University of Pennsylvania and the Historical Society of Pennsylvania; the Brown University Archives; the Maryland Historical Society, the Maryland State Library, the Hall of Records in Annapolis, and the library of the Anne Arundel County Circuit Court in Maryland; The University Library of Washington and Lee University, the Eggleston Library of the College Hampden-Sydney, and the library of the University of Virginia; the Transylvania University Archives in Lexington, Kentucky, the Centre College Library in Danville, and the State Archives and Record Center in Frankfort, Kentucky; the Education Library of George Peabody College of Teachers in Nashville, Tennessee; the South Caroliniana Library of the University of South Carolina; the University of North Carolina Library at Chapel Hill and the Manuscript Department of the Southern Historical Collection; the Williams College Library in Williamstown, Massachusetts; the Bowdoin College Archives in Brunswick, Maine; the Middlebury College Archives, the University of Vermont Archives, the Guy W. Bailey Library of the University of Vermont in Burlington, and the Vermont State Archives in Montpelier.

The many years of research and writing have been generously supported through leaves, grants, and fellowships from the Research Committee of the University of Wisconsin Graduate School, the Wisconsin Institute for Research in the Humanities, the John Simon Guggenheim Memorial Foundation, the National Institute of Education, the National Endowment for the Humanities, and the International Research and Exchanges Board. I thank them all.

Finally, in gratitude and love I acknowledge the uncountable and unmeasurable contributions of my wife throughout these many years.

# I

## Schools of the Reformation in the New World

THE EARLIEST American colleges were schools of the European Reformation. When in 1636 the General Court of the Massachusetts Bay Company agreed to appropriate £400 to contribute to the expenses of a school or college, when the English crown in 1693 granted a charter to the College of William and Mary in Virginia, and when in 1701 governor, councillors, and representatives of Connecticut chartered a school for the colony, these governing bodies laid the first foundation stones for the perpetuation of Europe's heritage of learning in the wilderness of the New World. The Puritans of Massachusetts told their English brethren that they had erected a college in order "to advance *Learning* and perpetuate it to Posterity; dreading to leave an illiterate Ministery to the Churches, when our present Ministers shall lie in the Dust." William and Mary, speaking on behalf of their subjects in Virginia, gave a charter for "a certain Place of universal Study"—in Latin they called it a *quoddam studium generale*—"to the End that the Church of Virginia may be furnished with a Seminary of Ministers of the Gospel, and that the Youth may be piously educated in good Letters and Manners." In Puritan Connecticut a group of ministers had asked for permission to found a "Collegiate School . . . wherein Youth may be instructed in the Arts & Sciences who through the blessing of Almightly God may be fitted for Publick employment both in Church & Civil State."[1]

For public employment in church and state—this phrase defined the traditional purpose of university education at it was transmitted to the New World from the medieval and Reforma-

1

tion centers of European learning. The medieval unity of *sacerdotium*, *regnum*, and *studium* — of church, state, and university — fragmented though it was into the many subdivisions of the empire, was nonetheless preserved within the various territorial sovereignties with their established churches and universities. The territorial ruler decided the state religion of his subjects and served as head and protector of his church. In Europe the territorial princes had assumed much of the secular and ecclesiastical powers previously held by emperor and pope.[2] In New England the Puritans had assumed that, under the general supervision of their respective provincial General Courts, Harvard and Yale would train ministers and magistrates in their Calvinist faith. In Virginia, similarly, the College of William and Mary was to be an Anglican school and seminary under the management of a local Board of Visitors with the Bishop of London as the chancellor. In kingdom, principality, or province, college and church served to enhance the secular sovereign's prestige.

As schools of the Reformation, the colonial colleges and their sister institutions in Europe had broken with the medieval conception of the university as an autonomous guild or corporation of masters or scholars. They did not follow the Parisian pattern, where the masters had relied on papacy and empire to defend them against bishop, king, and city. The Parisian masters had associated with each other in a guild for protection against the secular and ecclesiastical authorities in the city and had become a legally recognized corporation. Given this corporate autonomy, the masters saw their university as a *collegium scholasticum*. Though they depended for protection and support on pope and emperor, they wanted to be neither a *collegium ecclesiasticum* nor a *collegium secularium*. They cherished their independence as scholars.[3]

The Reformation universities and colleges, by contrast, had become territorial institutions. They resembled more closely the municipal universities of Italy, the royal foundations of Spain and Portugal, and the fourteenth-century German-speaking institutions in Prague, Vienna, Heidelberg, Cologne, and Erfurt. Though these academic centers had received papal charters, their students were not required to enter holy orders, laymen were not excluded from matriculation, and, legally speaking, these universities were secular, not ecclesiastical, corporations.[4]

In Calvinist academic institutions the transfer of power from the corporation of masters to an external agency was most advanced. The Harvard Board of Overseers and the ministerial trustees of Connecticut's Collegiate School represent this type of control. They continued a form of academic government practiced consistently among Calvinist-Reformed groups in Europe from Switzerland to the Netherlands and Scotland.[5]

The desire to bring universities under external control took somewhat different forms among Lutherans and Anglicans. Luther himself had attacked the universities for taking refuge behind imperial laws and papal privileges. He had expressed the desire to see territorial law and custom take precedence over ancient tradition, and to have local authorities regulate admission to the universities.[6] University administration eventually became part and parcel of the sovereign's bureaucracy. In Oxford and Cambridge the appointment of Regius professors and the centralization of administrative power in the heads of colleges assured the influence of the crown over the universities while at the same time it preserved, to a degree, the autonomy of the academic corporations.

In England a series of acts during the reign of Henry VIII replaced the joint authority of pope and crown with that of the crown alone, exchanged the ecclesiastical appeals courts for the Court of Chancery, and transferred the rights of university visitation from the papacy to the crown. In 1571 Elizabeth reincorporated the universities in the name of their chancellors, masters, and students, and in 1604 James I granted each of the two universities the right of representation in the House of Commons. By the end of the sixteenth century, Oxford and Cambridge had been transformed into territorial institutions under the ultimate control of their Protestant secular sovereign.[7] What was true for the two universities did not necessarily hold for the colleges within them, however, for they retained a strongly ecclesiastical character.

But by the middle of the seventeenth century, the common law courts had come to view the colleges as well as the universities as lay corporations, despite the continuing ecclesiastical appearance of the former.

For the first 100 years of continuous English settlement in the New World the Reformation heritage determined the shape of colonial college government. The settlers had brought with them traditions of classical learning, and they applied them in the defense of the Reformed faith. From Calvinist practice they had adopted the boards of external governors, and from every

Reformed tradition they had inherited the religious character of college life. Universities could no longer claim for themselves the status of *collegia scholastica*, nor did colleges function as church seminaries pure and simple. Together with civil state and established church, they constituted the three great public institutions of their societies. Distrustful as the colonists were of crown and archbishop and lacking an ample supply of responsible masters and professors, they placed their trust in the representatives of provincial civil and church government and thus kept ambiguous the status of their colleges as secular or ecclesiastical institutions.

# 1

## A PROVINCIAL SCHOOL
## IN THE WILDERNESS

When the members of the General Court of the Massachusetts Bay Company agreed in 1636 to contribute to a school or college, they did not envisage a municipal grammar school or a continental style *gymnasium illustre* under the supervision of local authorities. They intended to found a provincial school with its government and its future graduates tied to the leadership of church and colony. They themselves took a hand in its establishment and meant to remain involved in its fate. Just six short and cruel years of near starvation and physical hardships separated the Court's act of faith from the company's landfall in the New World. No commonwealth, it was felt, could survive in the wilderness unless its leaders were well trained for the offices of state and church. The General Court could not then foresee that for fifty-seven years Harvard would remain the only college in the English-speaking colonies of North America.

On October 28, 1636, the General Court voted "to give 400 lbs. towards a school or college." Half of this sum was to be paid the next year, and the remainder "when the work is finished." It was left to the next Court "to appoint where and what building."[1] Both the initial stimulus and the first pledge of financial support came from the colony's government, and it was thus the college founder.[2] The Court's pledge of October 28, 1636, can be considered Harvard's founding date, for although instruction did not begin until 1638, it is the date of issuance of a charter, papal bull, or first gift of revenues—not the first day of teaching—that determines the official date of founding.[3] The Court's role as founder has been questioned because of its inability to pay the £400 as specified in the 1636 resolve, and because of the far larger donation of £799.17.2 bequeathed by John Harvard upon his

5

death on September 14, 1638. The size of the donation, however, is irrelevant to the question; only its timing matters. Exact figures are not available in the receipts of the college before 1644. Before that year, it has been shown, the college received £79.3.3 from the tax levies of Watertown and Cambridge, and the colony's treasurer reported that in 1639, £50.12.00 had been paid to the college from the colony's funds. The Court acknowledged on October 27, 1647, that it still owed the college £190.16.00 of the original £400 grant, yet by October of 1650 the pledge appears to have been paid in full. Of John Harvard's gift, we know that Nathaniel Eaton, the college's first master, is reported to have received and spent £200 for the construction of the college house, and this appears to have been done in 1639. During the early months of 1644 the colony's treasurer acknowledged the receipt of £175.3.00 from John Harvard's legacy, but there is no indication that that money was paid over to the college.[4] In 1639, then, the college treasury received funds from the colony's treasurer and Mr. Eaton received funds from John Harvard's executor. Whether a claim to priority can be established between these two transfers of funds is doubtful. What remains unquestioned, however, is that the colony's grant was the first to be announced and pledged.

On November 20, 1637, the Court arranged for a committee "to take order for the college." The colony's governor, deputy governor, and treasurer, as well as three magistrates and six ministers, were to be responsible for the college — the word "school" now having disappeared in the colony records. As a provincial institution Harvard was to be distinct from the grammar schools in Boston, Charlestown, and Dorchester. It was to serve the cause of Puritanism in New England, taking students from all parts of the expanding colony and neighboring Puritan settlements. It was to house its students and to take them beyond their grammar schooling through the traditional curriculum of the *artes liberales* until they would equal in their academic accomplishments the graduates of the colleges at Oxford and Cambridge. In their most ambitious dreams, the colonists saw Harvard as the spearhead of a conquering worldwide Puritanism.[5]

This committee of the General Court, called Overseers in common speech and more formally *inspectores*, was not a governing board and had neither permanency nor autonomy.[6] It was precisely its ephemeral nature as a committee — at commencement in 1642 only six of the original twelve appointees were still present in the Bay Colony, and no provision allowed for the replacement of those who had left — that led to the eventual reconstitution of the Overseers in 1642 as a permanent board. The original committee, although a forerunner of the board established in 1642, possessed no independence. It was allowed to act only at the pleasure of the General Court.

The committee's limited authority became evident when the Court, not the committee, fired the college's first master and hired its first president. The committee had appointed Master Eaton and had watched the arrival of the first students and the beginning of instruction in the summer of 1638. But Eaton made his mark more on the backs than on the minds of his students. The Court intervened, ordered an investigation and trial, and fined and dismissed Eaton "for cruel and barbarous beating . . . and for other neglecting and misusing of his scholars." Left without a master, the college closed its doors in September 1639. The following August the Court, rather than the committee of Overseers, invited Henry Dunster to serve as president of the college. Dunster had just arrived in the Bay Colony from a position as schoolmaster and minister in England. He quickly and energetically seized the reins of the institution and in 1642 presided over the first commencement. He bestowed bachelor's degrees on nine young men, the college's first graduating class. Four days later, no doubt relieved and impressed by Dunster's vigor and success, the Court reconstituted the *inspectores* as a quasi-corporate board, allowing them a greater and more direct share in the government of the college.[7]

In their new form as quasi-corporation the Overseers functioned as a self-perpetuating board for the purpose of exercising delegated governmental functions of legislation and administration.[8] They consisted of the governor, the deputy governor, the college president, all nine assistants of the Court, and the nine pastors and teachers of the six adjoining towns. Like the *reformatores* of European universities, they were formally charged with drawing up, from time to time, the statutes of the college.[9] This gave them rights commonly reserved in England to college founders or their representatives. For the execution of their various duties they were empowered to act by majority vote, and a majority of their number could speak for the entire body. Thus, for all intents and purposes, the Overseers were a body politic and corporate, without, however, an explicit and formal act of incorporation. Their decisions remained subject to appeal by aggrieved parties and, if the appeal went unheeded, to action by the General Court.[10] They had gained power and prestige, but they still were far from being an independent college corporation.

The Court also had confirmed the Overseers as trustees of the college property, subject only to the equity jurisdiction of the Court. As unincorporated trustees they administered the college property as a public trust for the benefit of the present and future citizens of the Bay Colony. English settlers were familiar with this type of government for educational institutions. Though in England trusteeships did not reach their most widespread use until the second half of the seventeenth century, they had become important well before that time. With the 1601 Statute of Charitable Uses, educational trusts had come under the supervision of royal charity commissioners whose duty it was to protect the interests of the beneficiaries. These were rarely specifically named individuals, as the purposes of these trusts were supposed to benefit the public at large. Such a trust arrangement avoided the expense and time required for obtaining a charter and relieved the founder of the need to seek the approval and consent of royal officials.[11] In Puritan New England the trusteeship offered itself as a most convenient device to establish a public college without having to consider the Anglican crown authorities in any way. The unincorporated trusteeship offered maximum legal protection and permanence with a minimum of royal involvement. It was an ideal device for administering a public charity.

## A Matter of Degrees

Harvard was established as a public institution. Their poverty, however, prompted the settlers to look for support to private benefactors as much as to the public purse. In 1636 they had pledged tax funds, and four years later they added to these an annual income of £40 from the Charlestown ferry. In the next year they authorized two Massachusetts men to go fund-raising in England. A promotional pamphlet, *New England's First Fruits*, was to help the emissaries in their task by honoring John Harvard as the founder of the college and emphasizing the gifts of other private donors. It then simply acknowledged in passing that "the public hand of the State [had] added the rest." The pamphlet's aim, after all, was to aid in raising further funds, and the best way to succeed was to inform potential donors of precedents set by others and of the fame and gratitude earned by them. Harvard College, the pamphlet was to make clear, was both accomplishment and promise. It was the school of the commonwealth, but it deserved the support of individuals everywhere who desired the success of the Puritan experiment in the wilderness.[12]

The first proof of accomplishment had come with Dunster's commencement of 1642. Nine young men had spent three years in the study of the liberal arts, philosophy, the biblical languages, and catechetical divinity. They had been granted their bachelor's degrees, and were now ready to begin studies for their second degrees or to enter upon their responsibilities as leading citizens. The account in *New England's First Fruits* shows no evidence whatsoever that Dunster and the Overseers were conscious of violating "a jealously guarded prerogative of sovereignty, to be exercised only by express grant from pope, emperor, or king."[13] Such prerogative, if it ever existed with respect to the bachelor's degree, was a relic of the Middle Ages. It had disappeared or was being ignored by the confessional universities of the Reformation.

When Dunster granted to nine young men "the power to lecture publicly in any one of the arts which thou hast studied whensoever thou shalt have been called to that office,"[14] he did not usurp power not belonging to the college. He merely announced to the world that by its own decision Harvard College intended to be more than a collegiate English grammar school or a continental *gymnasium illustre*. Dunster entered Harvard into a tradition reaching back to the earliest universities at Bologna and Paris and continued in England at Oxford and Cambridge. In the arts faculty of these universities the baccalaureate had always been the prerequisite for an academic career and for candidacy to the master's license and degree. In Paris as well as at the English universities the bachelor's degree was in fact the equivalent of an apprenticeship diploma granted the aspiring candidate for the master's license by the accomplished practitioners of the guild under the sponsorship of the university. As such the degree signified certification by the profession. Recognition of the candidate's accomplishment or status in the eyes of secular or ecclesiastical authorities was neither implied nor thought necessary, the degree being primarily a guild or university matter. There is no reason to think that the baccalaureate was thought of in any other terms at Puritan Cambridge in Massachusetts. With the approbation of the Overseers, President Dunster granted the degree to the nine candidates. He did so as their teacher and master and as the chief officer of the college.

Within two or three years a different situation arose, when four of the nine bachelors of the class of 1642 applied to the college for their master's degrees. Of the next class of four in 1643, three returned for their master's degrees and two of them, Samuel Mather and Samuel Danforth, subsequently taught as tutors and were appointed fellows of the college in 1650.[15] The Harvard master's degree telescoped two medieval certificates into one: the new professor's license to teach and the degree of *magister artium*. It signified that the bearer had successfully terminated his apprenticeship and was duly licensed to give ordinary lectures in the faculty in which he had obtained his degree. Mather and Danforth were thus regarded as fully qualified teachers in the faculty of arts. In granting the degrees Dunster again did not usurp powers not belonging to him. He followed traditions established in England and acted solely as the highest officer of the university. As the college's chief officer, he presented the candidates to the Overseers. After having received their consent, Dunster granted the candidates their second degree in the arts. The newly licensed professors now had received the power to lecture wherever they should be called to that office.[16] Their degrees were not backed by a universally acknowledged apostolic authority; their value would depend ultimately on the prestige the college could command in the academic world outside the Massachusetts Bay Colony.

After the Reformation, degrees and licenses testified to the bearer's academic accomplishments as certified by a university. They provided him with a pass to preferment in the realm of his territorial sovereign. Beyond this, the recognition of the degrees of one university by another was a matter of academic courtesy and prestige. When President Dunster in the presence of Governor Winthrop and the Overseers bestowed degrees at the Harvard commencement in 1642 he did no more or less than the Protestant universities and colleges of Europe had come to accept as common academic practice.[17]

### The Incorporation of 1650

When within eight years of the formal constitution of the Overseers President Dunster petitioned the Court for a charter of incorporation, he moved boldly into new territory. In the spring of 1650 the General Court of the Massachusetts Bay Company received petitions for incorporation from both the town of Boston and Harvard College. The Court expressed its willingness to entertain these requests if the town's terms and privileges should appear "fit for the Court to grant," and if the Corporation would include neither magistrates nor unwilling ministers.[18] As it turned out, Boston had to wait for formal incorporation another 170 years.[19] The Court did not want magistrates to serve on the Corporation because as members of the General Court they were Overseers and thus would "be judges in points of difference that shall or may fall out" between the Corporation and the Overseers. Similarly, the Court suggested that ministers might want to refrain from becoming members of the Corporation since at least those in the surrounding towns served also as Overseers. With the Court's specific reservations and general willingness clearly expressed, neither Dunster nor the Overseers hesitated long. They prepared a draft charter and submitted it to the General Court. On May 31, 1650, the charter having passed the Court on the preceding day, Governor Dudley affixed his signature. Harvard College now was a corporation.[20]

The new college corporation did not enjoy the customary privileges of self-government of an English university college. The Corporation was to consist of president, fellows, and treasurer. They were to take corporate possession of the institution and its property and, as a corporate body, were to have the right to succession in perpetuity, to receive and hold property, to sue and be sued, to have a seal, to appoint officers and servants, and to be exempted from taxes, duties, and customs. As individuals the members of the Corporation as well as the students, officers, and servants of the college were to be exempted also from civil office, military service, and watch duty, as well as from personal taxes on their estates as long as these did not exceed £100. Yet the Corporation was permitted to exercise its right to perpetual succession only in the presence of and with the counsel and consent of the Overseers, and it could enact by-laws and decide disputes as well as "great and difficult" cases only with their consent when a general meeting of Corporation and Overseers had been called.[21] The charter in effect placed the Corporation under the supervising authority of the Overseers in all matters that went beyond routine questions of daily administration.

Concern for financial responsibility seems to have been the primary reason the Court gave the Overseers effective control over the Corporation. The charter had listed as grounds for incorporation the rapid accumulation of gifts, bequests, and revenues in the hands of trustees who met only infrequently. In order to remedy this defect and create a permanent body to receive funds and property, the Court established the Corporation. At the same time, however, the Court never dissolved the trusteeship of the Overseers over the college funds, but specifically affirmed the Overseers' supervisory powers.[22] Presumably, members of the Court placed greater reliance on the Overseers than on the Corporation. Consisting of president, treasurer, and five young men — only two of whom had obtained the degree of *magister artium* and thus qualified as teachers — the Corporation had no more than four members who inspired confidence in their abilities to manage and govern the college. Dunster, the Overseers, and the Court thus faced the question of whether they could or should transfer the trust funds and the powers of government without reservations or safeguards from the Overseers to the Corporation, from established and proven fiduciaries to largely youthful and untested scholars. Although they wanted more constant government and administration than the Overseers could provide, they nonetheless desired the guiding hand of age and wisdom. Thus they effected a compromise that limited the autonomy of the Corporation by placing the fellows under the trusteeship and cogovernment of the Overseers.

What then was the position in which the new charter placed the Overseers? Obviously they were not a New England version of the incorporated board of external governors that in England frequently controlled grammar schools, hospitals, or colleges. Not being incorporated they could not well apply to themselves the ruling in the 1612 Charterhouse case, which had held that "if no visitor had been appointed by the charter, the governors should visit." Besides, in English colleges the visitors were to safeguard the interests of the founder, the corporation's faithful observation of the terms of the original bequest, and the members' adherence to the statutes. If disputes arose within the corporation the visitors were to serve as a court of appeal and to settle such issues as had arisen. The Harvard Overseers, however, were far more intimately tied into the on-going operations of the Corporation than English college visitors normally were. As trustees and cogovernors they could be said to be themselves under the visitatorial jurisdiction of the General Court as both founder and highest court of equity in the colony.[23] There are no court rulings or legislation on these matters, but it does not appear that the Overseers could be viewed as visitors. The Court, rather than the Overseers, visited the college.

Within the college the Overseers functioned as unincorporated trustees sharing authority with the Corporation and exercising implicit veto powers over its major decisions. In 1657 the General Court confirmed these powers and the Overseers' continuing responsibility as trustees. It then issued an appendix to the charter which replaced the requirement of the Overseers' concurrent consent to Corporation decisions with a reminder of the Corporation's accountability to the Overseers and the latter's power subsequently to alter or veto Corporation decisions. The Overseers more than once exceeded their "consenting" function — whether concurrent or subsequent — and took the initiative in settling stipends and ordering the treasurer to disburse funds.[24] They acted very much as trustees and assumed full responsibility for the college's financial affairs. They rather than the Corporation elected Dunster's successors Charles Chauncy in 1654 and Leonard Hoar in 1672. They thus were the de facto, if not the de jure, governors of the college.

Why did Dunster, the Overseers, and the Court find it necessary to incorporate the college when at the same time they preserved the Overseers as unincorporated trustees and governors? Administrative and governmental convenience as well as the need for sufficient authority for the resident officers of the college appear as the primary reason for Dunster's request for incorporation. The charter had pointed to the intermittent attention paid by the Overseers to the trust as the ostensible reason for incorporation. The new arrangement responded to that situation by supplementing the Overseers and their occasional meetings with the permanently available administrative authority of the Corporation. Incorporation did not contribute to the legal permanence and financial security of the college, since these had already been guaranteed by the establishment of the company of Overseers in 1642 as governors and trustees.[25] Nor could the desire for prestige equivalent to that of an English college corporation have been a strong motivating factor. No doubt Dunster and the fellows appreciated the heightened esteem that came with their increased authority, but Dunster, the members of the Court, and the fellows as well knew that the Harvard Corporation did not equal an English college corporation in authority and power. The reasons for incorporating president and fellows were of a more practical nature.

From seventeenth-century conceptions of the common law we know that Englishmen viewed corporations primarily as governmental devices by which to achieve their purposes. With governmental and administrative convenience being a primary consideration and, at the same time, a traditionally recognized reason for legal incorporation, it becomes ever more understandable why Dunster and the Court raised no objection — at least as far as we know — to leaving ultimate authority over both financial and governmental matters in the hands of an external board of unincorporated trustees and governors. That the Massachusetts settlers were quite satisfied to leave matters thus is borne out also by the legal records in the *General Laws and Liberties* of 1660 and 1672. Here the act of 1642 establishing the unincorporated Overseers as trustees and governors is published, but no mention is made of the charter of 1650.[26] Whether the Puritans were anxious not to provoke the crown by publicizing their incorporation of a college, or whether they simply did not think very important the legal incorporation of president and fellows, the new arrangement of responsible supervision over a permanent corporation served their purpose. In short, it worked, or promised to work.

From the *Colony Records* it appears that the Court showed little or no hesitation in asserting its authority to incorporate the college. Some think that the Court acted audaciously, and that it was aware of the risks it ran. Other scholars, however, tend to diminish the boldness of the Court's break with English legal practice. They point out that as separatists and Congregationalists the New England settlers were firm believers in their right of free association for civil and ecclesiastical purposes, a right the Pilgrims had exercised with the signing of the Mayflower Compact and the Puritans practiced when they founded churches by covenant.[27] Yet others hold that the Court was little concerned with legal technicalities, and that it acted on purely pragmatic grounds to provide for a more efficient college government. With the king's decapitation, the argument goes, the Court no longer considered binding the dictum that one corporation could not create another unless specifically authorized by the crown. Instead, the Court could rely on royal statutes that provided for the general incorporation of hospitals.[28]

Did the Court act audaciously? Did it knowingly and deliberately violate the traditions of English law? All we know is that the Massachusetts settlers were not entirely ignorant of the common law, and that they might have known of Lord Coke's famous 1612 decision in the *Case of Sutton's Hospital* "that none but the King alone can create to make a corporation." But they might also have been aware of a 1568 case in the Court of King's Bench, where it was held that while a subject could not create a corporation, the crown could delegate such right, provided that the subject acted strictly in accordance with the royal grant. At such occasions, the Court had held, the subject's action will be seen as the crown's.[29]

Another argument, that the incorporation of Harvard was analogous to the establishment of churches, congregations, parishes, cities, towns, villages, precincts, wards, and other units of ecclesiastical and civil government and therefore legitimate, misses the point. None of these governmental units had been formally incorporated in New England. They were quasi-corporations without charter, similar in legal standing to the college before its incorporation in 1650. Yet after 1650 Harvard had become a fully chartered body politic.

One argument still to be considered is that one corporation cannot create another without the specific authorization of the crown, although it is uncertain whether that rule had been accepted as law in the first half of the seventeenth century. The rule was firmly stated by Chief Justice Lord Kenyon in a 1798 case, but before that date its validity was doubtful.[30]

Finally, did the general incorporation statutes for hospitals and houses of correction of 1597 and 1625 serve as authorization for the Court to incorporate Harvard College? The statutes were intended to encourage the founding of charitable institutions by relieving the founders of the high costs of incorporation and of the license of mort-main. They promised automatic incorporation by Parliament once the founder had registered a deed in chancery court. Nothing in these statutes detracted from parliamentary or royal authority to incor-porate.[31] Again, it is a question of whether the Court could have assumed this authority for itself.

The Harvard charter of 1650 tranformed the college from a quasi-corporation into a fully chartered corporation. The existing evidence neither unequivocally supports nor denies the claim that the Court possessed the power to issue charters of incorporation. It is likely that the members of the Court were divided on this issue. But given their desire to strengthen the school's administration, given their confident expectations that their hopes and plans for the college now were shared by the party in power in England, and given their conviction that their proposed act did not obviously violate a statute or an undisputably ac-cepted rule of law, they went ahead and incorporated their college. It was a bold move, and they had neither precedent nor map to guide them.

In the charter of 1650 the Reformation concern for the subordination of colleges and universities to the public authorities of state and church reemerged in the New World. The General Court created Harvard as a provincial institution, and the Overseers were to keep the Corporation under public scrutiny. The charter exemplified a carefully wrought compromise between a medieval tradition of corporate autonomy and a modern concern for territorial authorities over all matters of state and religion. The former was preserved, even though weakly, in the Corporation; the latter was institutionalized in the Board of Overseers.

# 2

## HARVARD COLLEGE:
## THE NEW WORLD'S OLDEST CORPORATION

Harvard College is the oldest corporation in continuous existence under its original charter in the United States today.[1] When it was incorporated in 1650 and during its first decade, however, the Corporation's survival was precarious, its authority often questioned. The colony's poverty made it impossible to endow and support adequately the five fellowships provided for in the charter. Of the first five fellows, only Samuel Eaton remained as a tutor after September 1650. He was joined late in that year by Urian Oakes and, in 1651, by John Collins, both of whom were appointed as fellows and tutors. For the next two decades the average length of a fellow's stay in the college as a tutor was two and one-half years. It soon became evident that a full complement of resident teaching fellows could not be maintained. Few fellows remained as resident tutors. Those who did were young and inexperienced. The treasurer remained largely inactive, and the college business was for all practical purposes carried out by the president and the Overseers. Except for Dunster, the Corporation was not involved.[2]

Even rule by Dunster and the Overseers was not allowed to remain unchallenged. When monetary difficulties became pressing in the early fifties and Dunster appealed to the General Court for help, the Court responded by ordering the Cambridge town rate to be paid to the college. It appointed a committee to draw up a report on all the income and expenditures of the college since the commencement of Dunster's presidency and on the money paid to president and fellows. It further charged the committee to recommend the allowances for the president and fellows and "to take cognizance of all and every matter or thing concerning the said college in reference to the welfare thereof in outward things, and to present a way how to regulate and rectify any thing that is out of order."[3] The Court assumed direct responsibility for virtually all college affairs.

Disturbed by the Court's apparent suspicions about the integrity of his administration, Dunster complained. In addition to his own teaching, he had been forced on many occasions to shoulder the fellows' burden and had also been obliged to supervise the construction of the college house and the accounts of the servants. He assured the committee that he had been a faithful steward of all the contributions made to the college, and suggested that they consult with college graduates or fellows to obtain a better understanding of college affairs. He asked them to settle the college's finances so as to obviate any future requests for supplemental appropriations, and to give him an associate to collect the funds due the college from the various towns.[4]

The commissioners reported to the Court on May 3, 1654, that they had found no fault with the college. They thought three resident fellows were sufficient and recommended excluding students from commons unless they paid their bills promptly. They declared the Corporation treasurer to be the proper person to collect and disburse the college funds. The Court accepted the report, but ordered the financial affairs of the college to be entrusted to the Overseers, "who have hereby power to give order to the treasurer of the college" and to "proportion" the annual allowances of the president and the fellows.[5] Thus the Court ignored the Corporation and deprived it and its treasurer of the right to take the initiative in settling finances. Whether or not the members of the General Court had acted deliberately, they had assumed visitatorial prerogatives over both Corporation and Overseers. The ink on the charter had hardly had time to dry before the Court began to modify the document's provisions.

Dunster resigned one week after the Court's order. His resignation was prompted above all by his unwillingness to compromise his right to question the scriptural authority of infant baptism. When on May 3, 1654, the Court had admonished the Overseers not to keep in office teachers "that have manifested themselves unsound in the faith," Dunster prepared his letter of resignation. But he said nothing of his Baptist convictions. He was going to resign, he wrote, because the promises made for recompense at the time of his appointment had not been kept, because destructive ordinances had been passed, and because "our former laws and orders, by which we have managed our place, be declared illegal and null."[6]

Dunster could not have survived in office if he rejected infant baptism. His constitutional reasoning was correct, however, and he had a right to be aggrieved over the Court's past neglect of the college. The committee report had justified his conduct in office. Above all, the Court had ignored the charter it had so recently granted. Dunster, in other words, was in a strong position as long as he stood on the charter; had he taken his stand on the theological controversy, he would not have had a convincing argument.

After Dunster's departure from office the Overseers seized the initiative and, in violation of the charter, elected Charles Chauncey president. Within less than three years Chauncey and the Overseers sought to redress the balance of power in favor of the Corporation. In 1657 they obtained from the Court an appendix to the charter. The Corporation was given permission to enact orders and by-laws and to call general meetings of Corporation and Overseers without the Overseer's concurrent or prior consent. The Overseers, however, retained the right to revoke such laws at their discretion. This veto and the 1654 Court order for the Overseers to take charge of the college finances contributed to their de facto and de jure exercise of trusteeship powers. For all practical purposes, the government of Harvard College in 1657 was divided between the members of the Corporation and the Overseers. The latter were nonresident trustees and governors, and with the Corporation fell under the visitatorial jurisdiction of the General Court.[7]

When in 1672, less than two months after the General Court had granted the College a new charter, Leonard Hoar succeeded to the presidency, he could work with a Corporation that had regained much of its authority. The document of 1672 included the treasurer as a member of the Corporation and thus dissociated him from the Overseers. It reaffirmed the Corporation's power over the college finances as well as the 1657 provision giving it the power to initiate by-laws and orders provided the Overseers did not subsequently exercise a veto. It concluded by emphasizing the legality of its provisions, "any law, grant, or usage to the contrary notwithstanding," thus invalidating the 1654 Court order to the Overseers to take charge of the college funds and repudiating any intimation that custom authorized the Overseers to elect the members of the Corporation. Now officially styled The President, Fellows and Treasurer of Harvard College, the Corporation had regained its authority over all matters assigned to it by the charter of 1650, and received increased powers over college members within and without the college yard.[8]

Not apparent immediately from the wording of the charter but highly significant for the prospect of its successful implementation was the change in the composition of the Corporation. Of its five fellows only two now served as resident tutors, Joseph Browne and John Richardson, 1666 graduates and M.A.'s. Samuel Danforth, Urian Oakes, and Thomas Shepard, graduates of 1643, 1649, and 1653, held ministerial appointments in Roxbury, Cambridge, and Charlestown, respectively, and had previously served as resident tutors and fellows. As ministers they also served as Overseers, giving rise to hopes for a smooth working relationship between the Corporation and the Overseers that may be seen as a first step toward amalgamation of the two boards. This arrangement foreshadowed a governing pattern that, though never adopted at Harvard, was to become standard for other American colleges: a corporation of nonresident governors under the visitatorial jurisdiction of a legislature. At Harvard in 1672 it represented a fusion of the English tradition of resident corporation with the continental preference for a board of external governors. It provided a workable means by which the Corportion was restored, albeit in changed form, to the place assigned it by the charter of 1650.

For reasons that remain obscure, students and fellows of the college soon found cause to be dissatisfied with President Hoar. They presented their complaints to the Overseers and, rebuffed by that body, called upon the General Court and again were rebuffed. Dissatisfaction with Hoar would not subside, however, so the Court then acted in its capacity as Visitor and asked all interested parties — president, present and former fellows, Overseers, graduates, and students — to appear for a hearing. The inquiry resulted in a probationary period for Hoar. As students continued to leave the college in the following months, Hoar finally submitted his resignation to the Overseers in March 1675. There followed the short-term presidencies of Urian Oakes and John Rogers; after the death of Rogers in 1684 the college found itself without a chief executive. In 1685, both colony and college charters were lost, and Harvard was without either charter or president; the basis for its constitutional government had abruptly disappeared.[9]

### Charter Mongering

The ensuing twenty-two years witnessed an intermittent struggle to obtain a new charter for the college. These years were dominated by the imperious and peevish Increase Mather, who became president in

1685. The next year he was confirmed in that office by the Council of the Dominion of New England, and in 1688, as agent of the Bay Colony, he moved to London. He continued as absentee rector and was reelected president in absentia in 1690. In England he toyed for a while with the idea of asking for a charter from the new monarch, but he was advised to have the General Court proceed with the incorporation and then to submit the charter to the crown for confirmation. When he returned to Boston in 1692, he had such a charter drafted and accepted by the General Court. Governor Phips signed it on June 27.[10]

Despite its ultimate rejection, the 1692 charter must rank as a milestone in the constitutional history of American colleges. By abolishing the Board of Overseers, it made the first attempt in America to dissolve the Reformation pattern of joint secular-ecclesiastic college government. This intended exclusion of government officials was prompted by the fear that "a few Anglicans or even Baptists might obtain ex officio seats." Mather and the established ministers were growing uneasy in the face of the increasing denominational diversity of the population. The 1692 charter named a Corporation of eight fellows with master's degrees in the arts faculty, only two of whom lived with students as tutors. The fellows had graduated eight to forty years earlier. Surely, this corporation of ministers and tutors was "respectable" enough, even though it no longer contained any magistrates.

To add further luster to the Harvard Corporation, Mather quickly utilized another novel provision written into the charter: the power of the college to grant degrees in all faculties. The new Corporation asked Mather to accept the Doctor of Theology degree and, invested with his new dignity, to confer upon the two tutors the degree of Bachelor of Theology. Besides these remarkable new provisions the charter granted the usual corporate privileges as well as tax exemption for the college and its officers, and release from civil office duty, military exercises, and watching and warding for the president, fellows, scholars, and fifteen officers and servants. The Mather charter was at once reactionary and revolutionary. With its "gestures of academic sovereignty" it borrowed heavily from the precedents of medieval universities. It broke with two-board government, created an English-style — albeit largely nonresident — college corporation of a pronounced clerical character, and elevated the college to the rank of institutions conferring degrees in all the faculties. Here was a bold declaration of academic independence under ministerial tutelage.[11]

For the next few years, neither the abolition of the Overseers nor the elevation of the college to a degree-granting university captured public attention. The issue of debate was the question of visitation. In England a private foundation would have visitors appointed by its founder. Where governors were incorporated rather than the beneficiaries, the governors themselves could serve as visitors. In public corporations, such as Harvard College, where the charter did not name visitors, the Court of King's Bench would carry out visitatorial functions.[12] Under the 1650 charter the General Court had in fact done so. The 1692 charter did not name Visitors, and by 1696 the colonists learned that the omission of king and governor had prompted the Privy Council to disallow the charter. If the college was to regain its legal footing, the effort of obtaining a charter had to be undertaken once more.

Mather's strategy had to reckon with the Corporation's desire to incorporate into the charter the crown's and the governor's power to visit as well as with the ill-will of the magistrates. Excluded abruptly from their position as Overseers, the magistrates insisted on their right to visit the college together with the governor. Members of both houses of the General Court tried their hands at charter drafting and produced their new version on December 17, 1696. The Visitors were to consist of the governor and his Council, the assistants in the upper house.[13]

Mather and the Corporation wanted the crown and governor to be visitors because they were remote and their power was restricted by English custom to occasional inspections and appellate jurisdiction. The Governor's Council, however, was close at hand and likely to exercise a far stricter and more frequent supervision. Protests to the draft charter came immediately from several Corporation members. They blamed the Governor's Council for having put "a peculiar disrespect . . . upon some of us." New members had been added to the Corporation, and their names preceded those of some of the older members. The president, too, had been demoted. He no longer held a casting vote, and he was made "as insignificant a member of the corporation as the most junior fellow therein." On November 9, 1696, Mather and the ministers agreed to send Mather on another charter mission to England. The news of this decision was enough to cause panic in the Governor's Council. To prevent Mather's departure, they agreed to drop the 1696 draft charter and to invite Mather to prepare yet another draft. The General Court then made one change, accepted that document, and had it signed by the governor on June 4, 1697.[14]

The change introduced by the Court replaced the crown with the Governor's Council, and Mather accepted the councillors as Visitors. He probably expected that this would lead to renewed disallowance and would brighten his prospects for a return to London to argue his charter preferences directly before the crown. The General Court, aware of Mather's intent, refused his request to be sent as charter advocate to London. Mather, however, accomplished his purpose by letter and obtained another royal disallowance.[15]

In a renewed try, the visitatorial power was assigned "to his Majesty and his Governor or Commander-in-chief" — thus respecting the crown's wishes — and five members of the Governor's Council were placed on the Corporation. Mather had been forced to back down from his desire to exclude the magistrates altogether from college government. But he demanded in return that all Corporation members adhere to the "principles of the Reformation which were espoused and intended by those who first settled this country and founded the college, and have hitherto been the profession and practice of the generality of the churches of Christ in New England." These churches were Congregational or Presbyterian. Mather, the Corporation, and the General Court appeared determined to preserve the influence of the Bay Colony churches on the college, which Mather had first secured in his charter of 1692 when, with the disappearance of the Overseers, the Corporation as the only governing board had come firmly under the control of ministers. In other respects, the 1699 draft was not too different from the 1697 draft. It was, however, the religious loyalty clause, a gross violation of the English policy of toleration, that led Governor Lord Bellomont to veto the bill. He could not accept the exclusion of Anglicans and others from the Corporation. He ordered the college to continue to govern itself under the 1697 charter and recommended to the General Court that they petition the crown for a royal charter.[16]

The governor's refusal to sign the 1699 draft should not obscure the appeal of this document to the magistrates and to Mather. The magistrates, to be sure, were to lose their place as Visitors, but their admission to the Corporation would have given them a check on the ambitions of Mather and the ministers. For them, this was an acceptable trade. Faced by the disagreeable prospect of increasing denominational heterodoxy, Mather, for his part, saw in the loyalty provision a potent means of stemming religious diversity in both college and colony. Thus he could persuade himself that even with the participation of magistrates on the Corporation, he and his friends could maintain doctrinal purity at the college. In the last analysis, Mather's underestimation of demographic change in the Bay Colony and of the crown's commitment to toleration brought about the defeat of the 1699 charter proposal.

With the opening of the new century, the General Court submitted another draft for royal confirmation. There was no mention of religious requirements, and the visitatorial power was lodged in the crown, the governor, and his Council. Governor Bellomont advised the Lords of Trade to give in on the Council's wish to share the visitatorial power. He saw the Council's determination to keep a hand in the college affairs as prompted primarily by religious considerations, and he accepted the Council's determination to defend the Congregational orthodoxy of the Bay Colony. He was prepared to face that eventuality. In the meantime he preferred that the charter draft of 1700 receive the royal blessing.[17]

Mather was now willing to give up the fight and turn the college "into a school for academical learning without privilege of conferring degrees." Such a school would not need a charter. Mather was disturbed over the reappearance of that apparently irrepressible demand for visitatorial power by the Governor's Council. Like Bellomont he saw in it religious motives, but he suspected stirrings of Congregational heterodoxy, perhaps even sympathy for Anglicans or Baptists. Thus while Bellomont assumed that the Council would, if pressed, resist the royal policy of toleration and defend Congregational orthodoxy, Mather fearing the opposite and envisaging the Council's capitulation before the crown, preferred to forego incorporation altogether and to reduce the college to an "academical school."[18] Mather's instincts are probably a better guide than Bellomont's of the Council's intent. To the magistrates of the Bay Colony the royal policy of toleration may not have been the overriding factor, but as politicians they saw the impact of religious heterodoxy and heterogeneity, and they knew what that meant.

The challenge to the participation of the magistrates in college government was thus defeated. The draft charter of 1700 was sent off to London, but was lost somewhere in the channels of the bureaucracy. Mather, reluctant as ever to reside in the college yard, was finally given leave by his Boston congregation to take his position in Cambridge. He did not last long on the campus. He resigned in 1701, and was followed in office by vice-president Samuel Willard. The college was now governed under a temporary settlement that, for all practical purposes, endorsed the Corporation as established under the draft charter of 1700.[19] When Samuel Willard resigned in 1707, the Corporation elected John Leverett president and, not being sure of its authority under the temporary settlement to authorize such election, submitted the results to the General Court. The Council accepted the election of Leverett; the Assembly refused concurrence.

Governor Joseph Dudley proposed a startling resolution: if the lower house would accept the election of Leverett, he and the upper house would resuscitate the charter of 1650 and declare it to be in force. The lower house could not possibly reject this offer. It meant that the crown's representative now acknowledged the colony's right to charter a college. This concession was worth the price of allowing the governor to pick the members of the Corporation and of having him and his Council again function as Overseers.

The only ones to lose under this arrangement were the Mathers, whose hope for a church-dominated religious school under the protection of a royal Visitor was now shattered for good. Angrily, Increase Mather remonstrated with Dudley for having acted contrary to his earlier assertions that the charter had died in 1684.[20] On December 6, 1707, both houses of the Court resolved to pay President Leverett's annual salary and to direct the president and fellows of Harvard College to govern themselves and the college under the provisions of the 1650 charter. This charter, they declared, "has not been repealed or nulled."[21] To be sure, it made no explicit provision for visitation by General Court or Governor's Council, but it brought the magistrates back into the government of the college as Overseers.

After twenty-two years of "charter-mongering" the college had revived its old constitution. More important, the colony had reaffirmed the principle of joint secular-ecclesiastical college government and had declared its intention to abide with this arrangement even when it could no longer be presumed to accurately reflect the religious composition of Massachusetts society.

### The Pierpont Affair and the Draft Charter of 1723

The Leverett years witnessed significant changes in the student body, reflecting demographic transformations in the Bay Colony. Attendance increased, and students became more diverse in background and purpose. Before 1719 no eighteenth-century graduating class had ever exceeded twenty. In that year twenty-three students graduated, and in 1723 forty-three received their degrees. Growing enrollments brought different motivations and behavior patterns. "The new crop of young men came to be made gentlemen, not to study," and as a result discipline soon became a troublesome issue.[22]

Not only were the students different. President Leverett himself was a new type of college president. His experience as politician, statesman, lawyer, and judge brought a different outlook into a presidency that, until then, had always been the province of respected ministers. Attuned to the interests and concerns of Boston's rising commercial elite and having participated intimately in the affairs of state, he understood and felt some sympathy for the community's growing taste for diversity, toleration, and secular pursuits. His own religious conviction as a liberal Congregationalist made him tolerant of the Anglican leanings of Boston's business leaders. He also knew that economically the college depended for its survival on Boston's wealth.[23]

The storm that was to consolidate Harvard's defenders around the liberal faction of Massachusetts' ministers and magistrates broke at commencement in 1718. Ebenezer Pierpoint, 1715 graduate of the college and schoolmaster at Roxbury, had complained bitterly that one of Harvard's tutors, Nicholas Sever, kept denying admission to Pierpont's students. President Leverett rushed to Sever's defense. He denied Pierpont his second degree for "his condemning, reproaching and insulting the government of the college." Pierpont protested to Governor Samuel Shute. On commencement day Pierpont appeared before the Corporation and, in what Leverett described as a "long and impertinent" talk, repeated his accusations against Sever and the college. The Corporation, however, refused to be moved and upheld Leverett's decision to withhold the degree.[24]

Pierpont now brought suit against Sever in Middlesex County Court in Charlestown. The Corporation requested a joint meeting with the Overseers and, behind the scenes, looked for some sort of accomodation with ex-Governor Joseph Dudley and his son, Attorney-General Paul Dudley, who were known to be influential with the orthodox churchmen. The fellows also asked Governor Shute to delay the case in the Charlestown court until the Corporation and the Overseers had met.[25] What was planned was an all-out effort to rally the combined resources of magistrates, churchmen, and judges around the embattled Sever, regardless of the merits of the case and of the personal feelings of the protagonists. The suit against Sever was perceived as an attack against the Bay Colony's liberal establishment of college, church, and commonwealth.

At the joint meeting of Corporation and Overseers on October 31, with Governor Shute in the chair, Sever and Pierpont were asked to state their respective cases. Leverett, supporting his tutor, characterized Pierpont's statement as impudent, impertinent, and confused. He spoke of Sever's presentation as plain, modest, and honest. Pierpont's sympathizers found their spokesman in Attorney-General Paul Dudley who, according to Leverett's somewhat jaundiced view, "gave himself great liberty to patronize Pierpont, and made sundry motions tending to embarrass the proceedings of this meeting, and while he endeavoured to hide he did but the more discover his partiality." The Overseers drafted a statement of apology to be signed by Pierpont. He was to promise to abstain from any further prosecution of Sever in the courts. Pierpont, however, refused to cooperate and Governor Shute adjourned the Council.[26]

Pierpont's refusal to apologize was but a repetition of his effrontery, now aimed directly at the highest dignitary of the Commonwealth. His attack was made even more insidious by the support he received from the Dudleys and from Cotton Mather. The latter had urged Governor Shute on the day of the meeting to grant Pierpont's degree or to allow the complaint to be taken up in court and suggested to the governor that he raise the question of the legitimacy of the college charter.[27] Leverett was fully aware that it had been Dudley to whom he owed the presidency of Harvard when he restored the 1650 charter. Knowing well that Mather and the Dudleys had been among the schemers against the Corporation, Leverett must have perceived Mather's plain hint that what one Dudley had done for the college, another Dudley might try to undo.

Disturbing, too, were the means Pierpont chose. An inquiry into the legitimacy of the college charter and the Corporation's disciplinary proceedings first launched in county court involved an inferior court in a constitutional question that traditionally belonged before the General Court. Fortunately for Harvard, the Charlestown judges held that Pierpont had received a proper hearing before the college authorities, and dismissed his complaint.[28]

Still, for Leverett and the college the affair had further ramifications.

The county court's interference, Cotton Mather's and the Dudleys' threats to the charter, and continued discontent among the tutors moved Leverett to consider an appeal to London for a royal charter. Governor Shute's departure for England in the spring of 1723 provided the opportunity and suggested the timing. Leverett's contemplated initiative represented a stunning reversal of positions. In the 1690s it had been the orthodox ministers led by Increase Mather who had sought to use the crown as an ally in their fight to keep the liberal magistrates on the Governor's Council from visiting the college. Now the liberal ministers led by John Leverett were ready to seek the help of the crown for keeping the orthodox ministers and their allies in both houses of the General Court from taking over the Corporation.

News of a scandal that broke at Yale in 1722 might have been what prevented Leverett from following through with his application. In Connecticut, President Timothy Cutler, a liberal Calvinist, had openly left the established church and declared his conversion to Anglicanism. His declaration threw the colony into an uproar and nearly destroyed the college. A petition to the king would have been likely to bring upon Leverett's head a similar flood of accusations of treason and apostasy.[29]

Leverett's royal charter draft was born out of momentary frustration and fear. It testified to the search for the secular backing, for protection against a takeover of the Corporation by orthodox clergymen. But the demographic tensions in the Bay Colony and the orthodox-clerical attack on the colony's liberal establishment notwithstanding, joint government by magistrates and ministers survived. The more heatedly the Mathers and the Dudleys fought for a clerical seminary, the stronger Harvard seemed to emerge as a secular school. Leverett's proposed charter proved to have been an unnecessary precaution. By the mid-1720s Harvard College had weathered all storms under its original charter of 1650. It was still the colony's and the Congregational churches' provincial college.

# 3

## THE COLLEGE OF WILLIAM AND MARY

Though the Puritans had been in New England only six years before deciding to build a college, the Virginia Anglicans required eighty more to obtain a college charter. One difference was the weakness of the Anglican church in Virginia, which was poorly staffed and ineffective in almost every respect; another was Virginia's legal status as a royal colony and its dependence on church and crown officials in London. New England's Congregational churches, by contrast, were strong and vigorous, and the Puritans, having taken their colony charter with them to the New World, were not inclined to ask London for permission. Geography supplies yet another explanation. Virginia was a land of dispersed settlement and plantations, lacking the town government of New England that could create municipal and other grammar schools. The provincial legislators, too, represented a dispersed population. As prosperous plantation owners, they were less impressed with the necessity of public education for public survival. Besides, they were not empowered to license schoolmasters, a function reserved to the Bishop of London.

The original charter for the settlement at Jamestown had enjoined the planters to bring the Indians "to human civility and quiet government," and had encouraged them to save the cost of sending their children back to England by providing schools for them in Virginia. But Indian resistance and the revocation in 1624 of the charter of the Virginia Company stymied these educational projects. An attempt in the mid-1620s to erect in Virginia an *Academia Virginiensia et Oxoniensis* also came to naught. The House of Burgesses tried in the early 1660s to order subscriptions for the purchase of land to erect a school and a college, but met with little response. In 1671 Governor William

29

Berkeley reported that there were neither grammar schools nor colleges in Virginia. This pleased him, since learning, he said, "brought disobedience and heresy and sects into the world."[1] To prosperous Anglican landowners and crown officials public education did not rank high on the list of priorities.

The initiative of Commissary James Blair, the representative of the Bishop of London and head of the Anglican church in Virginia, finally led to the opening of the first grammar school in Virginia in the 1690s. Founded as an integral part of the projected College of William and Mary, and constituting with the Indian School until 1729 the only physical evidence of the college, this school was an English grammar school, royally endowed and placed under the direction of a provincial board of lay trustees.

The members of the Virginia Assembly, encouraging and supporting Commissary Blair, preferred the incorporation of external governors to that of masters and fellows. They had no intention of handing either school or college over to clerical academics; besides, neither masters nor fellows were to be had in Virginia in 1691. The members of the Virginia Assembly also were reluctant to let the funds to be collected for the college slip out of their control into the hands of persons thought of as mere schoolmasters and schoolboys. And finally, as the endowed grammar school origin of the College of William and Mary suggests, the model for its government was England's sixteenth-century grammar school. These schools were supervised by external governors or trustees who also could sit as Visitors. In many instances this arrangement gave increased power to the school's principal while, at the same time, it made this official highly dependent on the school's board. When the headmaster was a forceful personality, he could assert his claim to the co-government of the school; when he was weak, the school was governed by outsiders. The position of the principal or headmaster thus foreshadowed the status of Blair and many other college presidents in the American colonies. But wherever an external board ruled, the faculty's role in college government was bound to be minimal.[2]

For the projected grammar school the Assembly urged Blair to bring back to Virginia a Latin master, an usher, and a writing master for the teaching of English and arithmetic. Intending also to hold fast to their purpose of training candidates for the ministry, the Virginians did not mean to forego their desire for a college and instructed Blair to ask that the governors receive power to elect a chancellor for a seven-year term. Having thus in their instructions to Blair provided for both a school and a university and having directed him to vest substantial power in the Board of Governors in Virginia, they advised him to "make it your business to peruse the best charters in England whereby free schools and colleges have been founded, . . . having always regard to the constitution of this country and government."[3]

## Charter and Statutes

Once in London, Blair soon learned that the projected school and college presented a problem more complex than first envisaged by the colonists. Crown and church officials preferred a college to a school. Governor Berkeley's 1671 report on the absence of free schools in Virginia accurately reflected the suspicions and fears of Anglicans; free schools and academies, many felt, had a way of avoiding the supervision of the church. The bishops thus preferred a college chartered by the crown to a school that might turn into a center of dissent. As Blair wrote to Governor Francis Nicholson in December 1691, they pressed him hard on the school's need for discipline. They were suspicious of schoolmasters, thinking them likely to indulge their laziness, to arrange matters to their financial advantage, to be unjust to their students, and to use "bad books" in their instructions. To forestall such undesirable developments the bishops and "a great many other skillful men" urged Blair to provide first for a college president who, in the manner of an English vice chancellor, could supervise and execute discipline "both among the masters and scholars."

Blair found the colleges in the two English universities nothing but public halls where students could come and go at their pleasure and the professors simply delivered their lectures. Whatever serious educational work was performed at Oxford and Cambridge was carried out by private tutors. In Virginia, there were no funds to endow fellowships for tutors, and the professors and masters would have to take on the work of the tutors. Blair doubted that such professors could be found and was skeptical of discovering a man capable of serving as college president. He was afraid that "if we take a man from either of the universities who never saw any such institution, but has been accustomed to a much more easy and idle way, that he will never bear it and will not at all be fit for such a small college as ours will be."[4]

The bishops were afraid that a locally supervised school in the colony would eventually turn into a center of dissent, and Blair was distrustful of the laxity he associated with an English university college. Was there a way to combine elements of these models to be acceptable in London as well as in Jamestown?

In his letter to Nicholson, Blair informed him that English bishops and friends of the college had suggested Blair himself for the post. Blair, it appears, favored the recommendation. If accepted, he pointed out, his appointment could save the Virginians £50 transportation costs and a new set of instructions. "Though I never sought a place in my whole life time, I could find in my heart to seek this, being well assured that . . . there is none to be found that has a greater zeal for the country, or that is more concerned in point of honor to see this work prosper than I am."[5]

Blair may well have been convinced of his suitability for the presidential post by his familiarity with the governmental practices of Scottish universities. Blair had been a student at Marischal College, Aberdeen, and had earned a master's degree at Edinburgh.[6] Marischal's charter did not stipulate whether Marischal was intended to be a full-fledged university; whether, together with King's College, it was to constitute the University of Aberdeen; or whether it was meant to be a collegiate school in the continental sense of a *gymnasium illustre*. It shared with all Scottish colleges the function of providing endowment support for a president, the members of the teaching faculty, and a number of students. But it also possessed such university officers as chancellor, rector, and dean of faculties, and it had the right to grant degrees in the Faculty of Arts. Blair saw in Marischal a possible model for the school in Virginia. With the functions, privileges, and responsibilities of college and university combined, a new institution at the edge of civilization might be better able to cope with the problems of discipline anticipated by Blair and the English bishops.[7]

The College of Edinburgh, created in 1582 by a royal grant to the government of the city, was governed by a town council. It did not have the university office of chancellor, and it had fused the offices of rector and principal into one. By the end of the seventeenth century Edinburgh appeared as "essentially an arts college with a divinity school attached," governed by the City Council of Edinburgh, and possessing on paper all the rights and privileges of a college.[8] It served as an example for Blair that a school with a board of external governors need not turn into a dissenting academy.

Blair convinced himself and his partners in the negotiations in London that a college governed after the fashion of the Scottish universities would be the ideal institution for Virginia. His earlier reservations about a collegiate institution and his preference for an incorporated grammar school gave way to the arrangements ultimately spelled out in the charter. The London authorities agreed that a provincial council could prevent a college from turning into a seedbed of dissenters. If, in addition, a trusted president, backed by a chancellor in London, acted as liaison between the secular board of control and the academic corporation of clergymen, joint secular and ecclesiastic government would be assured and both royal and Anglican interests well represented.

When Blair returned to Virginia he took with him the charter and a schoolmaster for the Latin school. The charter authorized eighteen Virginia gentlemen to act as college trustees, among them James Blair and the colony's lieutenant governor. The remaining members were to be nominated and elected by the General Assembly. Once the president and masters had arrived, they were to form a Corporation and take over from the trustees the responsibilities of government. The trustees or their successors would continue to supervise the Corporation as governors and Visitors. It was assumed that most, perhaps all, of the professors would be ministers, and that president and chancellor would represent the church. But the effective center of governing power was to be found among the Visitors and in James Blair. As member and first-year rector of the Board of Governors Blair was to have a hand in appointing the masters. As lifetime president he was to remain for many years the living embodiment of the Reformation ideal.[9]

There was plenty of time to study the charter, for incorporation did not occur until 1729. It was evident that the document of 1693 created tension between the Corporation's claims to university status and the powers granted to the trustees both before and after incorporation. The charter used the Latin term *studium generale* to suggest possible growth into a full-fledged university. It named the Corporation as the recipient of all property, land, and services belonging to the college, and gave it the right to perpetual succession, the power to plead and be impleaded, the power to sue and be sued, and the right to have a common seal. The charter further provided for such traditional university offices as rector and chancellor, and for the election by the Corporation of a representative to the Virginia House of Burgesses. With the grant of that privilege, the College of William and Mary was recognized by the crown as a civil corporation like the two universities at Oxford and Cambridge.

But the charter also curtailed the powers of the Corporation. The Virginia Visitors not only received the right to make the original college statutes and to elect the original members of the Corporation as well as their own successors, but also were given power to alter and add to the existing statutes and to continue to elect members of the Corporation and the rector and chancellor. These provisions effectively cut back the traditional powers of an English college corporation and placed them in the hands of the Board of Visitors. The resulting organization, particularly the functions of the rector, resembled that of Edinburgh rather than Oxford or Cambridge. In Edinburgh, as in William and Mary, the rector was not the elected representative of the student body and the faculty, but the spokesman for the board of control—the city council in Edinburgh, the Visitors in Virginia.

These deviations from the traditional English university model may be ascribed to the colonists' distrust of clergymen-professors, to their realistic appraisal of the abilities of "schoolmasters" who needed close supervision, to Blair's preference for the Edinburgh example, or to the more recent English practice of centralizing power in the heads of colleges and the vice chancellor. Whatever the reasons, by shifting so much power from the Corporation to the Board of Visitors, the Virginia college, in contrast to those at Oxford and Cambridge, was far less autonomous and more subject to local outside control.

In the college statutes approved in 1727, the Visitors were also named the Academic Senate. This was a curious and unusual designation for an external governing board. In the University of Cambridge the Senate consisted of the officers and masters of the university assembled as its governing body, and in the Scottish universities the term described the principal and masters meeting in formal session. Tradition suggests that the senate was a college's internal governing body and, with minor exceptions, identical with the college corporation.

In the William and Mary statutes, the senate of the college meant the Boards of Governors and Visitors. Was Blair still suspicious or contemptuous of his faculty? Did he have in mind the role of the city council of Edinburgh as government of that city's university? Or did the statutes represent the influence of the Bishop of London, who might have sought to assure equal authority to the representatives of church and state in college government? Intentionally or not, the 1727 statutes invested the lay board with far greater authority over the faculty than had been traditional in European universities.

Very little is said in the statutes about the faculty besides reminding them of their duty to carry out the educational design of the founders and enumerating the four schools: the Grammar School, the Philosophy School, the Divinity School, and the Indian School. These schools were ranked in something of a hierarchical order, as is indicated by the salaries paid their masters and the ranks assigned to them. The Indian School had a "master" to teach the three "R's" to Indian as well as white boys from the town. The Grammar school had a "school-master" and, if necessary, an usher. Once students graduated from this school they were promoted to the Philosophy School, which, under the guidance of "two masters or professors," allowed its students to work for a bachelor's degree in two years and for a master's degree in an additional two. The years required for the degrees followed Scottish practice, but were changed in the the second edition of the statutes printed in Williamsburg in 1758, when the time prescribed for the bachelor's degree was extended to four years and for the master's degree to an additional three, "according to the form and institution of the two famous universities in England." The Divinity School also was staffed with two professors to indicate its higher status.

The daily government of the college was entrusted to the president and the masters under the statutes promulgated by the senate. The masters were to participate in the election of college officials, such as usher, writing master, bursar, librarian, janitor, cook, butler, gardener, workmen, bailiffs, and overseers. "In lesser matters" the president could act alone. He was, in fact, the "supervisor of the rest." His power derived from the senate; he had to attend its meetings to report on developments in the college. If he disagreed with his faculty on important matters, he was required to ask for the decision of the governors. Again it was clear that the College of William and Mary was not to be governed by its Corporation, but by its senate of nonresident laymen. The one person who belonged to both worlds was the president. Ultimately his actions would determine whether the college faculty could maintain their authority as members of the Corporation or whether they would yield before the power of the governors assembled in the senate.[10]

## Old World Tradition and New World Conditions

The College of William and Mary owed almost everything to the labor and vision of one man, James Blair. In this respect it differed markedly from its Puritan rivals in the north. As schools of and for dissenters, Harvard College and the Collegiate School in Connecticut had to rely on the resources of their Puritan supporters, their secular governments, and their Calvinist churches. In Virginia, James Blair could count on aid from the mother country, on his own academic experience in Scotland, and on the Virginia gentry. Above all, he could rely upon himself. Almost single-handedly he not only created the college but also guided it through it first half-century.[11]

When Blair died in 1743 he had held at one time or another all of the important administrative offices of the college. His career reflected the centralization of governmental powers in the college heads and in the vice chancellors that had been introduced at Cambridge with the Elizabethan statutes of 1570 and at Oxford with the Caroline statutes of 1628 and 1631. Distrustful of the masters' ability to rule themselves and their scholars in a disciplined fashion, Blair had included in his charter proposal variations on these English models. He had supplemented them with provisions for lay government copied from Scotland. He evidently knew what he was doing, for his college survived and prospered.

Blair was also keenly aware that the College of William and Mary was not an integral part of one of the English universities. Not unlike the colleges of Scotland and Trinity College in Dublin, Ireland, it lay isolated in a foreign province.[12] It could not sustain itself on English tradition alone. It needed native support, protection, and direction. Using his instructions from the Virginia Assembly as a point of departure, Blair had asked for and received authorization not only for the initial eighteen Virginia trustees, but also for their continuance as governors and Visitors after the establishment of the Corporation. As in both Edinburgh and Massachusetts, the need for assuring the support of local authorities, civil and ecclesiastic, subordinated the corporate organization of the faculty to supervision and control by nonresident authorities. While the Visitors in Virginia closely followed the example of Edinburgh, the Overseers in Massachusetts had found their counterpart among the *inspectores* of continental Reformed universities. In both colonies similar circumstances led to similar solutions.[13] The governing practices of Reformed universities in Europe, the inexperience or absence of academic personnel, and the scarcity of funds in the New World combined to bring both state and church into the government of the colleges.

# 4

## CONNECTICUT'S COLLEGIATE SCHOOL

In Massachusetts and Virginia secular and ecclesiastic officials jointly participated in the government of their colleges; in Connecticut a collegiate school came into being under the exclusive direction of a group of Congregational ministers. These men had sought authorization from the colony's General Court to fit youth "for public employment both in church and civil state."[1] They were troubled over the expense of a Harvard education for their young men and by Harvard's remoteness from Connecticut. They were also disturbed about the charter difficulties encountered in Massachusetts during the 1690s, and uncertain of the religious orthodoxy of their brethren in the Bay Colony. They thought they had good reason to consider a college for themselves, and consulted with several Connecticut and Massachusetts men whose opinions they valued.[2]

Chief among their advisers was Increase Mather, the recently dismissed president of Harvard. He counseled his Connecticut correspondents to arrange for the government of their projected school by external inspectors who, preferably, should be ministers of neighboring churches. Without resident masters, fellows, or tutors, the Connecticut planners could run their institution like a continental university where the students would board in town. Financial support, Mather suggested, could be arranged on the French model. "The presidents and professors in the Protestant universities in France were maintained by the churches," wrote Mather, "and the several churches were directed by the synods what they should contribute in order thereunto."[3] Clerical control was considered essential.

Another issue for debate was whether the General Court should follow the Massachusetts example and incorporate the Collegiate

38

School as a college. Legal advice from correspondents in Connecticut, while divergent in many ways, favored caution. Gershom Bulkley, physician, lawyer, and politician of Wethersfield, told "the reverend elders deliberating of a college" that as dissenters they could apply for the protection of the 1689 Act of Toleration against possible actions under previous statutes barring nonconformists from teaching. He cited the Statutes of Incorporation of 1597 and 1625, and the 1601 Statute of Charitable Uses.[4] Bulkley did not express himself on the possibility of founding an unincorporated "school of learning" or "free school," but concluded that the General Court should not go ahead on its own with the incorporation of a college since "we all know that the King and Parliament are above us." The Court should apply to them for a charter.[5]

Eleazar Kimberley, the colony's secretary, and John Eliot, lawyer and politician of Windsor, pointed out that Bulkley's opinion was grounded on the mistaken assumption that all the statutes of England and the acts of Parliament were in force in the colonies. This, they said, was true only of those statutes in which the colonies were specifically named. Besides, added Kimberley, William and Mary, the current sovereigns, were known to promote literature and learning and had not raised any questions about the legal status of Harvard College. In addition, Eliot pointed out, colonial governments in New York and Massachusetts had created quasi-corporations to dispose of land, and these had not been questioned by the crown.[6]

Those who like Kimberley and Eliot wanted to explore the feasibility of incorporating the school faced the question of whether English law prohibited the incorporation of a college in the colonies unless a charter were issued by crown and Parliament. The only applicable ruling was the decision in *Calvin's Case* of 1608. Distinguishing between the "realm of England" and the "dominions of the King," the court had held that parliamentary acts and statutes enacted before the time of settlement were in force in the king's dominions only when they had been locally adopted or when the colonies had been specifically named. Even then the royal prerogative remained.[7] Since the presettlement statutes cited by Bulkley had never been adopted in and did not refer to Connecticut, the colonists were subject to the royal prerogative.

Furthermore, the question of the applicability of the English statutes and acts of Parliament to England's foreign plantations posed an uncomfortable dilemma for the the colonists. Unless the answer were qualified to apply to specific cases, it could easily prove to be a double-edged sword. In 1695, for example, a Massachusetts act of 1692 asking that the English habeas corpus act be applied in the colony was disallowed. The colonists resented this, but found it difficult in this instance to argue for an extension of English statutory authority when such extension would, at the same time, restrict their own legislative freedom. On the other hand, not to argue for this extension meant to acquiesce in a denial of constitutional privilege. Kimberley and Eliot felt it worthwhile to assert the colony's right to incorporate a school or college even if they had to face the challenge of a possible quo warranto. Nevertheless, when arguing that English statutes were not automatically in force in the colonies, they were liable to the accusation of consenting to the denial of the right of habeas corpus.

Although Kimberley could point out that Harvard's charter of 1650 had been uncontested, in 1701 the college's legal status was being questioned, and the inability of the Massachusetts authorities to draft a charter acceptable to the crown had caused much anxiety. Furthermore, when Eliot referred to quasi-corporations in New York and Massachusetts, he overlooked the fact that, though exercising many of the privileges of corporations, they were not fully and formally incorporated.

For example, when in 1652 several landowners on Boston's Conduit Street formed a company to supply houses on the street with water, this "incorporation" neglected to name the company and to give it the right of succession. Similar developments occurred with the founding of municipalities, counties, towns, religious societies, and charitable educational foundations. Joseph Davis found that in Massachusetts and Connecticut, in particular, the so-called incorporation of towns meant little more than the definition of geographical limits, the naming of the settlement, and the authorization of the owners to govern themselves. Davis also acknowledged that Connecticut had authorized religious societies and bestowed on them certain privileges of corporations without complete legal incorporation.[8] It would seem, then, that neither Harvard College nor the various quasi-corporations could supply incontrovertible proof of the right of Connecticut's General Assembly to incorporate a college.

There remained the possibility of establishing the projected school as a trust under the Statute of Charitable Uses. Would such action bring the school under the supervising authority of royal commissioners as provided in the statute, or could Connecticut's General Court, sitting as the highest court of equity, serve as visitor? The answer depended on the applicability of the 1601 statute to the colonies. If the school were set up as a public charitable trust, its purposes and effects would have to be "beneficial or . . . supposed to be beneficial to the community," and the trustees would be held responsible less for the welfare of its students than for the welfare of the public. Their fiduciary relationship would be with the public, who were the ultimate beneficiaries, rather than with the students, who were to benefit immediately. The public, in turn, could call on the Court to hold the trustees accountable.[9]

Of all the advisers John Eliot appears to have argued most strongly for the establishment of the school as a trust.[10] As he saw it, the trustees would not be founders, masters, scholars, or governors of the proposed school. Neither they nor the governors — if they were indeed to be distinct from the trustees — would have to be incorporated. Without formal incorporation the trustees could safeguard the property and the permanency of the institution in much the same way that the Overseers had protected Harvard as a trust before the incorporation of 1650. The case for the proposed Connecticut college as a charitable trust was strong inherently and by virtue of the Harvard precedent.

Anxieties concerning the permanency of the colony's chartered government and uncertainties over the school's legal status inclined the planners to reject Eliot's proposal to apply for the university privilege of sending two delegates to the Connecticut General Court.[11] His proposal pointed to the fact that all of the sixteenth-century colleges founded outside of England — Trinity in Ireland, Edinburgh and Marischal in Scotland — had been expected to grow into universities, and that even the seventeenth-century college founded in Virginia had raised the same hope. But Eliot's colleagues refrained from including such a provision in the charter of the Collegiate School, aware that, had they done so, they would have arrogated to themselves a royal prerogative.

Finally, caution also persuaded the ministers to omit any reference to the subject of visitation. To ask either crown, Parliament, or royal charity commissioners to appoint or act as Visitors would only bring the projected school to the attention of London. To embody in the charter a provision for visitation by Connecticut authorities might be an even greater mistake. In 1701, the Connecticut planners knew that twice within the last five years the crown had rejected a new charter for Harvard College because their charter drafts had not provided for visitation acceptable to the Privy Council.

Thus, when the draft charter was presented to the October session of the Connecticut General Court in 1701, it did not contain provisions for magistrates in college government, for incorporation of the school by either crown, Parliament, or General Assembly, for university privileges, or for visitation. It proposed in as inconspicuous a manner as possible to establish a collegiate school by legislative authorization.

## Quasi-Corporation or Partnership?

The charter adopted by the Court empowered ten Connecticut clergymen and their successors "to stand as trustees, partners or undertakers for the said school." The trustees received liberty to organize the school under such rules as would further the school's purpose, as long as they did not violate the established laws of the colony. They also were given power to manage funds and property already received and expected to be contributed by the Court or by others. Once the school had been established, the trustees had power to furnish and direct it, and to appoint a rector or master and officers. The Court promised to grant the school £120 in local currency annually. Finally, the trustees were empowered to grant degrees or licenses.[12] With the 1701 charter the Collegiate School added a new chapter to the history of Reformed academic institutions. For the first time a Reformed collegiate establishment declared its intention to operate without the direct participation of secular officials in its government, while it nonetheless expected to receive financial support from the General Court.

The omission of the magistrates from the governing board was not the only potential problem. The charter also left ambiguous the identity of the school's founder or founders. The preamble to the charter spoke of "several well disposed and public spirited persons" who had petitioned the Assembly to grant "full liberty and privilege . . . unto certain undertakers for the founding, suitably endowing the ordering a Collegiate School." From this wording it appears that the "public spirited persons" were not identical with the "undertakers." The latter were the ten ministers appointed as trustees or partners, but who were the "public spirited persons," and who provided the funds and thus could claim to be the school's founder? References to funding in the charter are to "moneys or any other estate which shall be granted by this Court or otherwise contributed," to the £120 the Court obliged itself to pay annually, and to lands, tenements, hereditaments, goods, chattels, and sums of money "as have heretofore already been granted, bestowed, bequeathed, or given" or would be given in the future. It could be argued that the General Court itself was the school's founder on account of the £120, or that it was James Fitch, who on October 16 offered glass, nails, and a farm.[13] The entire matter of the school's founder or founders remains obscure.

Another source of future trouble lay in the charter's definition of the ten ministers as trustees and partners. As trustees the ministers constituted a quasi-corporation and resembled the Harvard Overseers during the years from 1642 to 1650 as well as their contemporary fellow-trustees at the College of William and Mary. The charter, however, also called them partners and, by implication, permitted each of them to conduct the partnership's business on his own and to commit the other partners to his decisions. Such policy conflicted with the requirements of a quasi-corporation for majority approval.[14]

The question of the trustees' status as partners or as members of a quasi-corporation was stimulated by the controversy that arose in 1715 over the school's location. Since 1701, the students had been taught at various times at Killingworth, Milford, and Saybrook. When in October 1715 the General Court voted to grant £500 to the school for the construction of a house, dissatisfaction with the Saybrook site prompted interest in a change of location.

The initiative was taken by the two Hartford trustees, Timothy Woodbridge and Thomas Buckingham. Viewing themselves as individual partners, they organized a number of Hartford residents and petitioned the Court for assistance in establishing the Collegiate School in their hometown. They and some of their colleagues on the board believed that the choice of location would have to be unanimous to forestall intervention by the legislature. They pointed to the charter phrase that required all trustees "to erect, form, direct, order, establish, improve and at all times in all suitable ways for the future to encourage the said school." The majority of the trustees, however, thought of their board as a quasi-corporation and, also pointing to the charter, argued that only a majority was required "to furnish, direct, manage, order, improve, and encourage . . . the said collegiate school so erected and formed."[15] To them the search for a new location was not a new beginning, but simply an act of managing an already existing institution. Finally, the trustees consulted their by-laws. These specified that if a majority had assembled to discuss the "furnishing and the directing" of the school, their decision would have to be ratified by two-thirds of the members. If, however, less than a quorum had attended the meeting, the decision had to receive subsequent unanimous approval. Thus the presence or absence of a quorum at trustee meetings was to become a point of contention in the debates that were to follow in the next two years.

The site controversy with its constitutional issues soon deteriorated into a series of interminable wrangles that involved the General Court as well. The lower house generally agreed with the Hartford group and urged the trustee-partnership to put the question before the legislature. The upper house, by contrast, favored the view of the majority trustees that the board constituted a quasi-corporation. Legislative interference with a corporation, several trustees pointed out, was dangerous business. It was "contrary to the common law of England," and raised the specter of parliamentary annulment of the colony charter.[16]

Eventually both lower and upper house agreed to endorse New Haven as the permanent home of the college. The Hartford group and its partisans in the lower house had to yield on the location, and the upper house, by its participation in the decision, had in fact contradicted its own principle of noninterference. Tutor Johnson saw the outcome as a compromise achieved after "great throws and pangs and controversy and mighty strugglings." There had been no clear-cut victory for either party. Neither had their been a resolution of the constitutional question of whether the trustees constituted a partnership or a quasi-corporation. They continued to hold the somewhat unique status of partners associated in a quasi-corporation.

Another question, the relation of the trustees to the General Court, came to be much more significant than the nature of the trusteeship and was to figure prominently in later disputes. The Hartford trustees acknowledged readily that the Court had authorized the erection of the school and had contributed funds for that purpose. They also admitted that the school continued to depend on tax money. For these reasons they were inclined to let the Court have a say in the school's affairs, particularly when, as in the site controversy, the trustees could not reach agreement. The majority trustees acknowledged the reasons given by their Hartford colleagues, but they did not come to the same conclusion. They insisted on the chartered rights of the trustees to self-government and, in doing so, compared their partnership to a body politic. With this they overstated their case, but they nonetheless had legitimately raised the question of the General Court's power over the trustees.[17] Given the specific cause of complaint, the majority trustees felt that having a quorum present at all of their meetings precluded the need for unanimity in "furnishing" the school. There was thus no cause for legislative intervention. The Hartford trustees felt otherwise. In 1717 this issue remained unresolved, but the dispute was the exception to an otherwise untroubled relationship between college and Court. The trustees had been able to govern the college without interference, and the Court had supported the college generously with regular annual grants and occasional special contributions.

## A Charter for Yale College

Even after the animosities of the strife over location had subsided, the procedural questions of decision-making continued to haunt the trustees. The school had now been named in honor of Elihu Yale, a wealthy London merchant who had made his fortune in the East India trade and had become the collegiate school's first benefactor. Yale College was thrown into renewed turmoil when in 1722 its rector, Timothy Cutler, defected to the Anglican faith. The trustees were again obliged to look for a new presiding officer. They found it difficult to locate qualified candidates and to agree among themselves "concerning the rule of our practice" of arriving at decisions. The conditions laid down in the by-laws proved cumbersome, and the charter left several questions open to debate. In their quandary they turned to the General Court with a request that it "resolve" these matters, trustee John Davenport "freely consenting . . . in case the General Assembly be the proper seat to resolve said inquiries."[18]

Trustee Samuel Mather had become unable to participate in meetings because of senility, and the trustees asked the Court whether in such a case or in the case of a voluntary resignation they might proceed with the election of a new member. The Court said they could choose another trustee by majority vote, and the following year they elected Samuel Whitman. Next the trustees asked if a majority of the "trustees in being" constituted a quorum. Admitting that the school's charter did not clarify this matter, the Court declared that seven members constituted a quorum and that a majority of any meeting attended by a quorum was capable of making decisions. Unanimity was not required. Furthermore, the Court reduced the age requirement for a trustee from forty to thirty, and provided that the school's rector be a trustee during the period of his rectorate.[19] By authorizing majority decisions and voiding the by-law provision requiring the assent of absent members, the Court underlined in 1723 the quasi-corporate characteristics of Yale's governing board. Though this was helpful in answering the immediate questions, it still left in doubt the larger issue of the school's legal status.

The Assembly's relation to the school was questioned again in an indirect manner when in 1728 Rector Elisha Williams suggested that the trustees apply for a royal charter. It seems that despite their commitment to the Congregational churches, New England college presidents considered recourse to London a possibility of last resort. In Massachusetts Leverett had thus hoped to extricate Harvard from its charter difficulties in 1723, and now Williams considered the same step for Yale. In Connecticut the Episcopalians had challenged the colony's ecclesiastical establishment and had obtained the right to have the church tax of their members paid to them directly rather than to the established Congregational churches. In February of 1728 came news that the king in Council had annulled the Connecticut law of intestate estates, which provided that such estates be divided equally among the heirs and that a double share be given to the oldest son. Annulment threatened the return to the common law practice of primogeniture.[20]

Referring to these blows to colonial pride and self-government, Williams wrote in July of 1728 to trustee Woodbridge that he feared for the school charter as well as for Connecticut's ecclesiastical constitution. After all, he wondered, had the governor and the Court ever had the "power to make a body politic"? He suggested that the colony's agent in London be instructed to petition the crown for a charter of Yale College "and if it might be also, something in favor of our ecclesiastical constitution." The time for such a petition, he felt, was propitious. George II had ascended to the throne in June of 1727. With his annulment of the intestate estate law he had given "no small shock and grievance" to the colonists; thus, reasoned Rector Williams, he might now be ready to do the colony a favor, "since tis not uncommon nor disagreeable to the wisdom of a prince to show an act of grace when he has manifested severity." Williams hoped the Anglicans would not get word of his project because, he wrote, "our bigotted churchmen would endeavour all ways possible to defeat it."[21]

The trustees appear not to have endorsed Rector Williams's suggestion, and nothing ever came of it. A royal charter would surely have constituted a threat to the Connecticut establishment of General Court and Congregational churches. It would have superseded the charter issued by the General Court and, coming from the crown as protector of the Anglican church, would neither have allowed the continuation of an exclusively ministerial board of trustees nor accepted the colony's proposition that in all religious and ecclesiastical matters the Collegiate School was to be guided by the Saybrook Platform of the Connecticut Congregational churches.[22] A royal charter also would have brought to an abrupt end the hegemony of the ministers over the Collegiate School. That Rector Williams nonetheless was willing to run this risk shows how important he deemed it that Yale College be placed on secure legal ground, above the uncertainties of the partnership arrangement, above the vicissitudes of the jurisdictional disputes between trustees and Court, and above the growing power struggle between the Connecticut Congregational establishment and the Anglican church.

Under Williams's successor, Thomas Clap, the trustees were finally incorporated in 1745 as The President and Fellows of Yale College. The charter of incorporation, however, did not come from the crown, but was issued by the Governor and Company of his Majesty's Colony of Connecticut. It transformed the trustees into fellows, but in 1745, just as in 1701, all of them were ministers of Connecticut churches. As a corporation the president and fellows were presumably protected from the Court's interference in their business. But the charter also made it clear that the Court had the right, "as often as required," to inspect the college laws, rules, and ordinances, and to repeal or disallow them "when they shall think proper."[23] The charter thus upheld the ultimate authority of the Court over the college, but also guaranteed the school's autonomy within specific limits. It clearly was intended to clarify the issues that had arisen in the past. It also reaffirmed the original intention of the clerical planners of 1701 to protect the established religion while keeping the secular authorities out of the direct government of the college.

# 5

## THE TRIUMPH OF EXTERNAL GOVERNMENT

In the 1720s at Harvard and in the 1750s at William and Mary academic corporations attempted to reassert their chartered prerogatives as "masters of their colleges" and were defeated. Colleges in America were not to be governed by their teachers, but by the representatives of the civil society that supported and protected them. Secular leadership triumphed over clerical leadership. Whether as in Massachusetts the magistrates among the Overseers gained the upper hand over the ministers of the Corporation, or whether as in Virginia the Visitors of the gentry ruled over the Oxford-trained clerical masters, the results were the same. External governors, favoring landed wealth and secular interests, set the policies for higher education in the colonies.

With this development Harvard and William and Mary embarked on the same road already traveled by Yale and followed by all eighteenth-century colonial colleges. But the government that Yale and the other colleges had taken for granted as determined by their charters emerged only after vigorous battles at the Massachusetts and Virginia institutions. There the faculty, not the members of the external governing boards, made up the Corporation. The Harvard charter of 1650 had incorporated the president, five fellows, and the treasurer; the 1693 charter of William and Mary had incorporated the president and the masters or professors. At the same time, the teachers had to share their corporate prerogatives with the members of their respective external governing boards, the Harvard Overseers and the Visitors of William and Mary. These boards did not content themselves with an occasional investigation or arbitration of a college dispute. They acted as a second governing board and, more often than not, claimed superior wisdom and power in disagreements with the Corporation. In addi-

48

tion the Harvard teachers found themselves further limited in their governing function when the practice of appointing nonresident fellows to the Corporation and of appointing tutors without concurrent Corporation appointment began. Under these circumstances it was only natural that the Harvard tutors and the masters at William and Mary would demand their rightful voice in college government.

The battle of the teachers at the two colleges to regain for themselves a place in college government can also be seen as another attempt to break the Reformation pattern of external supervision and to reintroduce corporate faculty government on the model of the medieval universities or of the English colleges. It proved impossible, however, to turn back the clock and to revitalize the medieval corporations of masters and scholars.

### The Tutors of Harvard College

After Leverett's election to the Harvard presidency, the tutors took up the fight against nonresident governors. They were unhappy with the daily problems of discipline and with President Leverett's reluctance to support their request for greater authority. They found it easy to blame their unhappiness on the activities and sentiments of outsiders who, in their view, wielded authority in blissful ignorance of the consequences. Their disagreements with Leverett and the fellows originated in April 1716, when the Corporation began to distinguish its members as "Fellows of the Corporation" and the resident tutors as "fellows of the house," and when, with the election of Joseph Stevens, minister at Charlestown, they had deliberately broken with the custom of selecting resident tutors as Corporation members.[1] In addition, the Corporation imposed a three-year-term limit on newly elected tutors. By 1716 the Corporation consisted of four nonresident fellows and tutor Henry Flynt, who was serving his sixteenth year. The other two tutors, Thomas Robie and Nicholas Sever, were without Corporation appointment.[2] They were further offended when in 1717 two outspoken, liberal Congregationalists and supporters of President Leverett were chosen to replace Corporation members who had died. These new fellows, Benjamin Coleman, the minister of Boston's Brattle Street Church, and Nathaniel Appleton, the youthful inheritor of William Brattle's church in Cambridge, were also nonresidents.[3]

In the spring of 1718 Leverett interfered with Sever's administration of student discipline and reprimanded him for having signed the students' quarter bills. Leverett tended to take a less severe view of student misconduct than Sever, who, because of his advanced age — he was thirty-eight in 1718 — was determined to make up for any presumed loss of prestige by acting as a strict disciplinarian.[4] For another two years Sever and Leverett got along with each other, Sever being gratified by the support Leverett extended to him during the Pierpont affair. But by May of 1720 the old conflict had broken out again.

Tutors Flynt, Sever, and Robie petitioned the Corporation to appoint all of the tutors as fellows and to require them to live in the college. They argued that it had been the practice of the English universities and the intent of the 1650 charter to have the members of the Corporation reside within the college and to administer its daily government.[5] The Corporation, however, was not impressed with the tutors' arguments. As they saw it, tradition did not favor the tutors' case for five resident fellows. If they were to grant the tutors' request, the charter would require the replacement of three of the four nonresident fellows with tutors. No matter which of the four fellows were picked, such a move would be a heavy blow to Leverett's supporters. The only possible alternative was to petition the General Court for a change of the charter. But this soon after the Pierpont affair, the Corporation had reason to leave well enough alone. As long as Dudley and Mather had to be reckoned with, a move to alter the charter might result in a loss of that precious foundation on which the college rested. The members of the Corporation saw no pressing reason to consider seriously the tutors' memorandum.

Meanwhile the tutors and their supporters among Leverett's orthodox foes kept up the pressure. The president complained to John White, the Corporation's treasurer, that Paul Dudley had falsely accused him of neglecting his duties in the college and had claimed that he had been so informed by one of the tutors. All of the tutors, Leverett wrote indignantly to the Speaker of the House, had denied this, and he resented such rumors being used to undercut his urgent requests for increased appropriations. In May of 1721 two fellows of the Corporation came to his assistance and petitioned the General Court for an increase in the president's salary.[6]

Less than a month later Leverett heard the annoying news that the tutors had submitted their petition to the Overseers. However, a change had occurred among the signatories. Tutors Flynt and Robie had refrained from signing and Sever was now joined by William Welsteed, who had been elected in 1720. The Overseers referred the petition to a committee headed by Chief Justice Samuel Sewall, a friend of the Dudleys and Cotton Mather.[7]

In the meantime the Corporation went on with its business. In June of 1721 they elected Edward Wigglesworth to the newly endowed divinity professorship, and in September they chose William Cook as fifth tutor. In the following January they filled the vacancy left by the death of Joseph Stevens with Joseph Sewall, son of the chief justice and minister of a Boston church. In doing so they rebuffed the tutors by ignoring their petition.[8]

But the tutors had their supporters. When President Leverett in the spring of 1722 sought the Overseers' approval of Sewall's election, they told him to chose a tutor instead. The Corporation, asserting its charter right to elect its own members, elected tutor Robie. They claimed at the same time that their withdrawal of Sewall's election should not be viewed as a precedent. The Overseers, however, were not mollified. They apparently resented Robie's election and deferred his endorsement in order to discuss further the petition of Sever and Welsteed.[9]

While this matter was still pending, Sever's three-year term ran out in April, and the Corporation refused to rehire him. The Overseers interceded, asked the General Court to allow the inclusion of all the resident tutors in the Corporation, and ordered Sever to continue with his tutorial duties "notwithstanding what had been done with reference to him by the corporation." The fellows acquiesced.[10] In June the General Court responded to the Overseers' request with a recommendation that the Corporation consist of the resident tutors and that fellows not be permitted to serve on the Board of Overseers.[11] Only Governor Shute's added proviso that the current three nonresident fellows and Overseers — all liberal supporters of Leverett — remain as fellows of the Corporation saved the fellows from embarrassment and protected the president and his friends from their opponents. The changes desired by the Court would go into effect only after the current fellows' terms expired. In the face of repeated requests by the lower house to reconsider, Governor Shute held fast to his proviso, relying on what he called the "desire and intention" of his Council and the Overseers.[12]

Disputes and disagreements continued. At the beginning of the new legislative session in November of 1722, the House urged the Corporation to observe their charter and obey the resolution passed by both

House and Council the previous June. The Corporation asked for a meeting with the General Court. On December 12, 1722, the House rejected this request as "altogether groundless, and no ways to be justified," and urged the Council to join them in this declaration. But the upper house bided its time and did nothing. In February of the next year the fellows failed to elect a Corporation replacement for Thomas Robie, who had resigned from his offices as tutor and fellow. With the House pressing for the appointment of Sever and Welsteed, the Overseers known to be divided on the issue, and the governor and Leverett resisting such a move, the Corporation understandably hesitated to act. Instead they deferred the matter until their next meeting in April and, after further postponement, took it up on June 4. They then unanimously elected Edward Wigglesworth, the newly appointed Hollis Professor of Divinity, only to have their choice refused by the Overseers.[13]

Three days later, on June 7, the Overseers once more tipped their hand by advising the Corporation to improve the salaries of the resident tutors, Sever and Welsteed. These two gentlemen, in the meantime, had continued to further their own interests and again asked the Court to include them in the Corporation. The House asked for the Council's opinion, only to be told that it had done nothing on the matter. On August 7 the House then decided to revive its resolution that the tutors should be members of the Corporation and that no fellow should also be an Overseer. The Corporation reacted two days later by reviving its request to be heard before the General Court. On the same day the Overseers decided that they would visit the college in order to "serve the interest of religion and learning in that society." In the House on August 13 the Overseers' original petition to add the resident tutors to the Corporation was received from the Council and voted down. As matters now stood, the lower house as before was determined to oust the nonresident fellows from the Corporation and to replace them with the tutors; the upper house was willing to keep the nonresident fellows but would add to them the resident tutors. The Overseers had rejected the Corporation's choice of Professor Wigglesworth for the vacant spot on the Corporation and recommended improving the salaries of tutors Sever and Welsteed and they now pressed for a visitation of the college. The Corporation, uncomfortably situated at the center of the conflict, continued to request a hearing before the General Court.[14]

At this juncture the Council voted to receive the Corporation and grant it a hearing. In its presentation on August 23, 1723, the Corporation maintained that the original charter did not provide for the fellows to be residents of the college, but specified only that they be inhabitants of the Bay Colony. The Corporation, rather than the Overseers, had been given the right to manage the college funds and to fix salaries and allowances. They also were to make the laws of the college, while their execution was left to the president and tutors. The charter could not have meant, the fellows maintained, that the resident tutors had the power to elect the president, to choose and remove officers, to make the laws they were asked to administer, and to manage revenues and determine salaries. These were powers and responsibilities not lightly granted to "younger gentlemen of small experience." Sever's and Welsteed's contentions, they argued, were novel and contradicted the history of the college. The fellows ended by suggesting that the tutors would find little reason to complain "if they would, as become Christians, study to be quiet and do their own business."[15]

Then it was Sever's turn. His argument was based on his contention that the charter had placed "the execution of all orders and by-laws" into the hands of the Corporation, and that its members had no authority to delegate their powers to tutors and other officers and servants. For the fellows to withdraw from the college allowing others to manage its business was "to pretend to such a power as I believe was never granted to any college under the British dominion." Sever added that a feeble resident government entailed lack of decorum and discipline among the students. He protested the tutors' low salaries, the three-year tenure law, and the choice of nonresident fellows from among the Overseers, a practice that allowed the proposal of rules "by the fellows from themselves in corporation to themselves as overseers for confirmation." Sever's main point, however, was that the distinction between fellows and tutors — or fellows of the Corporation and fellows of the house — was unwarranted. Nonresident fellows were unknown in Britain except "in extraordinary cases," and their introduction here and their replacement by other persons "with only a title, and that are upon no foundation" was "a thing entirely new under the sun."[16] Sever wanted this practice stopped.

The Council now voted not to concur with the House resolves that had remained unanswered for so long. It did not approve of constituting the resident tutors as the Corporation and of preventing the fellows from serving on the Board of Overseers. The House then let the matter rest. The Overseers still proceeded with their visitation of the college.

They expressed general satisfaction with the instructional program, but complained about student immoralities, such as "stealing, lying, swearing, idleness, picking of locks, and too frequent use of strong drink." In December the Corporation for the second time elected Wigglesworth a member and, in addition, agreed that each subsequent holder of the Hollis Professorship of Divinity should be chosen as a fellow.[17]

The death of President Leverett the following May then changed the situation completely. On the day following the president's death, the Overseers accepted Wigglesworth's election as fellow to fill the vacancy left by Thomas Robie. The Corporation showed a willingness to end the strife of the last few years by electing Joseph Sewall, son of Chief Justice Samuel Sewall and a friend to the orthodox party, to the presidency. Sewall, however, declined the nomination and, after a second unsuccessful attempt to select Leverett's successor, Benjamin Wadsworth took over the reins of the college in July 1725. He was one of the three nonresident fellows whose eviction from the Corporation had been sought by the House, but his elevation to the presidency was balanced two months later by the unanimous election of tutor Sever to the Corporation. With that step the tutor controversy faded from view, and new issues — such as the claim of the Anglican ex-President of Yale, Timothy Cutler, to a seat among the Overseers — rose on the horizon.[18] For a century the questions raised by Sever were to remain dormant.

Did Sever accomplish what he had set out to do? To the extent that after 1724 the number of nonresident fellows and Corporation members on the Board of Overseers had been reduced to two and that in 1725 Sever himself became one of the resident members of the Corporation, he could be satisfied. The Corporation now had three fellows in intimate and daily touch with the affairs of the college. Only two of them, however, served as tutors. The third was Edward Wigglesworth, the Hollis Professor of Divinity. At the same time, Sever had failed in getting all of the resident tutors on the Corporation. Nathan Prince and William Welsteed remained without appointment to the Corporation.

The outcome of the controversy reaffirmed the Reformation type of college government. More significant, however, was the shift of relative power from the ministers to the magistrates. Sever had not intended to bring about such a result when he began his agitation, but given the religious and political situation in the Bay Colony it could hardly have been avoided. The fact that it was possible for Sever, with the help of disgruntled partisans among the ministers, to gain as much attention as he did indicates how weak the hold of churchmen had become on the colony's public affairs. Dissension in their own ranks coupled with the rise of heterodoxy in the commonwealth reduced their influence in politics and allowed the academics in the college to raise their claim for participation in college government. That claim itself was based on the far older tradition of the medieval universities' corporate self-government, but the tutors were unable to revive it. Boston's aristocracy of merchants and traders gained where the tutors and the orthodox ministers had failed in their bid for power.

## The Masters of William and Mary

Thirty years later a similar struggle between academics and representatives of secular interests began at William and Mary. The event that provoked the controversies between professors and Visitors was the passage by the Virginia assembly of the so-called Two Penny Act in December 1775.[19] In a time of rising tobacco prices, Virginians were permitted for a period of ten months to pay the clergy in money rather than in tobacco, as had been customary. The clergymen-professors of the college protested unsuccessfully to Governor Robert Dinwiddie. Their president, Thomas Dawson, who was also the commissary of the Anglican church in Virginia, asked for the intervention of Bishop Thomas Sherlock in London.[20] When three years later the Assembly passed another Two Penny Act, Professor John Camm was sent to London to bring the clergy's case to the attention of the crown. Bishop Sherlock aided his mission with a letter to the Board of Trade.[21] The Privy Council then disallowed the acts of 1755 and 1758, but upon his return to Virginia Camm was severely reprimanded by Governor Fauquier for having brought London into Virginia politics and for having delayed his appearance before Fauquier for ten months.[22]

A bitter pamphlet war broke out in the colony, making the Anglican clergy and the masters of the college exceedingly unpopular and contributing to the rising revolutionary sentiment. The crowning blow came in 1767 when Camm's appeal to the Privy Council was dismissed on a technicality. The affair served to identify the masters of the college as clergymen who had support in London and who stood apart from the main current of life in Virginia. This did not help to strengthen the college's political position.

Within the college itself the controversies surfaced in May of 1757 when the Visitors gave six months' notice of dismissal to Thomas Robinson, master of the grammar school, and asked the chancellor to recommend a layman as successor. Robinson protested to Bishop Sherlock, the college chancellor, and received the endorsement of his colleagues John Camm, William Preston, and Richard Graham, all masters in the college, and Emmanuel Jones, the master of the Indian school.[23] President Dawson, on the other hand, appeared reluctant to offend the Visitors and Governor Dinwiddie. The governor had charged Professors Robinson and Preston with drunkenness, irregular execution of duties, and marriage in defiance of college rules. Dinwiddie further censored the entire faculty for having called a clergy convention in 1757 and for having refused to aid President Dawson in his ministerial duties during a recent illness.[24] The lines of battle were now clearly drawn: the faculty on one side, and president, governor, and Visitors on the other.

At their meeting of November 1, 1757, the Visitors learned that James Hubard, the usher of the grammar school whose reprimand by Robinson was thought to have precipitated the latter's dismissal, had now been discharged from his job, allegedly "without any equitable cause." The Visitors appointed a committee to investigate the circumstances and to report four days later. They received help from neither President Dawson nor the faculty. Professors Camm and Graham and master Jones all claimed that according to the college statutes they could not provide evidence because the power of appointing or removing an usher belonged solely to the president and masters. In response the Visitors removed them from office as of December 14. Three days later, however, Mr. Jones had a change of heart and was reinstated by the Visitors.[25]

On campus it was left to President Dawson to enforce the Visitors' ruling. He met with master Jones, and the two demanded that their colleagues vacate their quarters and hand over keys and college papers in their possession. When Robinson and Graham refused—Camm was absent on that day—Dawson and Jones instructed the housekeeper and the steward to cease serving them. On the next day Camm returned and, upon being approached by Dawson and Jones, joined Robinson and Graham in their refusal to leave the college. Dawson and Jones now decided to consult with a lawyer, and to ask Graham to hand over the accounts of the college to them. Graham's answer was evasive. He would "go about them," he said, "when the weather was warmer," and, adding insult to injury, when "there was a society to examine them." A few days later Dawson ordered the doors locked and barred to all the faculty.[26] This action of late March 1758 appears to have ended the resistance of the dismissed faculty, and by 1759 all agitation appeared to have died down.

Robinson soon died, and in 1763 the Privy Council reversed the dismissals of Camm and Graham. When a new faculty assembled, the Visitors were again in control. They now claimed the right to inquire into the faculty's proceedings and the power to dismiss members of the Corporation. Whatever hopes for redress the masters might have cherished now rested on the appeals they had filed in London.[27]

The faculty's channel of communication to London was the commissary, who usually also served as the college president. This channel, however, was far from effective. The faculty resented Dawson's refusal to push their claims against the alleged illegality of the Two Penny Acts and to call a clergy convention. William Robinson, Virginia clergyman and aspirant to Dawson's office of commissary, wrote Bishop Sherlock in November 1760 that both as president of the college and as commissary of the church Dawson had become a "mere tool" of the Visitors. He was, said Robinson, "a false brother." Furthermore, Robinson accused Dawson of being "a very immoral man," frequently intoxicated and often found in public houses playing cards.[28] When Robinson succeeded Dawson, he was to be no more successful than Dawson had been. He was not a faculty member and did not receive the customary appointment as president of the college. He was, however, a close confidant of Professor Camm and, as such, cordially disliked by Governor Fauquier. Fauquier saw in him a mouthpiece of the faculty, and he advised the Bishop of London "to direct his commissary to break off connections with Mr. Camm who winds him about his finger just as he pleases." The bishop, of course, did nothing of the sort.[29]

For the faculty, matters went from bad to worse. The Visitors dismissed Jacob Rowe, the professor of moral philosophy, for drunkenness, and for having led students in a riot with apprentices of the town. They also censured Gronow Owen, master of the grammar school, for drunkenness and other indiscretions.[30] The final straw for the faculty was the elevation of James Horrocks, master of the grammar school, to the college presidency. Many felt that Graham and Camm had stronger claims to that office and were further incensed when they learned that Horrocks had obtained his appointment by taking an oath on a statute adopted by the Visitors on September 14, 1763. The Visitors had given themselves the right to discharge the president and masters by majority vote and to exercise direct and final authority over the internal management of the college. They also prohibited the masters from taking on a parish assignment while holding office in the college, required their residence at the college, and ordered the president and masters to take an oath on the statute. The statute severely infringed the charter rights of the Corporation. It placed the masters' tenure as members of the Corporation at the mercy of the Visitors, and it took from them their basic right to administer their own affairs. Opposition mounted quickly in the faculty and received support from the chancellor in London. President Horrocks, sensing that a fundamental point of college law was at issue, asked for a revision of the college charter in order to spell out more clearly the respective responsibilities and rights of Visitors and masters.[31]

When the Visitors asked Professor Camm to choose between his professorship and his parish Camm refused. He argued that he was confronted with a charge, and demanded the right to submit a written defense. When after considerable hesitation the Visitors finally agreed to receive it, Camm severely condemned the statute, chided President Horrocks for having taken an oath on it, and announced that he would appeal to the king, who was the supreme Visitor of a college founded by the crown.

Camm's threat was effective. The Visitors decided not to press their demands, and several of them asked Camm to tutor their children, who were not doing well under President Horrock's supervision of the grammar school.[32] Later, on May 1, 1766, they agreed to amend the statute. The day-to-day administration of the college was left to the faculty under the supervision of the Visitors, nothing was said about the Visitors' power of dismissal, and the prohibition of parish employment was not to be applied retroactively. The oath on the statute and the prohibition of future outside employment remained, however. The key issue of the right to dismiss faculty members was smothered in silence; the Visitors did not give up their claim to supervision of the Corporation's internal college government and, by keeping the oath, they upheld the principle of their action. Still, many observers would agree with Governor Fauquier, who complained that the Visitors had allowed "Mr. Camm [to] lead them by the nose."[33]

Little was to change in this perpetual tug-of-war between masters and Visitors in the years preceding the American Revolution. For a time both parties seemed to agree on the desirability of a charter revision.[34] Perhaps the matter was aided by Governor Fauquier's death early in 1768. President Horrocks appeared to draw closer to Professor Camm, and in a letter to Bishop Terrick went so far as to call the Visitors "ignorant and intemperate." He told the bishop at the same time that the faculty would soon present him and the Visitors with a statement of their position.[35] This statement was presented on May 4, 1768. It received a polite but chilly response. In it president and masters underlined their status as members of the Corporation who derived their powers from the charter and not, as the Visitors seemed to think, from them. The day-to-day government of the college belonged to the president and masters, and they carried it out according to the statutes promulgated by the Visitors. They, too, should have the power to award scholarships and to appoint officials and servants. As far as parish appointments to members of the faculty were concerned, the masters were competent to judge the appropriateness of such assignments. The Visitors, president and masters maintained, were judges in all cases of complaints submitted to them over questions of faculty government. They should refrain from making statutes upon mere rumors and "nameless information," and they should join the faculty in asking for help from London to suppress the smuggling of tobacco, an activity whereby the college lost much of its revenue.

In response the Visitors approved the faculty request to award one named scholarship, but added that they would "pay a proper regard to the recommendation of the said president and masters in all future appointments to scholarships they have a right to dispose of." They appropriated £50 to the president and masters for the purpose of awarding students, and they rescinded their order "that for the future, if the Masters desire hot suppers, they shall provide them at their own expense." But they refused to even accept the complaint referring to statutes based on "nameless information," and said nothing about the questions of delegated versus chartered powers for the faculty, of the faculty's power over the daily government and appointments to the staff, of keeping or accepting parish appointments, or of their right to administer the college revenues. Rector Fontaine, in fact, confirmed this essentially negative stance when he wrote Bishop Terrick that the Visitors reserved the right to grant or deny permission to the masters for outside employment.[36]

As might be expected, the faculty's reaction was one of disappointment and anger. Many now saw no other way but an appeal to the crown. They considered the concessions offered them by the Visitors inadequate and, in the case of the hot suppers, not even asked for. From President Horrocks they had learned that the Visitors' silence on the important issue of delegated power and control over the college's internal affairs had been deliberate. Many of the Visitors liked the term "delegated power" because it seemed to imply that the faculty's right to the internal government was limited to appearing before the Visitors "with their council." To vest the professors with the power to administer charitable scholarships, the Visitors were said to have remarked, would be "impiety to the dead and injustice to the living." President Horrocks reported further that the Visitors had in fact asserted their full control over the appointment of officers and servants and over acceptance of parish assignments by members of the faculty. The masters concluded that the Visitors meant "to keep the grand points of power . . . unsettled and in confusion," and asked Bishop Terrick for his advice.[37]

As the 1760s drew to a close, the chances for charter revision dimmed. While the masters felt as disaffected as ever, Virginians, excited by the tremors of the approaching Revolution, were ill-disposed to listen to the faculty's complaints, and Chancellor Terrick received nothing but negative advice from President Horrocks on the charter question. Horrocks had by now also been elevated to commissary of the Anglican church, and, after the arrival of a new governor, Lord Botecourt, aspired in addition to an appointment to the Governor's Council. His ambitions further strained his relations with his colleagues on the faculty, who would have preferred to see Professor Camm, over the years theirs and the clergy's most effective spokesman, appointed as commissary. When Horrocks aligned himself with the interests of the Virginia laity on the Board of Visitors and on the Council, when he refused to join Professor Camm in a request for the king's writ of mandamus to pursue one of the remaining complaints concerning the Two Penny Acts, and when he declined to transmit a report on this question as a petition to the governor, the break between him and the faculty became irreparable.

The Visitors saw no reason to desist from their attempts to place tighter reins on the faculty. In September 1769 they rebuked Professor Camm and grammar school master Josiah Johnson for having married and moved off campus, thereby neglecting their duties to the students. In December they resolved that in the future professors had to live at the college and to vacate their positions when and if they married. In the next year they debated new statutes that would give them greater and more direct powers in the administration of discipline and would reorder curricular requirements.[38] The faculty must have felt like a beleaguered minority in their outpost of academic learning. Within their college, however, they could still cherish a few instances in which they succeeded in keeping the Visitors from taking over. The two debated statutes apparently were never put into force; the masters kept their parishes notwithstanding the Visitors' displeasure, and Camm established himself as a married man outside the college walls.[39] Yet there could be not doubt that with or without charter revision, the college remained under the effective control of its board of external governors.

In Virginia as in Massachusetts, the teachers proved themselves inadequate to the demands of self-government. Though in their provisions for two-board government the charters of Harvard and of William and Mary differed from the constitutions of all other colonial colleges, the governmental practice of these two colleges soon lost its distinctiveness and came to resemble that of the one-board colleges. American colleges were to be ruled by powerful and respected citizens, who would govern them for their own and their children's benefit.

# II

## Cultural Pluralism
## and the Great Awakening

IT WAS the Great Awakening that set in motion the evolution of
college government from the Reformation style to the eventual
public-private pattern. That arousal of enthusiastic religiosity in
the 1740s shook the very foundations of some existing colleges and
was instrumental in founding new ones. The Awakening's
evangelistic spirit, stimulated by the expectation of population
growth and geographic expansion, demanded opportunities for
missionary work and welcomed students and teachers from all
Protestant denominations.[1]

In England, too, the new demographic realities in the colonies
were clearly perceived. In 1763 officials at the royal court warned
that "so mixed a multitude, if left destitute of the necessary means
of instruction, differing in language and manners unenlightened
by religion, uncemented by a common education, strangers to the
humane arts, and to the just use of rational liberty," would constitute a danger to His Majesty's plantations. They therefore sponsored a joint fund-raising effort in England for King's College and
the College of Philadelphia. The court pointed out that not only
Anglicans but also "the various denominations of other Protestants in his Majesty's colonies" vouched for the pressing need of
colleges, and were severally and jointly committed to "the support and extension of the reformed religion" in the colonies.[2] Such
common effort did not imply that the colleges were to deny or
give up the faith of their founders — neither Harvard nor Yale had
contemplated a break with the Congregational or Presbyterian
churches, and the new college in New Jersey was a decidedly New
Light Presbyterian institution — but it meant that such allegiances

63

would not stand as obstacles in the path of Protestants of other denominations.

At Harvard the effects of the Awakening were comparatively mild. The college gracefully adapted its century-old frame of government to changing conditions. The magistrates increased their influence on the Board of Overseers, and the liberal ministers gained strength on the Corporation at the expense of the orthodox.[3] At Yale, however, matters took a more dramatic turn. Initially Rector Thomas Clap had responded to the Awakening with a new charter that cemented the college firmly to the colonial establishment of church and state. But during the 1750s when he began to lose the support of the Assembly, Clap deliberately broke with tradition, reorganized the college as a religious society and seminary, and moved toward independence from state and church. This process reached its climax in his triumph over the Assembly in 1763, a political event of the first order, with repercussions in colonial politics for many years to come. But Clap's victory was reversed thirty years later when the General Court reorganized the Yale Corporation.[4]

In the Middle Colonies the Awakening was responsible for the founding of the College of New Jersey (Princeton) with a mixed board of ministers and laymen. As in Massachusetts, religiously motivated strife over the college was minor. Born into a heterogeneous society, the college did not have an ecclesiastical establishment to contend with. It was founded by laymen and ministers of various Presbyterian factions from New Jersey, New York, and Pennsylvania. It received no support from any of the colonies or from any church. Its charter forbade discrimination against anyone on grounds of religion or of residence outside the province, and it obliged the governor of New Jersey to enforce this provision for toleration. To have the governor appointed ex officio to the college board represented a compromise between the demands of the founders for independence and the insistence of Governor Jonathan Belcher on state representation. This was the kind of compromise Clap had not been able to achieve or to accept in Connecticut.[5]

In Pennsylvania's college-founding ventures, religion never quite aroused the same level of discourse and concern as it had in Connecticut. Here politics occupied the main stage. A municipal academy in Philadelphia grew into a college and in the process became deeply entangled in provincial politics and subject to a contest between a popular party and the representatives of the colony's proprietors. The College of Philadelphia thus came to play a major role in the political debates and struggles of the Revolution.

In New York, the college became a major issue in the 1750s. King's College lingered on as it became the victim of a power struggle between Anglican loyalists and their opponents, whose aim was complete separation of the college from denominational and religious interests. The struggle involved two clashing interpretations of toleration. The Anglicans in the city believed in a "preferred" toleration, while their antagonists stood for "equal" toleration or secularism. Toleration with preferment meant to open the door to members of all Protestant denominations while acknowledging the claims to special recognition of the Anglicans because of their contributions of property and service. The champions of equal toleration or secularism wanted, above all, to insure equal treatment for everyone. They therefore opted for a college under legislative supervision and supported by public funds. The irony in this situation lay in the fact that the Anglican claim to preferment had no basis in demography. The Dutch Reformed constituted the most numerous group in New York, but they became so disenchanted that they withdrew from the College of New York and eventually created a college of their own in New Jersey.[6]

By the end of the 1740s everywhere the concept of an established college tied to an established church had proved to be anachronistic. Contrary to the intent of its promoters, the Great Awakening had at this stage loosened the hold of organized religion on the colleges and set off a tumultuous search for new arrangements. During the following two decades politics rather than religion preoccupied the colonists. Legislators turned to college affairs not because they had become aroused by the spiritual agitation in the colleges, but because they became concerned over political strife and turmoil and alarmed by complaining parents who were upset over unrest in the colleges. If men of the cloth were slow to promote toleration and interdenominational cooperation, then laymen in the legislatures would seize the initiative and respond more quickly to changing popular moods.[7] Thus what had begun in the 1740s as a religious dispute provoked by the Great Awakening and as a widespread unwillingness to tolerate denominational exclusivity had, by the 1750s, become the stuff of colonial politics. The forces of American pluralism made themselves felt and began to shape the forms of American college government.

# 6

## YALE COLLEGE AND THE AWAKENING

The shift of focus from religion to politics took its most dramatic turn in Connecticut. There Thomas Clap, for a quarter century rector and then president of Yale College, through his determination first to integrate his school into the colony's secular and ecclesiastical establishment and then to break off that relationship, sought to gain a position of power for himself and his college. His efforts, however, only involved him in continuous battles with the Assembly, his students, and their parents. At the root of his troubles was his inability to come to terms with the enthusiasm aroused by the Great Awakening.

When Clap assumed the rectorship in 1740 he could justifiably expect to work easily and harmoniously with the Assembly and the colony's Congregational churches. In contrast to the liberal and tolerant Harvard, Yale College in 1740 was considered safely conservative for future Congregational ministers and worthy upholders of the established order. It "was a firmly established center of learning in the new world. The new rector had only to improve the college, not rescue it."[1] But the agitation of revivalist preachers, called New Lights, soon made improvement difficult. After having first welcomed the arrival on campus of George Whitefield and Gilbert Tennent, two of the most renowned awakeners, Clap came to regret his hospitality. The students' newly roused enthusiasm led them to ignore college rules. When James Davenport, a graduate of 1732 turned revivalist, denounced the New Haven minister Joseph Noyes from his own pulpit as a pharisee, Clap decided to call a halt to such proceedings. Other ministers and magistrates quickly came to his support. In May of 1741 the New Haven county association of ministers declared unanimously that it was "not well" for any clergyman to preach in a pulpit other than his own, unless he had first obtained the consent of the resident minister. In November a colony-wide consociation meeting of ministers at Guilford upheld these and similar sentiments.[2]

Upset over the influence exerted by itinerant ministers on the students the trustees resolved in September "that if any student of this college shall directly or indirectly say that the rector, either of the trustees or tutors are hypocrites, carnal or unconverted men, he shall for the first offense make a public confession in the hall, and for the second offense by expelled."[3] Clap soon found occasion to apply the ordinance and expelled David Brainerd for having said of his tutor that he possessed no more grace than a chair. But the turmoil persisted, split the New Haven church, caused Clap to send the students home, and threatened the ecclesiastical establishment of Connecticut. Alarmed that students had "fallen into several errors in principal and disorders in practice," a committee of the legislature recommended in April 1742 that the General Court grant funds to hire a college minister. In the next month the Assembly stepped in and with its "Act for Regulating Abuses and Correcting Disorders in Ecclesiastical Affairs" attempted to ban all but settled ministers and their supporters from Connecticut pulpits.[4]

Clap was wholly in sympathy with these repressive measures against the New Lights. He applied his conservatism with an even hand to both colony and college, and in so doing approved and relied upon an alliance of college and General Court. In a 1743 memorial the trustees stressed this alliance and emphasized that it had been "this honorable Assembly" which "of their fatherly care and concern for the religious as well as civil interest of the people of this colony" had been "pleased to found and establish Yale College."[5] In the early 1740s both Clap and the trustees favored a close relationship between college and legislature to uphold the Old Light establishment of state, church, and college.

The Court looked upon Yale as a provincial establishment and did not tolerate competitors. When in the summer of 1742 New Light ministers opened the Shepherd's Tent in New London as a seminary for the training of "awakened" ministers, the Assembly wasted no time in undercutting the new school. Fearing that the Shepherd's Tent would draw Yale's dissatisfied and restless students to New London, the legislators passed a bill in October, providing that unless a college, seminary, or public school was duly licensed by the Court, its teachers were subject to fines and its students and those who housed and fed them were to come under the provisions of the earlier act outlawing all but settled ministers.[6] Of particular significance for the status of Yale, however, was the preamble, which reiterated the assertion that "the well ordering of such public schools [as the college at New Haven and inferior schools in towns or parishes] is of great importance to the public weal." There is no reason to think that Clap or the Yale trustees were unhappy with this assertion of legislative direction over Yale College and its affairs.[7]

The most acute crises involving the college directly in the turmoil of the Awakening and highlighting the college-church-state nexus came in 1744 and 1745 and involved the English revivalist George Whitefield and the brothers John and Ebenezer Cleaveland, two students at Yale College. Whitefield had provoked the anger of the teachers at both Harvard and Yale when he had confided to his *Journal* that, "as for the universities, I believe it may be said their light is now become darkness, darkness that may be felt and is complained of by the most godly ministers." The Harvard faculty members charged Whitefield as "one that acts either according to dreams or some sudden impulses and impressions upon his mind," and as "an uncharitable, censorious and slanderous man." At New Haven, Clap and his tutors also issued a *Declaration* accusing Whitefield of vilifying and subverting the college and being responsible for "enthusiastic errors and disorders" and for students withdrawing "to that thing called the Shepherd's Tent."[8] Whitefield protested with some warmth that he had not come to "destroy the order of New England churches." But at the same time he did not retract his complaints about the lack of discipline at the colleges, and he was then censored once more in 1745 by Harvard divinity professor Edward Wigglesworth. As proof of Harvard's sincere efforts to discipline itself, Wigglesworth cited the dismissal of two tutors and one professor and the presence on its Board of Overseers of the colony's governor, lieutenant governor, and members of the Governor's Council and the Boston area ministry.[9]

The Cleaveland brothers' trespass consisted of their attendance with their parents at worship services conducted by New Light lay preachers when at home during college vacation. When Clap and the tutors heard of this, they charged the brothers with having violated the rules of the Gospel as well as the colony and college laws. They feared that now the two students "might infect and corrupt the college" with the heresies and errors propounded by lay preachers who claimed to have been divinely inspired. John Cleaveland apologized for his ignorance of the laws as Clap had defined them, but he was not willing to admit that the meetings he had attended were anything other than gatherings of a legally constituted church. He objected strenuously to what he considered the unwarranted application of college laws outside the confines of Yale during vacations.[10]

Clap's retort made it quite apparent how he viewed the college and its relationship with the affairs of state and church. "All college laws," he said, "excepting a few little ones extend farther than New Haven bounds." The reason for this lay in the "principal end and design" of the college, which was "to train up a succession of learned and orthodox ministers." This purpose excluded the educating of persons "directly subversive of the Visible Church of Christ."[11]

When questioned about the justice of punishing students for violating a law that could be said to exist only by implication, Clap asserted his own autocratic paternalism. The students, he was reported by the Cleaveland brothers to have said, knew that attending a lay meeting outside of New Haven was "contrary to my judgment, and if you do not go according to my judgment you can't expect to enjoy College privileges, but if it be so as you report of them [that they did not know], I suppose they do not think so honorably of my judgment as they ought. So be it. I'll make them know otherwise by my dealings with you."[12] The Cleavelands' account of Clap's words may not be letter perfect, but the note of personal hostility rings true.

Protests against the expulsion of the Cleaveland brothers remained largely ineffective. A letter to the editor of the New York *Post-Boy*, published on March 17, 1745, censored Clap for overstepping the bounds of his jurisdiction.

> You must excuse me, if I am a little warm upon this late stretch of college power; it is the utmost cruelty and injustice, take the thing in which light you please: Had the civil magistrates undertaken the affair, and punished them for a breach of the law of the colony (lately made to prevent the New-Lights from disturbing the government) that might have been just, but for a college to inflict so cruel a punishment for a crime not committed within their jurisdiction, and for which they had not the least glimpse of authority, is not a little surprising.[13]

When the Cleavelands petitioned the Assembly in April 1745, they pointed out that if Clap were right and a college ruling had indeed made the colony laws part of the laws of the college, then they should have stood trial in their home county. They also complained that Clap had refused to show them the college law by which the colony laws had been made to apply. In the Assembly, however, the upper house refused to take up the Cleavelands' plea, and at the college the students showed their feelings by publishing for distribution John Locke's *Essay on Toleration*.[14] College administration, Old-Light establishment, and General Court presented a solid front against schism and separation. The Cleavelands ceased their legal efforts at that point. Unlike Ebenezer Pierpont at Harvard in 1718 they did not challenge the Assembly's jurisdiction over affairs of the college by taking the matter to an inferior court. Nor did they threaten the college with an appeal to the crown, as one student had done when Clap refused him his degree in 1744 for having participated in the publishing of Locke's *Essay on Toleration* and having refused to confess publicly his part in the affair. The student forced the Corporation to relent and award him his degree. But in 1745 the college-state establishment stood its ground.[15]

## Charter, Laws, and Anglicans

The upheavals of the Awakening having crested in Connecticut by 1744, Clap sought to solidify and make permanent the position of the college as a privileged provincial seminary, backed by state authority and support, and yet largely free to administer its own affairs. The vehicle for achieving such permanence was the charter of 1745. Clap saw various liabilities that had become manifest in the college's forty-year history. There was the precarious legal existence of the trusteeship and the uncertainty surrounding its status as a quasi-corporation or partnership. More worrisome was the problem of the college's relationship to the General Court. The trustees conceded that the Assembly had authorized the establishment of the college and had contributed funds, but they could not agree on the extent to which the Assembly was free to intervene in the school's affairs. A step toward settling these questions had been taken in 1723 when, upon request of the trustees, the General Court had given the college an attribute of corporate power by ruling that the trustees could make decisions by majority vote. Five years later Rector Elisha Williams had considered applying to the crown for a corporate charter. The trustees, however, did not pursue this project, which, in all likelihood, would have opened the door to Anglican participation and would have ended the exclusive hegemony of Connecticut's ecclesiastical and secular establishment over the college. But Williams's desire for corporate status was taken up again by Clap. A chartered corporation with legal permanence and corporate powers of self-government, Clap felt, would stand a far better chance than a trusteeship of riding out such storms as the Awakening had brought and as might occur in the future. As toward the end of 1744 the excitement over itinerancy and separation died down, Clap laid before the trustees drafts of both a corporate charter and a new set of college laws.[16]

Drafted by Clap, the charter designated the president as a member of the Corporation, gave him a tie-breaking vote, incorporated him with the trustees and their successors as The President and Fellows of Yale College, and kept the crown and the Anglican church out of college affairs. While Clap thus had preserved the hegemony of the Congregational ministers, he had obtained the security of legal incorporation at the price of acknowledging the legislature's right to supervision of college affairs. "When they shall think proper," the Assembly members might inquire into or repeal the trustees' rules and ordinances. Perhaps Clap thought this an unavoidable and harmless concession. The legislators, after all, had pledged themselves to annual cash grants "to continue during the pleasure of this Assembly," and they were thought to be wholly in sympathy with the colony's Congregational establishment.[17] At any rate, Clap was determined to keep their supervision within the strictest possible confines, and whether he and the Assembly would always agree on just where the line separating college autonomy from legislative authority was to be drawn, only the future could tell.

The college Corporation did not include any tutors or professors. At Harvard at least some of the tutors and one professor were members of the Corporation, and at William and Mary all of the professors together with the president constituted the Corporation. Even in these two colleges the faculty's effective power in government was minimal, but at least they were recognized in principle as members of the body corporate. At Yale this was not to be, though Clap left the door open for the reappearance of teachers on the Corporation through the device of corporate self-perpetuation. In 1745, however, he barred teachers because he recognized that threats to the Old Light establishment were more likely to arise among young and inquisitive college tutors than among established ministers disposed to defend their pulpits. Perhaps, too, he was reminded of the defection of ex-President Cutler and tutor Johnson to Anglicanism and of the Harvard tutor rebellion in the 1720s.[18]

The college laws Clap compiled during the first years of his reign gave further evidence of his determination to anchor the college as a provincial institution securely in the establishment of state and church. The laws constituted a comprehensive codification of the rules by which students were to conduct themselves and the president and the tutors were to govern the college. The section on penal laws obviously reflected the turmoil of the early 1740s. For any student who was found to have libeled or to have spread a "false and scandalous report" concerning the president, a fellow or a tutor, or the minister of New Haven's First Church, or who "shall directly or indirectly say that either of them is a hypocrite, or carnal or unconverted," the laws required public confession and, for a repeat of the offense, expulsion from college. But Clap intended the laws to do more than check a temporary emergency. They were to express a way of life, prescribe conduct, and impress upon the students their total integration into an institutional and legal order including God's kingdom and their collegiate society, and embracing Connecticut's civil state and established churches as intermediaries.[19]

Based on these premises Clap gave himself blanket authority concerning crimes and infractions of the rules not specifically mentioned in the laws. He not only obliged the students to attend public worship on Sundays and on days of fasting and thanksgiving, but also required their attendance at public lectures appointed by the minister of New Haven's First Church. He viewed the minister as a public official who occupied a position of authority for the college. The integration of the students into this interconnected institutional framework was complete. The students were subject to the college and the church of New Haven and to the disciplinary and legal authority of president, tutors, fellows, and, ultimately, the General Court. They were also specifically prohibited from attending any religious services not appointed by public authority or approved by the president, and from taking any complaint or bringing any suit against any other member of the college to a civil court unless they had first obtained permission from the president or fellows. Clap wanted to protect the college's autonomy as a provincial institution from interference by municipal authorities or inferior courts. His laws were intended to keep the college a world to itself within the context of its associated institutions of church and state.

As the 1750s approached, Anglicanism gained ground in Connecticut. Until the apostasy of Cutler and Johnson not a single Anglican had graduated from Yale, but since 1724 one out of every ten Yale graduates had become an ordained Anglican priest. Clap himself had been relatively accommodating to Anglican students during his early presidency. He had permitted them to attend communion services at the closest Anglican church in West Haven and to listen to sermons by visiting Anglicans in other nearby churches, if such events did not interfere with their regular obligations at the college. But when in 1753 an Anglican church opened in New Haven, Clap abruptly changed his position. He terminated the relationship of the college to New Haven's First Church and ordered all students without exception to worship and receive religious instruction within the college. He obviously meant to respond to the Anglican threat by drawing the college community closer inward, even if that meant reversing the drift of his previous policy to integrate it into the existing establishment of church and state. When his instructions were met with vigorous protests by Anglicans he replied that no society could exist without enforcing uniform rules for all its members. But, he added, he was ready to continue the former dispensation for Anglican students to attend communion services and other special events outside the college.[20]

The Anglicans, however, were in no mood to accept such concessions. They insisted on strict enforcement of the policy of toleration. Samuel Johnson, since the 1720s the Anglicans' foremost spokesman in Connecticut and just then chosen as president of the new college in the Province of New York, warned Clap: "Tell it not in Gath! much less in the ears of our dear mothercountry, that any of her daughters should deny any of her children leave to attend on her worship whenever they have opportunity for it . . . For God's sake do not be so severe to think in this manner, or to carry things to this pass!" He reminded Clap that he and his brethren might have to complain of Clap's policies "to our superiors at home," and they, in turn, might conclude that the Corporation that had enacted the law, Yale College, was "a nullity in itself . . . inasmuch as it seems a principle in law that a corporation cannot make a corporation, nor can one be made without his Majesty's act." That was a potent threat designed to make Clap reflect on the uncertain legal position not only of the college but also of the colony itself.

And if that were not enough Johnson added that Yale College had been funded with the aid of such Anglican donors as Elihu Yale and Bishop Berkeley and, through the annual contributions of the Connecticut Assembly, of the colony's Anglican taxpayers. As much as Clap must have resented such lessons of contemporary history, which told him of Connecticut's changing demography, of English law, and of his own previous views of college-church-state relationships, he had no choice but to concede the point. Johnson's threat of appeal to the crown was too formidable to risk.[21]

Clap's retreat was more apparent than real. Once he had come to perceive the college-church-state relationship as a liability, he was determined to rid himself and the college of its obligations. His concessions came neither gracefully nor without reservation. They were coupled with a novel reading of college history. Despite the concessions he had been forced to make in practice, Clap roused himself to a spirited defense of his original position. He declared that the laws of the college and the rules of peace and charity demanded that the purpose and the order of the college as laid down by the founders be preserved. There was no violation of the liberty of conscience involved, he countered Johnson, since any Anglican who entered the college did so of his own free will and by entering accepted the college rules.

In a twenty-page pamphlet especially written and printed for the occasion, Clap argued that "the original end and design of colleges was to instruct, educate, and train up persons for the work of the ministry." Though ever since the Reformation colleges had received their charters from the civil government, they were nonetheless run by ecclesiastical persons for spiritual purposes. Thus they were religious societies and, because their purpose was to train ministers, they were superior to ordinary churches, which trained the common people. From this it followed, argued Clap, that colleges could carry on religious instruction, worship, and ordinances "within their own jurisdiction, by their own officers, and under their own regulation." He thus had provided a perfect argument to rationalize his withdrawal of the students from the New Haven church and the organization of a college church under his own direct supervision. He added that ever since 1746 the trustees had been accumulating a fund for the endowment of a professor of divinity and, in the meantime, had asked the president to perform that role. Regarding the contributions of Yale and Berkeley, they surely knew, wrote Clap, that they were supporting the intent of the original donors and could not expect to alter the founding principles. The tax-paying Anglicans had been amply recompensed by the education of Episcopal ministers.[22] Clap virtually ignored the effect of the Reformation on college purpose and government and, with his arrogant claim of superiority for colleges as religious societies, offended both the members of churches and the colony's representatives in the Assembly.

At the same time Clap continued to pursue his project for a college church. In March 1756 Naphtali Daggett was installed as professor of divinity, and on July 3 of the next year he preached his first sermon as the pastor of the newly established Church of Christ in Yale College. Within sixteen years Clap had thus succeeded in redefining the society over which he presided and in changing the character of its leadership. If Clap were to prevail, the college founded for the training of civil servants for state and church was going to become a church seminary, its first and senior professor its minister or chaplain. Doing this Clap had not only affronted members of the Assembly and others in Connecticut who believed in the original purpose of the college, but had also violated the Saybrook Platform, which gave the consociation of churches a voice in all matters of church separation.[23]

To make matters worse, in September of 1757 Clap then sought to oust Joseph Noyes, the minister of New Haven's First Church, from the college Corporation by means of a heresy trial. Here, however, he was forced to back down. By the mid-fifties a gathering storm of protest and resistance to his high-handed and arbitrary administration had begun to rise. The controversy, which had begun as a religious issue, spilled over into politics, and "in the course of the dispute, weighty questions were raised relative to the nature and purpose of Yale, the relationship of the school to the General Assembly, and the extent of authority of the Corporation and President Clap."[24] It was then in the political arena that Clap came to experience his greatest triumph and his ultimate defeat.

## College and Assembly

When in the 1750s President Clap sought to remove the surveillance of the magistrates from Yale College, he only provoked their renewed interest in the affairs of the school. His abrupt termination of the college's relationship to the First Church of New Haven, his order to students not to attend near-by Anglican services, and his establishment of the

Church of Christ in Yale College in violation of the Saybrook Platform, angered the lower house, and, pointing to the expenses of the French and Indian Wars, it refused the annual £100 grant to the college in 1755.

But more fundamental reasons were involved than the war and Clap's unpopularity with both New Lights and Old Sides. Dr. Benjamin Gale, physician and deputy from Killingsworth, rejected Clap's statement that Yale College had been founded "principally by the ministers." He accused Clap of falsely claiming that the Assembly had been "neither the founder nor visitor of that house," and he disputed the legal status of the college as a corporation or as a society of ministers. Gale concluded that Yale College had no right to a government appropriation. Instead he suggested that the Assembly should do something more for the "lower schools." "And is it no matter," he asked, "whether any of the children of our people be instructed but such as are sent to the college?" Gale's appeal to his colleagues in the Assembly was effective. For the first time in its history Yale found itself without the annual grant.[25]

Clap prepared a rejoinder to Gale's arguments. Citing John Ayliffe's history of Oxford University and Bishop Stillingfleet's argument on behalf of Exeter College, Clap repeated a claim he had established in 1754 that colleges were ecclesiastical societies "distinct from and superior to all other." This had remained true even after the Reformation. Predictably, he provoked a counterstatement from Gale, and the two pamphleteers engaged in a heated debate on legal and constitutional questions of college government. While both men gave skillful arguments, Clap went beyond exaggeration to deliberate omission of evidence and use of innuendo, skirting the boundaries of falsification of sources.[26]

There is no evidence that anyone besides Clap had read either Stillingfleet or Ayliffe, so he could misrepresent their statements without fear of being contradicted. He did so on the minor points of how consistently the majority of the members of a college corporation had enjoyed ecclesiastical status and of how long the English courts had recognized a college as a lay corporation.[27] He tried to do this also with the applicability of the canon law to the legal status of Yale, the basis on which he built his strategy. If he could get the Connecticut Assembly to accept the dicta of the canon law over the rulings of the common law, his case was made. Clap did indeed succeed in laying that issue like a smokescreen over the legal landscape, but Gale blew it aside: "The force of the canon law then will not make a college an ecclesiastical body, if the common law does not. And indeed, the canon law's making all colleges and universities spiritual bodies is agreeable to what I said in my letter: 'That the Popish clergy were resolved to monopolize all learning and knowledge.' " Clap was slowed, if not quite halted, in his attempts to reconstruct a legal history that would allow him to pull the college out from under the supervision of the General Court.[28]

In the meantime anti-Clap sentiment arose among the trustees as well as in the colony. In May, Corporation fellows Jared Eliot and Benjamin Ruggles asked the Assembly to visit the college, and on June 30 they and Joseph Noyes presented their fellow trustees with a protest memorial. In it they objected to the separation of students and officers from the First Church of New Haven and to the establishment of a college church. They rejected Clap's references to the examples of Oxford and Cambridge as inappropriate, since the two English universities, they argued, conformed to the rule of the Church of England, whereas Yale, like Harvard and the College of New Jersey, should take its cue from the dissenting academies in England. They called Clap's organization of the college church "a presumptious invasion of the rights of the legislature," indicating "an unwarrantable thirst of power and dominion." These were strong words, but in 1757 they remained ineffective.[29]

Two years later Gale again appeared in print. He belabored Clap for "dealing so very liberally in fines," which, Gale observed, "don't fall on the persons of the offenders, but on their parents." He objected to the students' having no recourse of appeal to the fellows from the judgment of president and tutors in cases of fines or even expulsion. He demanded that the votes and decisions of the Corporation become part of the public record and the "college laws be published in English for all to read." He conceded that a government over minors must of necessity be sovereign "in a great degree," but felt that Clap's regime "seems to be more so than is prudent or safe . . . For tho' it be true," he concluded, "that the corporation is invested with a legislative authority over the students by the government, yet they are not authorized to delegate any part of this power to the president, or any other man."[30]

The trustee memorial and Gale's pamphlets raised the issue of visitation. Whether the trustees knew it or not, by asking the Assembly to act as college Visitor they touched on a delicate and unsettled problem in English law. Generally speaking, in the mid-eighteenth century visitation referred to the supervisory power of a founder, patron, or donor of a charity over its members. This power, Chief Justice Lord Holt had said in 1693 "arises from the property which the founder had in the lands assigned to support the charity," and it was to descend upon the founder's heirs. Based on Holt's dictum, to know the founder was to know the Visitor. But there also was the earlier decision of the Charter-House case in 1612, which made the governors themselves the Visitors in cases in which the governors rather than the recipients of the charity had been incorporated, and where the charter did not appoint a Visitor. This decision seemed to apply to Yale College, since here the fellows had been incorporated, and not the students or the faculty.[31]

The circumstances surrounding the granting of the Harvard charter of 1650 were instructive for the Connecticut debaters. Few had questioned then that the Massachusetts General Court had founded the college and thus was to serve as its Visitor. The only contenders for that status were the nonincorporated Overseers, but they were in fact acting as trustees and, together with the Corporation, as cogovernors. Because of their intimate involvement in college affairs they were scarcely in a position to serve as arbiters of college disputes and as guardians of its charter provisions. With the Corporation they fell under the visitatorial jurisdiction of the General Court.

In Connecticut in 1759, then, Gale's party would point to Lord Holt's position and the Massachusetts situation and call on the General Court to assume its responsibilities as Visitor. Clap and his friends would cite the Charter-House case and vigorously reject the mere thought of visitation by the government. To forestall such a possibility Clap also began to concern himself with the question of who had been Yale's founder. If he could show that the General Court had not founded the college, then he could also undermine the applicability of Lord Holt's argument to Yale College.

In the years following the pamphlets and memorial of 1757 and 1759 the situation in the college deteriorated. It is hard to say to what extent the political history of Connecticut or the autocratic behavior of Thomas Clap were responsible, or what share might be attributed to general social unrest in the colonies. In 1759 Vice-Provost Francis Alison of the College of Philadelphia reported that President Clap had proposed a common plan of government for all the colonial colleges, including an agreement that students who had been expelled from or denied admittance to any college should not be admitted by another without prior consultation among the college officers. Nothing seems to have come of that scheme, but the Philadelphia trustees also expressed concern in these years over student disciplinary problems. They wanted a college lodging house in order to guarantee better supervision, and the faculty asked for more authority to discipline students. At Harvard a riot took place in 1766 over rancid butter and ended with an enforced confession of "irregular and unconstitutional" proceedings by 155 students.[32]

At Yale the Corporation complained in 1761 about "levity and whispering, . . . idleness, loud talk, and laughter . . . indecent and disturbing noises . . . and . . . many secret acts of wickedness done in the dark." It then voted itself the power to dismiss students "although they have not been guilty of any such great crimes as according to the laws of the college are worthy of expulsion." Within three months the Corporation's action provoked another memorial from citizens of the province. The memorial stated that "the highest academical punishments" had been so often repeated upon the students "as to serve only to irritate them into the highest outrage," and that the Corporation's latest edict had vested "the president with the supersedure and reversal of all the laws and make his will in effect the sole law." Then the petitioners went to the heart of the matter: the college, they stated, had been erected by the Assembly, and the Assembly were the proper Visitors. They therefore asked the legislators "to turn your eyes upon the society that you have founded, fed, and nourished, and for the honor of what is good, great, and noble, subject it to such like visitation as other collegiate schools in this land or devise some method of redress." As in 1757, both houses of the General Court "resolved in the negative," and once more Clap had avoided a legislative inquiry.[33]

Dissatisfaction and unrest reached such proportions that Clap, on short notice, changed the date of the 1762 commencement from September to July in order, as Ezra Stiles reported, "to keep the rabble from coming." A correspondent of Stiles referred to the occasion as "Mr. Clap's private commencement," adding, "Nothing looked to me more mean than to see a number of gentlemen of good sense so tamely noosed by the president, their country all the while cursing them for interrupting the joys of harvest." The sentiment was echoed by tutor Whittelsey, who bitingly remarked that he thought Clap "only aims by new things and unusual methods of managing, to make people attend to *him*, to render himself *somebody*." In November open rebellion engulfed the college. Students refused to abide by the 1761 Corporation law, which had, among other provisions, prescribed the taking of examinations as a means of ferreting out students "grossly defective in . . . knowledge" in order to expel them. After much debating and consulting following a series of further student outbursts of "great halooing in the yard in contempt and defiance . . . [playing] football in studying time in contempt . . . [absences] from the public worship on the Lord's Day," the Corporation ruled that all deserved to be expelled and demanded their confessions. They then placed several of the students on probation, suspended others, ordered some to be examined once more, and expelled two. This they did, they declared, that the "great ends of government and the reformation of this college . . . may be effected by the exemplary punishment of some, whereby others may hear and fear."[34] Surely, the fellows' application of selective discipline did not endear them to either the students or their families and did not help Clap's standing in the colony.

Matters finally reached crisis proportions early in 1763. In March the General Court received a memorial signed by three ministers and six laymen concerning "matters of grievance and misconduct in the government of the college." It was accompanied by a plea of five ministers — among them Stephen White, Clap's successor in 1739 at the parish at Windham, and Ebenezer Devotion, who had preached at Clap's ordination — who asked that the General Court "take the state of the college into their serious consideration." They spoke of the college's "deplorable state," of "notorious" facts, of the uneasiness of students and parents, and of "the resentments and prejudices the youth generally bring from thence." The petitioners offered a thorough review of the college's constitutional history and problems. They affirmed unequivocally that the legislature was the proper Visitor because the colony itself was the college founder and no Visitors had ever been appointed by law. They accused Clap of ignoring the fellows of the Corporation and illegally changing the date of commencement. They charged that the college law forbidding students and faculty to take complaints against the college to a civil court violated "the natural rights of Englishmen." They termed Clap's expulsion of the Cleaveland brothers during the unrest of the Awakening and his fining of students who worshipped outside the college "a most dangerous consequence and influence upon Christian liberty, as well as an open affront upon the laws of this colony." They thought college punishments unreasonable and injudiciously meted out and the monetary fines enormous. Besides, they charged, Clap taxed students and used fines to increase college buildings. He thus raised money without consent and account, which, they added, was "contrary to a fundamental principle of English government." Finally, they accused Clap of sitting in judgment on his own administrative and judicial actions, thus depriving his students of the right to appeal. They therefore petitioned the legislature to review all the college laws with an eye to approval or rejection, to ask for an annual accounting of the college for its laws and finances, to fix a maximum fine to be levied by the Corporation on students, to allow appeals of the Corporation's decisions to governor and Council, and to appoint a commission of visitation.[35]

The bill of particulars was comprehensive and impressive; the assaulting forces had wide backing in all parts of the colony. The key issues — visitation and the students' right of appeal — went to the heart of the matter. To what extent was a college a law to itself, and to what degree must it allow itself to be governed by the political body that authorized and supported it? The unrest spawned by the Awakening had now brought to the fore the most troubling aspects of political discourse: the nature of legitimacy in government and the rights of individuals in conflict with corporate authority. In New Haven these issues were raised in the context of a college. Throughout Connecticut and the other colonies the same issues were to be voiced as the Stamp Act Crisis developed and the colonists moved toward revolution.

# 7

## COLLEGE FOUNDING
## IN THE MIDDLE COLONIES

In the middle colonies Presbyterian ministers had become interested in a college of their own in the late 1730s. Some, chiefly members of the New York presbytery residing in East Jersey, thought of establishing a provincial school on the model of the New England colleges or the universities in Europe. Prominent among them were Jonathan Dickinson and Ebenezer Pemberton. One was a graduate of Yale, the other of Harvard, and both had been raised in the tradition of New England Congregationalism. In the early 1740s Dickinson and his colleague Aaron Burr had been active teachers of boys and young men in local academies at Elizabethtown and Newark. They labored in their own homes, teaching their students the liberal arts, the biblical languages, and evangelical divinity. But they were conscious of the inadequacy of this training and hoped eventually to be able to supplement their own and similar local efforts with a provincial educational establishment.

Others, residing in the presbytery of New Brunswick, had been deeply affected by the Great Awakening and were far more concerned with spiritual rebirth and evangelical fervor than with academic learning. They thought local academies were sufficient for intellectual preparation, and supported the so-called Log College, an evangelical school founded by William Tennent, Sr., between 1728 and 1730.

A third group, concentrated in the Philadelphia presbytery, were Old Sides suspicious of their enthusiastic brethren and adverse to founding a college. They preferred to have their successors taught and trained at the colleges in New England and Europe.[1]

In 1741 the Old Sides demanded that all ministerial candidates be examined by the synod and questioned the right of the New Lights in New Brunswick to vote in the synod. They also accused Gilbert Tennent, son of the Log College founder, of belittling the importance of studying physics, ethics, and metaphysics only "because his father cannot or does not teach them," and they asked for synodical examinations because they had heard reports "of Mr. William Tennent's great slackness in educating scholars under his care."[2] Their accusations and demands prompted the members of the New Brunswick presbytery to withdraw from the Philadelphia synod. The Philadelphians then began looking for a preparatory academy of their own and found it in Francis Alison's school and academy in New London. Alison, Presbyterian minister and classical scholar, had begun teaching in 1741, and the synod adopted his school three years later.[3]

The strains between the Old Sides of the Philadelphia synod and the New Lights of the presbyteries of New Brunswick and New York provoked a formal split in 1745, the latter two forming the new synod of New York. This development further lessened the prospect for joint efforts at college founding. The Old Sides complained that the New Lights "endeavoured to pour contempt on colleges and universities," and harbored "destroyers of good learning and gospel order." They wrote to President Clap of Yale in 1746 that Dickinson and Pemberton "whom we esteem with regard" had now "through some unhappy bias" joined forces with the Log College party, and they sought to strengthen their own educational efforts by seeking a formal alliance with Yale. They agreed with Clap that the graduates of their academy in New London should be admitted to Yale College upon examination by the president and fellows and there "be treated only according to their proficiency." The synod promised it would not recommend students who lived in or close to New England and would neither lend support to students expelled from Yale nor to such New Light institutions as the Shepherd's Tent. But there is no evidence that students ever moved from Alison's academy to the college in Connecticut.[4]

While the Old Side ministers sought to strengthen their academy, the moderate New Lights in the presbytery of New York held on to their college plans and hoped for reconciliation of the warring factions. In 1743 the New York presbytery had suggested to the synod that ministerial candidates trained in academies be sent to either Harvard or Yale, at synod expense if necessary. The synod, however, rejected the proposal.[5] When news came that President Clap had expelled the Cleaveland brothers for attending a New Light meeting, Dickinson, Pemberton, Aaron Burr, John Pierson, and others of the New York presbytery, took a more jaundiced view of the Connecticut college.[6] They consulted with three New York laymen, the jurist William Smith, the merchant Peter Van Burgh Livingston, and William Peartree Smith. The seven agreed that for training ministers they wanted a college rather than an academy. They knew that a college had to be incorporated to award degrees and that the legislature would not grant a charter to a synodical institution for the education of Presbyterian ministers. The seven planners thus declared: "though our great intention was to erect a seminary for educating ministers of the gospel, yet we hope it will be a means of raising up men that will be useful in other learned professions — ornaments of the State as well as the Church. Therefore we propose to make the plan of education as extensive as our circumstances will admit." Like the colleges in Massachusetts, Connecticut, and Virginia, the projected institution was to train leaders for public service in ecclesiastical and secular office. To draw into its classrooms young men of Presbyterian, Quaker, Dutch and German Reformed, and Anglican background, the curriculum had to compare favorably with that of Harvard and Yale. Finally, the planners felt, their chances for obtaining a charter would increase if they had proof of ready financial support. They therefore began a subscription drive in New York and New Jersey, which by March 1745 had netted pledges of £185 in New Jersey currency.[7] The New Lights of the New York presbytery had concluded that success could be theirs only if they avoided sectarian and exclusively religious objectives and proposed a college that would serve all sides and interests in the middle colonies.

Governor Lewis Morris refused to sign the charter because of anticipated protests from Anglicans in New Jersey and England. But Morris's successor, John Hamilton, serving as deputy governor and president of the Council, approved the document on October 22, 1746, and authorized the fourth college in the American colonies. The College of New Jersey was organized under a trusteeship familiar to Presbyterians from their academies in England and Scotland and the 1701 charter of Connecticut's Collegiate School. The seven promoters were named trustees. All of them were Presbyterians, three of them laymen, four ministers; four of them resided in New York, three held pastorates in New Jersey. None of them served in an ex officio capacity. The New Jersey trustees thus constituted the first intercolonial governing board of an eighteenth-century college. Their number was permitted to grow to twelve, the remaining five to be chosen by the original seven. They received the usual legal powers of government, of making college laws, of appointing and discharging president, professors, and tutors, and of granting degrees to the students. As in the Yale charter of 1745, no teacher had any claim to a seat on the board; the president also was left out. College government was in the hands of an exclusively external board.

The board represented a duly incorporated college that was neither a seminary of church or synod nor a school under the supervision of legislature or governor. The charter made no reference to either Presbyterian synod or presbytery, nor did it make any mention of the training of ministers. It declared the college to be for the instruction of New Jersey youths in the learned languages and the liberal arts and sciences, provided that "those of every religious denomination may have free and equal liberty and advantage of education in the said college notwithstanding any different sentiments in religion." The college received no promise of financial support from the colony and appeared independent from both the Old Side synodical academy in New London and the New Light Log College in Neshaminy. Authorized only by the governor and placed in the hands of an independent board of trustees, the College of New Jersey commenced its career without the benefit or hindrance of the traditional joint supervision of state and church.[8]

The college founders relied on the people of New Jersey and neighboring colonies. They sought support directly from subscribers and prospective students and their families rather than from the government. They obviously had little prospect of wooing Old Side members over to their cause, but they were more successful with friends of the faltering Log College. When in the summer of 1747 the seven original trustees announced their choice of colleagues on the board, they were five graduates of the Log College who represented the frontier areas of Pennsylvania and New Jersey.

If any one school can be said to have been the predecessor of this college, it was Jonathan Dickinson's classical academy in Elizabethtown. Its first president, Jonathan Dickinson, and his successor, Aaron Burr of Newark, may be considered the college fathers. The Log College, to be sure, predated Dickinson's academy, but its tradition merged with the Dickinson-Burr mainstream only after the college had received its first charter in 1746. The College of New Jersey did not grow out of one of the academies of the warring factions of either Old Side or New

Light Presbyterianism. On the contrary, it was nourished in its infancy primarily by the conciliatory and mediating spokesmen of middle colony Congregational Presbyterianism.

The less sectarian atmosphere of the New York presbytery of Dickinson and Burr is significant as the environment in which the Great Awakening made what was perhaps its greatest contribution to American history. It there fostered the growing tendency to inter- and intradenominational action within and among the colonial churches. It encouraged the Presbyterian ministers and the laymen of New York City to envisage a college rather than a synodical academy. Such latitudinarianism did not exist in either the Log College or Alison's academy at New London.

The College of New Jersey had broken with another tradition of earlier days when it modified its character as a provincial institution and moved toward intercolonial status. Though according to the 1746 charter the college was founded for the benefit of the inhabitants of the province of New Jersey, its trustees were drawn also from the provinces of New York and Pennsylvania, and no provincial official from any of the colonies received a seat on the board by virtue of his office.

While the principle of interdenominational and intercolonial service was to prevail, minor modifications of the governmental arrangements were unavoidable. When in May 1747 the college assembled for the first time in the home of its president, the Reverend Mr. Dickinson, the gathering represented only a slight enlargement of Dickinson's academy, with eight to ten students and a tutor. In August Dickinson welcomed Jonathan Belcher, the new royal governor, just arrived from Massachusetts. Like Dickinson himself, Belcher was a Congregationalist and anxious for the college to succeed. There were fears that Anglican foes of the college might question the validity of the 1746 charter authorized by Hamilton. Belcher, who spoke of the college as his "adopted daughter," was determined to forestall such an event and to issue a new charter. But before this happened, Dickinson died, and the college moved to Newark, the home of its next president, Aaron Burr.

Throughout the early part of 1748 the trustees negotiated with the governor over the terms of the new charter. Having in mind the constitution of Harvard College, Belcher insisted on ex officio membership on the board for the governor and Council members and on the role of board president for himself. Such an organization would resemble that of the Harvard Overseers, with four ministers and four councilmen balancing the interests of church and state. The New Jersey ministers, however, objected to the ex officio membership of magistrates. They did not mind Belcher's presence, but they could not be sure of his successors. Finally agreement was reached on a compromise that placed the governor ex officio on the board as its presiding officer, but named four councillors as individuals only.

The new charter increased the number of trustees from nine ministers and three laymen to twelve ministers, ten laymen, and the governor. Compared to the first charter, the 1748 document gave greater emphasis to secular and intercolonial representation by more than doubling lay members. It included the New Jersey governor and councillors and three prominent Pennsylvanians, among them the colony's chief justice. These men served in addition to the three New Yorkers already appointed under the first charter. The inclusion of the college president as an ex officio member of the board elevated him from the position of academy headmaster to one comparable to that of the presidents of other colonial colleges. In this and other ways Belcher's influence brought the new college more in line with its sister institutions. The traditional concept of a provincial college was not given up, for the second charter insured for New Jersey a constant voice in college affairs by requiring the presence of at least twelve board members from the colony.[9] The 1748 charter adapted traditional elements of college government to the diversity of interests then prevailing in the middle colonies. The college was designed to serve the inhabitants of at least three colonies and the members of diverse Protestant denominations without discrimination. Among these Protestant groups, New Light Presbyterians and Congregationalists were to have a major voice.

Soon after the signing of the second charter the trustees formally elected Aaron Burr president. For the next twelve years classes were held in Newark. The trustees' chief concern during this period was the financing of the new school. In this matter they received neither encouragement nor aid from the New Jersey legislature, not even an authorization to hold a lottery in the province. Proprietary interests in the Assembly and on the governor's council blocked any move to offer financial support. The college had to rely on gifts from its friends, on lotteries conducted outside of New Jersey, and on fund-raising efforts among English dissenters and among Presbyterians in Scotland and Ulster. Responding to a request of the trustees, the synod of New York in 1753 appointed Gilbert Tennent and Samuel Davies as emissaries to

Europe. The two ministers set out to plead the case for the college among sympathizers in the British Isles. They portrayed the college as a place of intellectual and moral education akin to the European universities and as a training ground for Presbyterian ministers in the colonies. Though they encountered competition from Old Side rivals and others who were on a similar mission on behalf of the Academy of Philadelphia, Tennent and Davies were successful beyond their own expectations. Their mission made possible the construction of Nassau Hall and, in November 1756, the college's move to its new and permanent home.[10] By the mid-1750s the fourth American college was firmly established.

### Franklin's Academy

In Pennsylvania the attempts to found a collegiate institution in Philadelphia were carried out by laymen rather than ministers. As a result, secular rather than ecclesiastical considerations prevailed, and rational rather than traditional institutional arrangements emerged. While the impact of the Enlightenment on matters of college government and constitutional reform was minor, the secularism, rationalism, and deism we usually associate with its climate of opinion helped shift the power from ministers to lawyers, businessmen, and politicians. When Philadelphians involved in college controversies expressed rationalistic ideas or deistic convictions, they did so out of impatience with the endless dogmatic quarrels of Christian ministers and the emotional excesses of the Awakening. They were confident of human capacity in general and, in particular, of their own abilities as colonizers, statesmen, and businessmen. Their rationalism and deism derived more from political and economic experience than from philosophical study.

In Philadelphia the roots of the municipal academy can be traced to the Great Awakening and to the activities of the famous English revivalist George Whitefield. Due in part to his efforts, a trust fund had been established in 1740 for a charity school. The building was completed the next year, but the plan for a free school for the poor was shelved. Instead Gilbert Tennent's New Light congregation took over the building in 1743. Six years later, a group of prominent Philadelphians sponsored a subscription campaign for a "public academy in the City of Philadelphia." The twenty-four largest subscribers, representing the city's leading citizens, functioned as trustees. Eight were wealthy merchants, four were well-known physicians, and many of the others were active in the political life of the city and the colony. Benjamin Franklin and Philip Syng were the only two artisans among them. Franklin, publisher of a newspaper and an almanac, prominent mason, deputy postmaster of the city, justice of the peace, city councillor, clerk of the colonial assembly, and parishioner of Christ Church, became the group's spokesman.[11]

In August 1749 Franklin printed in the *Pennsylvania Gazette* Pliny's letter to Cornelius Tacitus, urging the establishment of a public school where boys could be educated at home and their parents could save the expense of a foreign education. Franklin introduced the letter with the remark that the time had come for Philadelphians to provide for their sons at home "the culture of minds by the finer arts and sciences." A little more than a month later he published his *Proposals Relating to the Education of Youth in Pennsylvania*. In November the twenty-four trustees accepted and signed the "Constitutions of the Public Academy in the City of Philadelphia" and elected Franklin president. They acquired the building originally intended for a free school and with it an obligation to provide charity schooling. At the beginning of 1751, the Academy of Philadelphia began its operations.[12]

In his *Proposals* Franklin stressed what the trustees considered the chief end of all learning: the acquisition of the ability to serve mankind, one's country, friends, and family. For such public purposes, Franklin had written, "almost all governments have . . . made it a principal object of their attention to establish and endow with proper revenues such seminaries of learning as might supply the succeeding age with men qualified to serve the public with honor to themselves and to their country." In Pennsylvania the first settlers had been too busy to launch such an undertaking, and the provincial government had remained inactive. Franklin, however, now expected a response from the city council and from private citizens. The latter, he suggested, could pledge funds and apply for a charter of incorporation "with power to erect an academy for the education of youth." Franklin approached the council in July 1750 after the trustees had already received more than £700 in subscriptions. He listed the benefits to be expected from the academy and was rewarded with the council's gift of £200 and pledge of an additional £500 over the next five years in exchange for an academy scholarship for a graduate of the charity school. Franklin also hoped for support from Thomas and Richard Penn, the

the colony's proprietors, but, as he wrote to Cadwallader Colden in New York, the trustees did not count on any funds from the province.[13]

In relying on the generosity of private citizens and in providing for private trustees to govern the school and administer its funds, Franklin followed the examples of the Collegiate School in Connecticut and the College of New Jersey. But in contrast to these two colonial models, the Philadelphia scheme did not originate with a group of ministers. The Philadelphia trustees, many of them active in city and provincial politics, were men of business and members of the professions. Whitefield sensed correctly that the trustees had not contemplated placing the doctrines of Christianity at the school's center, and he complained to Franklin that "there wants *aliquid Christi* in it, to make it so useful as I would desire it might be." To be sure, the majority of the trustees were Anglicans and parishioners of Philadelphia's Christ Church. But as trustees they acted as laymen and prominent citizens rather than as representatives of a religious denomination or church.[14]

The lay, business, and professional character of the trustees appeared also in their policies concerning the academy's educational program. Best known of all their statements is the classic formulation Franklin penned in the *Proposals*: "As to their studies, it will be well if they could be taught everything that is useful and everything that is ornamental: But art is long, and their time is short. It is therefore proposed that they learn those things that are likely to be most useful and most ornamental, regard being had to the several professions for which they are intended." As Franklin told the city council, Philadelphia and the province could expect that such a curriculum would produce well-qualified magistrates and schoolmasters who could combat the ignorance of the country's laws, customs, and language so widespread among the foreign immigrants in Pennsylvania.[15] Of particular benefit would be the academy's English School. "Youth will come out of this school fitted for learning any business, calling or profession, except such wherein language are required; and tho' unacquainted with any ancient or foreign tongue, they will be masters of their own which is of more immediate and general use."[16] Next to the English language, Franklin singled out history and geography, arithmetic and accounting as the studies most useful for professional success and public service. History, he believed, would impress upon the students the necessity of a public religion, that is, standards of virtue and rational intercourse among men, with a shared belief in accepted social conventions and principles of moral conduct. Only when a society could assume the presence of such a public religion could it expect its politics and social life to contribute to the health and prosperity of the body politic.

Behind the trustees' endorsement of Franklin's *Proposals* lay hidden a dispute over the means to achieve the desired end, a dispute in which Franklin found himself in the minority. Most of the trustees believed that a traditional Latin academy would best prepare the sons of their city for careers in the ministry, law, medicine, and business. Franklin, however, was convinced that the city was best served by giving men of all ranks and occupations a thorough training in their native language and the useful arts. Anxious as he was to get the academy underway, Franklin was willing to compromise with the advocates of a Latin school and, for the sake of harmony and a broader appeal to potential subscribers and students, to provide for both an English and a classical education. But, as he related forty years later, he found himself out-maneuvered at every step. When in November 1749 the trustees adopted the academy's constitution they chose the Latin master, rather than the English master, as the school's rector, and they gave him twice the salary for teaching half the number of students assigned to the English master.[17]

On July 13, 1753, Lieutenant Governor James Hamilton signed the charter and the academy began its official existence. The trustees had received a gift of £500 from the proprietors, were pledged to public service in the widest possible geographic area, but had to live within five miles of the academy. It appears that trustees, proprietors, and lieutenant governor all thought of the academy as a local, rather than provincial, institution, as a municipal grammar school rather than a college. The charter empowered the trustees as a corporate body to support, maintain, and govern "an academy or any other kind of seminary of learning." There was no mention of a college in the document, nor was there any hint that anyone had considered granting academic degrees. This possibility, however, must have been in the mind of Benjamin Franklin, who had referred to it in 1750 when he unsuccessfully attempted to persuade Samuel Johnson, former tutor at Yale and then Anglican missionary in Stratford, Connecticut, to serve as master of the English school. In 1753 the Philadelphia school did not offer any college-level work.[18]

Franklin and some of his colleagues on the board kept the idea of a college in mind, however. Franklin in particular was encouraged when he read two pamphlets written by a Scottish schoolmaster who was interested in a college in New York. He was so impressed with William Smith's *Some Thoughts on Education* and *A General Idea of the College of Mirania* that he expressed his hope that their author could be persuaded to accept a teaching position in the Philadelphia academy rather than return to England. Smith shared Franklin's views on subordinating revealed to natural and public religion and on preferring Anglicanism as a more tolerant denomination to the "narrow" and strife-ridden Presbyterianism of New England and New Jersey. Both men agreed on the necessity of public educational institutions in a new country with a large and heterogeneous immigrant population. They appreciated the advantages of a centrally located provincial institution for the training of English teachers. Such a school, conducted in the capital, could in time become the fountainhead for the civic education of all the province's foreign-born children.[19]

Moreover, in the *General Idea* Smith had flattered Franklin's considerable pride. He had compared the division of the College of Mirania into the college proper and the mechanics school to the Philadelphia academy's division into the Latin and the English schools. There can be little question that Franklin recognized, or thought he recognized, a kindred spirit, and that he expected support from someone who referred to him as "the very ingenious and worthy Mr. Franklin." Franklin also approved of Smith's provision that all public acts, commencements, and declamations were to be conducted in English rather than in Latin.[20] The reservations implied in the *General Idea* concerning the sufficiency and appropriateness of an exclusively classical or Latin education and the explicit references to Franklin's 1749 *Proposals* go a long way to explain the receptiveness Franklin showed Smith and his educational ideas. Add to this that Smith's institution was from the start conceived as a college rather than as a municipal grammar school, and it becomes clear that his ideas served as a powerful stimulus for Franklin's hopes to transform the academy into a college.

## The College of Philadelphia

In May of 1755 the Philadelphia institution was incorporated as a college as well as an academy and charity school. The initiative had been taken by William Smith and Francis Alison. Smith had in the meantime been ordained as an Anglican priest and, upon his appointment as professor of natural philosophy, had left New York and begun teaching at the Philadelphia academy in 1754. Alison had given up his post with the Old Side synodical academy in New London in 1752 to take over the Philadelphia academy's Latin School. He also served as the academy's professor of moral philosophy. It did not take long for Smith and Alison to join forces. In December 1754 they requested a charter addition to allow the granting of academic degrees. This, they said, would serve as an added inducement to attract and hold students. For the same reason Smith sought to broaden the academy's appeal to Presbyterians and encouraged Alison in 1755 to promote a Presbyterian seminary in conjunction with the academy. The Philadelphia Old Light Presbyterians, wrote Smith, were "the most substantial and sensible people of this place," and included Pennsylvania's Chief Justice William Allen, another trustee of the academy. By thus flattering the Old Light Presbyterians, Smith at the same time undermined the influence of the College of New Jersey.[21]

By encouraging Alison, Smith also allayed reservations expressed by the Penns and Franklin, who worried about Smith wearing clerical garb as a professor. Smith was well aware that the Philadelphia school could not possibly have been chartered as a church establishment because of the necessity to appeal to a variety of denominational interests. Thus the cooperation of Smith, the Anglican priest, with Alison, the Presbyterian minister, helped pave the way for incorporation as a college. The trustees asked the two to prepare a draft charter, ordered its revision by the attorney-general, Trench Francis, and took their oaths under the newly adopted charter on June 10. Written into the document were the elections of William Smith and Francis Alison as provost and vice-provost respectively of college and academy, and of Alison as rector of the academy as well.[22]

With the signing of the charter of 1755 the College of Philadelphia was officially launched. The provost and vice-provost of the college and the rector of the academy were not members of the Board of Trustees, but together with the professors were established as the faculty. While the trustees had ultimate authority over the college, they could delegate governmental powers to the faculty. This they did in the "Rules and Statutes" with the proviso that all faculty-made laws had to be approved by the trustees. The faculty also were empowered to assess minor fines, but only the trustees could expel, suspend, or degrade students.[23]

In recognizing the faculty as a separate and duly constituted body with clearly defined governmental functions, the charter contained an innovation in colonial college government. Only the College of William and Mary had a faculty of masters. But there the masters constituted the body corporate. At the other colonial colleges professorships had been established or were to be founded on a case-to-case basis. In 1755 Harvard College had two endowed professorial chairs, the Hollis Professorship of Divinity and the Hollis Professorship of Mathematics and Natural Philosophy. At Yale President Clap had for a time performed the functions of a professor of divinity, but the first regular appointment to that chair was in 1756. The College of New Jersey had to wait for its first professorship until 1767 when a chair of divinity was created, and in New York King's College filled its chair of mathematics and natural philosophy in 1757.

How, we might ask, did the idea of a recognized yet nonincorporated faculty surface in Philadelphia? William Smith — not unlike James Blair of Virginia — was well acquainted with the Academic Senate of universities in Scotland. It is rather likely that it was this Scottish influence as well as a willingness among the Philadelphia trustees to recognize the presence of a community of qualified, mature teachers that prompted the college founders to acknowledge them as a faculty. After all, the Philadelphia teachers were neither foreign-educated clergymen-masters as at William and Mary nor young, inexperienced tutors as at Harvard. They were men recognized as equals by the leaders of Philadelphia society.

The trustees' task of providing the leadership and the financial support of the college was complicated by the constant threat of armed conflict at the province's frontiers and by the resulting political feud between the heavily Quaker-dominated Assembly and the proprietor's allies. Among the trustees themselves there were clashes over the provost's favoritism toward the proprietary party. In 1756 Smith was accused of having violated the trust of his office by partisan indoctrination of his students, but both trustees and students absolved him of the charge. When two years later the Assembly found the provost to be in contempt, the trustees again came to his support and authorized him to teach his classes in jail, where he had been confined by order of the Assembly. At the end of the year they gave him leave to go to England and present his case before the crown.[24]

Smith had a way of causing trouble for the trustees and antagonizing his sponsor Franklin. Though in his official actions and in his teaching Smith scrupulously adhered to a policy of toleration and nonalignment, he always remained a convinced Anglican clergyman and supporter of crown and proprietor. He was never adverse privately to helping the cause of the church and its influence in the college. In 1756, for example, he confided happily to an Anglican correspondent in England that "the Church, by soft and easy means, daily gains ground in it [the college]," and in the preceding year he had published two pamphlets that provided arguments and support for the proprietary party. These pamphlets aroused Franklin's ire and made him report irritably to Peter Collinson that Smith had "scribbled himself into universal dislike here; the proprietary faction alone countenance him a little, but the Academy dwindles, and will come to nothing if he is continued." In May 1756 Franklin had been replaced as president of the trustees by Richard Peters. Later he expressed his chagrin that "the trustees had reaped the full advantage of my head, hands, heart and purse in getting through the first difficulties of the design . . . When they thought they could do without me, they laid me aside."[25]

Others joined Franklin in his dissatisfaction with the academy. Late in 1758 Pennsylvanicus, an anonymous writer in the *Pennsylvania Journal*, attacked Smith's pamphlets, the practice of fund-raising by lottery, and the magistrates and ministers who had endorsed the latter. Faculty members of the academy and college felt threatened by these strictures and asked the trustees to be allowed to prepare a reply. The trustees, however, vetoed the proposal, arguing that it was undignified to respond to "low creatures who wrote from passion and resentment." Pennsylvanicus, however, broadened his attack, condemned the college charter as "narrow" and "confined" and the trustees as mesmerized by unlimited power. A few years later charges of undue Anglican influence surfaced, and friends and supporters of the college in England urged the trustees to reaffirm their commitment to a common Protestant cause. Lest jealousies arise, the Archbishop of Canterbury, the proprietors, and a representative of English dissenters recommended in a joint letter to the trustees that they make "some fundamental rule or declaration to prevent inconveniences." The trustees responded favorably. "Ever desirous to promote the peace and prosperity of this seminary," they wrote in 1764, they were willing to adopt the letter from their English friends, insert it into their minutes, and pronounce it to be "perpetually *declaratory* of the present *wide* and excellent plan of this institution."[26]

In religious and political affairs, the trustees tried hard to avoid causing offense. They were happy to have escaped a clear-cut identification of the college with a particular church, and they hoped to evade an open alignment of the college with the proprietary party. But they came to learn that the passions of political warfare were more encompassing and more destructive than denominational jealousies. In Philadelphia higher education was very much the public's business. The college's fate was bound up with the political fortunes of the colony.[27]

# 8

## A COLLEGE FOR NEW YORK

The history of a college in New York goes back to 1704. In that year a correspondent had informed the Society for the Propagation of the Gospel, the missionary arm of the Anglican church, that New York was "the center of English America [and] . . . a proper place for a college." But not until 1746 did New York's governor, Council, and Assembly authorize a lottery to raise £2,250 for founding such an institution. This was the year of the first charter for the College of New Jersey and three years before Philadelphians promoted the subscription campaign for their academy. The move was greeted warmly by Samuel Johnson, former tutor at Yale College. Johnson had defected with President Cutler to the Anglican faith and now served as missionary in Stratford, Connecticut. He wrote Cadwallader Colden that he hoped the new college would "not suffer the Jersey College (which will be a fountain of nonsense) to get ahead of it," for that school was "entirely in the hands of the most virulent Methodists."[1]

In 1746 and 1747 talk and legislation concerning colleges in the colonies provoked among Anglicans like Samuel Johnson both fear and determination: fear of further institutions spawned by the Awakening — whether they be New Light Presbyterian or Methodist — and determination to counter that threat with a college of their own. An anonymous contributor to the *New York Evening Post* of May 18, 1747, for example, expressed hope that the new college "sprung up almost instantaneously so near" might serve as an added incentive to endowing a provost and other professorships as well as to financing a library. He envisaged a Board of Trustees made up of the chief justice of the province, a councillor, an assemblyman, the ministers of the city parishes, the provost, and such others as these officials and ministers might choose.[2]

When in April 1748 the lottery was authorized again for £1,800 and then extended in October, the momentum increased. In March of the next year appeared William Livingston's *Some Serious Thoughts on the Design of Erecting a College in the Province of New York*. Livingston, reared in the Dutch Reformed church of Albany, thought that a college would "demolish enthusiasm and superstition," vice, drunkenness, and vandalism, and contribute to the welfare and virtue of the community. A graduate student of Yale College in 1741, he had been as much repelled by the orthodox Presbyterianism of Connecticut's establishment as by the outbursts of enthusiasm engineered by the itinerant revivalists. He objected to clergymen desiring to enlarge "the sphere of their secular business," and he hoped for a rational religion, which, joined to the liberal arts, would make the contemplated New York college a center of learning and enlightened politics.[3] Johnson and Livingston, the one a committed Anglican clergyman, the other a liberal layman impatient with theological controversies, both rejected the enthusiasm of the awakeners and the illiberalism of Clap. They therefore favored a new college in their province as an alternative to the schools to the north and south of New York.

However much opposition to the Awakening and anger with Clap's dogmatism influenced the advocates of a New York college, their chief motivations and arguments were not religious. Rather, they expected the college to bring prestige, wealth, and political stability to their province. They perceived higher education as an instrument of social control that would provide a well-educated leadership in civil and ecclesiastical offices. As Livingston put it, "the liberal sciences are vastly subservient to the cause of religion," and religion "is inseparably connected with private and social happiness . . . A well regulated academy will therefore cause a surprising alteration in the behavior of our young gentry." Anglicans like Johnson hoped that a college in such a religiously heterogeneous population center like New York could offset the Presbyterian schools in other provinces. But in the late 1740s this was a secondary consideration to the college's expected impact on the political, social, and economic life of the colony. Even Bishop Berkeley dissuaded Johnson from following the practice of the College of William and Mary and relying on Anglican professors trained at Oxford. Instead he suggested the New England colleges as recruiting grounds. The views on college government as they appeared in the *Evening Post* letter also were traditional. The New York college was to be neither an academy under denominational control nor a college with an incorporated faculty.[4]

The secular and political interests involved in its creation were demonstrated again in November 1751 when the legislature established a Board of Trustees for the lottery funds. To this board were appointed the colony's senior councillor, the Speaker of the Assembly, the judges of the Supreme Court, the mayor of New York City, the colony's treasurer, and James Livingston, Benjamin Nicoll, and William Livingston. All of the three named members were lawyers with diverse literary and trading interests. Nicoll, an active member of the Anglican church, was also the stepson of Samuel Johnson.[5] The board reflected accurately the realities of New York's political life, in which Anglicans exerted an influence quite out of proportion to their number. For them to claim a strong voice as the representatives of organized religion in the governing of the college would be simply to follow traditional policies in force at Harvard, William and Mary, and Yale.

But Anglican preponderance among the lottery trustees created uneasiness among non-Anglicans. Matters were not helped when in March 1752 Trinity Church offered a site for the college. In October followed the publication of *Some Thoughts on Education* by William Smith. Smith, later provost of the College of Philadelphia, was then a recent immigrant. A graduate of the University of Aberdeen, he earned his living as a private tutor. He argued strongly for an urban location because, he wrote, "such as are designed to be useful in society . . . ought to know men and the world." The argument for a city site aided the advocates of the Trinity Church offer, though non-Anglicans could take comfort from Smith's recommendations of the colleges in New England and New Jersey as possible models. A month later Smith anonymously endorsed his own proposal in the *New York Mercury*, suggesting that the city might furnish city hall as a place for the college "for some years," and that Trinity Church might employ the provost as their minister and thus relieve the lottery trustees from paying his full salary. Though Smith's recommendations thus balanced the scales between Presbyterian and Anglican as well as civil and ecclesiastic interests, he then gave a further boost to the Anglicans by warmly proposing Samuel Johnson as a likely candidate for the post of college provost and minister of Trinity Church.[6]

In the ensuing debates between the proponents of a denominationally neutral public college and the advocates of an Anglican institution,

William Livingston and William Smith were to become the chief spokesmen for their parties. Livingston published a series of essays in the *Independent Reflector* from March 22 to April 26, 1753, and Smith entered the debate in earnest with his *A General Idea of the College of Mirania*, published on April 11. Both authors agreed that a multi-denominational society needed a public college and a public religion for civic purposes of internal peace. But Livingston and Smith differed on the place of religion in the college curriculum and on how denominational interests should or should not be recognized in college government.

Livingston wrote his essays for the *Independent Reflector* together with William Peartree Smith, John Morin Scott, and William Smith, Jr. Neither of the two William Smiths was related to the author of *Some Thoughts on Education* and *A General Idea of the College of Mirania*. All four were Presbyterians and graduates of Yale, Livingston and Scott having changed their affiliation from the Dutch and French Reformed churches, respectively. They all objected vigorously to the orthodoxy of President Clap at Yale and agreed on the need for a liberal and nonpartisan college in the province of New York. Both William Peartree Smith and the father of William Smith, Jr., had served as trustees of the College of New Jersey. To all four the connection between the Anglican church and the crown spelled possible tyranny, and they championed the Assembly as the defender of the people's liberties.[7]

Early in 1753 Livingston outlined their program in a letter to another Yale graduate, Noah Welles. If the New York college were to fall under the management of churchmen, wrote Livingston, the consequence would be "universal priestcraft and bigotry in less than half a century." He complained that the men proposed as trustees were all Anglicans "and many of them the most implicit bigots" at that. He then gave his blueprint for a college established to avoid denominational strife: "I would have no charter from the Crown but an act of Assembly for the purpose. Nor, for the same reason should divinity be taught at college because whoever is in the chair will obtrude his own notions for theology. Let the students follow their own inclinations in the study of divinity and read what books they please in their chambers or apply themselves to it after they leave the college."[8]

Livingston's program constituted a sustained argument against the English policy of toleration. Toleration, he argued, was unworkable and infeasible. In moving away from the Reformation triad of established state, church, and college, one denomination could not be expected to govern a college and also to tolerate the presence and religious rights of other Protestants. There could be no such thing as nonsectarian religious instruction. Neither government by a religious group nor religious instruction were possible alternatives in a college intended to serve the interests of a religiously and ethnically heterogeneous society. Only a secular college with no official religious ties would do.

Livingston's opposition to toleration and religious instruction did not prompt him to ban religion altogether from the college. He explicitly justified regular attendance at church services of the students' choice and mandatory public prayers for all students. He insisted, however, on such nondenominational prayers "as all Protestants can freely join in" and on strict prohibition against public instruction in divinity, against the appointment of a professor of divinity, and against the rewarding of theological degrees.[9]

Livingston also demanded legislative control over the college and its Board of Trustees. He was ready to break with English concepts of corporate collegiate autonomy as well as with the independence of clerical or private trustees. In a pluralistic society, a board of control had to be representative of all factions and, to insure impartiality, the board should be supervised by the Assembly, which represented the various factions. It was precisely these factions that, far from wrecking or splintering the commonwealth, "would inevitably produce a perfect freedom from each particular party." Similarly, a royally chartered college would subvert the idea of an open and free seminary of learning by making the college subject to the whims of the sovereign, who could at any time threaten it with a quo warranto and annulment. Only under legislative enactment and supervision could the college be assured of truly fulfilling its public mission.[10]

Livingston admitted "that the creating of a body politic by act of legislation without a previous charter is unprecedented and an infringement of the prerogative of the Crown, and may possibly for these reasons be damned by the King." He asked that the legislature appoint all trustees; that governor, Council, and Assembly each have a veto over appointments and power of dismissal; that the legislature confirm the trustees' choice of president and their by-laws and that it settle all disputes arising among the trustees. He knew that with this plea he broke new ground.[11]

William Smith, too, had taken as his starting point the necessity for public education in a religiously heterogeneous society. His main concern, however, was to counteract that diversity by a deliberate attempt to socialize the future leaders of society. Referring to New York's immigrants, Smith wrote "that nothing could so much contribute to make such a mixture of people coalesce and unite in one common interest as the common education of all the youth at the same public schools under the eye of the civil authority." He thought it essential that the legislature suppress private schools in order for the public institutions to succeed. In a province such as New York it was possible to collect all the youth of the colony in one seminary of learning and place them under the immediate supervision of the legislature or of those commissioned by it. Further, a system of feeder schools would channel the province's most promising youths into the college.[12]

Smith's disagreement with Livingston came over the issue of toleration. Smith and other Anglicans like Samuel Seabury of Hempstead and Samuel Johnson thought Livingston's notion of equal toleration preposterous. As Seabury put it, it was impossible to agree on "a scheme of public worship for our college which shall not be liable to all the confusions in the building of Babel." Only the Church of England, he maintained, was disinterested enough to furnish an acceptable kind of worship. The dispute between the Anglicans and Livingston thus centered on the question of whether or not it was possible to have nondenominational worship and religious instruction in an institution intended to serve all members of the population.[13]

Smith wanted to replace the teaching of revealed religion — instruction in "the great uncontroverted principles of Christianity," he called it — as much as possible with natural or public religion. He wanted revealed religion to be restricted to Sunday evenings only, and he maintained that when teachers were committed to training virtuous men for public service, the teaching of natural science and of history would in themselves become exercises in natural and public religion. The former would bring "the deity before our eyes in the study of His stupendous works," and the latter would spur the students on to "enlist . . . for life under the banner of virtue."[14]

Smith's difference with Livingston again emerged in his willingness to acknowledge the claims of the established church to be the representative of the public religion. He pointed out that the neighboring provinces — New Jersey, Connecticut, and Massachusetts — all had colleges of their own "under the same narrow government." He meant, of course, Presbyterianism, and felt it was high time to establish a school that would attract Anglican students.[15] Smith thus clung to the English idea of preferential treatment for an officially established church with toleration of dissenters. For him religion and education were to be subordinated to the common weal, as church and college were to be the chief sources of spiritual nourishment for the body politic. Since, in Smith's view, of all the denominations the Anglican church was the least "narrow" and least rent by faction, it was the most likely to strengthen the general good.

## The Birth of King's College

In his letters to the *Reflector* Livingston had voiced what was perhaps the most advanced and radical thought of English Whig thinkers and had given the appearance of uncompromising rejection of every Anglican claim to favored recognition, but he took a far less extreme position as a member of the lottery trustees. The board was pleased to have received authorization for further drawings of £1,125 each in July and in December. On November 22, 1753, they chose Samuel Johnson as college president and Chauncey Whittelsey, tutor at Yale college, as an assistant master. From the correspondence of the men involved in these appointments it becomes evident that Livingston was not opposed to the selection of the Anglican Johnson, whereas some of the Anglicans had strong misgivings about the Presbyterian Whittelsey. Johnson himself seemed ambivalent. He was afraid that Livingston's objective was to make the college "a sort of free thinking latitudinarian seminary," but since he was involved at the time in a struggle with President Clap of Yale over his refusal to allow Anglican students to attend church services outside the college, Johnson was more concerned with Presbyterian conservatism than with Livingston's free thought. Henry Barclay, the minister of New York's Trinity Church, confided to Johnson that he and his friends "shall do what we can to prevent his [Whittelsey's] having any offer made him," and should they be unable to prevent a call to Whittelsey, the would hope that "such a subscription [i.e., oath] will be thrown in his way as his present principles, if he has any conscience, will not permit him to swallow."[16]

This Anglican ill will toward the Connecticut Presbyterian was not a reaction provoked by Livingston and other non-Anglicans on the board because these, Barclay told Johnson, "are notwithstanding very hearty for having you." Livingston himself was to prove that point when he wrote Johnson in early January on behalf of the trustees, telling him of the offer, apologizing for the small salary, and expressing the trustees' approbation of a concurrent offer by Trinity Church for Johnson to serve and receive a salary as an assistant minister.[17]

Johnson refrained during his career as president from turning his college into a sectarian school. He had prepared, for example, a liturgy for services in the college so as not to rely on the Anglican Book of Common Prayer, but was discouraged from introducing it by Henry Barclay. While neither Livingston nor Johnson could totally avoid becoming embroiled in partisan disputes, they were conscious of the ultimate futility of religious warfare in as heterogeneous a society as New York. Johnson's experience during the Cutler defection at Yale in the 1720s and his struggle with Clap in the 1750s, and Livingston's student days at Clap's Yale in 1740-1741 and his reading of English radical thinkers had convinced both men that toleration recognizing at least the principle of equality for members of all Protestant churches was a necessity. The college would never escape the vigilance and censure of Livingston, but from him it would not have to fear a threat to its existence.

The conflict between Livingston and the Anglicans flared up again when on May 14, 1754, the wardens of Trinity Church reaffirmed their 1752 offer of a parcel of land with the new condition that the president always be a member of the Church of England and religious services always be conducted in the Anglican manner. Two days later, at a meeting of the lottery trustees, the confrontation occurred. Several Anglicans, Johnson among them, had prepared a charter draft and submitted it to the trustees for approval. The draft proposed to build the college on the land donated by Trinity Church, to accept the church's conditions, and to ask the governor for a royal charter. Livingston entered a vigorous protest objecting (1) that the Church of England was not established in the colony of New York; (2) that the use of lottery funds for the support of a college with an Anglican president and liturgy was unjust to dissenters and violated their rights; (3) that the first unconditional offer of Trinity Church ought to be adhered to; (4) that only the legislature, not the trustees, could finally accept the offers made; and (5) that the charter ought to be submitted to the Assembly rather than to the governor. Livingston added fifteen further points, one of these charging that the acceptance of the Trinity Church offer turned the original design of a public college for the province into one for a college of Trinity Church.[18]

The lottery trustees paid Livingston no heed. They easily overrode his objections, refused to enter his protest in the minutes, and only consented to consider it at a later date. They then endorsed the proposed charter, accepted the Trinity offer to use their vestry room as a preliminary classroom, and on May 20 petitioned governor and Council for a charter of incorporation. Livingston, however, found allies among the councillors. While a majority of three quickly endorsed the petition, two of them, William Smith, Sr., and James Alexander, the latter an Anglican, objected vigorously. They backed Livingston's view that the proposed charter violated the rights of Protestant dissenters, that it offended and weakened the affection of many loyal supporters of the crown, that it was inconsistent with religious liberty, and that it encouraged youth to leave the province in search of education elsewhere. Smith and Alexander found it even more offensive that John Chambers and Edward Holland, lottery trustees and members of the governor's council, were sitting in judgment on their own petition. To add insult to injury, not only were their objections overruled, but the Council also refused to publish their views. On June 4 Lieutenant Governor James DeLancey ordered his attorney general to prepare a draft of a royal charter of incorporation.[19]

In the meantime Johnson had been persuaded by the trustees to get the college underway. He believed that with DeLancey's support the charter would eventually be granted and that the Assembly would allow the lottery trustees to pay out their funds to the college, but his son William counseled caution. The Assembly held the money, he wrote his father on May 31, "and there are corrupted Dutchmen . . . as well as Presbyterians." He thought the college would not be safe until the Assembly had passed the charter. But Samuel Johnson went ahead. He published an advertising circular, announcing entrance examinations to begin on July 1. He took particular care to assure parents that there was "no intention to impose on the scholars the peculiar tenets of any particular sect of Christians, but to inculcate upon their tender minds the great principles of Christianity and morality in which true Christians of each denomination are generally agreed." He promised parents liberty to choose the church in which their sons would have to attend Sunday worship. He attempted to give the requirement for daily

Anglican prayers as innocuous an appearance as he could. Within the bounds of his commitment to the Anglican church and its claim to preferment among Protestant denominations, Johnson sought to allow the greatest possible liberty of conscience.[20]

In this matter, as in his offer to include a variety of novel subjects, Johnson was responding to what he understood to be the wishes of New Yorkers. To the usual college instruction in the learned languages and the liberal arts and sciences he added surveying and navigation, geography and history, husbandry, commerce, and government. He promised instruction "in the knowledge of all nature . . . and of everything useful for the comfort, the convenience, and elegance of life, in the chief manufactures relating to any of these things."[21] Whether out of conviction of the fitness of these subjects or out of a calculating desire to attract the widest possible support for the college, Johnson here spoke as a modern man whose clerical robe and scholarly labors did not prevent him from taking advantage of the liberal elements and the mercantile and manufacturing interests of his province and city.

Livingston wrote Chauncey Whittelsey that Johnson promised "stupendous matters." He quoted from Johnson's advertisement and his intent to teach the knowledge of all nature, adding: "Whether he intends to descend as low as he soars on high, and conduct his disciples to the bottom of Tartarus, he does not inform the public." The college, in fact, never did introduce courses in navigation or surveying, although its more traditional academic offerings resembled those of William Smith's Academy of Philadelphia. This was particularly true for the instruction in moral philosophy Johnson was to offer his graduating seniors. The course brought together all the students' learning as a synthesis and stressed the supreme importance of religion for moral conduct without favoring any particular sect.[22]

The summer and early fall of 1754 were trying times for Samuel Johnson. Livingston and his friends were busily circulating petitions to persuade the governor to appoint trustees from all denominations and to give the Assembly a voice in the charter and subsequent amendments or additions. In October the Dutch Reformed church of New York petitioned the Assembly to allow them a professor of divinity in the college. They argued that they constituted "the greatest number of any single denomination of Christians in this province," and they received the happy approval of Livingston. If the Dutch were successful, Livingston reasoned, the appointment of a professor for them "would diminish that badge of distinction to which the Episcopalians are so zealously aspiring." If they are not, "that will animate the Dutch against them, and convince them that all their pretenses to sisterhood and identity were fallacious and hypocritical."[23]

Johnson did some scheming of his own since he was dissatisfied with his colleague Chauncey Whittelsey. Whittelsey so far had remained in Connecticut because of illness, and he had delayed answering the trustees' offer. From Henry Barclay, Johnson then learned in July that his objections to Whittelsey had been taken into account and that there had been a plan underway "to overset the proposal with regard to Whittelsey ever since he was thought of."[24]

By October 31, over the dissent of William Smith, Sr., the Council accepted the charter, and on the next day the Assembly received the trustees' report together with Livingston's protest containing his twenty points. On November 2 the governor signed the charter, and the College of the Province of New York, now to be known by the name of King's College, was duly incorporated by the crown "for the instruction of youth in the learned languages and liberal arts and sciences." In conformity with previous legislation and promises, the college was to use the lottery funds and the land given by Trinity Church. Its president was forever to be a communicant of the Anglican church and to arrange for morning and evening services at the college according to the discipline of that church. Its governing board was to consist of forty-one trustees, seventeen of them appointed ex officio, and twenty-four as laymen named in the charter. Of the ex officio members, ten were to represent secular and seven clerical offices, among the latter being the rector of Trinity Church, the senior minister of the Dutch Reformed church, and the ministers of the Lutheran, the French, and the Presbyterian churches in the city. Johnson was named in the charter as the first president, and as such he was also an ex officio member of the board. The governors were empowered to hire and discharge president, fellows, professors, and tutors as well as to make all the rules and laws of the college and to prescribe textbooks. As in New Jersey, the college governors were barred from excluding "any person of any religious denomination whatever from equal liberty and advantage of education, or from any of the degrees, liberties, privileges, benefits, or immunities of the said college, on account of his particular tenets in matters of religion."[25]

In many ways the charter provisions were similar to those of the College of New Jersey. Livingston's protestations to the contrary, King's College was not a church school. It was a public institution for the benefit of the entire province of New York, and neither church nor state assumed any financial obligations. As in New Jersey, the trusteeship form of government prevailed. The president was a member of the board, but the faculty was excluded from it. As at the College of William and Mary, crown officials residing in England were directly involved in the government of the college. The Archbishop of Canterbury and the First Lord Commissioner of Trade and Plantations were named to the board and empowered to appoint proxies to represent them at meetings. Though Anglicans were the dominant faction on the board, the charter provided for diverse religious representation and paid no regard to the denominational affiliation of the lay members. Unlike the New Jersey college, however, there was strong representation on the board by public officials. Had it not been for their largely Anglican affiliations and the suspicions these aroused, nobody would have been likely to question King's College's status as a provincial college.

But the college faced new difficulties. Petitions flooded the Assembly protesting confirmation of the charter and assignment of the lottery funds to the college. In early November the Assembly unanimously resolved not to authorize any expenditure of lottery funds other than by legislative act. It ordered printed a bill to establish and incorporate a rival college, and then resolved to delay discussion of the matter until the next session.[26]

The bill was the work of Livingston and his friends. With it they had mounted the most radical challenge to college government yet devised in the colonies. "The President and the Trustees of the Provincial College of New York," as they called their projected corporation, constituted a state institution in every conceivable way. The trustees were to obtain the consent of governor, Council, and Assembly for any grant or sale of college property and for the appointment of college officers. They were to submit to the three branches of the government their annual financial reports, by-laws, and other records as well as their plan of instruction and the forms of nondenominational worship. The government reserved the right to fix the location of the college, and declared that election to any of the twenty-four trustee seats should be by legislative act only. During recess of the Assembly a majority of the trustees might make temporary appointments for the offices of president and treasurer, but these had to be confirmed by the legislature at its next session. As one might expect, the bill made express provisions against religious tests for officers, teachers, or students and prohibited religious discrimination against any Protestant. There was to be no public instruction in divinity, but both the Anglican and the Dutch Reformed churches of New York were to be allowed to choose a professor of divinity who might then privately instruct those students who desired it. The bill assigned the lottery funds to the college, continued permanently the annual grant of £500 from the excise tax fund, and gave students and officers the right to sue officers, trustees, and president "in any court of law within this colony." By delaying final consideration of the bill to the following spring, Livingston hoped to buy time and persuade more people to support the Assembly bill rather than the governor's charter.[27]

While the Assembly was in recess another newspaper war broke out between the Livingston party and the supporters of King's College. Between November 25, 1754, and November 17, 1755, Livingston published fifty-two "Watch-Tower" essays in the New York *Mercury*, reiterating his belief "that the constitution of our college ought to be by legislative act, and not by charter." He continued to blast the Anglicans with his charge of their "dark" design "of appropriating the public moneys to private and sinister purposes." In the meantime Johnson placed his faith in the unassailable legality of the royal charter and remained confident that the Assembly would eventually authorize the transfer of the lottery funds. If this should not come about, he hoped that independent financing for the college could be found. He informed the Society for the Propagation of the Gospel of his intent to resign his Stratford post at Christmas 1754.[28]

Following the example of their rivals in New Jersey, the King's College governors opened a drive for subscriptions in June 1755 on the continent, in the West Indies, and in England. Johnson received a pledge of £500 from the new governor, Sir Charles Hardy, a sign, he concluded, of the governor's intentions toward the college, even though he and the Assembly were preoccupied with the French and Indian Wars and in no mood to concern themselves with the college. The impasse continued throughout most of 1756, when finally, in December, a compromise was reached. Weary of the issue, the Assembly divided the lottery fund between the college and the city and confirmed for a period of seven years the £500 annual subsidy to the college. The city used the money for a jail and a hospital, prompting William Smith, Sr., to remark that "the money had been divided between two pest-houses." It appears that many New Yorkers shared that sentiment.[29]

### Queen's College: Postlude in New Jersey

Before the affair had drawn to its close at the end of 1756, it had brought into its orbit rival factions of the Dutch Reformed churches in New York and New Jersey. A conservative group within the church resisted efforts of a New Light wing to form an American classis, and under the leadership of Domine John Ritzema, senior minister of the Dutch Reformed Collegiate Church in New York city, supported King's College. In October 1754 the ministers, elders, and deacons of the Collegiate Church petitioned the Assembly to fund a professor of divinity in King's College, who would be appointed by the church and serve the Dutch Reformed of city and province. The college charter, which had not originated with the Assembly but with the governor and Council, did not include a provision for a professor of divinity. It had, however, named Domine Ritzema to the Board of Governors. On May 7, 1755, Ritzema, on his own initiative, then requested the governor of New York to provide for a professor of divinity in the college, to be nominated and appointed by the Dutch church. The governor indicated his willingness to comply with the request if it were to come from the college Board of Governors. When this condition was met, he issued an additional charter containing the professorship as requested. Even though this new charter granted only what the church members themselves had requested of the Assembly, they now censured "the imprudent conduct of Domine John Ritzema" in obtaining a charter that "was prepared incontestably without our knowledge, advice, or counsel, and [which] in no respect answers to our conception of what would be advantageous for the upbuilding of our church."[30]

Ritzema immediately protested that he had done nothing for which he deserved "to be so miserably beaten and branded." He reported to the classis of Amsterdam that the censure really was meant to punish him for his opposition to an independent American classis and an associated academy. His main opponent, Domine Theodore Frelinghuysen, had called a convention in New York on May 27 that had unanimously endorsed a call for a Dutch Reformed college. Freling-

huysen confessed amazement "at the astonishing imposition of the en-
croaching party [the Anglicans] that would monopolize our intended
college" and at "our own infatuation, stupidity, and lethargy" that had
allowed Ritzema's project to proceed unhindered. He did not think
that either the New Light college in New Jersey or the Anglican college
in New York were worthy of Dutch support. The situation in the middle colonies appeared to him uncongenial to united efforts. "Let every
one provide for his own house."[31]

This, in 1756, expressed the disenchantment of a growing number of
Americans with the task of coping with diversity. As long as one church
or denomination was to remain predominant, the representatives of
other groups found it difficult to give the support a provincial college
demanded and had a right to receive. The English concept of toleration
with preferment was difficult to translate into practice in the pluralistic
society of the colonies. At the College of New Jersey the New Lights
were in command at Nassau Hall and had succeeded in holding down
the representatives of the government to a minimum of influence.
Could the Dutch Reformed create a college of their own similar in its
governmental arrangements to the Presbyterian foundation in
Princeton?

The Dutch Reformed did just that in 1766. Like the college in Nassau
Hall their new school at Brunswick had an intercolonial Board of
Trustees from New York, New Jersey, and Pennsylvania. At Princeton
all of the trustees were Presbyterians; at Queen's College they all
belonged to the Dutch Reformed church. In the words of the Queen's
College charter, both schools were committed "to promote learning for
the benefit of the community and advancement of the protestant
religion of all denominations."

But there were also significant differences. The founders of the college at Princeton had wanted their school to be New Jersey's provincial
college, and they had insisted on their independence from both church
and state. At Queen's, on the other hand, the charter specifically
acknowledged the college's mission to instruct "young men of suitable
abilities in divinity, preparing them for the ministry" of the Dutch
Reformed churches. But to balance the apparent tendency for the college to become a church seminary, the charter also required that no
more than one-third of the trustees could be ordained ministers. In addition, it placed among its lay trustees the governor, Council president,
chief justice, and attorney general of the province of New Jersey. Com-

pared to the College of New Jersey, Queen's College was at once more particularistic in its purpose of serving the members of the Dutch Reformed churches and more directly under secular, governmental control.[32]

How did Queen's College achieve this paradoxical status of being at once a college designed by and for a religious and ethnic minority and at the same time under close and direct governmental supervision? Of the colonial colleges founded in the aftermath of the Great Awakening, Queen's was the only one that did neither have from the outset nor later add a clause forbidding the discrimination of students on religious grounds, and only Queen's and King's made provision by charter for the appointment of a professor of divinity. It may well have been these specific denominational purposes which prompted Governor William Franklin to insist on effective secular management. In addition, Queen's College owed its birth to the efforts of a faction among the Dutch Reformed in the middle colonies. They needed all the support they could obtain from sympathizing Dutch Reformed inhabitants. As an ethnic as well as a religious minority, they depended heavily on the good will and favor of the secular authorities. Thus they were in no position to object to strong secular representation on their board.[33]

Those requesting the college charter were rewarded on November 10, 1766, when Governor William Franklin signed and sealed the document. The trustees commenced their work in April 1767 and turned their attention to choosing a location for the college and to fund-raising through subscriptions. They had to counter the continuing opposition of Domine Ritzema, who charged that Governor Franklin had granted the charter under the mistaken assumption that the applicants were subordinate to the classis of Amsterdam and had done so more to spite the Presbyterians than to aid the Dutch. They also had to contend with the suggestion of the classis of Amsterdam that the two Dutch factions join their efforts and unite their educational work with the college in Princeton. A second charter of March 20, 1770, then placed residents of New York and New Jersey on an equal footing in their relationship with the college, and with the appointment of a tutor in October 1771 the college began its work in New Brunswick. When it celebrated the graduation of its first student in 1774, Queen's College had set a precedent.[34] No longer need a colony be limited to just one college.

The strife over King's College had thus produced the colonies' first nonprovincial college and set the stage for the development of the

American system of higher education in which public and private institutions came to exist side by side. The underlying causes for this evolution were ethnic and religious diversity, and the inability of publicists like Livingston to gain acceptance for a truly nondenominational, secular college. The colonists in New Jersey acknowledged that with Queen's College they had authorized a school specifically and primarily for the benefit of the members of a particular church. Thus the new college was not to be a threat to the provincial collegiate monopoly held by the College of New Jersey, but it nonetheless constituted academic competition. At Queen's College the first steps were taken toward what eventually became the nineteenth-century private or denominational college.

# 9

## AUTOCRACY IN CONNECTICUT AND PLURALISM IN RHODE ISLAND

On Sunday, May 15, 1763, a momentous confrontation between Thomas Clap and the General Court of Connecticut took place. The General Court, having received petitions from ministers and laymen demanding that it review all college laws, ask for an annual accounting of the laws and finances, order the Corporation to permit appeals of its decisions to the governor and General Court, and appoint a commission of visitation, decided that they could no longer ignore these repeated complaints and ordered the New Haven County sheriff to summon the president and fellows of Yale College to appear before them in the meeting house at Hartford.[1]

The proceedings opened with the presentation of the petitioners' case by two former students of Clap. One was the forty-one-year-old Jared Ingersoll, Yale graduate of 1742; the other was William Samuel Johnson, Yale class of 1744, the thirty-six-year-old son of Clap's colleague and rival, Samuel Johnson. Both men were known as outstanding and accomplished jurists. They had been preceded three days earlier by the Reverend Mr. Stephen White, who in preaching the election sermon before the Assembly, had reminded the legislators of their duty to keep the college under proper supervision. His sermon had been a clarion call for a visitation.[2]

With the ground thus prepared, the petitioners and their lawyers entered. Some of their points were merely prods to the Assembly to review the college laws, rules, and ordinances "as often as required" to repeal or disallow them "when they shall think proper." But the two chief demands — for visitation by the General Court and for the students' right of appeal to governor and Council — were far from being mere insults to Clap and the fellows. They were grave threats to the autonomy of the college and the government of the Corporation, and Clap felt he had to address himself to these with particular care.

When it came his turn Clap first tackled the issue of visitation by neatly diverting the main thrust of the petitioners. He simply ignored their objection to the trustees visiting themselves and asserted instead that the question was not visitation, but the Assembly's authority as the colony's supreme legislative and judicial body over all persons and institutions in Connecticut. He referred the legislators to his 1754 pamphlet, *The Religious Constitution of Colleges*, and to his anonymously published pamphlet of 1755, *The Answer of the Friend in the West*. In them he had acknowledged the dependence of the college on the Assembly as the source of its charter and much of its support. He had written that the Assembly "necessarily have the same power over the college, as they have over all other persons and estates in the colony, and a greater power as constant benefactors." He had been unjustly accused, he maintained, when charged with claiming that the college was exempt from the supreme authority of the colony. He had meant only to refute the claimed right of visitation.[3]

His argument, Clap went on, rested on the common law as found in the Case of Sutton's Hospital, also known as the Charter House Case, and in Thomas Wood's compendium, *An Institute of the Laws of England*.[4] In these sources it was held that a college founder is he who makes the first donation of lands, funds, or other gifts and who prepares the first statutes for the government of the college. From such a founder the right to visit devolves on his heirs, successors, or appointees who, as Visitors, are to see to it that the founder's statutes are observed by the members of the college. Colleges may be founded, that is the first donation given, before or after they have received a charter of incorporation. Yale College, Clap stated, owed its origin to several ministers "who nominated and desired ten ministers to be undertakers, partners, or trustees." These ten ministers, said Clap, were a company or society by compact a year or two before they had a charter and as such consulted with each other and received small donations. They "each of them brought a large number of books principally out of their own libraries and in formal manner gave and laid them down together as the beginning or foundation of a library for the college." This event, argued Clap, was the foundation of the college and made the ten ministers the founders in law. Thus the trustees and subsequently the president and fellows derived the authority to visit the college.

As Clap pointed out to the Assembly, the 1701 charter acknowledged the prior existence of "goods, chattels, sum or sums of money," and in its preamble the 1745 charter recognized that the trustees had "founded a Collegiate School at New-Haven, known by the name of YALE COLLEGE." President and fellows, in short, were the legal Visitors of the college. Neither the common law nor "the nature and reason of the thing" allowed the Assembly to appoint a committee and invest it with the arbitrary power to visit and to report back to the Assembly. If ever there was reason for a body other than the college officers to look into the affairs of the school, then the General Court would have to exercise its general supervisory authority. The occasion, then, said Clap, "would be well worthy of the public hearing and determination of this honorable Assembly by themselves. And we shall always be ready," he added, "to give this assembly or to any one of them an account of the state of it whenever they shall please to desire it."[5] He returned to a point made before: the Assembly held a general supervisory authority; it did not have the right of visitation.

For Clap's argument to prevail he had to convince the Assembly that not they but the ministers had founded the Collegiate School. In the manuscript of his 1766 *Annals or History of Yale College* he repeated that the first trustees "by compact became a society or quasi-corporation (as my Lord Coke says) near two years before they had a charter," and that, through their formal donation of books "above a year before they had a charter," they had founded the college.[6] He sought to strengthen this point when he maintained in his manuscript that the trustees had received a gift of 600 acres and building materials "in the time of the sitting of the assembly in which the charter was given and as one motive to induce the Assembly to give it." The printed version puts the matter differently: the donation was made "in the time of the sitting of the assembly, some days before the charter was given. And this donation he made to the Collegiate School as already set up by the great pain and charge of the ministers."

Why was Clap so anxious, indeed overanxious, to assert again and again that all of these actions had occurred two years or "above a year" before the chartering? Did he protest too much? Part of the explanation lies in the fact that Clap himself had not always placed the founding of the college before 1701, the year of the charter. In his *The Religious Constitution of Colleges* of 1754 he had ascribed it to the ten ministers at their first meeting in Saybrook in 1701, at which time and place the donation of the books took place.[7] The *Annals* also give evidence that Clap had thought of 1701 rather than of any earlier date as the year of the founding. The subtitle of the manuscript had originally read: From the First Founding thereof in the Year 1701 to this Present Year 1757. The dates were later changed to read 1700 and 1765.

The change from 1701 to 1700 had, however, first appeared in Clap's 1755 pamphlet, *The Answer of the Friend in the West.* In that publication he described the ten ministers in much the same way as he was to do in the 1766 *Annals.* They were "a company or society by compact a year or two before they had a charter, in which time they . . . received sundry donations for [the erection of a college]." During these same years the society constituted in fact an unincorporated school, and "in this less perfect state" they received their charter.[8] Also in 1755 Clap refined his definitions by distinguishing between the founding and the erecting of the Collegiate School. He attributed the former, "done before the charter," to the ministers, and the latter, done in 1701, to "the fathers of the colony."[9] In the printed 1766 edition of his *Annals* Clap then wrote of the nomination in 1699 of "ten of the principal ministers . . . to stand as trustees or undertakers to found, erect, and govern a college." Proceeding with the marginal notation 1700, he continued, "The ministers so nominated met at New Haven and formed themselves into a body or society, to consist of eleven ministers, including a rector, and agreed to found a college in the colony of Connecticut; which they did at their next meeting at Branford, in the following manner . . . " And now Clap again tells the story of the presentation of the books as the official act of founding the college. In the *Annals*, then, as published in 1766 Clap announced: Yale College had been founded in Branford, Connecticut, in the year 1700.[10]

Next in importance to visitation was the issue of the students' right of appeal to governor and Council from the disciplinary decisions of the Corporation. On this point Clap refused to budge. All he was willing to grant was a student's right to appeal his and the tutors' judgment to the fellows of the Corporation. That, he maintained, was not innovation anyway, and "was never desired above once, or twice, and then it was allowed." But an appeal to authorities outside the college was out of the question. "For this would occasion a great delay in government and mispence of time." The same disadvantage of "a great expense of time and money and . . . many mischiefs and confusions" would result, Clap held, if students were allowed to sue each other or the college officers in court.

Clap also rejected scornfully the charge that he functioned as both accuser and judge in cases involving disobedience and misbehavior toward him, and that he denied his students the right to counsel. "This is the case of all judges," he maintained, "and absolutely necessary in such a society as this." He scoffed at the petitioners' charge that the "very young without advice" were peculiarly subjected to his rule as master and judge, and warned that for the students to be allowed to introduce counsel could only lead to formal indictments and court costs far exceeding any fines he had levied.[11] With that he had disposed of the students' right to hire attorneys, to engage in law suits, and to appeal to governor and Council. Such supposed rights, he said, threatened the academic integrity of the college, violated English academic precedent, and ignored the common law.

The petitioners denounced Clap's presidency as an arbitrary and autocratic rule in an enclave of privilege liberally supported by public funds. Clap denied that he acted as an autocrat, because he consulted "in all difficult and important cases" with his tutors and "in all cases of extraordinary importance" with members of the Corporation as well. He also denied that the fines he levied were excessive and that the college did not keep accounts. He explained that the alleged tax imposed on students for college buildings was used to erect and maintain "a necessary house for the college, called and known by the name of Joseph." Addressing himself to the Assembly, he asked facetiously whether such policy was "a infraction upon the privileges of Englishmen?" As to the complaint of the multiplication of college laws Clap pointed out that the accusation used to be the scarcity of laws. He stoutly defended his philosophy that severe laws were the best prevention of disorder, and that the prevalent vogue of student play-acting called for a close supervision of their activities. He laid the blame for whatever problems the college experienced "principally to the instigations and insinuations of designing men," men who in a later century would be called outside agitators.[12] Clap denied that he had failed to consult in the proper manner other members of the Corporation, and none of the fellows present contradicted him.

Clap's strategy, played to perfection against the background of long-standing partisan divisions in the General Court, was successful. He had counted heavily on the soundness of his conviction that the Assembly would do nothing to endanger the colony's charter, and he saw correctly that visitation and appeal were issues inextricably linked to each other. He wagered correctly that nobody would insist on the petitioners' demand that students be granted the right to appeal to governor and Council. Not even Gale pursued this point any longer and appeared willing to concede to the Corporation the right of parental superintendence over the students. Clap's intransigence was not just a show of bravado or the result of confidence in his considerable legal knowledge. He was aware that the question of appeal could also be used to put the General Court on the defensive. Should the Court decide on a visitation or permit the students to appeal Clap's disciplinary judgments to the governor, Clap warned the legislators, the college might file a complaint with the crown authorities in London. A visitation of the college by the Assembly would open the door for visitors from England "with full power in themselves to redress everything in our laws or courts which they might esteem to be abuses."[13]

The threat of royal interference in the affairs of Connecticut and of Yale College had a long history. It hinged on the question of whether or not the colony had the legal right to create a corporation. When Yale was formally incorporated in 1745, lawyers agreed that the English statutes did not apply to the colonies unless they were specifically named. Thus it was no longer necessary to apply for incorporation to the king in Parliament.[14] As the person mainly responsible for the Yale charter of 1745, Clap shared these sentiments, but now, in 1763, he reminded his listeners that their status was uncertain. Not being confronted with a royal quo warranto was not the same as being in possession of a royal endorsement. While the risk of royal interference may have been small, it was a risk nonetheless, and Clap made the most of it. On May 15, 1763, the victory was his.

### Exit Thomas Clap

Contemporary and later opinion has, by and large, upheld the contention that Clap had won a decisive and lasting victory over the General Court. In 1766 Clap reflected that "the question never will be publicly moved again." In 1818 Benjamin Trumbull, author of a two-volume history of Connecticut who is said to have been an eye witness to the 1763 proceedings in the state house, summed up his impressions. "The memorialists, and their whole party, were greatly disappointed and chagrined, and the president got much honor by the defense which he made of the college . . . The question relative to the assembly's being the founders of the college, and having a right of visitation, has never been publicly disputed since, and it is believed that it never will be again." Franklin Bowditch Dexter, college archivist and historian of early Yale, virtually echoed Trumbull's judgment in 1896: "The result of this open struggle was an utter defeat for the opponents on their own ground, and a deeper respect for the ability and learning of the sagacious old President. He was abundantly justified in the quiet comment with which he dismisses the subject in his Annals."[15]

Yet subsequent events in college and colony contradict the "quiet comment" that the subject "never will be publicly moved again." The confrontation of 1763 constituted at best the battle that, while won, signaled the turning point in a war that was about to be lost. The students accomplished what the legislature had been unable to carry out: they brought down Clap's administration in utter ruin a few years later.[16] But more was involved than student high jinks and adolescent rebelliousness directed against an obstinate old man. Behind the students stood their parents and, with them, the people of Connecticut. Gale and the petitioners expressed sentiments that enjoyed a wide currency beyond the immediate vicinity of the college and even the colony. When the petitioners objected to Clap barring the students' access to the courts and to his charging them for erecting college buildings, they referred to the natural rights of Englishmen and spoke of taxation without representation. Clap's defiance constituted a victory for the concept of a college as a sectarian seminary and of college government as paternal absolutism. Neither concept blended in well with the prevailing temper of the times.

Upon his return to the college from his bout with the Assembly, Clap addressed himself to the problems raised by the rebellious students. Flushed with the elation of victory and incensed over the continuing affronts to his authority he determined to spell out clearly the relationship he wanted between himself and his young charges. The Assembly had allowed him to have his way on the matter of visitation. Now he was going to tell the students just how far they might take their claimed right of appeal.

He let it be known that there was no such thing as a natural right to appeal. Any right of appeal was subsequent, not antecedent, to the laws of the particular community in which it was claimed. Thus the right depended in each case on the likelihood that its exercise would inconvenience or damage the community less than that its suppression would hurt the appealing party. "Universal experience teaches," Clap remarked, "that men will appeal when they may, unless the charge and trouble of it is more than the thing is worth."[17]

Clap's insistence that the rights of the college were superior to the rights of individual students was coupled also with his view that students were minors without the rights of adults. As he spelled out in his Observations Relating to the Government of Yale College in 1764, the need to maintain order placed the immediate legislative and judicial powers firmly in his hands. This is, perhaps, one of the clearest and most explicit early statements of a college's right and obligation to stand *in loco parentis*. For purposes of good order and government it was assumed that parents and guardians delegated their parental rights to the college officers when their sons enrolled in the college. Families, it was further assumed, were governed by mutual love, respect, and parental authority. They were essentially private communities in which there was no room for visitations by outsiders or legally sanctioned appeals from the father's judgment.[18]

Both Clap and the petitioners prepared further written material on their positions. Clap published his *Annals or History of Yale College*, and an anonymous author wrote a twenty-six-page letter in which he showed that "Yale College is a very great emolument, and of high importance to the state."[19] But the decisive events occurred in the college itself.

In February of 1766 in a petition signed by all but two or three, the students demanded Clap's ouster. They accused him of being in his dotage and showing arbitrariness and partiality in his administration. When the Corporation did not act on the petition, the students went wild. They damaged college buildings, burned boards and furniture, threatened the tutors with bodily harm, and drove them out of the college. Clap faced a mutiny with only the assistance of Naphtali Daggett, his professor of divinity. In April the Corporation ordered an immediate vacation and abolished the system of placing undergraduates by social rank. In May only about one-third of the student body was at the college, and in June James Dana reported that Clap had "arrived to his *ne plus ultra*." With only Clap and Professor Daggett attempting to teach, Chauncey Whittelsey reported that "the good old lady seemed just to breathe, but ready to expire." In July Clap offered his resignation, which the Corporation accepted as effective at commencement in

September. On the tenth of that month he gave his valedictory address, maintaining to the last his view of Yale as a religious school for the education of gospel ministers. With the college nearly in ruins, the Clap regime had come to its end.[20]

But the "grand old lady" had not expired after all. In fact she was soon to be revived and restored to her old stature. The resignation of Clap ended the attempts to take Yale out from under the supervision of the legislature and led to a renewed affirmation of its role as a provincial college. In October the Assembly resolved to recommend to the Yale Corporation that the college laws be revised and printed in English as well as Latin. The legislators expressed their hope that a mild paternal government would impose as few pecuniary fines as possible and inform the parents of fined students of both crime and punishment. Then they ordered that "for the continual support of college their [the corporation's] accounts be annually laid before the General Assembly of this colony in the October sessions." Clap's nightmare had become reality. John Devotion wrote to Ezra Stiles: "Their Reverends submitted, *lamb like*," and then added, "A certain gentleman says, AYE, you have given up all." That gentleman was Benjamin Gale, who also wrote to Stiles of "our gentle visitation of Yale College, in which we touch'd them so gently, that till some time after the assembly, they never saw they were taken in, that we had made ourselves visitors, and subjected them to an annual visitation . . . a very considerable share of which policy your humble servant claims as his own."[21]

Gale and his friends had reason to be jubilant. Clap's victory of 1763 had been short-lived. Everything the old president had resisted, with the sole exception of the students' right of appeal to the General Court, had now been accepted. Even the right of appeal was eventually conceded, when in May 1792 the Assembly adopted an act amending the college charter to include in the college Corporation the governor, lieutenant governor, and six senior Council members.[22] Through that act the students gained access to state officials and their appeals would be heard by the highest secular magistrates. But by 1766 most of the vestiges of Clap's opposition to the General Court had been overcome. Yale College, a publicly supported corporation for the training of Connecticut's leaders in state and churches, had been placed under the general supervision of the legislature and was recognized by all as the provincial college of the colony.

*Rhode Island Baptists and Ezra Stiles's Pluralistic College*

Eighty miles to the northeast the people of Rhode Island wrestled with similar problems of denominational diversity in their attempt to found a provincial college. Rhode Island was particularly open and vulnerable to all the challenges of a pluralistic society. Throughout its history the colony had cherished hospitality toward all varieties of Protestant Christians. Claims for ecclesiastic or educational privilege were foreign to its traditions, and religious diversity characterized its population. Ezra Stiles estimated that in 1760 there were 16,200 Baptists in the colony, living in harmony and legal equality with 6,420 Quakers, 5,100 Presbyterians, 1,800 Anglicans, and 11,000 "Nothingarians."[23] Though the Baptists represented the largest denomination, they had not asked for, either formally or informally, any kind of preferment.

It was in this setting in 1760 that Stiles, a Yale graduate and minister of Newport's Second Congregational Church, delivered a call for unity among all Calvinist-Reformed churches. His sermon was printed a year later in Boston as *A Discourse on the Christian Union.*[24] In order to add institutional support to his vision of interdenominational cooperation, Stiles began to discuss with friends the desirability of incorporating trustees for a college in Rhode Island. When it became known that the Philadelphia Baptists were contemplating the establishment of a college somewhere in the colonies Stiles saw a possibility for a joint venture. James Manning of the Philadelphia Baptist Association "made the design known" and received a favorable response from local Baptists. Negotiations then began between the Philadelphia and Rhode Island Baptists and Ezra Stiles and his friends. As a result the Rhode Island Assembly in February 1764 granted a charter for a provincial college in Rhode Island. The seventh colonial college was born.[25]

The charter proceedings illuminate the changing and conflicting conceptions of a college. At issue was the question already posed in the preceding decade in New York during the controversy over the founding of King's College: what kind of control could or should be devised for a college in a religiously heterogeneous colony?

In Rhode Island there was no established church and, consequently, there existed no policy of toleration with preferment. But the colony's Baptists based their case for the control of the college on their role as sponsors and chief supporters. Though they viewed the college as a provincial institution, they maintained that it was *their* college for which they had taken the initiative in the Philadelphia Association and among the colony's Baptists. Ezra Stiles and his friends, on the other hand, saw in the college a means of uniting the representatives of several Protestant denominations and churches.[26]

Stiles and William Ellery, a lawyer and one of Stile's parishioners, coauthored a draft charter and submitted it to the Rhode Island Assembly in August 1763. They had tried hard to devise an instrument acceptable to both sides and had provided for a corporation of two branches, the trustees and the fellows. Of the thirty-five trustees, nineteen were forever to be elected from among the Baptists, seven from among Congregationalists or Presbyterians, five from among Quakers, and four from among Episcopalians. The Corporation's second branch was to consist of twelve fellows, one of whom was to be the president of the college. Eight of the fellows were always to be Congregationalists; the remaining four could be of any denomination. The charter declared that there should never be any religious tests in the college, and that the school should "be free and open for all denominations of Protestants," with no proselytizing or insinuating "the peculiar principles of any one or other of the denominations."

Stiles and Ellery had striven valiantly to combine the Baptists' desire for dominance with their own ideal of a harmoniously balanced representation of the several denominations. The two-branch Corporation was the device by which they sought to achieve this aim. Of the forty-seven members, at least nineteen were always to be Baptists and at least fifteen Congregationalists. The Baptists controlled the trustees, and the Congregationalists were dominant among the fellows. This caused James Manning to complain that this was unfair to the Baptists since the fellowship — the group empowered to grant degrees — was the "soul" and the trusteeship the "body" of the institution. But the two branches had to concur in their decisions and the trustees elected the president. Stiles and Ellery had tried their best to produce an equitable solution to a difficult problem.[27]

In the Assembly accusations were levied that "trechery" was involved in designing the fellowship in such a way that no Baptist need sit on its board. The clamor led to a postponement of action and to the subsequent introduction of a modified charter. It passed the Assembly in February 1764, and was signed by the governor on October 24, 1765.

This charter assured that the Baptists would be in control of the college, with a forty-eight-member Corporation, thirty of whom were to be Baptists, twenty-two to sit as trustees and eight as fellows. The Congregationalists were to have a minimum of four representatives, all of them trustees. And the president was always to be a Baptist. Apart from these changes, however, and the omission of the passage proscribing proselytizing and insinuating the principles of any one denomination, the charter remained largely as Stiles and Ellery had drafted it. There would be no discrimination against students and professors because of their denominational allegiance. As in the colleges in Connecticut and Pennsylvania, representatives of the civil government were absent from its governing boards.

The College of Rhode Island was thus in every respect a model example of an eighteenth-century provincial college. Its founding illustrates the triumph of traditionalism over idealism. Like Stiles, the Baptists conceived of the college as a Christian institution to help unify the colony by training its future political and professional leaders. But like the Anglicans in New York and the Presbyterians in New Jersey, the Rhode Island Baptists believed in toleration with preferment. Stiles' proposal for an equitable representation of all the major denominations seemed unworkable and therefore utopian, just as William Livingston's concept in New York had appeared un-Christian and therefore pernicious.

Ezra Stiles and William Ellery were not yet ready to concede. Stiles refused to yield to Baptist overtures and twice turned down their invitations to serve as Corporation fellow of the new college. He and Ellery then resurrected his plan for a multidenominational college in February 1770. This was to be a college in Newport "on the plan of equal liberty to Congregationalists, Baptists, Episcopalians, [and] Quakers."[28]

The project quickly became embroiled in local rivalries between Providence Plantations and the city and island of Newport. In Providence as in the colony as a whole, Baptists and their sympathizers constituted the dominant religious group, whereas in Newport Presbyterians and Congregationalists ranked first in numbers.[29] Given these circumstances, Stiles and Ellery had good reason to push for a multidenominational college as an alternative to the College of Rhode Island. What distinguished their project from all previous attempts at chartering a college in the colonies was the unconventional and rather complicated way by which Stiles and Ellery sought to give institutional and legal assurance to their hopes for equity in college government. This they did by introducing radical changes in the manner of selecting trustees, fellows, presidents, professors, and tutors. They provided for a Corporation of forty-nine members divided into forty trustees and nine fellows, with the president of the college being one of the fellows. Trustees and fellows were to sit on one board, with the president as moderator having a casting vote. Ten of the trustees and two of the fellows each were to come from one of the four named denominations: Church of England, Friends, Baptists, and Congregationalists. Their numerical relationship was to be fixed and to remain "to perpetuity immutably the same." The charter assigned the president's choice by lot to one of the four denominations and provided that for any subsequent election a lot should be drawn among the denominations not yet having furnished a president. This system was to continue until each denomination had supplied a president, and the order of rotation established by lot would thereafter have to be observed.

Stiles and Ellery applied the same system to the choice of professors and tutors, provided, however, that the first tutor should not be of the same denomination as the president. In order to guarantee further a continuing equitable representation, a president or teacher was to be removed from office if he changed his denominational affiliation or accepted regular or occasional paid duties as a minister. The two charter drafters sought to make it nearly impossible for a particular denomination to capture the proposed college. They devised their own affirmative action program, eighteenth-century style.[30]

The Stiles-Ellery plan was submitted to the February session of the Rhode Island legislature. Less than a week after the lower house first conferred on the matter, it resolved on March 1 to grant the petition and sent it to the upper house. That house on the next day referred the bill to the next session, which was to open on May 2.[31] But before the matter could be taken up again, the Corporation of the College of Rhode Island petitioned the legislature to reject the application. They claimed that the College of Rhode Island had been erected "for the education of youth . . . to be effected chiefly, if not altogether, by the application and at the cost and expense of the Baptist churches." In this college the Corporation stated, "the youth of every denomination of Christians are fully entitled to, and actually enjoy, equal advantages in every respect, as the Baptists themselves, without being burdened with any religious test or constraint whatsoever." They expressed their anxiety over the possibility of a second college being chartered by the Assembly and set forth the argument that "large sums of money have been given, and more subscribed, toward this intention . . . should a charter be granted for erecting another corporation of the same kind in this colony, all those who have been benefactors to this will think themselves deluded and deceived; notwithstanding we have acted under the faith of the government; and all those that hereafter might become benefactors will be discouraged and hindered."[32] The legislators agreed and decided to defend their provincial school. No word appears of the Newport college in the legislative records of the May session.

Ostensibly the Stiles-Ellery proposal collapsed because it threatened the monopoly of Rhode Island's provincial college. More likely, however, regional and denominational jealousies condemned Stiles's equitable scheme as impractical and utopian. Even in Rhode Island the wishes of a powerful majority prevailed over the claims for equitable representation for minorities.

# 10

## THE AMERICAN PROVINCIAL COLLEGE

By the middle of the eighteenth century the provincial college had become the standard institution for higher education in the American colonies. It enjoyed the official sanction, if not always the financial support, of the colonial legislatures, and from them derived its claim to a monopoly on higher education. In its government and policies it also reflected the colony's majority denomination, though the British policy of toleration and its own interest in attracting students persuaded it to recognize the presence of governors, teachers, and students of other denominations and to grant them freedom of conscience and worship. By 1768 provincial colleges under Presbyterian auspices existed in Massachusetts, Connecticut, and New Jersey. Anglicans dominated in Virginia and New York. In Pennsylvania Anglicans and Presbyterians struggled for control. In Rhode Island the Baptists were in command. Only Queen's College in New Jersey, established to meet the special concerns of the Dutch Reformed church, did not fit the mold of a provincial college.

In 1770 when Ezra Stiles learned of the chartering of Dartmouth College in New Hampshire and of plans to establish other new colleges in Georgia, South Carolina, and Rhode Island, he commented wryly in his diary, "College Enthusiasm."[1] Yet of the four institutions he had mentioned, only Dartmouth was to survive and succeed as New Hampshire's provincial college. Its origins may be traced back to the missionary labors of Eleazar Wheelock, a Congregational minister and Yale graduate. Under the impact of George Whitefield and the Great Awakening, Wheelock had taken Indian boys into his parish home in Lebanon, Connecticut, to educate them as Christian missionaries and send them back to their tribes on the frontier. With the support of a

local landowner, Colonel Joshua Moor, and several missionary societies, Wheelock broadened his work in 1754 and organized it as
Moor's Indian Charity School. In the early 1760s he sought to obtain
for it a charter of incorporation from the Connecticut General Court.
He was turned down, however, by the upper house, apparently because of fears that the Charity School might compete with Yale for
white students. Needing funds for his growing academy, Wheelock
sent two emissaries to England from 1765 to 1768. They closed their
successful drive with the organization of two trusts, one in England
and one in America. The board in England was to continue receiving
funds, and the board in America was to manage the property and supervise the school. Just as these financial and administrative arrangements promised to give greater stability to Wheelock's enterprise, there
was a rapid decline in Indian admissions, and the survival of the school
under its original purpose appeared problematical.[2]

Wheelock had previously considered a reorganization and relocation
of the school because of his inability to obtain a charter in Connecticut
and the distance from the Indian territories. In addition, he faced
growing competition for his missionary efforts from the Anglican Society for the Propagation of the Gospel, despite the fact that by 1765 he
had trained eight white students, twenty-nine Indian boys, and ten Indian girls. In 1766 President Myles Cooper of King's College had revived plans for attracting Indian students to King's, and it soon became
evident that Sir William Johnson, the crown's Superintendent of Indian Affairs, preferred Anglican missionaries among the natives. Despite his personal friendship with Wheelock, Johnson opposed his
influence as a dissenter. Then, too, many of Wheelock's Indian graduates had ceased to work effectively as missionaries.[3] This "most melan-
choly" experience persuaded Wheelock "that a greater proportion of
English youths must be fitted for missionaries."[4] If white students were
to take a more prominent place in the school and its affairs, then incorporation as a college rather than as an academy seemed preferable.

The rumors that Wheelock had set his mind on the creation of a college thus proved not altogether groundless. Early in 1768 John Devotion had written to Ezra Stiles that speculation had it "that Wheelock's
school will drain the blood of Yale, draw in the present administration,
and finally be [established?] as a college or academy at Lebanon."[5] Indeed, when in 1769 Wheelock and the English trustees accepted an
offer of land and a charter from Governor John Wentworth of New

Hampshire, Wheelock added a postscript, as if an afterthought, "Sir, if you think proper to use the word *college* instead of *academy* I shall be well pleased with it."[6] The governor, it turned out, thought it proper, and Moor's Indian Charity School of Lebanon, Connecticut, was transformed into Dartmouth College in the province of New Hampshire. Two years later James Manning, the president of the College of Rhode Island, commented that, from what he could gather, Wheelock's project was "to be a grand Presbyterian college, instead of a school for the poor Indians."[7]

The charter issued by Governor Wentworth in the name of the king gave to the trustees of the new college a freer hand than Wheelock had dared hope. All it required of the college with respect to the English trustees was for the president to report the use of the funds received from England, annually or whenever requested, as long as the English trust existed and there were Indian students at the college. The charitable trust thus was a legal entity distinct from the college. The charter defined the college's purpose as "the education and instruction of Youth of the Indian tribes in this land in reading, writing, and all parts of Learning which shall appear necessary and expedient for civilizing and christianizing children of pagans as well as in all liberal arts and sciences; and also of English Youth and any others," and "to supply a great number of Churches and Congregations which are likely soon to be formed in that new Country with a learned and orthodox ministry." It spelled out the traditional purpose of promoting learning and the liberal arts and sciences for the education of youth and the training of future ministers.

The governing board consisted of six magistrates and six dissenting ministers. Among these were the governor of New Hampshire, a member of the Connecticut Assembly, and Eleazar Wheelock, who was also named as president. State and church were equally represented, and the British policy of toleration was safeguarded by prohibiting the exclusion of "any person of any religious denomination whatsoever from free and equal liberty and advantage of education." The trustees were to have the right to grant degrees and to enjoy perpetual succession. They were responsible for the education and government of the students, and were to elect presidents, professors, tutors, and all other college officers. Only Wheelock's immediate successor was to be chosen by Wheelock himself. Eight of the twelve trustees had to be residents of New Hampshire, seven of them laymen.[8] Despite its origin as a missionary academy for the education of Indians, Dartmouth College emerged in 1769 as a provincial institution with secular interests and clearly defined responsibilities toward the public.

Initially the trustees in England had protested the new arrangements. They complained justly that few Indian students were continuing at Hanover, and that the disposal of their funds in New Hampshire had been taken out of their hands. It took all of Wheelock's powers of persuasion to keep them from dissolving the trust. He convinced them that he, and not the college trustees, could draw on the English funds and put them to the use of Moor's Indian Charity School. This he did with remarkable success in the next few years, although it was nearly impossible for him or anyone else to be certain that only the Charity School and not the college was the beneficiary. From 1770 to 1774 Wheelock drew £6,467 sterling, and then was notified that the fund had been exhausted. For the results of this investment Wheelock could point to the educational record of the 1770s: approximately 40 Indians and 120 whites had been educated at Hanover, the numerical difference between Indians and whites calling into question the fidelity with which the trust funds had been expended.

Dartmouth's character as a provincial institution was underlined in 1773 through a grant of £560 from the New Hampshire Assembly, and in 1775, 1776, and 1778 by actions of the Continental Congress. Twice the Congress appropriated $500 and then an additional $925 to aid the college in its efforts of defending and pacifying the Indian frontier. Even after the war such public support continued. New Hampshire authorized lotteries in 1784 and 1787, appropriated £361 in 1790, and granted land in 1791. The State of Vermont, too, aided the college when in 1785 it gave 23,000 acres.[9] At the century's end, the college played the customary role of an incorporated institution serving as the province's training ground of future professionals, civil servants, and ministers. While there was never any doubt that Dartmouth College was run by Congregationalists, it was also evident that it served all the Protestant denominations of the province. Dartmouth, like the College of Rhode Island, stood firmly on the toleration with preferment tradition of the eighteenth century.

## College Plans That Failed

Anglican suspicions, threats of armed conflict, and opposition by established college interests prevented the creation of other colleges in the years before the Revolution. The Anglicans used their influence among royal officials to block new colleges in at least three colonies. When in 1758 the ministers of the dominant Congregational churches in New Hampshire proposed at their convention to found a provincial college or academy under the toleration plan, Governor Benning Wentworth refused the charter because of his uneasiness over the proposed college's Congregational sponsorship.[10]

In the next decade Anglican authorities blocked George Whitefield's plan to enlarge his Savannah orphanage into an academy or college. In 1764 Whitefield petitioned Governor James Wright for a land grant in order to provide "for the education of persons of superior rank who thereby might be qualified to serve their King, their country, and their God either in Church or State."[11] The governor and both houses of the Georgia legislature granted the request, but opposition arose in England where the Archbishop of Canterbury and the Lord Commissioners of Trade and Plantations objected to Whitefield's unwillingness to give explicit assurance of preferment for Anglicans. The crown officials were suspicious of Whitefield's evangelism and the support he received from dissenters. Whitefield, in fact, later told Thomas Secker of Canterbury that "by far the greatest part of the orphan house collections came from Dissenters, not only in New England, New York, Pennsylvania, South Carolina and Scotland, but in all probability here in England also." In addition, he told the Archbishop, he had assured his contributors from the pulpit that his intended college "should be [founded] upon a *broad bottom, and no other*."[12] To Anglican officials such liberality was the project's fatal flaw.

The specific objection which moved Secker to veto Whitefield's college was that it had been modeled on the Presbyterian foundation of the College of New Jersey. Secker preferred King's College as a model with its Anglican president and Anglican liturgy at religious services. But Whitefield told Secker that these Anglican requirements had "greatly retarded the progress of the College of New York." By contrast, he went on, the understanding obtained for the College of Philadelphia that there be no charter preference and no preferential policy, had been of great advantage to that college. Whitefield reminded Secker that even though the charter had not forced the Philadelphia trustees to appoint an Anglican president, they had done so anyway. The same development, he suggested to Secker, might safely be expected for the college in Georgia. But Whitefield's arguments accomplished nothing.[13]

A similar situation obtained in 1771 in North Carolina. Here the legislature in January incorporated The Fellows and Trustees of Queen's College, to be located in Charlotte. The Assembly nominated a board of fourteen trustees, twelve of whom were Presbyterians. In exchange they accepted the requirement that the president be an Anglican and be licensed by the governor. Neither governor nor Assembly insisted that the charter carry the usual clause prohibiting discrimination against students on religious grounds.[14]

When Governor William Tryon recommended incorporation to the Board of Trade and Plantations he explained his readiness to accept the heavily Presbyterian board by acknowledging the Assembly's aid in past political difficulties.[15] But again Anglican and royal officials disagreed with their representatives in the colony. If this college were allowed to be incorporated, they told the crown, it would "in effect operate as a seminary for the education and instruction of youth in the principles of the presbyterian church." Even though, they said, they approved the "tolerating spirit" manifest in the king's dominions and appreciated the "loyalty and zeal" shown by the North Carolinians, they felt that a royal charter would simply grant "great and permanent advantages to a sect of dissenters." They therefore advised the king to disallow the incorporation, and he did so on April 22, 1772. Queen's College, however, did not thereby disappear. It conducted its operations as an unincorporated academy, until it was incorporated as Liberty Hall Academy by the new state government in 1777.[16]

In South Carolina, however, the failure of yet another provincial college project seems to have been caused by excitement over the Stamp Act and rising revolutionary agitation rather than the influence of Anglican officials. In this colony, bills to establish a college by action of the legislature had failed in 1723, and again in 1765. The first died apparently because of lack of funds, the second because of neglect during the Stamp Act crisis. A third attempt in 1770 was part of a more comprehensive bill to expand the free schools of South Carolina. It was first proposed by Lieutenant Governor William Bull on January 30 and introduced into the lower house on March 31. When the Governor dissolved the Assembly, renewed efforts were made to reintroduce the bill in August 1770 and again in January 1771. But these efforts failed as legislators turned their minds and attention to the conflict with England.[17]

Even though the 1770 bill asked for private donations for the construction of a college building on land appropriated by the legislature in Charleston, it proposed the College of South Carolina as a provincial school. The trustees were to consist of the lieutenant governor, the governor, the Council president, the speaker of the house, and an unspecified number of unnamed individuals. These gentlemen were to enjoy perpetual succession, to serve as recipients of all funds given to the college, and to have the power of appointing president and professors, of making the college laws and statutes, and of bestowing degrees "as are usually granted at either of the Universities in Great Britain." The legislature committed itself to supply any necessary public funds in case private donations should prove insufficient for the completion of the building, and to endow the college and pay for its president and professors. The 1770 bill did not contain a phrase making illegal any discrimination against students on grounds of their religion. With its insistence "that the president of the said college shall be of the religion of the Church of England and conform to the same," it must have pleased a royal governor and London officials.[18] Next to the charters of the College of William and Mary and King's College, the South Carolina charter draft provided for one of the most thoroughly Anglicanized provincial colleges in the colonies. The bill, however, never cleared either house of the legislature before the Revolution swept away the necessity of submitting it to London. In 1770 the College of South Carolina remained stillborn.

The final instance of an unsuccessful attempt to charter a college during the colonial period occurred in Massachusetts in 1762. Here the college promoters were dissident orthodox Congregationalists who sought an alternative to the liberal establishment institution in Cambridge. They collaborated with small farmers, wealthy landowners, and entrepreneurs of western Massachusetts who were also dissatisfied with the dominance in politics and social life of the province's eastern section. Harvard College did not have a good reputation in the Berkshires and along the Connecticut River. Westerners felt that their sons were discriminated against in the college "placing system" whereby all the members of a class were ranked by social origin and scholastic achievement. There were the disadvantages of distance and travel expense, and the suspicions of a predominantly rural and religiously orthodox population toward an urban, cosmopolitan, and religiously liberal community. As the 1750s and early 1760s brought reports of riotous student behavior, the people of western Massachusetts decided that they needed a college of their own.

Responding favorably to a suggestion to use the bequest of Ephraim Williams for "the support and maintenance of a free school" or "for schools on the frontier" as an appropriation for the founding of a college, a committee of seventy-four interested persons met in January 1762 under the leadership of Israel Williams of Hatfield and prepared a charter for the proposed college.[19] They were assisted by William Smith, Jr., a New York lawyer and close friend of Williams. Smith had had long experience with college affairs. His father was a trustee of the College of New Jersey, and he himself was a Yale graduate and one of the collaborating authors of the *Independent Reflector* during the battle with the Anglican supporters of King's College.

Smith and Williams drew up a charter that stressed the increasing population in Hampshire and Berkshire counties and their distance from existing New England colleges. They announced the willingness of six laymen and six ministers "to found and endow a college or collegiate school within the said County of Hampshire," and asked that a president and fourteen fellows — of whom at least seven had to be laymen — be incorporated by royal letters patent as "The President and Fellows of Queen's College in New England." This Corporation was to have the powers of making and altering statutes and laws and of appointing and setting salaries for a master, tutors, and other college officers. Crown and governor were named as Visitors. There was no reference to religious services and to the church membership of president or fellows, teachers or students. The silence on religious matters and the naming of crown and governor as Visitors were intended to protect the orthodox Calvinists of western Massachusetts against interference by the Bay Colony's liberal establishment.[20]

Smith and Williams, however, soon doubted that they had followed correct procedure in applying to the governor in view of the plenary powers given to the General Court in the province charter. They therefore recommended that the proponents also prepare a petition to the General Court to bring in a bill "for incorporating a society for the founding and regulating an academy in the western part of this province." In this bill the applicants named Northampton, Hadley, and Hatfield as possible locations for Queen's College, and specifically authorized the president and eight of the fellows to confer bachelor of arts and master of arts degrees to qualified students.[21] Governor Bernard had no objections to this procedure, and stood ready to grant a charter even if the legislature were to pass the bill.[22]

This, however, did not come to pass. Though the lower house accepted the bill on its third reading on February 24, the upper house refused to give it a second reading and thus killed it. Three days later Governor Bernard signed the charter, only to come under intense pressure from his Council to retrieve it for further consideration. The Council, as Williams stated, "make part of the Board of Overseers of Cambridge College" and opposed the chartering of another college in Massachusetts as "greatly prejudicial to Harvard College." They appointed a committee to prepare a statement of their objections to the college in Hampshire County. The Assembly, too, then asked Bernard to withhold the charter until the next session of the Court.[23]

No document gives better insight into the eighteenth-century conception of a college as a provincial center for the training of society's leaders than the remonstrance of the Harvard Overseers against the establishment of a college in Hampshire County. Harvard College, their argument ran, was a provincial monopoly, funded and supported by the General Court for reasons of state. To preserve it and enable it to carry out its function meant to shield it against the competition of similar seminaries of learning, even to the extent of prohibiting any attempts at incorporating a new college. Harvard, the Overseers stated, was "properly the College of the Government," and for another college to be established "exactly, or nearly upon the same footing with that at Cambridge . . . would not only be quite unnecessary, but really prejudicial to Harvard College." It was quite immaterial, the Overseers contended, whether the new institution was called a college or a collegiate school, since there was "no real difference between [them]." Unlike the collegiate schools of England, which were nurseries for the university colleges, Queen's College was to be Harvard's rival, not an inferior preparatory school. Its establishment would make Harvard lose potential and existing friends and benefactors, and the "multiplying [of] colleges without having a single one well endowed" would have "pernicious consequences."

Furthermore, the Overseers hinted, the governor's proposed charter for Queen's College might arouse the displeasure of the crown. They also intimated that Queen's College might not be as open to youths of various denominations as had Harvard, where, they said, "the rights of conscience were duly preserved." Above all, however, they stressed repeatedly that at Queen's College "the means of education . . . will doubtless be far inferior" than they were at Harvard College, and that therefore it must be the primary aim of the governor, just as it was of the Overseers, to preserve Harvard's unrivaled position in the colony.[24]

The Overseers' remonstrance achieved its purpose. For another thirty years Harvard was to enjoy its monopoly in the Bay Colony. In March of 1762 Governor Bernard notified the Harvard board and also the two houses of the General Court that he would neither issue a charter nor assist any group in applying for a charter in Massachusetts or England. He advised the Overseers to send their memorial and an accompanying statement to London to counteract any further action on the part of the Hampshire petitioners.[25]

The friends of Queen's College, however, were unwilling to give up. They now turned to General Jeffery Amherst, commander-in-chief of the British forces in North America, and hero of Louisburg, Ticonderoga, and Montreal. Israel Williams submitted to him a petition for a royal charter for a collegiate school with the request that Amherst endorse it and transmit it to the crown. The petition played heavily on the royal sympathies for the plight of a frontier population "exposed to the invasions and depredations of our French and Indian enemies," and flattered the king with an account of his military successes in Canada. Unfortunately for Williams, the king never read the colorful document. General Amherst was unwilling to circumvent the governor and Council of Massachusetts, and only assured Williams of his support in London once the petition had been submitted there through the Massachusetts authorities. Williams and his friends then embarked on a letter-writing campaign to potential supporters in England.[26] But all of this was to no avail. The Queen's College project was dead, and no other college was erected in western Massachusetts until Williams College was chartered in 1793 and Amherst College in 1824. Harvard kept its lonely eminence until the century's last decade.

## The American University in the Province of New York

While the Stamp Act crisis and Anglican anxieties prevented the creation of new colleges in the years before the Revolution, that same unrest and uncertainty were responsible for an ambitious Anglican academic venture, an attempt to transform their provincial college in New York into the center of a university on the English model. King's College was to be the system's foundation stone. Through the university the Anglicans hoped to gain academic hegemony over the colonial colleges and to train a civil service loyal to the British crown. This

American university was to take its place as a dominant intellectual center over all the provincial colleges.

King's college had not fared well. During the 1750s and 1760s attendance had hovered consistently around the mid-twenty mark, except for an early peak in 1757 with thirty-three students. During those years the governors had repeatedly appealed to Anglican dignitaries in London for support, and President Samuel Johnson had complained over the lack of a good preparatory grammar school. For replacements of tutors and professors as well as the president, Johnson had corresponded with Archbishop Thomas Secker and had asked for candidates to be sent from either Oxford or Cambridge. In 1762 Myles Cooper of Queen's College, Oxford, arrived to begin his labors as professor of moral philosophy and administrative assistant to Johnson. By March 1 of the next year he took over the reins of the college. The promulgation of new college laws and the opening of a grammar school followed. But not until 1771, when more than forty students attended, did Cooper feel encouraged by the rising enrollment.[27]

The college carefully nurtured its close connections with the Church of England. Upon Cooper's urging, the new statutes introduced such Oxford customs as the wearing of gowns, and the governors ordered a fence built around the college and a porter stationed at the gate to keep the students under tighter discipline. Of great help to Cooper was the upturn in the college's financial fortunes. Collections in England, Scotland, and Ireland netted £6,366 sterling or £11,500 in New York currency. These funds and other gifts made King's College in the mid-sixties "the wealthiest of the American colleges" in endowment and provided the means to hire a medical faculty of six professors who began their work in 1767. Though the grammar school did not keep its promise of supplying large numbers of well-prepared students and caused anxiety in the late 1760s, the other indicators of college life pointed to prosperous times and good fortune.[28]

Under these circumstances Cooper entertained and vigorously promoted the university project. His intent was to make King's College the fountainhead of a resurgent Anglicanism in the colonies and the means for "diffusing principles of loyalty, affection of the parent kingdom, and of spreading the light of the Gospel among the native heathen."[29] As head of the college and leading Anglican clergyman he saw himself as the rejuvenator of plans for educational missions among the Indians and for a colonial episcopate. In September 1771, the governors authorized Cooper to travel to England and to request from the crown a charter that would make the college a university.[30]

Alas, in 1772 Cooper returned without a charter. He reported that the governors had "not furnished him with a copy," and he had not dared to have one drafted on his own authority "lest some part of it might not be agreeable to the present governors, whom in any article he should be extremely unhappy to offend."[31] The governors immediately ordered a committee to prepare a charter draft, but it took nearly two years for the document to be composed, approved, and forwarded to the crown officials. By then — August 1774 — political considerations weighed heavily. Lieutenant Governor Cadwallader Colden, pointing to the Presbyterian colleges in other colonies, urged that "a seminary on the principles of the Church of England be distinguished in America by particular privileges not only on account of religion but of good policy, to prevent the growth of Republican principles which already too much prevail in the colonies." Governor William Tryon likewise endorsed the project, writing that he could testify to "the attachment to his majesty's person and government, which has always distinguished the governors, professors, and members of King's College," and which "renders them truly deserving of the Royal attention and countenance." Certainly the prospects for obtaining the royal document looked good.[32]

The draft charter was a remarkably ambitious blueprint. It declared King's College to be "the mother of the American University in the Province of New York," in the same words that Trinity College, Dublin, had been incorporated as the cornerstone for a university in Ireland in 1592. The original college was expected to be joined by several others to constitute a university on the model of Oxford or Cambridge. King's College was to remain the leading college, its board of governors, suitably enlarged over the existing one, to serve at the same time as the university's Board of Regents. King's president was also to be the university's president and a communicant of the Anglican church. Cooper and his friends had also side-stepped the vexing problem of a provincial college monopoly. As members of a province-wide university, colleges presumably would not compete with one another, and the provincial Board of Regents could adjust conflicting claims and avoid or settle rivalries. Certainly the King's College trustees, being themselves university regents, had nothing to fear from the projected arrangement.

But with the draft charter Cooper and his backers sought more than academic hegemony in New York. Through strong ties with the mother country and the Anglican church they wanted to give the American university as much political influence as the English universities enjoyed. They thus gave the regents and officers of the university power to elect two representatives to the New York Assembly. In an obvious approximation of English custom, they also granted voting rights to the holders of advanced degrees who had kept their name on the roles of the university for an annual fee of five shillings. These voting graduates were, in effect, the equivalent of Oxford's nonregent masters. In addition, they expanded the King's College board by ex officio appointments of six overseas dignitaries of state and church and by the regents' election of a university chancellor. The university's board was to consist of the original King's College trustees and others yet to be elected. Altogether it would number fifty non ex officio members and the original and new ex officio appointments. With this preponderance of royal and Anglican officeholders and with the injunction that president and vice-president of each of the colleges be practicing Anglicans, the university was sure to fit the English pattern of an establishment institution. The charter also acknowledged the policy of toleration by prohibiting discrimination in all academic matters against persons of any religious denomination. In every conceivable way it provided for the Anglicanization of the American university, while it made sure that King's College would remain the center of this English university system in New York.[33]

The drafters sought to combine wide and powerful support for the university with effective leadership and administration. To do this they differentiated the university regents from a smaller subdivision in the university — the Academic Senate — and from subordinate senates in the colleges. Expecting the regents to have access to or to participate in the secular and ecclesiastical establishment of province and empire, the drafters viewed them as a political body par excellence. To insure their efficiency, however, they permitted them to meet annually with a quorum of fifteen and to elect from among themselves an Academic Senate of twelve, all of whom had to be residents of New York City and had to include the university's vice-chancellor and president. Of these twelve men, seven constituted a quorum, and by a majority vote of four could thus carry out the business of a fifty-man board responsible for the university's internal affairs.

In the colleges the minor senates were to have delegated power over student affairs. They were to consist of president, fellows, professors, and tutors. On the college level, then, there was to be the appearance of faculty government on a restricted basis, corresponding to the "immediate government" at Harvard and other American colleges. For the university, however, even this immediate government remained in the hands of external governors. The charter was patterned on diverse systems from European and American academic traditions. The demands of imperial relations and internal administration were both well provided for.[34]

Despite the endorsements the charter had garnered from crown officials, the times were not propitious for its passage. Though the news reached New York in the winter of 1774-1775 that the crown was willing to appoint a regius professor of divinity, the closing of the port of Boston and, in April of 1775, the armed clash at Lexington rudely spoiled the plans of the academic imperialists. In May, Myles Cooper, Tory sympathizer that he was, had to flee for his life to escape tarring and feathering and other indignities. He left New York on board a British warship. The college continued to operate until April 1776 in its accustomed quarters. Thereafter the building was requisitioned as a hospital, and classes were held for another year in a private home. In 1774 King's had celebrated its last public commencement, and the last bachelor's degrees were given privately to six graduates in 1776. All class activity seems to have ceased in 1777.[35] Not until 1784 were actions taken to bring the institution back to life, and not before 1788 could the college again confer degrees. By then there was no longer any thought of King's College becoming the mother of an English university in the New World; the American university would appear only with the new American nation.

# III

# From the Revolution
# to the Dartmouth College Case

BY THE 1760s the American provincial college had become the characteristic educational institution in the colonies. Except in New Jersey where the Dutch Reformed had obtained a charter for Queen's College as a rival to the College of New Jersey in Princeton, each provincial college claimed a monopoly on higher education in its colony. In their practice of college government, Americans had adapted to their own circumstances the British policy of toleration with preferment. In each colony they placed the college in the hands of clergymen and laymen of the dominant denomination. Thus Anglicans and Presbyterians shared in the government of the College of Philadelphia; in all other colonies one denomination was in control. In Virginia and New York Anglicans played that role, in Massachusetts, Connecticut, New Jersey, and New Hampshire the Presbyterians, and in Rhode Island the Baptists. In educating a colony's future leaders these churchmen acted as stewards for all other Christian groups, and in Rhode Island they embraced Jewish students as well.[1] Toleration and preferment together had achieved a modus vivendi for the citizens of a new country marked by religious and ethnic pluralism and for the representatives of particular churches and denominations eager to take responsibility for higher education. Under this policy the American provincial college had come into its own.

Half a century later, at the beginning of the 1820s, the American college scene had changed dramatically. Whereas in 1770 there had been nine colleges, eight of which were provincial schools, this number had grown to over forty. In terms of ownership and government, they were of a bewildering variety. The concept of a provincial or state monopoly held by a college or university was no longer viable. Though before the Revolution attempts to open up rival colleges succeeded only in New Jersey and failed in Massachusetts and Rhode Island, after the war, one or more new colleges appeared in Maryland, Virginia, Pennsylvania, Kentucky, Massachusetts, Tennessee, and New York. Some of these institutions preserved the toleration with preferment concept as state colleges or universities, while others took up their responsibilities as public institutions without any ties to organized religion. Still others viewed themselves as private, rather than public, institutions, sometimes expecting to enjoy the benefits of preferment, and sometimes not. It became increasingly difficult to define the rights and responsibilities of these schools in relation to the public, and it remained unclear whether public and private institutions enjoyed the same legal standing and whether they were accountable to the people.

Although the decades after the war witnessed far-reaching changes in the history of American higher education, the direct effects of war were minor. All nine colonial colleges survived. In marked contrast to what had happened so frequently in continental Europe, the Revolution did not permanently abolish a single college or university, nor did it subordinate these institutions to the direct authority of the states as administrative departments or agencies. American colleges exhibited a remarkable resilience, though many saw their students and faculties dispersed and their buildings destroyed, and all had to adjust to the changes in territorial sovereignty.[2]

The Revolution also heralded the introduction of professional studies and the creation of state-wide systems of university education. Medical instruction had begun by the 1760s in Philadelphia and New York. In the next two decades professorial chairs in many new fields and faculties of law and medicine were added in several states. In New York, Georgia, Kentucky, and Vermont ambitious proposals were advanced for state systems of Latin preparatory, collegiate, and professional education under public direction and control. During the early years of the Revolution, there was a growing demand for facilities for higher education at the most advanced level. Though the numerical impact of these innovations was limited and insignificant in relation to population growth, and though many of these projects never moved beyond the planning stage, their existence testified to an initial determination among the revolutionary generation to expand and improve the institutions of higher education.

In several colonies the Revolution challenged charter rights disputed the colleges' claims to immortality and invulnerability under the law, but an English tradition of the common law sanctity of corporate institutions survived the revolutionary turmoil. There were disputes between governing boards and revolutionary legislatures, to be sure, but in the end the colleges survived with their charters intact. Where changes had been made, it was with the consent of the college governing boards. Significant for the legal history of American higher education, however, was the fact that the conflicts over charter rights and state power were fought in the legislative bodies of the states, and not in the courts of law. Having commenced their careers as provincial institutions, most colleges functioned as public bodies under the supervision of their respective assemblies and turned to them not only for financial support but also for the settlement of their jurisdictional and legal disputes.

In the years following the war the dependence of the public colleges on their legislatures was to make them exceedingly vulnerable to the extravagances of partisan politics. The Smith-Livingston debate in New York and the attempts to seize the colleges in New York and Philadelphia during the Revolution highlighted the perils awaiting the colleges in the midst of political warfare. Given the strong ties to the parties in power that the colleges enjoyed as provincial institutions and training grounds for political and professional leaders, it is not surprising that they were denounced as bastions of aristocratic privilege and Federalist power. In many states, both North and South, the champions of town schools and county academies appropriated revolutionary rhetoric to denounce the colleges and their defenders and demand that the state's resources be used for educational institutions below the collegiate level. They discomforted such college advocates as Thomas Jefferson, Ezra Stiles, and Benjamin Rush, who, to many "republican" partisans, appeared to favor privileges for an elite. Spokesmen for the common people were simply not impressed with the demands for professional training and certification in law and medicine that accompanied the pleas for college reform. They perceived certification as an infringement rather than a protection of their rights.

The sudden appearance of private colleges in the 1780s was a direct reaction to the plight of the old provincial and new state schools. In the frontier areas of the South and West, from South Carolina through Tennessee, Kentucky, and Virginia to western Pennsylvania, Presbyterian clergymen founded, governed, and taught in preparatory schools and academies. These schools were close to the people. They functioned as centers for local and regional development while they supplied to a select number of rural boys the rudiments of a Latin preparatory education. Once these academies were incorporated as degree-granting colleges, their trustees gained independence from supervision by presbytery or synod. Though most of the governing boards could be expected to remain sympathetic to Presbyterian interests, they were nonetheless autonomous legal bodies, independent of state and church control, except for the general supervisory authority of an elected legislature over all corporations. There were no ex officio state officers on the board of Presbyterian colleges, nor did the charters require ex officio membership of Presbyterian clergymen. Where, as in Pennsylvania, the charters asked for the replacement of the original Presbyterian ministers by other ministers, they referred to Christian clergymen without specifying a particular denomination. In these colleges, then, ministers took prominent places without claiming to act as public officials.

In other parts of the country, clergymen of other denominations played the same role. In Maryland, Catholics and Methodists founded academies and colleges; in Massachusetts, New York, Pennsylvania, and Ohio, Congregationalists did so; and in Maine, Baptists did likewise. Private colleges were not founded exclusively by clergymen and sponsored by a church or denomination. Civic and professional associations, sometimes in league with denominational groups and sometimes not, engaged in the same endeavors. Impatient with the slowness of legislative negotiations, distrustful of politicians in far-off eastern or southern capitals, fearful of being exposed to the retributions of political and ideological warfare, the people on the frontier created their own institutions of preparatory and collegiate education. The result was a phenomenal growth of private foundations and, as a consequence, further questions on the legal status of college corporations. Did public and private colleges have the same standing in law? Did the public colleges, as civil corporations, enjoy greater legal protection than the private foundations, or were they more vulnerable to legislative interference?

The end of legal uncertainty came when Chief Justice John Marshall delivered the Dartmouth College decision of 1819.[3] Though Marshall did not prescribe the rights and privileges a legislature should write into a college charter, he did shore up the legal foundations of all colleges by placing their charters under the protection of the constitution's contract clause. For the private colleges this meant that, based on contract and property law, their standing was equal to that of any business corporation. Marshall's decision could not protect the public colleges from governmental neglect or the private colleges against partisan attacks, but it assured them both that the courts would guarantee their charter rights and privileges. Since businesses and churches had begun to compete with government in sponsoring colleges and universities, this was no small matter. It ensured that higher education, partaking aggressively in the development of the country, would draw on the strengths and suffer the liabilities of laissez-faire capitalism.

# 11

## WAR AND REVOLUTION

Gowns give way to arms — this Roman saying applied to the colleges in war. All the colleges except Dartmouth were forced by armed confrontations to cease their normal operations for a time, and all lost lives and treasure. Interruptions included student boycotts of tea, the wearing of homespun clothes and the use of homemade paper for diplomas, the formation of college military companies, the occupation and destruction of college buildings, the suspension of classes and commencements, and the outbreak of actual warfare on the campuses. In Connecticut an Assembly committee urged the removal of the students from New Haven because of the "peculiar advantages the enemy may derive from the capture and detention of such a number of young gentlemen from the principal families in the state." They thought the colony's future leadership too valuable a prize to allow it to be plucked by the British.[1] Although the immediate threats of physical damage and forced closure were real and acutely felt, the more far-reaching effects of the war on the college constitutions were to come later.

### Old Struggles, New Conditions

Fundamental changes in American college government had already begun to appear before the outbreak of the war and initiated a reorganization of American higher education in the 1780s. In New York and Philadelphia the Anglican party in college government was quickly drawn into the revolutionary tumult. In the City of Brotherly Love religious rivalries simmered beneath the apparent calm and accompanied the open political debates and struggles between the proprietary party and their opponents. Richard Peters, the chairman of the trustees and an Anglican clergyman, professed to be uneasy over what he saw as the disproportionately weak representation of Anglicans among the faculty. He complained to the Archbishop of Canterbury in 1763 that of five professors, four tutors, and two writing masters the Anglicans furnished only one each, "and this," he added, "from downright necessity, no churchman offering when there was a vacancy." The archbishop, however, let it be known that he preferred a policy of cooperation that would hold suspicions and jealousies to a minimum.[2] The college vice-provost, the Old-Side Presbyterian Francis Alison, believed conversely that the college had been "artfully got into the hands of episcopal trustees" and its graduates had got "a taste for high life." Thus these young men were regarded with suspicion by the New Light Presbyterians, had difficulties finding preaching positions, "and under that discouragement . . . are flattered and enticed by their episcopal acquaintances to leave such bigots and go to London for orders."[3] Such developments only increased the unpopularity of the college among the revolutionaries who castigated it for its Anglican connections.

In Virginia the Revolution was bound to put the Visitors fully in command of the college's Anglican masters. With the elevation in 1772 of John Camm to the college presidency, the church commissaryship, and membership on the Governor's Council, it looked as though this champion of faculty and clergy rights had gained the advantage. But the growing rift between the colonies and the mother country discouraged any action on the part of the professors. A strange and uneasy silence came to characterize their relations with the Visitors. On one occasion they censored an usher and several students for their participation in patriotic military exercises, only to have the Visitors come quickly to the aid of the students. Under these circumstances both parties sought to avoid political quarrels.

Once the colonists declared their independence, the professors' position became precarious indeed. Camm did not help matters when with his customary persistence he protested the removal of all references to the crown from the surveyors' commissions issued by the college.[4] To nobody's surprise the Visitors finally acted in 1777 and dismissed Camm and his colleagues Jones and Dixon. Now only James Madison was left as the new president and John Bracken as master of the Grammar School. Two years later, upon the urging of their newly elected colleague Thomas Jefferson, the Visitors wrote the concluding chapter to the institution's history as an English college corporation in the New World. They revamped the curriculum and gave themselves a decisive and direct role in college government.[5] Thus Anglican dominance had come to an end in New York, Philadelphia, and Williamsburg.

At Harvard the Overseers asserted their authority in disputes concerning the college's constitutional government. These occasions began in 1727 when Timothy Cutler, ex-president of Yale College and then rector of Boston's Anglican Christ Church, and Samuel Myles, Anglican minister of King's Chapel, sought membership on the board.[6] With their petition Cutler and Myles attacked the traditional toleration with preferment principle of college governance. They argued, in fact, that toleration not only applied to students but to members of the governing boards as well. Yet the Overseers, with the backing of both houses of the General Court, rejected the request and insisted that under the preferment principle the college had been placed under the joint supervision of magistrates and ministers.

Another vexing problem concerned the relationship between the two boards of the Harvard College government. The issue arose first over the repeated drunkenness of Isaac Greenwood, the Hollis Professor of Mathematics and Natural Philosophy. The Corporation had taken the initiative and had recommended Greenwood's dismissal; the Overseers temporized and only agreed to the recommendation more than half a year later.[7] A similar situation then occurred a few years later in the case of Nathan Prince, who had served as resident tutor since 1723. When in 1728 tutor Sever resigned his seat on the Corporation, Prince, as the senior tutor, had been expected to be elected in Sever's place. But there had been talk in Cambridge of filling seats on the Corporation with non-residents rather than with tutors or professors, and on June 24, 1728, an advertisement appeared in the *New England Weekly Journal* protesting such rumors. The statement — according to President Quincy "probably the work of Prince himself" — achieved its desired effect, and Prince was elected.

As time went on Prince's behavior came to resemble Greenwood's. Prince, too, took to the bottle, and in October 1741 the Overseers felt constrained to ask the president and tutors for a written report on Prince's bahavior. In November they called Prince three times to appear before them and reply to the charges. Prince refused, but later submitted a written defense. In a series of meetings lasting until April the Overseers rejected several of Prince's appeals, and then dismissed him from his offices as college tutor and Corporation fellow.[8]

The dismissal of Prince by the Overseers did not turn into a constitutional cause celebre mainly because the Corporation was only too happy to leave the disciplining of one of its members to others. Had they exercised their jurisdiction, they would have acted as an aggrieved party and as judge at the same time. They thus did not object when the president and tutors complained to the Overseers rather than to them.

Prince rightly insisted that the initiative for disciplinary proceedings against tutors should be taken by the Corporation and not the Overseers, who held appellate rather than original jurisdiction. He protested repeatedly to the Overseers and appealed to the General Court as college Visitor.[9] But all was in vain. His actions produced no further investigations or reconsiderations. His case remained closed and the Overseers' decision unchallenged.

More threatening to the Corporation and to the faculty was the Overseers' politically motivated enforcement of censorship. In April of 1776 they required that members of the Corporation and the faculty declare their political principles. The officers and instructors complied, and the Overseers accepted their report. Two years later a similar inquiry brought on a clash between the two governing boards. The Corporation had elected William Kneeland as college steward. Unfortunately for Kneeland, the Overseers thought he opposed independence for the colonies. "Reserving to themselves the right they have by the charter of approving or negativing the election of a steward made by the corporation," they therefore recommended that the fellows elect someone else. The Corporation, however, disputed the charter claim, and the Overseers, debating the matter once more, conceded the point to the fellows. The Corporation then proceeded once more to elect a steward without submitting their choice to the Overseers.[10]

Paralleling the situation at Harvard, constitutional issues within Yale College were less disruptive in the 1770s than they would become in the 1780s and 1790s, but they were of greater and more lasting significance for the history of the institution than the disturbances caused directly by the war. Beginning in the 1760s students, their parents, and members of the Assembly viewed Yale as a public institution created to serve the entire commonwealth with scrupulous regard for the rights of all its members. They clashed with President Clap and the fellows, who saw the college as a religious seminary with parental authority over the students. This conflict had come to a head, but was by no means resolved, when President Clap resigned in 1766 and, in return for the resumption of legislative grants, the Assembly obliged the college to submit its accounts for an annual inspection.

When Naphtali Daggett took over from Clap, Yale had again become more responsive to the needs of the commonwealth.[11] But within the college the fellows of the Corporation regarded with suspicion the efforts of the tutors and Daggett to infuse the curriculum with new life, and they decided to get rid of the innovators. Finding himself in a cross-fire from students and fellows — the students petitioned for his removal in 1776 — and beset by food shortages and suspension of Assembly grants, Daggett gave up the presidential office in 1777. He continued, however, to serve as professor of divinity. The tutors were next. Timothy Dwight resigned in 1777, and Joseph Buckminster and John Lewis followed in short order. The cause of their departure was the Corporation's apparent displeasure with literary studies. Although they had allowed Dwight in 1776 to teach history, rhetoric, and belles-lettres, their reported remark that Daggett and the tutors had turned the college into Drury Lane and "left the more solid parts of learning and run into plays and dramatic exhibitions chiefly of the comic kind" had made clear their true feelings. At a time of grave military and economic crisis the Corporation became a conservative, clerical society unresponsive to students, faculty, and the people of the colony.[12]

The first rumbles of the conflict had been heard as early as 1771 when in response to the appointment of Nehemiah Strong as professor of mathematics and natural philosophy a complaint appeared in *The Connecticut Courant* on April 16 over the signature of "Timothy Bickerstaff." Bickerstaff felt that "although the knowledge of mathematics and natural philosophy tends as much as any of the arts and sciences to dissipate superstitions, chimeras, and old women's fables," the college was neglecting medicine, a field that in Philadelphia and New York had received its proper recognition. Bickerstaff was soon seconded by "Parentes" and "Misericordia" as well as "X," who revived old complaints of arbitrary corporation government, accused the steward of enriching himself at the expense of the students, and charged the college with unfitting rather than fitting youths for business.[13]

The confrontation began in earnest during the summer of 1777. A committee of the Corporation suggested to a committee of the Assembly that they consider doing "something . . . to put the education of youth in that seminary upon a more extensive plan of usefulness consistent with the original design of the institution." In their answer the Assembly members paid lipservice to the fellows' reservations and expressed their belief that improvements could be made "without departing from or relinquishing the original design of the institution." Their concrete proposals, however, cleverly turned the Corporation's reservations against the Corporation itself by agreeing not to interfere with "the education of youth to supply the churches with able orthodox ministers." The Corporation should remain in full possession of its powers to elect the professor of divinity, to supervise his work and his department, and to administer religious tests to college officers.

But they also proposed that the Assembly appoint a second governing board, somewhat akin to Harvard's Board of Overseers, with veto powers over the Corporation's election of president and tutors. This they justified with the remark that the duty of president and tutors "extends to every branch of literature as well as the science of divinity." They further suggested that the new board together with the Corporation elect all professors, except the divinity professor, set their salaries, and direct their teaching assignments. No professor thus elected could be dismissed from his office without the consent of the new board. This new board also was to be involved in student appeals in cases of degradation, suspension, rustication, expulsion, and corporal punishment, and in the financial management of the college. Finally, the Assembly committee proposed that the state endow and establish professorships of law and medicine "as soon as conveniently may be and other necessary professorships from time to time."[14]

Here was a detailed proposal for placing Yale under the supervision of a state-appointed board. The Assembly would assume financial responsibility for college expenses that exceeded the Corporation's revenues, and—most extraordinary of all—would take a direct hand in setting the curriculum and appointing, endowing, and regulating the professors. For all intents and purposes this plan proposed a Connecticut equivalent to the regius professorships at Oxford and Cambridge. It was an ingenious scheme to take over the college by surrounding its traditional members with state appointees.

The Corporation's response to these proposals was predictable. They thankfully acknowledged the Assembly's offer of financial support and professed their readiness to comply "with whatever measures tending to the real benefit of the college" as long as these did "not imply an abdication and resignation of the trust reposed in us as successors of the original partners and undertakers." They expressed their willingness to let an Assembly-appointed board take over the financial management of the professorships, except divinity, and to share with the Corporation the powers of election, dismissal, and supervision of the instruction of Assembly-supported professors. But they insisted that all professors, including those introduced by the Assembly, were to govern and instruct the students under rules established by the Corporation, and were to be subject to religious tests set and administered by the Corporation as well as to abide by "that soundness of faith which it is the especial duty of the corporation to propagate." They reserved for themselves the right to establish professorships under their sole control, and they refused to merge their revenues with contributions from the Assembly. They expressed grave reservations but nonetheless agreed to subject the election of the president to an Assembly veto, because "the head of college should be acceptable not only to themselves and the ministry, but to the General Assembly and State." That reason, they added, obviously did not apply to the tutors.[15]

To these counterproposals the Assembly made no response. They remained unsympathetic to the clerical and conservative character of the Corporation, whose members also were responsible for the departure of the fourth tutor, Abraham Baldwin, in 1779, and for the ouster of Nehemiah Strong, their professor of mathematics and natural philosophy, in 1781. When the Corporation then offered Daggett's former professorship of divinity to Abraham Baldwin they received his polite refusal. At the same time the Assembly, despite their dissatisfaction with the Corporation, were unwilling to provoke a serious conflict over the college charter. There is some indication from the diary of Ezra Stiles that they were mollified somewhat by the Corporation's offer of the presidency to Stiles, a Yale graduate and Congregational minister in Newport, known for his conciliatory endeavours in mediating sectarian strife.[16] Stiles accepted the presidency in March of 1778, and was inaugurated the following summer. With a new president in office, the British raid on New Haven taking place a year later, and in 1781 the century's largest freshman class arriving at Yale, no more was heard of a Corporation—Assembly dialogue. The issues raised in their 1777-1778 conferences remained below the surface until resurrected in 1792.

## Student Unrest and the Curriculum

The growing clamor for colonial independence and self-determination found echoes within collegiate halls. At Yale, dissatisfied students began a sustained effort to create for themselves an extracurriculum. They had nurtured an interest in literary societies ever since the 1750s. Linonia had been founded in that decade, and was opened to freshmen in 1767. In the next year the Brothers in Unity was created as a rival. The tutors encouraged their students to try their hands at poetry and dramatic performances, and in the fall of 1767 asked the junior class to recite English grammar. President Daggett encouraged these endeavors, as he strongly believed in the value of literary training for future ministers and public servants. The tutors, however, placed a different value on literature. For them the study of English language and literature took on intensely nationalistic and patriotic overtones and contributed to the growing revolutionary fervor among their students. Noah Webster's later efforts to create an American language had their inception during his student days at Yale, and the literary work of Yale tutors Timothy Dwight and John Trumbull–both appointed by Daggett in 1771–has become associated with the fame of the Connecticut Wits.[17]

Yale was not alone in experiencing curricular changes, student unrest, and the founding of student societies. At Harvard the Overseers in May 1766 endorsed recommendations to give up the familiar system of assigning each class to a tutor for instruction. Instead they asked one tutor to take over instruction in Latin for all classes, another in Greek, a third in logic, metaphysics, and ethics, and a fourth in natural philosophy, mathematics, geography, and astronomy. All four tutors, however, were to remain responsible for instruction in belles-lettres, including elocution, English composition, and rhetoric. As before, the professor of divinity and the professor of mathematics and natural philosophy would lecture in their fields.[18]

In 1766, too, the first great student rebellion occurred over rancid butter at commons. "Behold, our butter stinketh," was the battlecry, and the subsequent commotion in the yard resulted in demands by the Corporation and Overseers for a humble confession. It was answered, in turn, by the students' complaints of unconstitutional oppression. In the end the students were obliged to admit to irregular and unconstitutional proceedings on their part, and the matter subsided. But not for long. In 1768 the students passed resolutions against one of their tutors, and in the next year during their protests against faculty rules the sheriff of Middlesex County was called in. Other signs of change were in evidence as well. As at Yale, "placing" students by their social standing was abolished, and students were now listed in alphabetical order.

Soon thereafter, on September 11, 1770, the first literary society was born. The Speaking Club was followed quickly by the Mercurian and, in 1774, by the Clintonian. Similar groups had come into being at William and Mary, the College of New Jersey, the College of Rhode Island, and Queen's College.[19] The organization of these societies was the students' declaration of independence from the curriculum of tutors and professors and, to some extent also, from the supervision of their governors. College life had entered a new phase.

In Philadelphia the Trustees were confronted with demands by parents for stricter disciplinary supervision. In response the trustees opened a lodging house in 1765 to provide "a collegiate way of life" for their students. But not all students could be accommodated, and complaints continued that the faculty allowed truancy to persist unchecked. In 1773 the college then instituted a policy of certifying private boarding houses for use by students.[20]

In Princeton the students' literary and political interests received the enthusiastic support of President John Witherspoon. The American Whig and the Cliosophic societies had been founded in 1765, three years before Witherspoon's arrival from Scotland. Their debates and orations were just as effective in turning the college into "a school for statesmen" as were the lessons in classics, philosophy, and science presided over by Witherspoon.[21] In nearby Brunswick instruction at Queen's College was in the hands of two Princeton graduates, the tutors Frederick Frelinghuysen and John Taylor. Both men had been deeply influenced by John Witherspoon's learned patriotism, and in 1773 they organized a literary society, the Athenian. They saw to it that their charges imbibed their learning and their patriotism in the classroom as well as in the society.[22]

The demand for institutional and curricular innovation voiced within the colleges by students found expression outside also. Professional education, begun in medicine in New York and Philadelphia in existing colleges during the 1760s, appeared in independent institutions for the training of ministers and lawyers and in plans for a national scientific institution and university. In New York the synod of the Dutch Reformed churches on October 5, 1784, commissioned John H. Livingston, pastor of the city's Dutch Reformed church, to act as the synodical professor of sacred theology. They encouraged him to train candidates for the ministry in his study at his church, and gave him an assistant to teach the biblical languages. When Livingston delivered his inaugural lecture in May of 1785 the Theological Seminary of the Dutch Reformed Church was born. Only when Livingston was elected to the presidency of Queen's College in 1810 was the seminary joined with an institution of higher education. Until then apprehension that the seminary might make the college suspect in the eyes of those who distrusted clergymen as college teachers or opposed Professor Livingston on theological grounds kept college and seminary separate.[23]

In Connecticut a proprietary law school evolved in 1784 out of Tapping Reeve's apprenticeship arrangements with his clerks. When in 1798 Reeve was appointed to the Connecticut Superior Court, James Gould joined him as a second instructor. Throughout the last fifteen years of the eighteenth century the Litchfield school remained the only training ground for young lawyers, offering lectures and moot courts.[24] In the second decade of the nineteenth century, divinity chairs at the colleges were replaced with college-related seminaries at the College of New Jersey and at Harvard. While there had been law professorships before 1800 in Virginia, Pennsylvania, and New York, after the turn of the century they would also appear in the colleges of New England. In the 1780s, however, the synodical theological seminary and the proprietary law school stepped in where the colleges had failed to tread.

Perhaps the most unusual initiatives for the establishment of post-collegiate education proposed during the 1780s were the projects for a national scientific academy and a federal university. The academy was the brainchild of a French officer serving in Virginia in 1777-1778. Chevalier Quesnay de Beaurepaire envisioned an Academy of Sciences and the Fine Arts in Richmond, Virginia, with branches in Baltimore, Philadelphia, and New York. With the national academies in London, Paris, and Brussels it was to engage in an international exchange of scientific and scholarly information and research. In Richmond and its American branches it was to offer advanced scientific instruction to graduates of American colleges and other interested persons. These plans were ambitious, and due to insufficient financial backing they remained, as Jefferson had warned, "but a project in the air." When the revolution engulfed France and de Beaurepaire returned to his native country in 1789 the project collapsed.[25]

The idea of a federal university seems to have been first suggested in 1775 around the fires of Washington's army camped on the Harvard college grounds. A decade later Benjamin Rush became a persistent advocate of such an institution. He saw it as the best way of providing the finishing touch of republican education to young Americans destined to lead the new nation. As he said in his famous remark of 1786, he considered it possible "to convert men into republican machines." Only the graduates of a federal university, he believed, should be eligible for national honors and offices.[26]

The idea of a federal or national university for the new states found advocates as far away as Germany. At the University of Halle, Johann Reinhold Forster had prepared a plan that he hoped to get into the hands of Benjamin Franklin. The national university was to consist of thirteen residential colleges, one for each of the states. It was to be located in Pennsylvania and to be directed by a chancellor appointed by Congress. Forster's plan, however, never seems to have reached Franklin and was not discussed in the United States.[27] Benjamin Rush's scheme, though, was taken up by the constitutional convention in 1787. Those who thought a federal university unnecessary because its establishment was already included in the power of the Congress over the seat of government, were joined by those who objected to it because of their fear of federal power. Jointly they defeated the proposal.[28] Public institutions for the postgraduate education of young Americans were thus excluded from the realm of Congress and confined to the initiative of the states. There they would be created through the establishment of professorships in the professions at the states' colleges and universities and in the opening of professional schools.

# 12

## THE BIRTH OF THE
## AMERICAN UNIVERSITY

Revolution and independence created the American university and brought to a close the era of the colonial college.[1] The colleges had usually asked that upon entrance their students be acquainted with the Latin language, even if only to a modest degree. Where they could not take for granted such familiarity, they had organized their own preparatory departments or grammar schools. In their collegiate curriculum, then, they had adapted the medieval trivium of grammar, rhetoric, and logic as well as the quadrivium of arithmetic, geometry, astronomy, and music. In addition they introduced their students to natural philosophy or physics, mental philosophy or metaphysics, and moral philosophy or ethics. In some cases, as at the College of William and Mary, critics had charged that the entire college resembled an English grammar school or dissenting academy, albeit with the right of granting baccalaureate and master's degrees, both earned and honorary. Other colleges could more justifiably be described as *gymnasia academica* or incomplete universities, consisting of an arts faculty but lacking the higher faculties of theology, medicine, and law. When, however, in the 1760s the colleges in Philadelphia and New York added medical faculties to their instruction in the arts, a new stage had been reached. The appearance of professional studies signaled the transformation of American colleges into universities.

Not all new universities, however, evolved from colonial colleges through the addition of one or more professional chairs or faculties. In New York, Georgia, and, for a few years toward the end of the century, in Kentucky, the term university meant a state-wide administrative system of Latin preparatory and collegiate education. These first state systems of education did not include elementary or vernacular schools, but comprised the institutions of secondary and higher education. The first model of this type had been proposed in 1775 as The American University in the province of New York. The outbreak of hostilities aborted the project, but parts of it were revived in 1784 and 1787 with the creation of the regents of the University of New York.

## Professorships in the Professional Fields

In the American colonies university studies had first made their appearance through the establishment of professional chairs in divinity. Harvard had created such a chair as early as 1721; the College of William and Mary had been assigned two of these professorships in its statutes of 1728; the Yale trustees had appointed their first divinity professor in 1756; and the College of New Jersey had elected its first in 1767. These professorships represented little more than a potential nucleus for the creation of a professional faculty. Their incumbents taught students in the college and served as college chaplains or ministers. The case was different, however, with the first professorships of medicine in Philadelphia and New York. Pressure from professionals and citizens for medical education in a college-related public medical school offered the colleges an opportunity for growth in self-respect, financial base, and service opportunities to the local and national community. Trustees and professors could now establish their institutions as universities in the traditional meaning of the term. The colleges that chose to grasp such opportunities laid the foundation for their subsequent expansion as American universities. The colonies — and later the states — that encouraged their provincial colleges in this undertaking thereby encouraged the development of professional education as a university responsibility.

In Philadelphia and New York medical instruction was first proposed by foreign-trained physicians concerned over low standards and lack of proper training.[2] The young doctors who had studied in Scotland and England and on the European continent had to compete with men who frequently practiced medicine as a side-line and whose education, such as it was, derived only from observations made as apprentices. Motivated thus by self-interest as much as by concern for others, these young doctors looked for ways of providing standardized, regulated, and universally acceptable medical training. In 1765 John Morgan proposed in Philadelphia "a scheme for transplanting Medical Science . . .

and for the improvement of every branch of the healing art."[3] In New York a group of doctors suggested a plan in 1767 to rescue medicine "from the obscurity which still continues to veil it in this place, and [to] prevent for the future if possible the many scandalous and pernicious abuses in the practice."[4] In both cities the doctors succeeded in launching institutions for the proper training of medical practitioners.

In both cities, too, the medical schools sought and obtained the support of already existing institutions of higher education. In Philadelphia John Morgan insisted from the beginning that his own medical professorship or, later, the medical school be affiliated with the city's college. He had in mind the examples of Edinburgh and Leyden, and he desired for medicine all the advantages of public recognition as a learned profession through a connection with the city's college. Besides, Morgan insisted on the indispensability of the liberal arts for a well trained physician. "We can go but small lengths in natural or medical inquiries without their assistance. Happy are we to have all these taught in such perfection in this place."[5] The founding doctors in New York held similar views. They too looked to Edinburgh and Leyden and now Philadelphia and, with a bit of envy in their hearts, requested of the governors of King's College that even if their professorships were "not attended with the emoluments and advantages arising to them in other colleges, [they] shall at least have all that exterior dignity, and every honorary mark of respect, which is in your power to bestow."[6]

The doctors' connection with a college allowed them to proclaim their trade to be a public rather than a merely private concern. This redefinition permitted them to announce standards of admission and performance and publicly conferred honors for meritorious achievement. Requirements for admission and graduation in Philadelphia and New York were similar. Both institutions demanded a college degree for entrance or satisfactory competence in Latin, mathematics, and natural philosophy. Students had to matriculate and take courses with the professors in the various branches of medicine as well as engage in hospital or apprentice work. Within three years the student could obtain a bachelor of medicine after proper examinations, and after a three-year interval in Philadelphia and a one-year interval in New York he could obtain a doctorate of medicine.[7]

Much importance was assigned to the awarding of degrees. The New York petitioners viewed them as a means of gaining public recognition for the profession, and John Morgan saw them as a stimulus to raise the level of accomplishment and performance among the practitioners.[8] By 1776 the two medical schools had conferred a total of forty-nine medical degrees, thirty-five in Philadelphia and fourteen in New York. Though the war would cut off this encouraging development, and American medical education would revert, with a few notable exceptions, for another century to private proprietary schools and apprenticeship, the gains made in the 1760s and 1770s had prepared the ground on which the university movement would gather strength in the 1780s.[9]

While medical education had obtained a foothold in Philadelphia and New York, university plans were taking shape in the fall of 1777 in New Haven where Ezra Stiles was about to take over the presidency of Yale College. To legislative inquiries Stiles responded with a detailed university plan. Creating professorial chairs would strengthen the college rather than weaken its position by the establishment of rival schools or faculties, and would allow Stiles to stay within the financial limits of college and state. Since he could not add chairs in Hebrew and Oriental languages, ecclesiastical history, civil history, oratory and belles-lettres, law and medicine to the already existing professorships in divinity, mathematics, and natural history, he gave priority to the professorships in law and medicine for which there was popular demand. His views on medical education did not vary greatly from those held by the doctors in New York and Philadelphia. He suggested three series of lectures in anatomy, *materia medica*, the nature of diseases, *ars medendi*, and surgery. Upon completion of the course, students would receive a bachelor of physic. Then would follow an apprenticeship and a year of lectures on practical subjects. Further evidence of proficiency could be rewarded with the doctor of physic degree. The law professorship, Stiles thought, was to offer instruction in the civil and the common law, the codes of the new states, and in the forms and policies of governments.

Behind Stiles's proposal for a college enlarged by professional studies was a civic purpose. As Stiles saw it, an American university was to grow organically out of the college, not to be superimposed on it and allowed to destroy it. The college was to remain "soul and body" of the institution, and general studies in the liberal arts were to constitute the heart of its curriculum. Legal studies were not designed for "educating lawyers or barristers"—that, Stiles thought, could best be accomplished through apprenticeship—"but for forming *civilians*." The graduates of Yale College were to be given "the discipline and education . . . in that knowledge which may qualify them to become useful members of society as select men, justices of the peace, members of the legislature, judges of courts, and delegates in Congress." Therefore, he wrote, the appointment of a law professor, "will very much supersede the present necessity of a history professor." Legal instruction in government, he continued, "is itself *civil history* of the best kind. It is not a dull an unanimated narrative of events—it is tracing great events, great political phenomena to their operative and efficient causes—it is the *true spirit of history.*"[10]

In Virginia also college reforms and the introduction of legal and medical instruction were demanded in the late 1770s. The reformers stressed the competitive disadvantages of Virginians whose sons were lured to Europe, Philadelphia, or New York in search of medical training. They complained of quacks and imposters and asked for medical as well as legal certification and education. One of them wanted in addition to the existing professorships in the grammar, philosophy, and divinity schools appointments to chairs in astronomy, modern languages, history, botany, and chemistry.[11]

The masters of the College of William and Mary resisted these criticisms, however. They were fully convinced that the Oxford and Cambridge models for their classical and mathematical curriculum were superior to any other. The students in the grammar school provided an important part of their livelihood that they were loath to give up. Routine instruction and surveillance of the boys in grammar school and college did not pose inordinate problems or demand exacting duties of the professors.

Thus many of the critics concentrated their attacks on the presence of the grammar school and the masters' tolerance and humoring of the school boys. One writer wanted "young gentlemen" at the college; boys should be prepared for the college at a public grammar school "upon nearly the same plan as Eton or Westminster." Another seconded that view. Removal of the school boys would permit the college students to gain a "higher idea of the dignity of a student. They would look upon themselves as entering upon a nobler scene of action; a scene wherein puerility was to be exchanged for the manly and philosophical life."[12]

The long-standing dissatisfaction of the Visitors with the masters and their growing frustration over their inability to discipline the faculty then merged with the clamor of the reformers and the surging demands of the colonists for self-rule. In 1777 the Visitors dismissed the staunchly loyalist professors Camm, Dixon, and Jones for "neglect and misconduct."[13] On December 4, 1779, they placed the college under a new form of instruction and government. They abolished the grammar school because, as Jefferson wrote, it "filled the college with children" and rendered it "disagreeable and degrading to young gentlemen already prepared for entering on the sciences." For the two chairs in divinity and the chair in classical languages the Visitors substituted professorships in law and police, anatomy and medicine, and modern languages. To the professorship of moral philosophy they added the laws of nature and nations and the fine arts, and to the chair of mathematics instruction in natural philosophy.[14] The Visitors had taken advantage of the disappearance of crown and Privy Council as the masters' ultimate court of appeal, had realized their long-standing desire to rid the college of the professors of divinity, and had responded favorably to the often heard demands for instruction in law and medicine. With the 1779 statute they had begun the transformation of their college into a modern university.

The actuality of professional training at the college, however, was less than impressive. The professor of modern languages appears to have dealt mainly with private students, and the medical school disappeared from the college in 1783 with Professor McClurg's removal to Richmond. George Wythe, the first man to hold a professorship in law at an American college, combined his teaching career for eleven years with his duties as judge on the Virginia High Court of Chancery. In 1790 he resigned his chair at the college and opened a law school of his own in Richmond. Despite his eventual departure from Williamsburg, his teaching of law at the College of William and Mary must be considered as the school's most fruitful venture into professional education.[15]

In Connecticut and Virginia, as in Pennsylvania, Massachusetts, and New York, curricular reform in the wake of the Revolution meant the establishment of new professorships. By 1782 the reorganized University of the State of Pennsylvania had professorships in natural philosophy, mathematics, moral philosophy, the classics, Oriental and German languages, English and oratory, and history. Again the appearance of studies in belles-lettres and history indicate the turn away from the scholastic curriculum toward a growing interest in contemporary problems. By 1783 the medical school also was back in operation and after the interruption of the war years granted its first degrees in 1786.[16] At Harvard the Corporation decided in 1782 to found medical professorships and sponsor clinical instruction. In the next year Harvard's "Medical Institution" began its work with three professors in anatomy and surgery, theory and practice of medicine, and chemistry and *materia medica*. In 1788 the university granted its first medical degree.[17] In New York in 1784 the governors of Columbia College, the revived and renamed King's College, endorsed the establishment of seven chairs in a faculty of arts, eight in medicine, three in law, as many in divinity as would be furnished by sponsoring religious societies, as well as ten additional ones ranging from ancient and modern languages to history, architecture, commerce, agriculture, music, painting, and natural history. In the next few months ten gentlemen were appointed to fourteen of these chairs, but then funds gave out and other, more pressing issues were being held up to the regents.[18] Though in many cases the initiatives here recounted remained plans and projects, they indicate nonetheless the pervasiveness of the conviction that the new states had to go beyond the traditional collegiate training in the liberal arts, and that the establishment of professorial chairs was one of the most useful means toward that end.

### State Systems of Higher Education

In 1755 in a book published in Boston, William Douglass had proposed that the English colonists on the American mainland erect a comprehensive system of township schools for an English education, town grammar schools for the classics and divinity, a college or *schola illustris* of the arts and sciences for each province, and "near the center of the North-American continent colonies . . . an university or academy to be regulated by the board of plantations, to initiate young gentlemen in the learned professions of divinity, law, and medicine; in the modern, commercial and travelling languages of French, Spanish, and Dutch; in other curious sciences of mathematics, belles lettres, etc. and gentlemen exercises of riding the great horse, fencing and dancing."[19] Nothing came of this suggestion, but twenty years later President Myles Cooper's plan for an American University in the province of New York showed some similiarities. When after independence Thomas Jefferson prepared a three-stage system of elementary English education for all children, colleges for "all who were in easy circumstances," and "an ultimate grade for teaching the sciences generally, and in their highest degree," the idea of a state system of education gained another hearing. Jefferson's "Bill for the More General Diffusion of Knowledge" expressed its author's conviction that preparatory and collegiate education were a public responsibility the state owed its gifted boys regardless of their families' circumstances. Sectarian jealousies, however, and financial considerations prevented its adoption in the legislature in 1778 and 1780 and again in 1785 and 1786. In the eighteenth century Jefferson's vision of a comprehensive system of public education remained just that.[20]

It was in Maryland that the first steps were actually taken to erect a university on the English model as a confederation of colleges. William Smith, author of the 1753 *General Idea of the College of Mirania* and in 1779 the just-deposed provost of the College of Philadelphia, established himself on Maryland's eastern shore as the master and Visitor of the Kent County School, an incorporated Latin academy, and as rector of the Chester parish. He promoted the enlargement of the school into a college, and in November of 1782 obtained final incorporation by the Maryland Assembly for the Kent Visitors and others as The Visitors and Governors of Washington College.[21]

The college charter stated that the geographic division of the state in the eastern and western shores had prevented the establishment of a state university. Instead the legislature was persuaded to permit the inhabitants of each shore to found and endow a college. Later, it the situation warranted it, the two colleges could "be united under one supreme legislature and visitatorial jurisdiction, as distinct branches or members of the same state university." Smith's project resembled that of Myles Cooper, that other Anglican college president ejected from office by the revolutionaries. Like the 1775 American University in the province of New York, the state university of Maryland was planned as a confederation of colleges separated from each other by many miles of land and water.[22]

Washington College got off to a good start. At its first commencement in May 1783, five regular bachelors and one master as well as one honorary bachelor and one master *ad eundem* received their degrees. In November of the next year the Visitors petitioned the legislature for a permanent revenue and gained the government's backing for the principle of "public instruction for the education of youth under the care and patronage of the state." A house committee recommended public funds to pay the salary of professors and tutors, and both house and senate committed themselves to provide a permanent fund of £1250 annually. That accomplished, the house in December ordered a bill prepared for the founding of a college on the western shore to be combined with Washington College into the University of Maryland. Early in 1785 St. John's College was chartered, granted an annual and perpetual fund of £1,750 and joined with Washington College. The provisions of its charter were similar to those of Washington College.[23]

For the University of Maryland the charter prescribed government by chancellor, vice-chancellor, and convocation. The state's governor was to serve as chancellor, one of the two college principals as vice-chancellor, and at least seven Visitors and two faculty members of each college should compose the convocation. By the spring of 1785 Maryland's state system of higher education was thus designed and funded. St. John's College, however, was hampered by defaulting subscribers, and opened for classes only in 1789 after its funds had been merged with those of King William's School, a preparatory academy. The university did not fare well either. In the 1790s interest in it as a separate institution began to wane. The two colleges, instead of cooperating with each other, became rivals for the legislature's attention. Smith, who had returned in 1789 to Philadelphia, was no longer present to keep the university in the public eye, and the institution gradually faded away. In 1805 the legislature voided the act of its creation.[24]

The first state university to succeed as an administrative system of preparatory and collegiate education was established in New York. Acting in response to the request of the thirteen surviving King's College governors, the legislature created a state university system and resuscitated the remains of King's College as Columbia College, without submitting the new charter for the formal approval of the King's College governors. Perhaps they thought this unnecessary since no protest was heard from the thirteen petitioners, six of whom were directly involved in preparing or endorsing the charter. These six were Governor George Clinton, Chief Justice and presiding officer of the council of revision; Richard Morris, the chairman of the senate committee of the bill; James Duane, the State Treasurer; Gerard Bancker; the Attorney General Egbert Benson; and the Secretary of State, John Morin Scott. Besides, it could be argued that with only thirteen governors left in the city the legislature could reorganize the corporation, which, under its charter of 1754, required a quorum of fifteen governors to conduct its business.[25]

168

FROM THE REVOLUTION TO THE DARTMOUTH COLLEGE CASE

The act passed on May 1, 1784, transferred the rights and privileges of the governors of King's College to the regents of the University of the State of New York. That body was to consist of the governor, lieutenant governor, senate president, speaker of the assembly, attorney general, secretary of state, the mayors of New York City and Albany as ex officio members, two representatives each of twelve counties, and one clergyman. The state's governor was to have the right of appointing successors to the regents representing the counties. The regents were to make the laws and ordinances for any of the colleges and to have the right of dismissing college officers after a hearing. The colleges to be established were permitted to grant bachelor's degrees and were to be under the general supervision of the regents. Privately endowed colleges could, upon application of their founders or trustees, join the university and send a representative as well as their president to the Board of Regents.

The regents were to choose the president and professors of Columbia College, and to insure that no professor be discriminated against on religious grounds or be compelled to take a religious test oath. They reserved to themselves the power to grant degrees. Finally the charter declared all fellows, professors, and trustees to be regents of the university ex officio "and capable of voting in every case relative only to the respective colleges to which they shall belong, excepting in such cases wherein they shall respectively be personally concerned or interested."[26]

In its early years the Board of Regents did not function as administrators of a state system of preparatory and collegiate education, but as governors of Columbia College. In November of 1784 both houses of the legislature amended the charter and added thirty-three appointed regents, twenty of whom were to be from New York City and thus likely to favor the college.[27] To overcome this preferential treatment of Columbia College a legislative committee recommended in 1787 that each college of the university system have a corporation of its own, subject only to a "wise and salutary" supervision by the regents. The same should be granted to private academies. Furthermore, they added, the regents should take responsibility for the state's elementary schools.[28]

On April 13, 1787, the legislature repealed the acts of 1784, reorganized the regents of the University of the State of New York, and clearly separated them from the trustees of Columbia College. It reinstated the King's College charter of 1754, but changed the institution's name to Columbia and eliminated ex officio trustees as well as stipulations concerning the president's religion, test oaths, and chapel services. The number of the trustees was set at twenty-four and their quorum reduced from fifteen to thirteen. The university regents were to consist of twenty-four individuals of whom the governor and the lieutenant governor were always to serve ex officio. Vacancies on the board were to be filled by the legislature. The regents' chief task was "to visit and inspect all the colleges, academies, and schools" in the state and to incorporate newly founded colleges and academies under boards of trustees of their own. These boards were to be self-perpetuating, and the regents were to function as Visitors and general superintendents over them all. They also held the power to raise academies to the status of colleges and to grant the higher academic and professional degrees.[29] In contrast to the acts of 1784, the new legislation did not provide for any clerical representation. The regents were established as the state's secular supervisory agency for all matters concerning preparatory and collegiate education. Schools, academies, and colleges, however, could retain their corporate autonomy including denominational leadership or influence to whatever extent their founders and trustees stipulated.

The act of 1787 was New York's answer to the question of how denominational and social heterogeneity could be harmoniously combined with the new state's search for secular cohesion. Its inspiration was English, deriving from William Livingston's admiration of the radical British thinkers Thomas Gordon and John Trenchard, and from Myles Cooper's Oxford-based vision of the American University.[30] The specific arrangements of 1787 constituted a compromise between the friends of Columbia College and the champions of academies and schools in the state. They struck a balance between the university as a secular administrative system and the colleges as state-approved autonomous corporations for educational purposes. Balance and compromise rather than subordination and centralization characterized the New York solution.

In the development of Georgia's state university system several dissident graduates of Clap's Yale played a decisive role. They were Lyman Hall, Yale graduate of 1747 and governor of Georgia, Nathan Bronson, Yale graduate of 1761, physician and ex-governor of Georgia, and Abraham Baldwin. Baldwin, a lawyer, had finished his student career at Yale in 1772, served there as a tutor, and declined his election to the chair of divinity. In 1784 all three were placed on the Georgia state university Board of Trustees. They remained in touch with President Stiles in New Haven and, considering the struggle between the Yale Corporation and the Connecticut Assembly, went along with Baldwin's insistence that, in order to avoid similar troubles in Georgia, the university be placed under secular oversight. In marked similarity to Jefferson's 1779 plan, Baldwin's proposal was for a state system through which the legislature could "unite [society's] literary concerns and provide for them in common."[31] As in New York, the university was to encompass preparatory and collegiate education. A state Board of Visitors, consisting of the governor and his Council, the speaker of the house, and the chief justice, was to oversee its work and cooperate with the trustees. Together the two boards would make the laws and appoint the president of the university, keep themselves informed about the schools in the state, and be authorized to create new ones.

The Georgia legislature adopted Baldwin's scheme on January 27, 1785. It confirmed and enlarged the Board of Trustees of the college and established it together with the Visitors as the Senatus Academicus of the University of Georgia. The General Assembly reserved to itself the power of repeal of the senate's legislation; all officers of instruction and government were to be "of the Christian religion;" president, professors, students, tutors, officers, and servants were to be excused from military duties; the trustees were forbidden to discriminate against students on grounds of their religion; and the senate was to be responsible for the state's schools as Baldwin had specified. Baldwin served as the trustees' president from May 1785 until June 1801, but called them into session only twice within the first twelve years. During all this time the board concerned itself mainly with the academies, rather than the college. By 1794, reported Ezra Stiles, six academies had been opened, yet only three of them could be said to flourish. The senate did not meet until November of 1799, but in June 1801 a location was selected for the college, a president was elected, and Baldwin retired from the Board of Trustees. Within another year instruction began at the college.[32] The University of Georgia, consisting of a number of preparatory academies and Franklin College at Athens, was finally under way.

Among the proposals for a state system of education, the scheme projected by Benjamin Rush for the state of Pennsylvania must rank as the most farsighted and encompassing. Disaffected as he was with the influence of the revolutionaries' radical wing, Rush had proposed in 1782 the founding of a college to educate the state's future political leaders in conservative republican principles. When on September 9 of the following year the Pennsylvania legislature chartered Dickinson College, Rush prepared an essay that was published in 1786 as "Thoughts upon the Mode of Education proper in a Republic," and issued together with his "Plan for the Establishment of Public schools and the Diffusion of Knowledge in Pennsylvania."[33]

Rush's "Plan" resembled Jefferson's proposals of 1779 in Virginia. It envisaged free schools for all children in every township, county academies to prepare youth for college by teaching the learned languages, four colleges in different parts of the state for young men to be instructed in the liberal arts, and one university to present lectures in law, medicine, divinity, the law of nature and nations, and political economy. "By this plan [Rush predicted] the whole state will be tied together by one system of education. The university will in time furnish masters for the colleges, and the colleges will furnish masters for the academies and free schools, while the free schools, in their turn, will supply the academies, the colleges, and the university with scholars, students, and pupils."[34] Like Jefferson's plan, Rush's was never translated into reality. When the University of Pennsylvania appeared, it was the successor institution to the College of Philadelphia, not a state system of common schools or of preparatory and collegiate education.

The most unusual proposal for designing and administering a state system of higher education was submitted in northern New England by John Wheelock, the president of Dartmouth College. An out-of-state corporation, the trustees of Dartmouth College, would train and staff Vermont's system of preparatory and collegiate education and thereby prevent the creation of a Vermont state college. Wheelock's maneuvers grew out of rather complicated territorial disputes and boundary changes involving New York, Vermont, and New Hampshire.[35] Between 1778 and 1782 Dartmouth College was twice claimed by Vermont. When in 1779 the college found itself for a time in no-man's land and the Vermont legislature considered a request to charter a state university, the Dartmouth trustees tried unsuccessfully to obtain legislation favorable to their interests.[36] They pursued their endeavours during the next few years when the college belonged again to Vermont and, after February 1782, to New Hampshire. In 1785 they received from Vermont a grant of 23,000 acres.[37]

Ironically enough, it was the land grant of 1785 and the fear that once Vermont had created a state university of its own all such gifts would cease that prompted Wheelock and the Dartmouth Trustees to try to prevent the establishment of a university in Vermont.[38] Already £2,000 had been offered privately to the Vermont legislature in October of 1785 "as an encouragement to literature for the purpose of founding a university." The donor intended the institution to be endowed "with all the power and privileges which the University in Cambridge in the Commonwealth of Massachusetts at present possesses." It was to be located in Vermont. The legislature, however, postponed action since resources were still insufficient and arguments about a location within the state seemed unavoidable.[39]

Dartmouth trustee Bezalell Woodward and President Wheelock in the fall of 1786 then asked the Vermont legislature for the use of land rights once granted to the Society for the Propagation of the Gospel. The trustee assured the legislators that the college was not likely ever to become "subservient to the sinister views of sect or party." If the legislature were to grant this request, Wheelock added, Dartmouth College would educate Vermont residents free of charge and might join with the proposed Vermont state college "in one band of union."[40]

A few days later Wheelock offered an even more extraordinary proposition to the chairman of the Assembly committee to whom his and Woodward's earlier letters had been referred. He wrote that "the trustees will engage to undertake, so soon as may be consistent, to carry on and support one public school or academy in each county of this state, and to furnish the same with good skillful instructors free of all expense to any inhabitant in the respective counties, who may either be a member or send his son or friend to the same." He added that the trustees of Dartmouth College "would also undertake and carry on an institution or university in the state, whenever the legislature should think it proper, and all instruction at Dartmouth College or said institution shall be free and without expense to every citizen of the state." In exchange Wheelock wanted "the foreign public rights within the state, and also the state and county rights for the promotion of literature." The Dartmouth trustees would take on the function of a public board for the state of Vermont and would carry out their administration of the university "under the inspection or visitation of the state."[41]

Wheelock managed to persuade the Assembly committee, which

recommended on October 20 that favorable consideration be given to the proposal "as thereby the poor may not only have better but also cheaper education."[42] The Assembly, however, postponed discussion of the matter and ordered the proposal printed in the state's newspapers. Their publication brought forth a sharp outcry accusing Wheelock of attempting to undercut the creation of a state university in Vermont and leading in March of 1787 to a rejection of the plan.[43] Thus ended the abortive attempt of the Dartmouth trustees to prevent the founding of a state university in Vermont. When such an institution was chartered in 1791 it was a state college rather than a state system of preparatory and collegiate education. The Dartmouth trustees played no part in its creation.

# 13

## THE PEOPLE VERSUS THE COLLEGES

Underneath the struggles for curricular reforms and the development of state systems of higher education lay a fundamental question concerning the place of the colleges in the life of the new nation. Were the colleges independent, autonomous bodies, created and supported by their private sponsors and benefactors? Or were they creatures of the political communities now called states, responsible to the people and subject to their wishes as proclaimed in the legislatures? Expressed in legal terminology the question was whether the colleges resembled English eleemosynary corporations for the education of young men, or whether they functioned like civil corporations as incorporated towns. If they resembled charitable foundations like the colleges within the English universities, they fell under the exclusive visitatorial jurisdiction of their founders or their designated successors and could keep the legislatures at arm's length. If, on the other hand, they were civil or public corporations, they would have to recognize their legislature as founder and Visitor and, their chartered rights notwithstanding, acknowledge their continuing dependence on the legislature's authority.

The question of the legal status of the college had already been raised during the eighteenth-century struggle at Yale between Thomas Clap and Benjamin Gale. By 1766 the General Court had reaffirmed Yale's position as provincial college and civil corporation under its supervision. During the 1770s the court was willing to concede trustee autonomy only in the area of the college's "original design," that is, the teaching of divinity to ministerial students. Apart from this, the legislators wanted to establish a second governing board and appoint its members in order to safeguard the public interest. As the war soon posed problems of another sort, the Court did not press its point but bided its time. This came in the early 1780s when student dissatisfaction with the dismissal of their tutors vented itself in the destruction of Old College Hall. Then, in February of 1783, a series of letters, signed anonymously by Parnassus, appeared in the *Connecticut Courant and Intelligencer* and signaled the onset of a new wave of attacks.

Parnassus castigated the Corporation's dismissal of Professor Strong and the tutors, their failure to fill the vacant professorships, their bungling in not accepting donations and gifts, and their maintenance of a college church and separate congregation. He charged that their instructional program was frozen into a limited curriculum of a heavily clerical cast. "Theology does not belong to academic instruction more than physic, jurisprudence, or civil polity," he wrote. "Why should not professors in these branches be appointed as well as in *that*?"[1] Parnassus supported President Stiles's endeavors to broaden the curriculum and transform the college into a university. But above all, he wanted to slay the ghost of Thomas Clap and insure that Yale was to be after the Revolution what it had been when it was founded in 1701: a civil corporation devoted to the education and training of the state's professional leadership. "Those gentlemen who were first nominated for trustees were not founders considered as an *eleemosynary* corporation. No other appelation than a *civil* corporation can therefore be claimed by their successors." The Revolution having cut off the English derivation of their charter's legitimacy, and the Declaration of Independence having "disannulled part of it [the charter]," the General Assembly should now see to it that public officials — civilians, in the terminology of the day — be added to the Corporation.[2]

In 1784 the Connecticut Assembly deferred consideration of the issues raised by Parnassus and others.[3] But in the early 1790s the struggle began again with an unsuccessful attempt in the lower house to order another visitation of the college. Though the upper house had stopped the move, the Yale Corporation thought it the better part of wisdom in 1791 to show their willingness "to lay before said Assembly . . . all the information in their power, relative to the state and condition of said college, and all the funds and revenues thereof."[4] This was done in joint meetings of the Corporation and a committee of the General Court in January and May of 1792.

The main subject of debate was the addition of civilians to the Yale Corporation. Stiles was determined to resist such a change in the original charter arrangements. Yale College, he wrote in his diary, "is and doubtless always will be the only American college in the hands of ec-clesiastics. If well conducted, it may exhibit a noble example and be a standing monument and proof that ecclesiastics can conduct an institu-tion for the highest literature, with a success and glory equal to the other sister colleges, tho' all governed by a mixture of civilians and ec-clesiastics." Moreover, with the memory of his charter fight at Newport on his mind, he feared that civilians on the board would open the doors to jealousy and strife over the proportional representation of the vari-ous denominations and would eventually abolish religious tests for students, tutors, professors, and the president. The addition of civil-ians, he wrote, will "bring the deistical and mixed characters hereafter ascending into the [Governor's] Council to such a control and influence in this institution as to neutralize and gradually to annihilate the reli-gion of the college, and so to lower down and mutilate the course of ed-ucation, and model it to the taste of the age, as that in a few years we shall make no better scholars than the other colleges, or the universities of Oxford and Cambridge."[5] Such prospects were intolerable.

All the more surprising, then, to read Stiles's happy satisfaction when he learned that at its meeting of May 31, 1792, the Assembly had placed civilians on the Yale Corporation. The legislators did not nullify Yale's charter, but simply tied the acceptance by the Corporation of a revenue grant to the addition of the governor, lieutenant governor, and six members of the Governor's Council to the Corporation. The entire proposal depended for its enactment on the consent of the Corporation "in legal meeting assembled." That agreement was unanimously given on June 26. On September 12 the eight civilians joined Ezra Stiles and his ten clerical trustees for their first Corporation meeting under the new dispensation. Stiles now called the assembly act "a grand and liberal donation and a noble condescension beyond all expectation! Es-pecially," he added, "that the civilians should acquiesce in being a minority in the corporation. It will do; and will be finally adopted and closed with."[6] Clap's contention that the college was a religious society under the administration of an exclusively clerical board was dead and buried.

*The College of Philadelphia: Victim of the Revolution*

A similar though more dramatic battle was fought in Pennsylvania. It began when the British occupation troops left Philadelphia in June

1778, and in a report of March 16, 1779, the trustees of the college of Philadelphia told a distrustful Assembly committee that the college and academy constituted a charitable corporation under their exclusive jurisdiction. They maintained that their charters of 1753 and 1755 "treat the seminary as a private foundation . . . wholly exempt from any state-direction or control." Their institutions had been designed "for the common benefit of a *mixed* body of people," and had been governed by them in a nonsectarian manner on a "catholic plan."

The trustees' view was not shared by many in Pennsylvania's government. On July 8 a request of Joseph Reed, President of the State, persuaded the trustees to postpone commencement exercises and to express their hope that the government speedily proceed in a *legal way* to question their rights. Only then might they be able to "take the proper steps to defend their charter according to law."[7] Matters appeared even more threatening when on September 9 President Reed in his message to the Assembly chastised the trustees for not having "sought the aid of government for an establishment consistent with the Revolution, and conformable to the great changes of policy and government." He suggested that "an institution framed with such manifest attachment to the British government and conducted with a general inattention to the authority of the state" did not deserve the government's protection nor enjoy the people's approbation. He added that corporations that "compose a species of internal government" should be subordinate and obedient to the legislature.[8]

For three days the house debated the question of the college's relationship to the state, and on October 2 passed a motion to prepare a bill that would "confirm the estates and interests of the College and Academy of Philadelphia and . . . alter and amend the charters of the said institution, so as to make them conformable to the revolution, and the Constitution and government of this State." The Assembly refused to refer the question to the judges of the Supreme Court and rejected a request to present to the house the relevant documents on which the action was based.[9]

In a dissent to the Assembly ten legislators pinpointed the constitutional issues raised. The house, not having had an opportunity to study the committee report on which their vote was based, was not sufficiently informed of the facts. Though the judges of the Supreme Court had been invited to attend the proceedings, they had not been permitted to state their views on the law of the case. There had been no evidence supporting the charges against the college and good reason to think that many legislators were motivated by a spirit of vindictiveness toward individual trustees. Above all, the Assembly had violated the separation of legislative and judicial powers. Quoting Montesquieu and Blackstone, they warned that a union of judicial and legislative power was a threat "of the most terrifying nature" to liberty and the rule of law.[10] But their efforts were in vain, as were further attempts by Provost William Smith and the trustees to gain another hearing.[11] A bill to amend the college charter was passed on November 27, 1779, and only one lonely legislator filed a dissent protesting the haste with which the measure had been rushed through on the last day of the Assembly session.[12]

Nothing illustrates better the partisan intent of the Assembly than their statement of reasons for repudiating the trustees' declaratory act of 1764 in which the trustees had committed themselves in accordance with the English policy of toleration to uphold the original numerical representation of Anglicans and various dissenters on the board and faculty. Their motives at that time had been mixed. Some genuinely believed in the desirability of interdenominational harmony and cooperation; others thought the agreement was to their denomination's advantage. All found it advisable to humor the English authorities and donors and therefore accepted their suggestion. Thus they had signed their names to a statement of intent not to narrow the plan of their institution, only to be faced in 1779 with an unabashed and deliberate misconstruction of their words. Implying that the trustees were "dangerous and disaffected men" such as had "troubled the peace of society, shaken the government, and often caused tumult, sedition, and bloodshed," the Assembly charged them with having "departed from the plan of the original founders and narrowed the foundation of the said institution." Therefore the present Board of Trustees was to be dissolved and vacated, the declaration of 1764 voided, the charters of 1753 and 1755 amended and confirmed in their amended state, and the college expanded into a university.[13]

The new board was to be made up of six public officials: the president and vice president of the Supreme Executive Council of Pennsylvania, the speaker of the house, the chief justice, the judge of admiralty, and the attorney general. To these were added the senior ministers of six denominations, including the Episcopal, Presbyterian, Baptist, Lutheran, German Calvinist, and Catholic churches, but omitting the Quakers, ostensibly because they had no official ministers. In addition the charter named thirteen individuals, among them Benjamin Franklin, the state's representatives to the Congress, and two state Supreme Court justices. The trustees were empowered to elect successors to the non-ex officio positions, subject to a veto by the Assembly. The act also provided for an oath of allegiance to the Commonwealth of Pennsylvania and for financial accountability of the trustees to Visitors to be from time to time elected by the legislature.[14] Expressed in their new title, "The Trustees of the University of the State of Pennsylvania," was the central significance of the change. The legislature had asserted that by virtue of the Revolution and the change of government in Pennsylvania and the new confederation, the College of Philadelphia under the autonomous rule of its trustees had been transformed into a university under public supervision carried out by public officials on the Board of Trustees and by state appointed Visitors.

The trustees' expropriation in 1779 did not end the matter. The college's legal status as a corporation soon became a point of protracted controversy. As had Thomas Clap and Ezra Stiles and their trustees in Connecticut, ex-Provost William Smith and his former colleagues on the board of the College of Philadelphia insisted that their charter rights had been violated. They referred to section 45 of the Pennsylvania Constitution of 1776, which specified that "all religious societies or bodies of men heretofore united or incorporated for the advancement of religion and learning, or for other pious and charitable purposes, shall be encouraged and protected in the enjoyment of the privileges, immunities and estates which they were accustomed to enjoy or could of right have enjoyed under the laws and former constitution of this state."[15] If, as Smith and his trustees believed, the college was a charitable corporation like the colleges in the universities of England, the legislature was bound to safeguard the college charter in accordance with section 45. If President Reed was right and the college was a civil corporation like the two famous universities themselves, the Assembly could rely on its inherent powers of legislative regulation and expropriation.

During the decade's early years, ex-Provost Smith and his trustees did not meet with much encouragement in their efforts to regain their charter rights. In 1780, 1781, 1782, and 1783 they bombarded the legislature with protest memorials, but the Assembly only referred them to a committee and turned to other business. A similar fate awaited petitions Smith and the trustees submitted to the Council of Censors on December 4, 1783, and July 16, 1784. The trustees claimed again that they had been disenfranchised "without any misdemeanor, offense, neglect of duty or breach of trust in any manner proved against them," and all of this was done "without their consent."[16] The Council ordered the memorial read and laid on the table. In their review of all legislation on August 27, 1784, Council members argued that the college Corporation had expired long before 1779 for want of a requisite number of qualified trustees to elect successors. The trustees' by-law of 1764, requiring the provost to be a member of the Anglican Church and the vice provost to be a dissenter, had narrowed the original plan of the constitution and had thus brought about "a forfeiture of the said charters [of 1753 and 1755]." Council members further reasoned that it was the legislature's duty "after so recent and great a revolution" to place the education of youth "under the direction of gentlemen, not only of education, but of known republican principles, and of tried virtue." The great majority of the former trustees, they held, were men "hostile to equal liberty, or inimical to the revolution and independence of this state . . . [and] abettors of the cause of the King of Great Britain, and totally disqualified for such a trust under our present government."[17] Clearly, the trustees had few friends among the Council members and could not hope to have their cause considered favorably.

On the legal issue of the sanctity of corporate rights the defenders of the act of 1779 maintained that they had "no idea that corporations, which are the creatures of society, can, under the bill of rights, plead any exemption from legislative regulation." In a peroration the councillors defined their view of corporations and explained the necessity of their subordination to the people's will:

> We consider that these *imperii in imperio*, these governments within the government of the state, holding common estates of large value, and exercising the power of making *bye laws*, as against the spirit and the policy of democracy, and only to be endured in order to obtain advantages which may greatly counterbalance the inconveniences and dangers which accompany them. In Pennsylvania we have not a sole executive officer of permanency and weight, sufficient to restrain, and whose interest it is to keep those communities in awe; they may, therefore, gradually produce an indirect, yet firm aristocracy over the state, before we be aware of the mischief.

They went on to say that although in England the misuse of a charter could lead to dissolution by a jury or the Court of Chancery, in Penn-

sylvania only the legislature could repeal a charter. For the Assembly
to await the verdict of a judicial decision, they objected, "involves this
absurdity, that one House of General Assembly can enact a law that no
succeeding General Assembly can alter, amend or repeal, without the
consent of the corporators, who may be highly interested in opposing
the interposition of the Legislature."[18]

A minority on the Council defended the trustees and objected to
dropping the question of the constitutionality of the 1779 act. They
cited section 45 of the constitution of 1776 and indignantly rejected the
contention that the by-law of 1764 limited the charter as "the specious
coloring to a scene of pre-determined injustice" never subjected to judicial proceedings under oath. They called the charge that the corporation had lost the requisite number of qualified members "frivolous and
equally unsupported." Calling into question centuries of tradition in
which the bond between universities and established authorities of state
and church had been forged, they recommended the college charter for
its lack of ties to state and church: "The care of education is best confined in private hands. Servants of government, and even ministers of
religion, have been, in all ages and in every country, the interested
tools and favorers of power. To make any of these trustees, ex officio, is
to create a dangerous alliance between the institution and the state, by
which the dogmas of a slavish obedience may come gradually to dis-
place the pure and exalted precepts of liberty, and learning itself be
made instrumental to the purposes of tyranny and oppression." Their
efforts, however, were in vain, and the Council refused to consider the
act of 1779 unconstitutional. The trustees, nonetheless, gained one
small victory. The Council ordered their memorial of July 16 printed in
the minutes. At the same time, it refused to include in the record ex-
Provost Smith's similar petition of the previous December.[19]

Matters began to look up for Smith and the trustees when in the fall
of 1784 hearings were held before the Assembly sitting as a committee
of the whole. Counsel for the college denounced the act of 1779 as "contrary to the principles of equal government . . . [and] natural justice"
because the college trustees had not been heard before the legislature;
their charter allowed a small quorum and assured the corporation's
continuance, and the by-law of 1764 — "the great charge of all!" —
broadened rather than narrowed the base of the corporation by permitting the addition of a Baptist. Counsel for the university stressed the
legitimacy of the Revolution and the necessity for curbing corporations

"unfriendly to the genius of the government." He held the by-law to be an unwarranted addition to the charter and repeated the contention that the corporation had lost its quorum. He argued that there had been no jury trial called "because it was not [the] intent to crush or destroy it [the college], but to revive and to cherish it, and put it again on the broad bottom of Catholicism — and to put it into proper hands — friends of independence." The complaints of Smith and the trustees were illegitimate since Smith was neither "founder, patron, nor Lord," but an employee of the corporation, and the trustees held neither estates nor profit in the college. Besides, he added, the Council of Censors had decided the matter, and the Assembly ought to abide by its verdict.

The committee of the whole now found in favor of the college and held that only a court, and not the legislature, could change or abolish a charitable corporation. It recommended that part of the act of 1779 be repealed to reinvest the college trustees with their former rights and franchises. But they also suggested that the university trustees be allowed to continue their trust.[20] When the matter came to a final vote, nineteen members of the house walked out to prevent any action being taken.

Not until four more years had passed and conservatives were in control did the Assembly again consider the matter. In his *Address to the General Assembly* William Smith reiterated his contention that the college was a private, not a civil, corporation "wholly subject to the rules, statutes, and ordinances of the founders and the Visitors whom they appoint, and to no others." Following Thomas Clap's example, he added that the college was a religious institution and therefore protected by the constitution. The act of 1779 was an instance of legislative tyranny, not an act "of men governing according to law."[21] Smith's argument now carried the day. In its act of March 6, 1789, the legislature cited section 45 of the constitution, related the deprivation of the college trustees "without trial by jury," and then restored the rights of the college trustees while preserving those of the university trustees. The College of Philadelphia and the University of the State of Pennsylvania now were to exist side by side.[22]

Finding themselves competing for limited resources, college and university began to negotiate with each other within little more than two years. On September 30, 1791, they joined their resources under the direction of the trustees of the University of Pennsylvania. The university was recognized as a self-governing corporation under its own board of self-perpetuating trustees, consisting of twelve trustees from each of the merged schools and of the governor of the state as their president. Its connection with the state was through the governor and the requirement of annual financial reports.[23] No one said in 1791 whether the newly constituted university or its two predecessors were charitable or civil corporations. As an interested party, the legislature could not have done so. The question would ultimately have to be answered in a court of law.

## The Encounter with Class Bias and Religious Prejudice

During the 1780s, and 1790s hostility toward higher education flared up in the legislatures of several other colonies. In Maryland, William Smith, in his role as president of Washington College from 1782 to 1789, had become an ardent champion of publicly supported colleges, despite his equally ardent commitment to the privately governed College of Philadelphia. By 1785 he also aroused a great deal of suspicion and animosity when he attempted to gain legislative backing for the Episcopal churches. There was resentment in the state against public expenditures for colleges when veterans remained unpaid, and a wide-spread feeling grew that the state was being drawn into the denominational rivalries of Episcopalians and Presbyterians. Finally, the college bills were condemned as class legislation. "Let anybody show what advantage the poor man receives from colleges, who is scarcely able to feed and clothe his family, pay his public just and necessary demands, and teach his children to read the Bible and write their names; what are colleges to these? Why should they support them?"[24] In the end the debtor-creditor conflict was a more potent obstacle to state aid for the colleges than the religious issue.

For the next ten years the visitors of the colleges fought repeated attempts to repeal public funding. In 1796 they were powerless to stop the legislature from authorizing the establishment of grammar schools in each county.[25] In 1798 the legislature cut £500, "part of the sum heretofore appropriated to Washington College," and in 1806 Washington College's remaining annual grant of £750 and St. John's appropriation of £1750 were suspended and ordered to "remain in the treasury, subject to the appropriation of the legislature to literary purposes, and for disseminating learning in the several counties of this state, and not to other or different purposes." In the same act the legislature also abolished the University of Maryland by dissolving the union of the two colleges.[26] The colleges were permitted continued existence only under their individual charters. The idea of a state university annually supported by state tax funds had been given the coup de grâce.

The decisive element in this development had been the growing popular resentment of colleges as institutions for the state's elite, paid for annually by public taxes. Even before 1785 Maryland's debtors had agitated against the colleges and demanded that the appropriations be spent for the relief of the poor instead.[27] Yet it was not for poor relief but for the support of county academies that the college funds were diverted in 1798 and 1806. Ignoring the agitation of the 1780s, the legislators took up the cause of Maryland's middling people, which had been expressed most thoroughly and thoughtfully by Samuel Knox in 1797. Knox, an Irish-born and Scottish-trained Presbyterian minister in Bladensburg, had entered his "Essay on the Best System of Liberal Education Adapted to the Genius of the Government of the United States" in a contest sponsored by the American Philosophical Society. Emphasizing the need for preparatory education, Knox deplored the contrast between "one or two pompous edifices and expensively endowed seminaries" and the absence of "means of establishing and providing proper subordinate nurseries of students prepared for entering and attending such dignified seminaries." In excoriating the state of Maryland, Knox minced no words: "In all ages it has been the policy of those governments that existed by the slavish ignorance of the people to establish one or two sumptuously endowed schools for the sons of fortune and affluence, the expecting brood of despotical succession, leaving the canaille, the ignorant herd, to live and die, the *profanum vulgus*, the despised, enslaved, and stupid multitude."[28] By 1806 Knox's appeal bore fruit.

In Virginia pressure on the College of William and Mary was felt in November of 1776 when a correspondent in the *Virginia Gazette* demanded that the college be made accountable directly to the Assembly. The Visitors should cease to be a self-perpetuating body, he declared, and vacancies in their board should be filled by the legislature.[29] Three years later the Visitors asserted themselves. Prompted by their colleague, Governor Thomas Jefferson, they decreed changes in the professorial chairs and by college statute assigned to themselves a participatory role in curricular decisions. This was not a charter revision, however, and the Corporation's privileges were largely untouched.

Jefferson confided later that through a bill he had prepared for passage in the legislature he had sought to turn the college into a public university and to remove the Anglican influence.[30] He wanted the Visitors to be appointed by both houses of the legislature, and a group of three chancellors, appointed in like manner, to serve as a court in disciplinary matters concerning the faculty.[31] With this bill Jefferson intended to reaffirm the Reformation concept of public responsibility for higher education, and sweep away the anachronism of an autonomous corporation of Anglican masters. As he saw it, the Revolution had replaced crown and church with the people of Virginia as represented in their Assembly. The legislature was to claim no more than its legitimate role in college government.

But opposition now arose from different quarters. The Anglican origins of the College of William and Mary had alarmed the Presbyterians, who feared that the college would become a state university with the Episcopalians in control of preparatory and collegiate education. Referring to Jefferson's proposals for the diffusion of knowledge, a companion piece to the college bill, Samuel Stanhope Smith, 1769 graduate of the College of New Jersey and rector of the Presbyterian academy at Hampden-Sydney, warned Jefferson in 1779:

> Whatever party enjoys the preeminence in [the higher schools, academies, and university] will insensibly gain upon the others, and soon acquire the government of the state. This contest will chiefly lie betwixt the Presbyterians and the Episcopalians. The Baptists and Methodists content themselves with other kinds of illuminations than are afforded by human science. In the scheme, I observe that William and Mary is to be the university; and her visitors and professors will enjoy the power of appointing the academical and other masters, and of prescribing the system of education. Be assured Sir, that while she continues under her present influence, the proposal will alarm the whole body of Presbyterians. In their view it will be erecting a noble fabric upon too contracted a bottom, and they will oppose it.[32]

As a result of this Presbyterian opposition, Jefferson gave up his hopes of transforming the College of William and Mary into a state university. Instead he began to contemplate such an institution away from "the bilious diseases" of the James River country in a more central location further north. Thus began his campaign for the University of Virginia.[33]

In Massachusetts, defenders of Harvard in the General Court deflected demands to assert legislative control and to turn the college into a state university. In the state constitutional convention they requested that the Harvard Corporation and the Overseers propose the necessary changes, and they then proceeded to adopt these proposals in the new constitution. The Corporation thus was confirmed in all its rights and privileges and in the possession of its property. The only significant change was the reconstitution of the Board of Overseers. It was now to consist of ex officio public officials and Congregational ministers and to include among the former the entire Senate and Council. In addition the General Court reserved the right to alter the university's government "as shall be conducive to its advantage and the interest of the republic of letters." They added that this right was not an innovation, but that it could have been invoked by any previous legislature. Harvard College, they implied, had always been a civil rather than an eleemosynary corporation. They obliged the "legislatures and magistrates, in all future periods of the Commonwealth, to cherish the interests of literature and the sciences and all seminaries of them; especially the University at Cambridge," and included president, professors, and instructors among magistrates and other office holders who, because of their public duties, were forbidden to serve in the General Court. They further acknowledged and protected Harvard as a state university by devoting to it an entire section of the state constitution.[34]

Harvard's recognition, however, was problematical. Popular distrust of the institution as a citadel of aristocratic privilege was expressed in the town debates on the adoption of the constitution. Many objected to the confirmation of the college's privileges and felt that it was "unreasonable for men to enjoy every privilege of free citizens without bearing a part of the burdens of the community." Others asked that such privileges be tied to an annual accounting to the General Court. The citizens of Middleborough stated pointedly what was on the minds of many: that legislators and magistrates, pledged by the constitution to the support of literature and the sciences and "especially the University at Cambridge," might find it difficult to be as diligent or enthusiastic in the support of town schools.[35] Here was the issue also raised in Maryland and Virginia. Colleges served the elite; academies and town schools aided the many. Why, then, should public funds be spent for the benefit of the few?

This popular distrust of higher education was translated into legislative hesitation or refusal to grant the university additional funds. After the Corporation had created three medical chairs in 1782 and sponsored clinical instruction, the opponents of legislative funding argued that medical professors could support themselves through fees. Though the General Court responded intermittently with salary grants for the president and the professors in the college, it turned down in 1781 a petition of the Corporation for "a permanent and adequate salary for the President." After 1786 it ceased even its occasional grants and left the Corporation to wonder what had happened to the constitution's charge that the Court be "the encouragers of literature . . . for the honor and reputation of the new constitution."[36] The initial legislative support for Harvard as the state's university began to fade.

Popular distrust of aristocratic class interests in higher education hampered Federalist efforts to found a university in North Carolina. In 1784 a bill was introduced to fund a university through a tax on tradesmen and officials. President and trustees were to be public officers, incorporated by the General Assembly to administer the university under the visitatorial  oversight of the governor and his Council.[37] This measure was blocked by the anti-Federalist Assembly. Barely three weeks after the ratification of the Federal Constitution in 1789, a new Federalist legislature passed a bill authorizing a self-perpetuating board of forty trustees to include twenty-eight members of the constitutional convention. Since twenty-one of the forty also served in the legislature, the impression was that the university trustees were serving as public officials, and that the university itself was a public corporation under Federalist control. The charter permitted any number of the trustees, however small, to be a quorum so long as the president and the treasurer were among them; if these two officials were absent, the quorum was defined as a majority of the board.[38] Subsequently the Assembly assigned to the university all debts owed to the state as well as all property that had escheated or would escheat to the state, and it exempted all university property from taxation.[39]

Few North Carolinians doubted that the university was organized and supervised by a tightly knit group of legislators, many of them Federalists and their sympathizers. When the board met for the first time in November of 1790 with six of its seats vacant, four were filled with replacements from among the members of the legislature. An attempt by anti-Federalists to prevent such double service failed.[40] Attacks and difficulties continued. Funds were lacking, and the sums collected through debts and arrearages to the state amounted to only $7,362. As if to counteract the partisan stigma, friends of the university in 1793 appealed to the various denominations, "Episcopalians,

Presbyterians, Methodists, Baptists, Universalists, and Society of Friends, peaceful Quakers, give!" When in December of 1794 the General Assembly granted to the trustees all unsold confiscated lands, more resentment was created among those who now had to expect eviction from this property. As classes commenced in February 1795 in what is now Chapel Hill, the university was at last in operation, but its base of support was shallow at best.[41]

But not every state witnessed conflict over its college or colleges. In 1780 in New Jersey the General Assembly endorsed the 1748 charter of the College of New Jersey, requiring only that tutors and officers who were inhabitants of the state take an oath of allegiance to the state instead of to the crown. On June 5, 1781, the legislature removed a provision in the 1770 charter of Queen's College that had restricted the number of ordained ministers to one-third of the Board of Trustees, and asked the governor, when present, to preside over the trustees.[42] In Rhode Island state action followed a request by the Corporation of the College of Rhode Island in 1782 to adjust the oath of allegiance for Corporation officials to the changed political circumstances. The members of the Corporation referred to their institution in these documents as "the College, or University, in the State of Rhode Island and Providence Plantations," but did not persist long in using this appellation. There was little in the curriculum to justify university status, unless one were to rest that claim on the appointment in 1784 of unpaid lectureships in experimental philosophy and natural history.[43] In both New Jersey and Rhode Island the identification of the colleges with denominational interests—Presbyterian, Dutch Reformed, and Baptist respectively—provided them with a group of committed supporters, and their avoidance of ambitious state-wide university schemes shielded them from hostile public scrutiny.

# 14

## THE PRIVATE COLLEGES

The 1780s and 1790s witnessed the emergence of the American private college. Like Queen's College in New Jersey, most, but not all, of these new institutions were staffed, governed, and funded by a church or denomination. Most frequently they were promoted by Presbyterians, but Catholics, Methodists, Dutch and German Reformed, and Congregationalists were also active. Others were sponsored by local developers and businessmen or, as in Baltimore, by civil leaders of various professions and denominations. While such colleges were dependent on their legislature for incorporation, their trustees did not usually apply for public support. When they did, they had no guarantee of obtaining it. Almost always they refused to see themselves as part of the state's official establishment. This, above all, distinguished them from the governors of the former provincial colleges and new state universities.

The American private college originated because of disenchantment with the aristocratic flavor of political leadership in the colonies. For many Americans, particularly in the southern and western regions, the Revolution meant independence from eastern as well as British rule, and from cultural as well as social and economic domination by the established families of business and finance. They wanted educational institutions to be under their own control, and expected the frontier colleges to guarantee social stability and economic prosperity. These colleges were promoted as cultural outposts in the wilderness, as points of attraction for families "of the better sort," and as inducements for white settlers. The appearance of private colleges thus came to signal the effectiveness of local efforts at development.

On the frontier the private denominational and booster colleges outdistanced their public counterparts.[1] Under the conditions of American

189

ethnic and religious heterogeneity, public institutions depended on compromise and were plagued by continuous bickering and battles for supremacy. Legislative agreements demanded inordinate amounts of time and energy. Once they were achieved, they were likely to be questioned again and subjected to renewed negotiations. Theodore Frelinghuysen's "Let every one provide for his own house" expressed well the exasperation of potential college founders with the unwieldiness of interdenominational and factional debates.[2]

Cohesive groups promoting private colleges encountered no such difficulties. They had few problems persuading various proponents to join forces. If they represented a church or denomination, their task usually was to persuade their own members to risk investing their resources in a college. If they were civic promoters, they advanced their case in the language of business profit, civic pride, and civilization's advance. To the extent that they needed to bring together students of varied backgrounds, they promised nondiscrimination within the college. But they did not have to subject themselves to the suspicions of others in legislative debates and popular discussions. Those who did not agree with them stayed away; those who came more than likely were ready to lend hand and purse. It was precisely the partisan nature of the private colleges that allowed them to surpass the state institutions. Philip Lindsley, president of the public University of Nashville, put it well when he said that public institutions with neither sect nor party "to praise, puff, glorify, and fight" for them were in "the worst possible position." They were neutral and therefore trusted and regarded by no one.[3] The private colleges, meanwhile, surged ahead with the frontier and became a potent attraction of western developers.

*Presbyterian Pioneers*

In the years from 1780 to 1820 the Presbyterians became college founders par excellence. Their drive to establish academies and colleges was spurred by their desire to revive the seventeenth-century notion of ministerial responsibility for the spiritual and moral unity of the commonwealth. Like the New England Puritans, they regarded clergymen as public servants, though no public authority had issued ministerial commissions and no secular power had confirmed them in office.[4]

On the southern and western frontier, Presbyterians were active as college founders in Virginia, Kentucky, Pennsylvania, South Carolina, and Tennessee. Generally speaking, their collegiate foundations were most successful where they adapted the provincial college concept of toleration with preferment. Toleration, of course, was an absolute necessity. Without it the institutions would have resembled seminaries for the training of ministerial candidates, and the legislature would have refused a college charter. Preferment was a matter of prior possession rather than entitlement. Since most of the Presbyterian colleges in the five states grew out of academies, their boards had been raised to the rank of college Corporations. Their charters never formally recognized any influence or rights of a church judicatory. Preferment, then, was a matter of silent acceptance, not of legal acknowledgement.

But not all Presbyterian colleges gained such preferred status. In western Pennsylvania denominational concerns became so inextricably interwoven with community interests that Jefferson and Washington colleges were robbed of much of their power to attract potential supporters. In Kentucky the Presbyterians jeopardized their preferred position by their repeated attempts to gain complete control of the state's university system. When they failed in this, they sought in 1819 to gain incorporation for a college and several academies, only to be again stymied by the legislature. In South Carolina Presbyterians faced local poverty and disinterest and never managed to gain a permanent foothold. In Tennessee those Presbyterian institutions fared worst that had been incorporated as colleges through legislative initiative. By contrast, those first promoted for incorporation as colleges by Presbyterian ministers with the support of their churches prospered and embarked upon fruitful careers. A willingness to shun entanglements in local rivalries and to forgo special prerogatives gave denominational interests their best assurance of success.

The collegiate source of the Presbyterians' educational efforts had been the College of New Jersey. Wherever they went in the West, Princeton graduates established grammar schools and academies.[5] When these subsequently were incorporated as colleges, the Presbyterians acquired their reputation as college founders. This sequence of events unfolded for the first time in 1749 when Princeton graduates established Augusta Academy near Greeneville in Virginia. In 1776 it was recognized as Liberty Hall Academy and governed by a board of twenty-four trustees, all of them Presbyterians. The right to visit and to appoint the rector and assistants was given to the presbytery. When in 1782 the Virginia Assembly incorporated it as a degree-granting academy, its board became independent of any church group.[6] The trustees had avoided identifying the institution as a college, because they were afraid that as a public body it would invite legislative interference in its affairs. That such interference was no empty threat was to be demonstrated in the 1790s when the legislators attempted to change the academy into a college without the trustees' consent.

Princeton graduates were active also in Prince Edwards County, Virginia, where they founded an academy as a Presbyterian alternative to the Anglican College of William and Mary. At the same time they sought the cooperation of Anglicans to avoid that "too contracted a bottom" of which Samuel Stanhope Smith, the academy's rector, had written to Jefferson.[7] To assuage the fears of parents the Hanover presbytery announced "that no undue influence [would] be used by any member of this presbytery, the rector of the academy or his assistants to bias the judgement of any of the students; but that all of every denomination shall fully enjoy their own religious sentiments, and be at liberty to attend that mode of public worship that either custom or conscience makes the most convenient to them."[8] When in May 1783 the legislature incorporated the academy as Hampden-Sydney College, it recognized the trustees as a self-perpetuating society intended to provide a liberal arts education to academically qualified young men, independent of either church or state, and subject only to the general superintending power of the courts over all corporations.[9] The charter did not mention the Hanover presbytery, did not acknowledge its earlier right to select forever trustees, president, professors, and tutors, and did not allude to any obligation to church or religious doctrine. But in leaving unchanged the twenty-seven-member governing board it nonetheless insured Presbyterian control.[10]

The Virginia legislature pursued the same policy of incorporating previously existing groups in the state's western province of Kentucky when it empowered the Presbyterian trustees of Transylvania Seminary to confer bachelor's, master's, and honorary degrees.[11] It established the seminary as a public institution of learning without special rights or privileges reserved to members of any denomination. It held the trustees accountable to the public rather than to a church.[12] Though instruction at the seminary did not begin before 1789, Presbyterian unhappiness with Transylvania Seminary as a public institution was expressed in 1787 by a trustee writing pseudonymously in the *Kentucky Gazette*. "Catholicus" stated that a strong religious influence in the educational program of the college would be "far more safe and rational than that of discarding all religion from seminaries of learning through fear that the students may embrace that which is erroneous."[13] He therefore refused to consider the Jeffersonian suggestion of dissociating religious tenets from moral instruction and of apportioning an equal number of professorships to the various accepted protestant denominations. Instead he favored a diversity of sectarian views, and proposed to ignore the protests of Unitarians and Deists. As long as the board remained in Presbyterian hands, the views of Catholicus prevailed.

After Kentucky achieved statehood in 1792, the Presbyterians lost their majority on the seminary board. In 1794 they could not prevent the choice of Harry Toulmin, a Baptist Unitarian minister, as president, but managed to persuade the legislature to invalidate Toulmin's election and force his resignation two years later.[14] While Toulmin was in office, the presbytery withdrew its support of Transylvania Seminary and organized a grammar school and a seminary under auspices of their own. The grammar school opened in December 1794, but the seminary, called Kentucky Academy, had to wait until the fall of 1797. It was placed under the direction of a board of twenty-one trustees of whom at least half had to be Presbyterian ministers of the Transylvania presbytery. Within another two years, however, Kentucky Academy and Transylvania Seminary joined forces and on January 1, 1799, became Transylvania University. The legislature granted a new charter under which were to serve an equal number of ex-trustees of the two parent institutions and several well-known citizens. Among them was Governor Garrard who, however, did not serve in an ex officio capacity. The trustees were empowered to open one or more preparatory schools, and the Assembly passed another act establishing and endowing nineteen academies in various counties.[15]

The Kentucky legislature thus had created, on paper at least, a wide-ranging system of preparatory and collegiate education, comprising the university and its feeder schools as well as the nineteen planned academies in addition to those already in existence. Though this scheme resembled the state systems of Georgia and New York, it also differed from them since it did not involve the ex officio participation of

public officials.[16] More important, it was built on and around the previously existing institutions. It thus gave the opportunity to a minority
of highly influential Presbyterians during the next two decades to seek
the domination of the system and to put the government of Transylvania University and the county academies under severe strain.

With the arrival in 1818 of the Unitarian Horace Holley as president
of Transylvania University, the Kentucky Presbyterians decided to create a collegiate institution outside the university system. While synod
members agreed that the academic work should be free of denominational direction or influence, they wanted to reserve for themselves the
right to add a theological course "according to their own peculiar principles."[17] When they examined the charter of Centre College, which
the legislature had granted on January 21, 1819, in response to their petition, they found that it said nothing of biblical classes, instruction in
church history and the evidences of Christianity, the possibility of adding a theological department, or of the synod's right to confirm the
trustees—all items they had desired and expected. Instead the charter
ruled out the "inculcation" of religious doctrines "peculiar to any one
sect of Christians," and announced that "whenever the legislature shall
find it expedient to adopt the said college as a state institution, and endow it, in aid of the funds which shall have been furnished by private
donation, it shall thereafter be subject to such laws and regulations as
may be enacted for the government of the same." To leave no misun-
derstanding the legislators added these words, "Nothing herein contained shall be so construed as to take away the right which the legislature possess to repeal, alter or amend this charter."[18]

If the Presbyterians had harbored hopes of gaining a foothold in
three academies raised to collegiate rank through incorporation on
February 9, 1819, they were to be disappointed here also. With only
minor exceptions, the charters of the Southern College of Kentucky
near Bowling Green, of the College of Urania in Glasgow, and of the
Western College of Kentucky in Hopkinsville were identical to the
charter of Centre College. None of the four institutions was authorized
to grant degrees, and all were ordered to refrain from sectarian religious instruction.[19] As the 1820s began, a largely Republican legislature
had managed to hold at bay Presbyterian attempts to gain control over
the state's colleges.

In Pennsylvania a Presbyterian effort to found a college was similarly
blunted by the legislature. The charter of Dickinson College at Carlisle

as passed by the legislature on September 9, 1783, gave the institution the appearance of an eighteenth-century provincial college under the toleration with preferment scheme. It allowed for neither magistrates nor ministers to serve ex officio among the trustees, though it placed John Dickinson and James Ewing, the president and vice-president of Pennsylvania's Supreme Executive Council, on the board together with twenty-three laymen and fourteen clergymen. Any minister had to be replaced "with another clergyman of any christian denomination," and neither college principal nor professors could serve as trustees. The charter was declared to be inviolable except "by an act of the legislature of this state."[20] It repeated the nondiscrimination clauses of colonial college charters, and contained no guarantee that the Presbyterians would preserve their majority among the ministerial trustees.

Benjamin Rush, who as prime mover behind the scene had viewed Dickinson College as a Presbyterian counterweight to the newly created University of the State of Pennsylvania, was concerned not to antagonize Pennsylvanians by founding a purely denominational college. Thus he wrote to his friend John Montgomery that the professors at Dickinson College had to be chosen from several different religious persuasions. "It will help to remove the prejudices which Dr. Ewing & Co. [the provost of the University of the State of Pennsylvania] have raised against our society. A German Lutheran or Calvinist teacher will allure us many pupils and connect us with their people in government. An Episcopalian will draw pupils even from this city [Philadelphia]. It will be enough for us that the principal and a majority of the trustees are Presbyterians."[21]

Rush and his friends opposed the revolutionary or, as they were called, the Constitutionalist party. He disliked radicals in politics as much as in the church, and he took it for granted that a conservative view on social and political affairs had to be grounded in an equally conservative religious position. While a multi-denominational faculty might be advisable for tactical reasons, he much preferred Presbyterian direction for the college. This would enable the school to serve as an asylum for the youths of Presbyterians and would protect students from the clash and confusion of doctrinal strife.[22] Rush preferred "the patronage of particular societies." On March 19, 1783, he wrote to John Armstrong that "instead of encouraging bigotry . . . it prevents it by removing young men from those opportunities of controversy which a variety of sects mixed together are apt to create and which are the certain fuel of bigotry." Such denominational direction, Rush maintained, did not by itself place the college on a "narrow bottom." Support had come, he assured Armstrong, from "men of every political and religious party in the frontier counties of Pennsylvania." The trustees included Constitutionalists and Republicans, Old and New Light Presbyterians, Episcopalians, and Lutherans, and yet the college was firmly in the hands of a particular group claiming to act as stewards for all. In this fashion Dickinson could best serve the interests of all Pennsylvanians.[23]

Initially Rush had hoped that the legislature would fund the college and pay its faculty. But since such a proposal would have provoked much opposition, Rush decided to omit this request at the time of chartering the college.[24] But he never gave up the concept justifying public aid. Within three short years he was to see his original hope fulfilled when the legislature, on April 7, 1786, voted to give the college £500 and 10,000 acres. In subsequent years further appropriations were passed until it could be said that Dickinson College of all of Pennsylvania's colleges chartered before 1837 "received the largest share of the state's bounty and attention."[25] During its first forty years it functioned as an eighteenth-century provincial college under strong, though not exclusive, Presbyterian influence.

In Tennessee — the Territory of the United States South of the River Ohio — the legislature raised three Presbyterian academies to collegiate status and granted them the right to confer degrees. On September 3, 1794, Hezekiah Balch's academy became Greeneville College; on July 8, 1795, Martin Academy was changed to Washington College; and in September 1794 the legislators converted Carrick's Academy near Knoxville into Blount College. At Greeneville and at Washington the trustees were independent of church or state, preventing denominational ownership of the colleges. But because Carrick's Academy had been a relative newcomer, the legislature placed Governor Blount and the territorial secretary on its board in an ex officio capacity.[26] While legally these institutions were now recognized as colleges, they continued for the most part to offer preparatory rather than collegiate work. Blount College admitted women as well as men and granted its first bachelor's degree in 1806; Greeneville followed suit in 1808; only Washington College turned immediately to collegiate work and granted its first degree in 1796.[27]

After Tennessee gained statehood in 1796 the legislature responded to a Congressional land grant and took steps to charter a college in both eastern and western Tennessee.[28] On September 11, 1806, Davidson Academy near Nashville became Cumberland College, and on October 26, 1807, thirty trustees were issued a charter for East Tennessee College.[29] In a supplementary act the board members were individually named, and the legislature, with the consent of the trustees of Blount College, incorporated the funds of Blount College into those of East Tennessee College. Instruction of the new college was to be carried on in the buildings of Blount College, and the latter institution was formally dissolved.[30] In 1809 the legislature ordered the Presbyterian trustees of these two colleges to present at every stated session "a full and complete statement of the situation of said college, and the state of their funds, and in what manner they have appropriated such monies as they may have expended."[31]

Before 1820 these Tennessee colleges of Presbyterian origin were in no sense denominational institutions. All were governed by independent, self-perpetuating corporations that were held accountable to the legislature. None of them had ex officio representation on their boards. But there was a marked difference in their progress. Greeneville, Washington, and Blount had been relatively successful. Their prosperity must be ascribed to the reputation and financial backing they enjoyed among Presbyterians and non-Presbyterians. By contrast the two colleges founded upon public initiative were always in financial straits. Cumberland College had to close in 1816, and East Tennessee could not begin its work before 1820 when it merged its assets with those of the Hampden-Sydney Academy in Knoxville.[32]

As in Kentucky, the legislators in Tennessee remained suspicious of Presbyterian intentions. Despite their unwillingness or inability to grant financial aid, they nonetheless reaffirmed their ultimate responsibility over the state's colleges and academies. In 1817 they declared that these "should ever be under the fostering care of this legislature, and in their connexion with each other form a complete system of education." The state's academies, the act read, were to be considered as preparatory schools for the colleges, and the state's colleges were once more granted the right to give academic degrees.[33] The latent and occasionally open hostility between Presbyterian college sponsors and state legislators was to remain a permanent feature and keep the Presbyterian colleges from becoming truly private schools under complete denominational control.

Western Pennsylvania and South Carolina, finally, present a different version of Presbyterian collegiate history. One hundred and fifty miles west of Carlisle in Pennsylvania's southwest corner, two colleges grew out of academies founded there by Presbyterian clergymen. The state Supreme Court incorporated one of them in 1787 and the other in 1791.[34] Both received legislative appropriations and were chartered as Washington College in 1806 and Jefferson College in Canonsburg in 1802, no more than nine miles apart.[35] The state incorporated the academy trustees as college governors and, as in the Dickinson charter, insisted on a prohibition of denominational discrimination against trustees, principal, professors, and students. In each college the ministerial trustees could be of any Christian denomination.[36]

In subsequent merger negotiations between the two colleges a pronounced local partisanship became evident. Neither of the two schools would yield to the other on the question of a future joint site. The Washington trustees insisted that the college remain where it was, and their Jefferson counterparts resolved that they would not leave Canonsburg "except the hand of Providence is clearly discernible in such a measure, either by casting lots, or leaving it to the decision of the legislature."[37] Providence did not show itself, but the Washington trustees persuaded the principal of Jefferson College to become their college president. This coup, the Jefferson trustees noted angrily, had "in some degree destroyed that harmony that ought to subsist amongst those, whose peculiar office it is to promote pure and undefiled religion."[38] Controlled by trustees residing in close proximity, dependent on the good will and financial support of their neighbors, and viewed by them with pride, these two colleges were unable to protect their common denominational commitment against their separate community interests.

Community support or its absence is illustrated well in the different fortunes of Allegheny College, Meadville, in Pennsylvania's northwest corner, and of the Western University of Pennsylvania in Pittsburgh. Timothy Alden, the founder of Allegheny College, was a Harvard graduate and Congregational pastor. While his Presbyterian neighbors supported the colleges in Washington and Canonsburg, Alden relied on his connections in the Northeast and gathered a board of trustees from far and wide. The college charter of March 24, 1817, accompanied by a legislative appropriation of $2,000, listed fifty trustees, including Pennsylvania's governor, chief justice, and attorney general, all serving ex officio, and thirty-six laymen and eleven clergymen. It contained the usual phrases barring religious discrimination. But no further funds were forthcoming, and Alden failed to interest other teachers and churches in his school. Allegheny College barely survived as the 1820s began.[39]

By contrast, the Western University was a successful enterprise. It grew out of an academy chartered in Pittsburgh in 1787 by some of the same Presbyterian ministers who had helped found the schools in nearby Canonsburg and Washington. It combined the advantages of an urban location and support by a strong Presbyterian community. Its university charter of 1819 assigned five Presbyterian ministers to its twenty-six-member board of trustees, and four of its first five professors belonged to the same denomination.[40] In later years it was to overshadow its Presbyterian competitors in Canonsburgh and Washington and, strengthened by the cosmopolitan flavor of Pittsburgh, would thrive and eventually become the University of Pittsburgh.[41]

In South Carolina rural poverty and disinterest bedeviled Presbyterian efforts to open colleges. In 1777 the Mt. Sion Society had opened a school at Winnsborough in the center of the state. After the war it reopened in 1784 "upon the plan of the college of New Jersey" with the Reverend Thomas Harris McCaule as president, and a year later was incorporated as Mt. Sion College.[42] "It was restricted to no particular Protestant denomination," writes the historian of South Carolina's Presbyterian Church, "but it so occurred that its first teachers were Presbyterians, and its influence tended to promote the interests of this branch of the church." In the 1790s Mt. Sion College ran out of funds, and was then continued as an elementary school only.[43] Its charter of 1785 had also incorporated a college in Cambridge that had originally been founded as a Presbyterian school. There is some question, however, whether it ever functioned as a college. An act to establish a lottery for its financial support in 1792 described the school's funds as "considerably deranged," and an act of 1797, incorporating another group of Presbyterians as the trustees of Alexandria College near Pinckneyville, reported that "all the seminaries of learning which have been established in the interior part of this State" had "from some fatal cause become extinct."[44] That fate, too, overcame Alexandria College itself. Its twenty-one Presbyterian trustees never could raise enough money to open the school as a college.[45]

## The Varieties of Private Foundations

Presbyterians were not the only beneficiaries of privately founded colleges. In fact, one of their staunchest representatives, Benjamin Rush, took it upon himself to promote a college for the German Lutheran and Reformed settlers in Pennsylvania. Rush believed that denominational or ethnically-related colleges conformed best to the demographic realities of Pennsylvania's pluralism. He remarked in 1785 that it had "been found by experience that harmony and Christian friendship between the different religious societies is best promoted by their educating their youth in separate schools." Such colleges would not increase separation because, wrote Rush, "it is *ignorance* and *prejudice* only that keeps men of different countries and religions apart. A German college, by removing *these*, will prepare the way for the Germans to unite more intimately with their British and Irish fellow citizens and thus to form with them one homogeneous mass of people."[46]

The result of Rush's endeavours was the chartering of Franklin College in Lancaster on March 10, 1787. The forty-five trustees represented some of the state's more notable politicians and statesmen, though none of them served ex officio. Among them were Thomas Mifflin who, in the next year, was to succeed Benjamin Franklin as president of the state, Thomas McKean, the chief justice, Peter Muhlenberg, and Joseph Heister. There were Philadelphia lawyers and financiers as well as many of Lancaster's leading citizens. The largest group of clergymen came from Lutheran and Reformed churches. They were joined by Lancaster's Moravian pastor, Episcopal rector, and Catholic priest. A newspaper account of the opening festivities on June 6, 1787, captured well the spirit of cooperation prevalent at the occasion. "It was a spectacle beautiful in itself, and which we may with certainty pronounce, no age, or country, nor any set of people, ever held before . . . On the *same* day, in the *same* church, and to the *same* set of Christians, the ministers of *four* different religious persuasions successively joined in the worship and adoration of the Supreme Being."[47]

With the charter requirement that both the Lutheran and the Reformed churches were to furnish fifteen trustees each as well as the principal by rotation, Franklin College was the first college to be explicitly and legally church-related. It was to provide theological instruction in addition to languages, the arts and sciences, and literature, and its charter did not contain a clause prohibiting discrimination on religious grounds. Though the college was not in any direct manner subject to the authority of a church consistory or synod, it encouraged ecclesiastical opinion and authority through its announced service to the German churches.[48]

The widest variety of private colleges can be found in Maryland. Besides the two public colleges at Chestertown and Annapolis, the Methodists and Catholics each founded two; one was created by a civic association, and two owed their origins to professional proprietors. In none of these did public officials serve ex officio on the governing boards. The Methodists had asked that Cokesbury Academy be incorporated as a college in the hope of attracting state aid for their faltering school. Though the academy trustees were reconstituted as The Trustees and Governors of Cokesbury College on December 26, 1794, state funding did not follow, and the trustees were forced to suspend their collegiate department within a few months and to confine instruction to the English school. In December of 1795, when their building went up in flames, they moved the college to a new location in Baltimore. Again fire struck in December of 1796, and three years later the legislature permitted the trustees to dispose of the college property.[49] In 1818 the Methodists tried once more. Asbury College was chartered in Baltimore as successor to Cokesbury, and was to be conducted "for the benefit of youth of every religious denomination." But like its predecessor, it was forced to close sometime in the 1830s or 1840s.[50] The Maryland Methodists had neither the human nor the financial resources to compete with the Presbyterians in the field of college founding.

Where the Methodists failed, the Catholics eventually succeeded. With the struggle of Washington and St. John's colleges on his mind, Bishop Carroll shrewdly concluded that Marylanders distrusted the elitism of colleges but were willing to support preparatory academies. Knowing also that in Protestant countries Catholics could not expect enthusiastic support for Catholic colleges, he kept to himself his desire to found a college "which might at the same time be a seminary for future clergymen," and moved to establish an academy.[51] Not requiring state authorization to confer degrees, such a school could remain under the control of the church. A college, on the other hand, not being under exclusive church direction, could expect a wider base of support than an academy or a seminary. And was it not advisable for Catholics to join in community ventures? "Being admitted to equal toleration, must we not concur in public measures, and avoid separating ourselves from the community?"[52] Carroll resolved the dilemma by founding in 1791 an academy that, like a college, admitted students of all Christian denominations but allowed them to attend worship services at their own churches. Intellectual training and moral discipline were its announced aims.[53]

On March 1, 1815, Carroll's academy was chartered by Congress as Georgetown College. The charter left unchanged the academy's governmental structure, included no prohibition on religious discrimination against trustees, teachers, or students, and gave degree-granting power to "the President and Directors of the College of Georgetown."[54] Thus a privately founded and governed academy had received the rights and privileges of a college without explicitly acknowledging its obligations to public authority. Of the private colleges, Georgetown with its federal charter was the most private of them all.

In the same year that Carroll had established his academy in Georgetown, a group of three Sulpician priests and five students recently arrived from France opened a seminary in Baltimore for the training of Catholic clergymen. Their problem, as Carroll warned them, was to be the scarcity of sufficiently prepared students.[55] Not even the Georgetown academy could provide enough candidates for admission to the seminary. The Sulpicians had no students from 1795 to 1797, and then decided in 1799 to open a preparatory academy of their own.[56] There Father Du Bourg taught Cuban and French boys the elements of a classical education, until in 1803 the Spanish government recalled the Cubans to Havana. To compensate for this loss Father Du Bourg opened St. Mary's Academy to American students. The implications of this move were momentous. Both Protestant and Catholic students entered the academy, most of them having no intention of preparing for the priesthood, and the way was paved for the incorporation of the academy as a college.[57]

On January 19,1805, the Maryland legislature authorized Father Du Bourg and the associated professors of St. Mary's Seminary to admit students to degrees "in any of the faculties, arts and sciences, and liberal professions." It specified that students could not be subjected to religious tests, except those who were admitted to special certificates testifying to the completion of a partial course.[58] The charter thus recognized a distinction between the college and the academy and seminary. In the next year the Sulpicians officially adopted college, academy, and seminary as their own. There were plans under way in 1807 to incorporate a projected College of Medicine of Maryland into St. Mary's College and Seminary and thus to raise the Sulpician institution to the rank of a university. The legislature, however, refused to endorse the project. Seminary and college nonetheless fared well, the former now deriving support and candidates from the latter.[59] In 1822 the college received a papal charter permitting the bestowal of degrees in divinity. For many decades it was to serve Catholics and non-Catholics alike.

In Baltimore, too, efforts were made to create a college as a civic venture sponsored by an interdenominational group of clergy and laymen. Chartered in January of 1804, Baltimore College was to provide a liberal education "for the benefit of youth of every religious denomination . . . without requiring or enforcing any religious or civil test, or urging their attendance upon any particular plan of religious worship or service, other than that they have been educated in." The thirty-seven trustees elected Bishop John Carroll as chairman and proceeded to assemble a faculty without regard to religious preference. Their charter empowered them to admit the students to the degrees normally given in American colleges and universities. The college president was to serve as trustee ex officio.[60] Little is known of the history of Baltimore College. Apparently it never bestowed degrees and, for all practical purposes, functioned as an academy until in 1830 it was merged into the University of Maryland.[61] Lack of funds and of continuing commitment on the part of the sponsors account for its demise.

Finally, Maryland's medical practitioners added to the state's collegiate variety the independent proprietary school. Baltimore doctors had been concerned with competition from quacks and had sought to provide professional training and certification as early as the 1780s. During the 1790s their project began to look promising. In 1798 one hundred and one medical practitioners of various counties were incorporated as the Medical Chirurgical Faculty of the State of Maryland.[62] To protect citizens from "ignorant practitioners or pretenders to the healing art," they were empowered to establish a Medical Board of Examiners. That board could license candidates who had passed an examination or could show a diploma "from some respectable college."[63]

In 1807 the members of the examining board and other physicians were incorporated as president and professors of The College of Medicine of Maryland. For reasons not now known, the legislature refused an affiliation with St. Mary's College. Instead the professors remained in close union with the Medical and Chirurgical Faculty. Its members were to be patrons and Visitors; its president was to serve as the college chancellor.[64] The college opened promptly in 1807 and graduated its first medical doctors in 1810.[65]

Contrary to their expectations, the doctors did not find their enterprise profitable. They therefore sought to transform their medical school into a university and thus to add prestige and larger enrollments.[66] On December 29, 1812, the legislature authorized the medical college "to constitute, appoint and annex" three faculties. The faculty of divinity was to consist of a professor and six ordained ministers, the faculty of law of one professor and six qualified members of the bar, and the arts and sciences professors were to be joined by the principals of any three academies or colleges in the state. The regents were given the power to grant degrees, and anything in the act thought to be inconsistent with the 1807 charter of the College of Medicine was declared to be null and void. A new University of Maryland had been born.[67]

It was a remarkable institution. Despite its name it was not a state university, but a private corporation of professionals associated around the pre-existing College of Medicine. It resembled the *studia generalia* of the Middle Ages. Its members, governing themselves collectively and separately within their four faculties, were accountable neither to an external board of governors nor to the state government. Consequently, they could not lay claim to state support. They expected to be autonomous and self-sustaining as a proprietary business. It soon became evident that, though the 1812 charter appeared to have terminated the patronage of Maryland's Medical and Chirurgical Faculty over the medical college, members of the state medical examining board still served on the college faculty, and the new faculties remained mere appendages to the medical college.[68] Before the 1820s began, the College of Arts and Sciences managed to offer no more than a few desultory lecture series, and the divinity professors preached only occasional sermons. Instruction in law did not begin until 1823. For all practical purposes the College of Medicine was the university.[69]

Maryland thus presents a paradigm for the development of higher education in the decades after the Revolution. From an initial enthusiasm for public colleges and a public university, the people of the state backed off quite early and eventually repudiated their first state university. The elitist nature of colleges and universities had been the persistent theme of public agitation. Despite populist rhetoric, however, the counterproposals had little to do with education for the common people. Instead, after 1806 the legislature channeled the appropriations for the university colleges to the support of academies in the counties. These institutions were by no means intended to help the poor. Rather, they were seen as a means for the "middling classes" to challenge the hold of a native aristocracy on professional positions. The same intent motivated various groups to conduct collegiate ventures. We find it in evidence among the Methodists at Cokesbury and Asbury, among the multi-denominational founders of Baltimore College, and among Baltimore's Sulpician Fathers and Maryland's physicians. By 1820 collegiate and professional education in Maryland was in the hands of incorporated private trustees or regent-proprietors. Only Washington and St. John's Colleges, the two eighteenth-century survivors, received state support, and even that was on a reduced scale. In Maryland as in Virginia, Kentucky, Pennsylvania, South Carolina, and Tennessee, private academic corporations successfully challenged the traditional view that higher education was a responsibility belonging exclusively to the public. The private American college had arrived on the scene as a permanent part of American higher education.

# 15

## STATE COLLEGES AND UNIVERSITIES

Immediately after the Revolution, Americans had believed that public institutions were in the best position to imbue young men with republican principles and to prepare them for their roles as leaders of the new nation. Thus they founded state universities and state university systems in Pennsylvania, Maryland, Kentucky, New York, and Georgia. In the 1790s and later they continued similar efforts in North Carolina, Vermont, South Carolina, Tennessee, Louisiana, and Virginia. Some wanted to see traditional colleges like Harvard and Yale take on the role of state universities, though Harvard had to share its monopoly with newly chartered regional colleges in the west and north. In New Hampshire and Rhode Island the provincial colleges served as state colleges until the legislature's expropriation of the trustees of Dartmouth College turned the question of the private or public nature of colleges over to the United States Supreme Court for a resolution.

Compared to their competitors in private colleges, the spokesmen for the public institutions were essentially conservative. They took it for granted that after independence Americans would depend on a government by men of virtue and talent. When Jefferson asked John Adams whether it could not be said that "that form of government is the best which provides the most effectually for a pure selection of these natural aristoi into the offices of government,"[1] he implied that government-sponsored state colleges would assure just that "pure selection" of the natural aristocrats. For men educated in colleges that had served a highly select governing class, the view of colleges as training grounds for society's elite was accepted as a commonplace. The novelty of Jefferson's proposals lay in the insistence that virtue and talent rather than wealth and birth determine selection.

In the Southern states public universities and state university systems received their strongest backing. The first state university to open here was the University of North Carolina.[2] After an unsuccessful attempt in 1784 it was chartered in 1789 and began instruction in 1795. A child of North Carolina Federalism and home of several radical faculty members, it was unpopular in the rural areas. Its professor of humanity, the Reverend Mr. David Ker, was known as "a violent Republican," and its tutor, Charles W. Harris, announced his conversion to Mary Wollstonecraft's belief in the equality of women in intellectual pursuits.[3] With such sentiments in vogue at Chapel Hill, the university soon suffered a backlash of antirevolutionary opinion. Presbyterians like Joseph Caldwell, professor of mathematics and graduate of Princeton, compared the quiet orthodoxies of many a Presbyterian college unfavorably with the multiplicity of religious and political opinions at the University of North Carolina.

The rechartering in 1799 of Transylvania University as part of a Kentucky state system brought to Lexington quarrels and disturbances that resembled those in Chapel Hill. In the summer of 1801 they centered around the Reverend Mr. James Welsh, a staunch Presbyterian and professor of languages, whose insensitive and overbearing demeanor prompted students to ask the trustees for his dismissal. They accused him, among other things, of harassing and ridiculing students who expressed Republican or deistic sentiments. Though the trustees first supported the professor, the threat of student withdrawals persuaded them to accept his resignation.[4] Throughout the following months they denied the influence of "skeptical principles" among the students, and affirmed instead "that the grand leading Doctrines and duties of Christianity be warmly inculcated both by precept and example."[5]

Renewed conflict broke out in 1815 when another Presbyterian clergyman, the university's acting principal, James Blythe, in a sermon condemned the nation's leadership as heathen and the separation of state and church as "rocked in the cradle of French atheism."[6] Pressures built up to appoint a new president for the university and thus to terminate Blythe's tenure as acting principal.[7] The trustees stood behind Blythe, and condemned as "impudent" and "highly censurable" a set of student resolutions criticizing their support of Blythe.[8] Seventeen days later they rescinded their condemnation and adopted instead a new bylaw urging the students to "forbear from the public expression by way of resolution of their approbation or disapprobation" of actions taken by the board, president, and professors.[9] Still they retained Blythe as acting principal and voted to invite Horace Holley of Boston, Massachusetts, to become president. When subsequently it became known that Holley was a Unitarian, they revoked his election.[10] By then, however, public uneasiness over the trustees' management of the state's university had reached such proportions that the Kentucky legislature established a committee to investigate the university.

The committee condemned the board's religious and political partisanship as "an ulcer cancerous in its nature." The trustees had withdrawn the call to Holley, they stated, "not because the capacity or talents of Doctor Holley were doubted, his moral conduct reproachable, or his christian deportment called in question, but merely because it was reported that he had adopted some sentiments formerly entertained by the celebrated orator Priestly, which did not exactly quadrate with Calvinistic orthodoxy."[11] In addition, the committee reported, the "politics taught in the institution have not been pure." Faculty members had described the British constitution "as possessed of beauty and excellence," and had neglected to discuss American political institutions.

Considering the fact that in a state of over 500,000 only 3,000 were members of Presbyterian churches, it is remarkable how long the trustees persisted in their struggle against the heavily Republican legislature.[12] They did not protest the committee's recommendation to restrict the terms of trustees to two years and to elect the members biennially by a joint vote of both houses.[13] They themselves suggested that the legislature "render the institution more ostensibly a state concern" by adding the governor, the speakers of both houses, and the judges of the court of appeals as ex officio trustees.[14] In his messages of 1816 and 1817 Governor Gabriel Slaughter recommended state support to county seminaries and schools as well as to Transylvania University.[15] In March 1817 the trustees accepted the resignation of acting principal Blythe, and in November they again elected Holley president.[16] With the governor's signature on the Act Further to Regulate the Transylvania University on February 3, 1818, the original trustees were replaced with thirteen appointed members who were to serve for two years and be subject to new elections by the legislature.[17] By an overwhelming margin of 102 to 19, both houses had abolished the autonomy and self-perpetuation of the board. The liberals were now in control of the university.[18]

Georgia, too, presents the familiar picture of Presbyterians and secularists fighting over control of the university. In 1801 the trustees elected Josiah Meigs as president. Meigs was then professor of mathematics and natural philosophy at Yale and an admirer of Jefferson. He began his instruction in Athens in 1802, and did well enough under a board sympathetic to the Yale of Ezra Stiles and with a curriculum modeled after Yale's.[19] But his outspoken Republicanism did not endear him to Federalist sympathizers. As Presbyterians and other orthodox Christians began to feel uneasy over the growing number of Baptists in the state and enrollments began to decline, Meigs resigned the presidency in 1810. A year later the trustees dismissed him as professor, suspended the university's operations for a few months, and in December reopened with a Presbyterian minister at the helm. The Reverend Mr. John Brown managed to last until May 1816, and his resignation was followed by another suspension until January 1, 1817. A new president, the Reverend Robert Finley, a Presbyterian clergyman and Princeton graduate, died that same summer shortly after his inauguration. Not until 1819 did the university make a new beginning, and then its newly appointed president was again a Presbyterian. The Reverend Mr. Moses Waddel raised attendance within three years from 7 to 120 students, and he refashioned Georgia's state university in the image of a Presbyterian college.[20]

In South Carolina the College of Charleston, chartered in 1785, managed for a time to play the role of a quasi-established provincial college. On its Board of Trustees served twenty-three laymen and one minister, as well as the state's governor and lieutenant governor in an ex officio capacity. But when the state constitution of 1790 granted freedom of religion and abolished the requirement that state officials be Protestants, a new college charter removed the minister and the two ex officio officials from the board. It thus eliminated any legal connection of the college with either the state or a church.[21] The board's one minister had been the Episcopalian priest Robert Smith, who also served as principal and teacher. When in 1798 he was forced to resign as president because of his election as the Episcopal bishop of South Carolina, the school's fortunes declined. It ceased to function on its own and rented out its rooms to private teachers.[22]

It was then that the legislature chartered South Carolina College. They gave it a governing board of ex officio state officers and of lawyers and ministers nominated by the legislature. They supplied a building fund and provided for annual appropriations to pay faculty salaries.[23] Conservatives of both parties agreed to locate the college in the center of the state, and South Carolina College opened its doors in 1805. Its good fortune derived to a large extent from the state's initial refusal to sponsor a public institution and its willingness to charter Presbyterian and other colleges. When nearly all of these failed, the demand for a state university arose almost spontaneously. Federalists and Republicans, up-country democrats and low-country aristocrats joined forces and assured South Carolina College of its future. Though Episcopalians and Presbyterians dominated the state and the Board of Trustees, the college's first president was a Baptist.[24] Denominational jealousy and rivalry were happily absent. South Carolina thus constituted the exception to the rule that public institutions generally fared worse than the denominationally sponsored and community-based colleges.

Louisiana followed the familiar pattern. Up-country citizens resented the establishment of the College of New Orleans as the capstone of a public education system called the University of New Orleans. The university had been chartered by the territorial legislature in 1805. On its board of regents the governor, the judges of the superior court, the judge of the United States district court, the mayor and recorder of the city, and the council president served ex officio together with seventeen named individuals.[25] Due to opposition from up-country legislators the college did not receive its first appropriations until 1811, and by 1826 it was forced to go out of existence. The university regents, too, were abolished in 1821. The plan of a university system of public education for Louisiana was too ambitious and had failed to take into account the diverse interests of Creoles and French, Spanish, and English settlers. After 1826 other colleges were to supply the needs for higher education.

Jefferson's long-lasting endeavours on behalf of the University of Virginia illustrate most clearly the antagonism between Republicans and religious liberals favoring a public university and Presbyterians promoting their own colleges. Jefferson's initial hope to resuscitate the College of William and Mary as the state's public institution and his subsequent campaign for a new state university were revived in 1814 when the trustees of Albemarle Academy — an institution then existing on paper only — nominated him and several other Virginians to their board. When two years later the legislature incorporated the academy as a college, Jefferson helped draft its charter and laws. The charter left little question that Central College was meant to be a state institution. Its Visitors were to be appointed by the governor and were empowered to select the college officers and to fill professional professorships. Neither faculty nor trustees were incorporated but received their powers from the governor through the Visitors.[26]

Several plans for a state university were now prepared in quick succession. As president of the state literary fund, Governor Wilson C. Nichols recommended a form of university government that was remarkably similar to that at Central College.[27] Jefferson himself devised a new plan that placed the university Visitors under the control of the Board of Public Instruction.[28] Next, the Visitors of Central College offered to transfer to the state all property and rights of their institution, if the legislature were to establish a state university at the site of Central College.[29] On February 21, 1818, the legislature appropriated part of the income from the literary fund for "The University of Virginia" as soon as a board of commissioners had agreed upon a location. President and directors of the literary fund were to appoint thirteen Visitors for seven-year terms, and they were to elect one of their own as rector of the university.[30] Under the chairmanship of Jefferson the commissioners quickly agreed on the site of Central College, and listed as objectives of the university the education of statesmen, legislators, and judges. They signed their report on August 4, 1818.[31]

On January 25, 1819, the bill passed into law. It placed the university under a government of seven visitors appointed by the governor with the advice of the Council. The Visitors were to elect a rector from among themselves, and the university was to remain "in all things, and at all times . . . subject to the control of the legislature."[32] The transfer of authority from the Visitors of Central College to the Visitors of the University of Virginia was accomplished by March 1819, but several years passed before instruction got underway. On March 7, 1825, the university opened its doors to students.

With Jefferson as rector, the university at Charlottesville closely approximated the ideal type of a state university in a republican society. Students were permitted to elect their studies, and professors were challenged to devise the best and most appropriate ways and means of teaching their specialty. Only in the School of Government, comprising the study of political economy, the law of nature and nations, history, politics, and law, was Jefferson unwilling to give the faculty a free hand. Here, he wrote to his friend Joseph C. Cabell, "heresies may be taught, of so interesting a character to our own State, and to the United States, as to make it duty in us to lay down the principles which shall be taught."[33] To James Madison he wrote a year later that it was the supreme mission of the University of Virginia to keep alive "that vestal flame" of republicanism.[34] The university was to be, in effect, a secular church, independent of the state's denominations and churches, and a zealous guardian of republican political philosophy.

## Harvard and Yale: Tradition Continues

In New England's two oldest colleges traditional views of higher education as a public responsibility received new viability during the early years of the Revolution. At Yale the charter change of 1792 had brought governor, lieutenant governor, and six Council members into the Corporation in exchange for a promise of more than $40,000 in uncollected tax funds. While the ministers retained a majority and the right to elect their successors, the presence of state officials aided Yale in holding its monopoly in Connecticut until the founding of Washington, now Trinity, College in Hartford in 1823.[35] But the college paid a price for its supremacy. Its adherence to Presbyterian orthodoxy isolated it from dissenters and Republicans, and it began to feel keenly the competition for students with such newly opened institutions as the University of Vermont, and Williams, Middlebury, Union, and Hamilton colleges. As the 1820s began, Yale's curious nature as a Presbyterian state college constituted the heart of its problem.

In Massachusetts, Harvard was recognized as the state's institution in the constitution of 1780. Governor, lieutenant governor, and all the members of Council and Senate together with the college president and the ministers of the Congregational churches of six adjoining towns now constituted the Board of Overseers. The General Court reserved the right to alter the college government, and both Overseers and Corporation came increasingly under the influence of non-resident officers.[36] Professional men, state officials, and ministers, frequently members of Boston's leading families, strengthened the connections between college and community. In 1781 the Corporation declared that state financial assistance "would characterize the General Court as the encouragers of literature and be for the honor and reputation of the new constitution."[37]

Harvard was soon drawn into the state's politics. During the first decade of the new century Federalists and Unitarians came to dominate the Corporation, the Overseers, and the faculty. They reflected the politically conservative and religiously liberal temper of Boston's leadership. In 1806 the Corporation elected the Unitarian Henry Ware to the Hollis Professorship of Divinity and four years later John Thornton Kirkland, another Unitarian, to the college presidency. The Federalists, however, saw danger on the horizon. They felt threatened by the activities of Republicans in the state, and they were suspicious of the growing dissatisfaction among orthodox Congregationalists with the Unitarian character of Harvard. Thus when the Federalists took over the state's government in 1810 they passed a statute that removed the Senate and added fifteen Congregational ministers and as many laymen to the Board of Overseers. Except for its ex officio members, the Board was now self-perpetuating.[38]

The Corporation found it necessary to combine corporate autonomy with recognition as a public university. Private benefactions would help to guard against total dependence on the state, but they should not persuade the legislature to cease its appropriations. Could private funding and public protection be kept together without conflict? Partisan battles over Harvard's government returned the Senate to the Board of Overseers in 1812 when the Republicans regained power. The old board grudgingly acquiesced, "reserving to themselves and to each of them all the rights of contesting the validity of said Act."[39] In another two years a Federalist Senate and governor returned matters to the status of 1810, but then again added the Senate to the Board of Overseers, making the validity of the act dependent on the approval of Corporation and Overseers.[40] When this was given, the Federalists had restored Harvard's status as the state's university. The legislature underscored this recognition for the next ten years with an annual appropriation of $10,000, which exceeded the combined value of $3,000 each voted for Bowdoin and Williams.

Resentment and dissatisfaction began to grow among Republicans and orthodox Calvinists. If Harvard was indeed a public institution, a writer in the *Boston Patriot* said, then let all the people participate in its government. He blasted the Harvard Corporation as "a body made up of the priesthood and of lawyers . . . who make laws, confer honors, grant money, and raise it too by most extraordinary assessments, and who are anxious to teach our children what to think and how to vote, and when to act."[41] The *Patriot's* attacks rallied orthodox Calvinists and Boston's Republican voters against the city's elite of Federalists and Unitarians. They helped to preserve the requirement that the ministerial seats on the Board of Overseers be reserved for Congregational ministers and led to the defeat of a constitutional amendment to open these seats to ministers of all Christian denominations. Harvard was caught in a tug of war. Both parties wanted to keep it as a public university, the Federalists and Unitarians because they held the balance of power in the state, the Republicans and orthodox Calvinists because they hoped to gain possession of both state and college.

## New England's Regional Colleges

While Federalists and Republicans, Congregationalists and Unitarians battled each other over the government of Harvard, the challenge to the university's academic monopoly in Massachusetts was renewed in the 1790s. The trustees of Ephraim Williams's free school again sought a college charter. They called attention to the "temptations and allurements which are peculiarly incident to seaport towns" and to the "large sums of money" that could be saved by keeping boys away from Dartmouth College and Yale.[42] On June 22, 1793, they were incorporated with four additional laymen as The President and Trustees of Williams College. The charter gave the legislature the right to make future alterations and "more especially . . . [to] appoint and establish overseers or visitors, of the said College, with all necessary powers and authorities for the better aid, preservation and government thereof." The legislators committed themselves to pay £1,200 in equal installments over the next four years. In 1796 they gave the college two townships, in 1805 they added one more, and in subsequent years provided occasional grants.[43]

The chartering of Williams College and the legislature's subsequent debates about relocating the college in the center of the state demonstrated vividly the confluence of local and state interests. The people of Williamstown, vigorously resisting any move, emphasized the college's nature as a local, civic institution; the legislators, making use of their charter rights to intervene, highlighted their conception of the college as a provincial, or regional responsibility. The issue had arisen when a decline in graduation figures from thirty in 1814 to seven in 1817 prompted the Williams board in 1818 to listen to overtures of the trustees of Andover Academy to open an institution "for the classical education of indigent young men of piety and talents for the Christian ministry." The Andover trustees wanted to incorporate a theological seminary together with their Academy and Williams College in the town of Amherst.[44]

After some hesitation the Williams trustees expressed their readiness to consider a move to Northampton, but the Andover trustees declined. The Massachusetts legislature, responding to petitions from the people of Williamstown and the western border areas of the state, refused to give its consent for the move.[45] The legislators agreed with the petitioners that private donations depended on the inviolability of chartered rights, which included the permanency of the Williamstown location. They also brushed aside as specious arguments that the opening of Hamilton College and Union College in New York and the University of Vermont and Middlebury College had deprived Williams College of students. By February of 1820 both houses had overwhelmingly endorsed a committee recommendation that Williams College remain in Williamstown.[46] The town had won its case; and the legislature had demonstrated its ability not only to take responsibility for the public university at Cambridge, but also to assert its role in the joint administration of local and regional colleges.

At roughly the same time as the incorporation of Williams College in western Massachusetts, similar attempts were begun to charter a separate regional college for the district of Maine. On February 7, 1788, the *Cumberland Gazette* proposed to charter a college with a governmental system modeled on that of Harvard. There was to be a corporation consisting of a chancellor, a president, a treasurer, professors and tutors, as well as a board of overseers composed of the members of the corporation, the governor and his Council, and the ministers of seven adjoining towns. The college was to be "equally open to people of every class and denomination" and to serve especially "the poorer classes in the community." Later in the year the associated Congregational ministers of Cumberland County and the county's justices of the peace sent similar petitions to the General Court.

On March 2, 1791, the Senate received a bill to incorporate the seventeen trustees of Maine College, "a majority of whom shall be lay men." The bill stated in very general terms that the college should enjoy all "the advantages, privileges, immunities, franchises, and exemptions" granted to Harvard College, and that it was to submit its accounts to the Massachusetts legislature "once in every seven years." In he summer of 1794 a joint committee of both houses unanimously reported in favor of Brunswick as the location, and on June 24, governor and legislature approved the Bowdoin charter.[47] The document established two corporations, one to consist of no more than thirteen and no fewer than seven persons, including the college president; the other to be staffed by the president and the secretary of the trustees together with twenty-eight named laymen and fourteen named clergymen. These Overseers had the right to elect their own successors and to endorse most elections of personnel and decisions pertaining to college property and finances. The legislature, however, reserved the right to "grant any further powers to, or alter, limit, annul or restrain any of the powers by this Act vested in the said Corporation, as shall be judged necessary to promote the best interest of the said college."[48] The legislators looked upon Bowdoin as a public institution, granted it land in the charter and in special acts of 1804, 1806, and 1808, and, together with Harvard and Williams, included it in an annual state subsidy.[49]

As the century's second decade drew to a close and the separation of Maine from Massachusetts seemed likely to become a reality, the friends of Bowdoin began to worry whether the college would continue to receive state subsidies once the heavily Federalist legislature in Boston had been exchanged for a predominantly Democratic assembly in the new state. Maine Federalists were reluctant to see the new legislature succeed to the reserve powers the Massachusetts house held over the college. Through the help of friends in Massachusetts they sought to block the Maine legislature from altering the college charter. This they did by adopting on October 19, 1819, an act that subsequently became part of the Maine constitution. It assured the continuing validity of grants of land, franchises, and immunities made before the separation of Maine from Massachusetts, "except by judicial process, according to the principles of law."[50] This act could be modified or annulled only by agreement of the legislatures of Maine and Massachusetts.

Despite their best efforts, the Maine Federalists were quickly outmaneuvered by the Democrats. Through a provision in the new constitution the Democrats did not so much defeat Bowdoin's defenses as erect an effective checkmate. Article VIII prohibited any legislative endowment or grant to any literary institution "unless, at the time of making such endowment, the legislature of the State shall have the right to grant any further powers to alter, limit, or restrain any of the powers vested in any such literary institution as shall be judged necessary to promote the best interests thereof."[51] Bowdoin's trustees could govern their college without legislative interference and forgo any grant of state funds, or they would have to accept the likelihood of state aid together with alterations in their rights. They chose money over independence. Their request for financial aid was warmly supported by a joint committee of the Maine legislature and favorably decided by both houses when trustees and Overseers consented to allow the legislature the right to "alter, limit, or restrain any of the powers vested in the institution."[52] A persuasive stimulus had been a legislative charter and financial grant for a medical school to be established under the control of Bowdoin College. In June of 1820 the legislatures of both Massachusetts and Maine consented to alterations in the Bowdoin College charter of 1794, and in the spring of 1821 the Maine Assembly enacted a revised charter increasing the number of trustees and Overseers.[53] These new members were Democrats. Their addition gave the board a bipartisan flavor and, for the next decade, much needed stability to the college and protection against outside interference.

In January 1812 several Baptist associations attempted to found a college in northern Massachusetts. These endeavors resulted in a bill to incorporate the president, fellows, and trustees of the Maine Literary and Theological College. The bill was lost when the house rejected an amendment giving the legislature the power to alter and annul the charter and prohibiting a majority of the corporation from belonging to the same denomination. Undaunted, the Baptists tried again in the next session. This time the prohibition against a majority of the corporation was omitted, though the legislature's annulment powers remained. But now the bill excluded the fellows from the corporation and deprived them of the right to confer degrees. The bill as passed on February 27, 1813, established an academy, called the Maine Literary and Theological Institution.[54] The Baptists still did not have a college.

When the state of Maine came into existence in 1820 the Baptist academy had been open for classes at Waterville for nearly two years. "Though under the direction principally of one denomination," the trustees had written, it was "nevertheless open to persons of every religious sect." The school was an institution in which "the means of acquiring a liberal education should be made accessible to the middling classes of citizens as well as the more opulent." They formally requested the right to open a college with the power of bestowing academic degrees.[55]

The Maine legislature did not hesitate to grant the petition, and only added clauses prohibiting discrimination against trustees and students on the basis of religion. Eight months later, in February 1821, the name of the Maine Literary and Theological Institution was officially changed to Waterville College.[56] When by 1820 Maine's legislature granted an annual subsidy of $1,000 for a period of seven years, Waterville College — later to be known as Colby College — began its career as Maine's second regional institution.[57] The Baptists were in control at Waterville, and the Congregationalists at Bowdoin, but neither school was formally affiliated with or dependent on its parent church. Both were public regional colleges in the tradition of the provincial colleges of the colonial period.

# 16

## NOVUS ORDO COLLEGIORUM

A new configuration of American higher education began to evolve in the aftermath of revolution and the battle for independence. In the established provincial colleges an initial enthusiasm for professional studies and belles lettres had set in motion ambitious planning for new state universities and state university systems, but the spontaneous appearance of new colleges under private sponsorship proved to be the far more significant long-range result. It represented, in J. Willard Hurst's felicitous phrase, a "release of energy."[1] In higher education as in other areas of life this energy derived from the pent-up hopes and expectations to promote settlements and develop the land stretching out before the settlers in the West. Colleges were to play an instrumental role, and the result was something new in higher education, a pattern of public and private colleges, in competition with each other and developing side by side. The newer institutions served essentially local and diverse interests and this supplemented the public colleges and universities in their traditional role as shapers of a country's professional leaders, politicians, and statesmen.

As this pattern emerged legislatures and courts were called upon to keep order, clarify definitions, and arbitrate the many disputes that arose. While state legislatures bore the brunt of these efforts, state courts were called upon in two important instances. In Virginia, John Bracken, the former master of the grammar school of the College of William and Mary, protested his 1779 dismissal by the college Visitors. He filed suit in 1787, alleging that the Visitors had violated the college charter. The Virginia Court of Appeals rejected Bracken's contention and denied a writ of mandamus "on the merits." The judges noted that the Visitors had acted within their charter rights, and that it was not necessary for the court to rule on a question that, to their minds, was tangential to "the merits" of the case. Bracken, however, was not so easily put off, and in 1797 filed a second suit for recovery of his salary. He lost this suit also on appeal.[2]

The interest of the case lies in the remarks of the court's president. Edmund Pendleton emphasized that Bracken had lost his first case on the merits, not on the strength of the reasoning of his opponent's counsel, John Marshall, the future Chief Justice of the United States. Marshall took issue with the Jeffersonian notion of the college as a civil corporation. Citing numerous English cases he affirmed the College of William and Mary as an eleemosynary corporation under the exclusive supervisory jurisdiction of its Visitors.[3] There was, in short, no relief to be had from a legitimate exercise of visitatorial authority. But had this authority been exercised legitimately? Was the College of William and Mary an eleemosynary corporation? John Taylor, attorney for Bracken, thought not. Disputing Marshall's claim, he said that the college was "a corporation for public government, and whose proceedings must therefore be subject to the control of this Court. It has a right to a member of the Assembly."[4] The judges on the Court of appeals favored Taylor's view, but declined to rule on the issue. Had they done so, they would have had to acknowledge the court's power to issue a writ of mandamus to inquire into the action of the Visitors. They would then have come to the same conclusion and also have held that, on the merits of the case, the Visitors had acted within their rights. John Marshall, in other words, did not need the argument for the college as an eleemosynary corporation in order to win his case. For a verdict "on the merits" it was immaterial whether the college was a charitable or a civil corporation. In refusing to speak on that question the judges left the issue as clouded as before.

The second case came before the Supreme Court of North Carolina. In that state a heavily Republican legislature had become increasingly irritated over the "aristocrats" at the university and the self-perpetuating Federalist trustees, and repealed and declared void two acts. The first, passed in 1789, had assigned to the university all lands that had or would escheat to the state; the second, enacted in 1794, had granted to the institution all unsold confiscated Tory lands.[5] When in 1800 all escheated or yet unsold confiscated lands had been returned to the state, the university's sources of income were effectively blocked. The trustees filed suit to recover the lands escheated before the repealing act had been passed, and in the November term of 1805 won a judgment in the North Carolina Court of Conference in Raleigh.[6]

In its decision the court based its argument on the North Carolina Bill of Rights, which protected any person against seizure of his liberty and property without due process of law. It recognized the university as a person in law, and it addressed itself to the question left unanswered in Pennsylvania in the 1780s. Could a state legislature interfere with the property rights of a college corporation? The Bill of Rights and the common law, the court said, answered no. But the university claimed more. Its establishment had been decreed directly by the people of the state in their constitution, and the legislature, in chartering it, had only acted in accordance with the constitutional mandate. Thus, concluded the university's attorney, the university "stands upon the same basis as the Legislature itself does." The court agreed: "We view this corporation as standing on higher grounds than any other aggregate corporation; it is not only protected by the common law, but sanctioned by the constitution."[7]

Few American colleges and universities, however, were established by constitutional mandate, and since the decision was specifically based on the North Carolina Bill of Rights, it was of limited immediate value to institutions in other states. In addition, the legislature appropriated to itself the power of electing the trustees, and the University of North Carolina remained under heavy legislative oversight. Still, the principle of judicial review had been recognized, and the university's dependence on the legislature was no longer total.

Elsewhere in the new states, colleges and universities encountered hostile legislatures without the assistance of courts of law. The experiences of Yale and of the College of Philadelphia remained typical. In what has been called "Virginia's Dartmouth College Case," the Virginia legislature attempted to transform Liberty Hall Academy into the College of Washington without considering the wishes of the trustees.[8] The occasion was President Washington's surprise gift of one hundred shares of stock in the James River Company and the trustees' decision, in acknowledgement of the gift, to rename their seminary Washington Academy. Ignoring the trustees' protestations, the Assembly, on December 21, 1796, ordered Liberty Hall Academy to be "erected into a college" of four schools, each one with a professor and as many tutors as necessary. The Assembly also appointed a board of self-perpetuating Visitors that included the governor serving ex officio, but not a single clergyman.[9] The trustees denounced the legislative act as "an unjustifiable infringement of the rights of the corporation of Liberty Hall and an instance of tyrannical imposition in the legislature." They pointed out that in their haste the legislators had not bothered to repeal or annul the academy charter, and that the trustees therefore would continue to function as an academy board. They resolved to resist the confiscation of their property and to consider themselves "culpable if we suffer it tamely to be taken from us."[10] In this they received the support of colleagues at the College of Hampden-Sydney, and on January 19, 1798, were gratified to hear of the Assembly's repeal of the act of 1796. Washington Academy continued under its old charter until in 1813 the trustees themselves requested that the legislature change the academy into a college.[11]

Six years later a similar clash occurred in Tennessee when the legislature on October 25, 1803, tried to raise the trustees of Davidson Academy near Nashville to collegiate status.[12] Here, too, the trustees first protested, the legislators repealed their act, and subsequently the trustees reconsidered their refusal to accept incorporation as a college.[13] The occasion for the reversal was a Congressional land cession to Tennessee on the condition that the state establish county academies and two colleges.[14] The Davidson trustees asked that the property and funds of their academy be merged with the newly chartered Cumberland College. When this was done on September 11, 1806, the trustees had won their point.[15] They had preserved their autonomy from legislative interference, and they had received their college charter upon their own terms.

In New York, finally, the trustees of Columbia College turned back a legislative move of 1807 to deprive them of their right to elect their successors. This they did with the help of the Council of Revision, a quasi-judicial body created to check the constitutionality of state legislation. The Council declared that it was "a sound principle in free governments, and one which has received frequent confirmation by the acts of the Legislature, that charters of incorporation, whether granted for private or local, or charitable, or literary or religious purposes, were not to be affected without due process of law, or without the consent of the parties concerned."[16] The trustees were vindicated in their determination to defend their charter against unilateral changes by the legislature.

## Public-Private Competition in Vermont

With the emergence of the private colleges, pressures were felt in the states to cut the support for older provincial institutions and the new state universities. Vermont presents a particularly revealing example. Here John Wheelock had lost his ambitious struggle to make Dartmouth College a state university. When in 1789 Ira Allen subscribed £4000 for a state university on condition that it be located in Burlington, the legislature chartered the University of Vermont on November 3, 1791. Seventeen trustees were to serve on the governing board, among them the governor, the speaker of the house, and the university's president ex officio. They were to be joined by a clergyman of the Baptists, the Episcopalians, the Congregationalists, and the Quakers, and by six gentlemen of secular occupations.[17]

Little was accomplished in the next decade. The trustees quarreled with General Allen over his desire to have the university named after him, and they applied for the land rights of the Society for the Propagation of the Gospel. The legislature, however, passed these on to the county grammar schools.[18] Then, toward the end of the century, Yale's President Timothy Dwight visited the incorporated trustees of the Addison County Grammar School in Middlebury, who subsequently petitioned the legislature for a college charter. In response, the university trustees, in October 1800, elected Daniel Clarke Sanders as university president. Sanders, a Unitarian clergyman and Harvard graduate who had been teaching boys and girls of a preparatory school in Burlington, commenced instruction at the University of Vermont. The legislature wasted no time either and on November 1, 1800, a few days after the university had opened, incorporated The President and Fellows of Middlebury College. These men constituted a self-perpetuating board of sixteen men on which there were no ex officio members. They immediately began a collegiate program with five freshmen and two sophomores. They celebrated their first commencement in 1802, conferring one bachelor's degree and one master's degree to a graduate of Yale College. In Burlington the university bestowed its first bachelor's degrees to four of its graduates in 1804. Local competition had produced results.[19]

As the new century got under way the state of Vermont was host to two collegiate institutions. The university was established as a modern provincial college, replacing the eighteenth-century toleration with preferment policy with a concept of equitable cooperation of the various denominations. This liberal policy had been promoted in Burlington by Samuel Williams, Harvard graduate and Hollis Professor of Mathematics at his alma mater from 1780 to 1788. Williams had written that it was "not barely *toleration*, but *equality*, which the people aim[ed] at," and that the people of Vermont were determined "to leave to every man a full and perfect liberty to follow the dictates of his own conscience."[20] The supporters of Middlebury College, President Dwight of Yale among them, by contrast viewed Williams's philosophy as anti-Christian, dangerous to the morals of students, and conducive only to clamor, confusion, and chaos. They wanted the college to be firmly rooted in the soil of Presbyterian or Congregational orthodoxy. Like many of the Presbyterian colleges of the South, Middlebury College had begun as an academy. Its Corporation represented community interests and the town's Congregational Society, to whom the university's scheme of management appeared imprudent. Asa Burton, the Congregational clergyman on the university's original board, reported that whenever the board met for business "we were afraid of each other, and there was no harmony and unity of design." Burton thought no better of President Sanders, "who should be so lax in sentiment as to favor one sect no more than another." He was "the most unfit person they [the board] could well have appointed." This state of affairs, wrote Burton, prompted the adoption of a plan to erect a college in Middlebury.[21]

But there were other dimensions to this conflict than the clash between state university ideology and private college philosophy and the disaffections of orthodox Congregationalists. One concerns the differences between Unitarian Harvard and Presbyterian Yale, between liberalism and orthodoxy. Through Samuel Williams and David Clarke Sanders the university was linked to Cambridge, whereas Middlebury, having received its decisive counsel from Timothy Dwight, drew its first two presidents, Jeremiah Atwater and Henry Davis, from New Haven. Then there was the rivalry between Middlebury and Burlington. Many citizens in Middlebury saw in the availability of academic buildings and the inactivity of the university trustees an opportunity to exercise control and surpass Burlington.[22] If graduation figures can be taken as an index of success or failure in this competition, then Middlebury must be handed the prize. Between 1804 and 1820 there were 314 bachelor's degrees awarded at the college, whereas in

Burlington the university granted 103 such degrees. The Yale tradition of a religiously "safe" college, made safer yet by its independence of direct state influence, and strengthened by community backing—Middlebury residents had provided most of the library and the philosophical apparatus—showed the precariousness of the state university's dependence on the legislature. In Vermont as elsewhere a college fared better when it relied on local support rather than on the state.

Developments in the century's second decade only heightened the sense of precariousness felt by trustees worried by low enrollments and lack of funds. In August of 1810 they and the legislature worked out a charter amendment and raised the number of board members to eighteen. As in North Carolina, all future vacancies on the board were to be filled by a joint ballot of both houses, and the terms of the trustees were fixed at three years.[23] A few months later the trustees adopted new by-laws that ordered the president to hold worship services in the university chapel every Sunday.[24] By taking the students out of the local churches they hoped to pursue a policy of deliberate neutrality toward the Burlington churches and thereby to lay greater claim to legislative support.

President Sanders's position was difficult, since he was opposed not only by "rigid" Congregationalists but also by Republicans. As a Harvard Federalist, he felt uneasy about the support he received from those Republicans in the legislature and among the university trustees who shared his liberal religious views though they disagreed with him in politics. One of them, Sanders wrote President Kirkland of Harvard, had attacked him "chiefly on account of political opinions," and since he, Sanders, was "almost the only Federalist who has not already been made a sacrifice," he felt his dependence on the Republicans in university matters "too great to be pleasant." Besides, reported Sanders, his salary was in arrears, and he had begun looking for more promising employment elsewhere. The presidency of a state university in a society rent by religious and political divisions was not a bed of roses. With a sigh Sanders told President Kirkland that although opposed by rigid Congregationalists in religion and by Republicans in politics "I have still persevered, zealously 'contending for the faith once delivered to the saints'."[25]

Throughout the 1810s the university languished. The war of 1812 brought military occupation and cessation of instruction from March 1813 to September 1815. A legislative committee report cited the handicaps: indebtedness to the faculty, a drop in real estate values, and dispersal of the students.[26] President Sanders resigned in 1814, and in 1817 another committee raised the specter of withdrawing the legislature's support altogether by suggesting the repeal of the 1810 charter.[27] The desperate position of the university comes into focus most vividly when one compares its faculty and enrollments with those at Middlebury College. At Burlington there were the president, four professors, one tutor, and 28 students; at Middlebury the president had charge of five professors, two tutors, and 90 students.[28]

The university trustees, however, were in no mood to give up the fight. Undaunted by repeated attempts of Middlebury College to obtain state funding[29] and scornful of suggestions to merge the two institutions,[30] they reminded the legislators that the state had assured the university that it "would be the only institution of the kind in the state." A second chartered college, the trustees added, could "rise only upon the ruins of the university."[31] They were determined to keep on fighting the battle for a public university.

### New York and Ohio: Colleges on the Northern Frontier

In the frontier areas of New York and Ohio a pattern of college development emerged that was to become characteristic for the midwestern states prior to the Civil War. In almost every case opportunistic college founders and promoters responded to local interests, ignored doctrinal distinctions in order not to endanger financial, material, or personal support, and actively sought and accepted state aid and control. Under these circumstances it becomes meaningless for the historian to insist on sharp distinctions among denominational, community, and private colleges. Colleges related to churches or denominations often were tied more closely to their locality than to their church, and community colleges, though often incorporated and funded initially by civic groups, viewed themselves as public institutions. Difficult, precarious, and uncertain as existence was for the presidents, teachers, and students in these colleges, they relied on the promise that somewhere on the outside there was a band of supporters — however small, however impecunious, however fickle — who were committed to the college by bonds of common faith and economic interest.[32] That was more than the spokesmen for the state universities could claim.

Union College in New York presents a good example of a college first created through the efforts of several civic and one denominational group and then, in exchange for legislative patronage, transformed into a public institution. Together with the citizens of Schenectady the inhabitants of the state's northern counties approached the legislature in August 1779 to ask for the incorporation of a college.[33] Governor Clinton responded by authorizing the incorporation of the Trustees of Clinton College in Schenectady. The board was to consist of the governor serving ex officio and thirty-two trustees.[34] The college, however, remained a paper project, and a second attempt, made three years later, failed also. Then, in 1785 Dirck Romeyn, the pastor of Schenectady's Dutch Reformed church, dissatisfied with the faltering efforts of Queen's College in New Jersey, persuaded his church to sponsor and support an academy in Schenectady. After several unsuccessful attempts to receive land or incorporation, the regents incorporated the institution as "The Academy of the Town of Schenectady" in 1793.[35]

When the trustees petitioned for a college charter two years later they encountered competition from a similar academy in Albany. The regents were slow to decide between the two. Hoping to win stronger support from the Dutch Reformed congregation, the Schenectady supporters dropped a provision prohibiting the majority of the trustees to come from any one denomination and preventing the institution's president and its professors from accepting a pastoral charge. But they held fast to the proposition that the college be a community venture rather than a denomination-sponsored school.[36] Their strategy worked, and the regents incorporated Union College on February 25.[37] The academy property was transferred to the college trustees, and John Blair Smith, the new college's first president, stated in his inaugural that "men of diverse religious convictions, having set aside faction and division, are united in governing this institution and in spreading the benefits of the college, which is auspiciously called Union College."[38]

Subsequent events in the history of Union College before 1820 emphasize its public character. By 1804 financial contributions from private sources amounted to $42,000, but the state's various grants added up to $78,100.[39] President Eliphalet Nott began his sixty-two-year career as Union's president by obtaining authorization to raise $80,000 in state-controlled lotteries in exchange for the trustees' charter right to self-perpetuation. The state's chancellor, secretary, comptroller, treasurer, attorney-general, and surveyor-general, as well as the five justices of the Supreme Court, all serving ex officio, were added to the board. Its sitting members were gradually to be reduced to ten, and thereafter their successors were to be chosen by the New York Regents.[40] In 1814 Nott repeated this offer and won a lottery authorization of $200,000. Thanks to his formidable skills of persuasion and maneuvering there was at least one local college of which it could be said that its determined drive to throw itself at the mercy of a legislature had paid off handsomely.[41]

A quite different story has to be told of New York's Hamilton College on the Mohawk River. Like so many of the private colleges in the South, Hamilton began as a Presbyterian academy. It was founded by the Reverend Mr. Samuel Kirkland, a missionary among the Indians who had been educated at Eleazar Wheelock's school at Lebanon, Connecticut, and had graduated from Princeton College. His original plan, not unlike Wheelock's, had been to found a school for the education of Indian and white boys together. In January 1793 the Regents granted his petition for an academy in Herkimer County. Nineteen years later they incorporated twenty-four trustees to receive property of the Hamilton-Oneida Academy and to govern the institution as a college. The charter contained the usual phrases against discrimination on grounds of religion, and it established the trustees as a self-perpetuating board without ex officio members. The college's first president, Azel Backus, was a New Light Presbyterian from Yale and a Federalist. "For more than seventy years," states the official history of the college, "every principal and teacher in the academy and every president of the college, with one exception, was a graduate of Yale."[42] Like Middlebury in Vermont, Hamilton clung to its independence from state support and control and showed no inclination to imitate the course pursued by its sister institution in Schenectady.

Further west, the early history of Ohio University demonstrated once more the conflicting pulls of state university and private college. The roots of the university reach back to a contract drawn in 1787 for the Ohio Company by the Reverend Manasseh Cutler in negotiations with the Congress of the Confederacy. By 1799, when the advancing tide of white settlement justified the surveying of university lands in the vicinity of what is now Athens, Cutler drafted a charter for the "American University." Its board was to be self-perpetuating, and neither ecclesiastical nor secular officials were permitted to serve ex officio.[43] But when on January 9, 1802, the territorial legislature incorporated the "American Western University," it reserved the right to fill any vacancies on the Board of Trustees and to "grant any further and greater powers . . . or alter, limit or restrain any of the powers" given to the Corporation.[44] No action was taken, however, and a second charter was issued by the new state of Ohio on February 18, 1804. The state this time omitted the reserve clauses, but now placed the governor as ex officio member on the board, and gave the legislature the right to fill vacancies among the trustees.[45] While Ohio University thus was severely limited in its independence, it functioned for all intents and purposes like a private college. Its early presidents and all of its faculty members before 1843 were members of the Presbyterian church.[46]

Like Ohio University, Miami University traced its origins to a Congressional land grant. On February 17, 1809, the Ohio legislature incorporated a president and fourteen trustees, who were permitted to fill vacancies subject to the subsequent approval of the legislature. Again, the legislators reserved the right to grant additional and greater powers, and to alter, limit, or restrict the existing ones. The war of 1812, however, delayed construction and opening, and the first students enrolled in a preparatory school in 1818. By 1821 the school was forced to suspend its operations, and only by 1824 did a four-year collegiate department get under way. Two years later, twelve graduates were awarded their first bachelor's degrees.[47] As at Ohio University, legislative demands to supervise the college and denominational moves to assert Presbyterian dominance were in conflict. Though Miami University was created "by the Federal Congress and established by the State of Ohio, it could not have been more Presbyterian if funded by John Knox," wrote Walter Havighurst.[48] Of its eighteen board members five were of unknown religious affiliation, three were Baptists, and ten were Presbyterian or of Scottish ancestry.[49]

Community ventures in collegiate education made their first appearance in the Ohio valley in Cincinnati. An association of private citizens called for subscriptions for a college, promoted a lottery, and on January 23, 1807, received a charter from the legislature. Forty-nine incorporated persons and their associates were annually to elect nine trustees and necessary officers for one-year terms, and those elected were to carry on the business of the college. But the college never became a reality. The depression of 1807 and the loss of the college building in a tornado in 1809 forced the Corporation to give up its plan for establishing the University of Cincinnati.[50]

Plans were resurrected ten years later when a Lancasterian school, begun in 1815, gave promise of successful transformation into a college.

Again subscriptions were advertised and, on January 22, 1819, the state legislature granted a charter for Cincinnati College. Twenty trustees were incorporated to be annually elected by the shareholders of the Corporation. They were authorized to "cause the principles of morality and of the christian religion to be included but the religious tenets that may be peculiar to any particular sect or denomination, shall never be taught or enforced in the college." The college opened its doors in November 1819 with Elijah Slack, a Princeton graduate, as president and with three professors and a tutor. Here, too, the Presbyterians were the dominant group. In 1821 President Slack could bestow the first three bachelor's degrees on his graduates, but after four more years of reasonably successful operations, economic conditions again forced the college to close.[51]

In the center of the state near Columbus a similar community venture into collegiate education resulted in the incorporation on February 8, 1819, of Worthington College. Here the institution grew out of a previously existing academy, and its supporters were largely members of the local Protestant Episcopal church. College board members were to serve three-year terms, and their successors were to be elected by the subscribers and donors. Worthington College appears to have been unable to attract students, and the trustees offered their charter and building to the Reformed Medical College of Ohio. This group accepted the proposal and the school opened in December of 1830 as the Medical Department of Worthington College.[52]

The early collegiate ventures in Ohio suffered primarily from the unsettled conditions of the country, and from the intense local rivalries in promoting colleges and universities as a means of economic development. It made little difference whether, as with Ohio University and Miami University, the college derived its original stimulus from the federal government through the Northwest Ordinance, or whether, as in Cincinnati and at Worthington, it embodied the hopes and ambitions of municipal promoters. The chances of survival were equally precarious. Of the four institutions, Ohio University and Cincinnati College opened their doors before 1820, and only Ohio University bestowed degrees. In three of the four institutions Presbyterians were in command; the fourth in Worthington was an Episcopal creation. Whether or not state officials were ex officio on the boards did not appear to have made any appreciable difference in the day-to-day administration of the school or in its ability to survive. Nor did the fact that the legislators had reserved the right to alter the charters at Ohio and Miami universities help or hinder the institutions or diminish in any way the strongly Presbyterian influence. In the new country in the West questions of legal control were of minor importance. In Ohio, certainly, the state legislature paid little attention to the institutions of higher education. The source of all initiatives was the desire of religious and economic interest groups to extend their influence. The criterion of success or failure lay in the trustees' ability to raise funds from various sources.

# 17

## DARTMOUTH COLLEGE:
## THE SUPREME COURT SPEAKS

Rivalry, competition, legal and financial insecurity, and seemingly unbounded enthusiasm and energy characterized American higher education in the late 1810s. Colleges were to grow with the country, share its chaotic and spontaneous development, and lend respectability and staying power to an otherwise restless and often transient population. Such a conception of a college was a far cry from the traditional understanding of a university as a central authority whose purpose was to train a provincial governing elite, to help fashion public policy, and to set standards of taste and morality. As they spread out along the western and northern edge of settlement, the new colleges inevitably lost in traditional moral and intellectual authority what they gained through their closeness to the more immediate needs of a frontier population. Under these circumstances many asked, Was a college still a college?

To answer that question and to define the nature, rights, and obligations of a college necessitates a review of the institution's charter, as the battles at Yale, the College of Philadelphia, Liberty Hall in Virginia, Davidson in Tennessee, and Columbia College in New York have shown. The final and decisive controversy of this kind took place in New Hampshire and involved Dartmouth College. In essence this case did not differ from its predecessors. It, too, revolved around a legislative challenge to a college charter. But in finding its way from the Superior Court of New Hampshire into the United States Supreme Court it assumed direct precedential value for all subsequent cases of a similar nature. The decision in this case became the law of the land.[1]

In *The Trustees of Dartmouth College versus Woodward*, Chief Justice John Marshall ruled that the charter of Dartmouth College was a contract in the meaning of the United States Constitution, and that any impairment of its obligations was a violation of the Constitution. Dartmouth College was a private, rather than a public, foundation, and the legislature could not alter or revoke the college charter without judicial proceedings. That Dartmouth College was a private corporation was not to be understood as a result of a priori assumptions or historical traditions that affected all colleges alike. Marshall recognized from a review of the charter "that the funds of the college consisted entirely of private donations." He held that while the Earl of Dartmouth and other English trustees were the largest contributors, "the legal conclusion, from the facts recited in the charter, would probably be, that Dr. [Eleazer] Wheelock was the founder of the college." Dartmouth College, said John Marshall was "an eleemosynary, and so far as respects its funds, a private corporation." He distinguished it from a civil institution whose employees might be public officials and whose funds, given by the government, were subject to legislative management.[2] In thus acknowledging that colleges could claim judicial protection under their charters as private corporations, existing side by side with the public state colleges and universities, John Marshall laid the legal basis for the two-pronged system of American higher education.

The historical significance of the Dartmouth College decision for American higher education is to be found in Marshall's rejection of the notion that degree-granting institutions were necessarily chartered as publicly funded civil corporations. This assumption, commonly held in the seventeenth and eighteenth centuries, reached back to the beginnings of the universities in the Middle Ages. It had been confirmed during the Reformation when colleges and universities, like the territorial churches, became established institutions in their respective kingdom, principality, or province. In the colonies, where private surplus wealth was in short supply, colleges were aided through grants of public lands as well as through authorization of public lotteries and fund drives at home and abroad. While private donors to the colleges were known in the New and the Old World, the colonial colleges functioned as provincial institutions, and their governors seldom hesitated to appeal to public authorities for support and protection.

The crux of the matter rested with the institutions' right to grant degrees. In England this right had been bestowed on the publicly funded civil corporations of the universities in Oxford and Cambridge, not on the privately endowed charitable college corporations. Yet outside of England colleges were sometimes founded as arts faculties with the right to grant degrees in the hope that the professional faculties would be added later. Such foundations — Trinity College in Dublin or some of the *gymnasia illustria* on the continent are examples — were seen as "mothers of universities." In time these appeared in the New World also. The College of William and Mary, for example, had been granted the university privilege of representation in the Virginia House of Burgesses, and the 1775 plans for the American University in the province of New York had included a corresponding right for King's College. Seen in this light, the American colonial colleges appeared as civil corporations like the universities of England. Their inability to house and board teachers and students and provide for them an incorporated self-governing and financially independent fellowship strengthened that appearance and diminished any presumed likeness to an English university college. Their chartered right to grant degrees then clinched the argument that they were civil corporations.

In his decision in the Dartmouth case John Marshall pushed aside the historical foundations of this argument and considered contemporary economic developments. An inherited English classification of corporations into civil and eleemosynary that assigned private initiatives to charity and treated corporate investment in economic enterprise as essentially public business ill served the country's needs. Post-revolutionary America demanded incentives for capital to invest in expansion and development. Though in the past turnpike, canal, and bridge companies had been viewed as civil corporations performing a public service, they now were considered private businesses shielded from government interference. Marshall took these views of corporate enterprise and applied them to the colleges. Citing the Charter House decision of 1612 in which it was said that "he who gives . . . [the first gift of the revenues] is the founder in law,"[3] Marshall decided the question of Dartmouth College's nature as a private or public corporation by looking to the private source of its original funds rather than to the public purpose for which it was established.

## Who Governs a College?

In 1819 it was hardly possible to view the Dartmouth case with the historical significance it would assume in subsequent decades. In Hanover, New Hampshire, it was very much a local, at most a state, issue that involved the community's educational, religious, and political life. The original question facing the college had been a simple one: who was to govern on campus, the president or the trustees?[4] That such a pointed and limited question on a remote college campus should bring in its train matters of fundamental constitutional import should not surprise anyone who has perceived the reflection of the nation's destiny in the changing realm of college campuses. Not only do legislators, reformers, and rebels turn our colleges and universities into laboratories for national life-and-death issues; but the campuses themselves, far from being ivory-tower retreats, also generate and present problems society has to solve. In much the same way, a campus quarrel at Hanover, New Hampshire, set the stage for the discussion and legal determination of national policy.

The controversy began with a dispute between President John Wheelock and the college trustees over the appointment of the professor of divinity, the students' attendance at chapel and local churches, and the divinity professor's services to neighboring congregations. It reached a climax when the trustees fired Wheelock in 1815, and they in turn were accused by Wheelock and others of irresponsibility, illiberalism, and "unbridled aristocracy."[5] In terms reminiscent of the Pennsylvania constitutionalists of the 1780s, Elijah Parish, a Wheelock supporter, lashed the trustees as an *"imperium in imperio,"* and warned that they would "soon become an organized aristocracy, extending its influence with hallowed pretensions under a Sectarian banner."[6] These attacks soon mobilized the Republicans, who called for legislative intervention. Now lines of battle began to be drawn around political issues involving questions of college government and religious loyalties. The dismissal of Wheelock was portrayed as a Federalist criticism of Republican demands for democratic control of higher education. When the Republicans won in the spring elections of 1816 the issue emerged in its classical form. What degree of autonomy could a college claim from interference in its affairs by the legislature?

The newly elected Governor William Plumer, a friend of Thomas Jefferson's, believed wholeheartedly in the obligation of colleges to respond to the people's needs. He had little sympathy for classical curricula and for colleges as retreats for the training of an aristocratic elite. He preferred practical training in agriculture, mechanical arts, and commerce. In previous legislative sessions he had favored the maintenance of the public interest by inserting reserve power clauses into corporate charters. In his inaugural address of June 6, 1816, he attacked the principle of self-perpetuating trustee government at Dartmouth College as "hostile to the spirit and genius of a free government," and he urged the legislature to alter the Dartmouth charter.[7] The legislative investigating committee seconded his views. They refused to blame either President Wheelock or the trustees for the difficulties at the college, and pointed to the charter instead. They, too, recommended that it be changed.[8] From Virginia arrived a message of support:

> The idea that institutions established for the use of the nation cannot be touched nor modified, even to make them answer their end, because of rights gratuitously supposed in those employed to manage them in trust for the public, may perhaps be a salutary provision against the abuses of a monarch, but is most absurd against the nation itself. Yet our lawyers and priests generally inculcate this doctrine, and suppose that preceding generations held the earth more freely than we do; had a right to impose laws on us, unalterable by ourselves, and that we, in like manner, can make laws and impose burdens on future generations, which they will have no right to alter; in fine, that the earth belongs to the dead and not to the living.[9]

Jefferson stood with Plumer on the side of the living.

Matters then proceeded quickly. On June 27 Governor Plumer signed a bill transforming the Trustees of Dartmouth College into the Trustees of Dartmouth University, increased their number to twenty-one, and added a board of twenty-five Overseers with the power to confirm, disapprove, or veto proceedings of the trustees. Among them were to serve as ex officio members the president of the New Hampshire Senate and the speaker of the House as well as the governor and lieutenant-governor of Vermont. College president and trustees were accountable to governor and Council, and the latter were authorized to fill vacancies on the Board of Overseers and to appoint the newly added trustees.[10] For some ardent foes of the trustees the new charter proved to be a disappointment. It neither deprived the trustees of their power to select their own successors, nor did it reinstate President Wheelock. The fate of Wheelock and the right of the trustees to self-perpetuation had become quite unimportant. The central issue now was the legislature's assertion of power to alter the charter.

Even before the bill had passed the General Court, several of the trustees indicated by petition and counterproposal to Senate and House that they, too, understood the changed nature of the case. They no longer argued about their feud with Wheelock, but protested the legislature's intrusion into their affairs. They pointed out that the bill under discussion did not just alter the charter but replace it with a new one. There had not been any detailed consideration of the legislature's own investigating committee report, and the trustees had never been granted a hearing. They remonstrated against the bill, they said, "on the ground of want of legitimate power to dissolve, in this manner, the Corporation of a literary institution, not founded by the State, without judicial inquiry." Such a course, they reasoned, "effectually blends judicial and legislative powers, and constitutes the Legislature a judicial tribunal." Such an action was unprecedented, and the trustees could not silently accept it.[11]

The subsequent failure of the trustees' counterproposal to the legislature's college bill made a confrontation in court probable. Intending to keep the college out of "the vortex of political controversy," the proposal suggested "the passage of a law connecting the government of the State with that of the College" through a Board of Overseers to consist of the councillors and senators of New Hampshire and the speaker of the house serving ex officio. This board was to meet once a year at commencement and pass on the actions and the legislation of the trustees.[12] The emphasis of this proposal was that these and other charter changes were to have the prior approval of the trustees. By this simple expedient of prior consultation and agreement the proponents hoped to avoid a constitutional crisis. Had they succeeded they would have postponed once more a judicial answer to the question of the rights of a chartered college vis-à-vis a hostile legislature. Since they did not, events now moved toward a judicial settlement.

## The Decision

The decision, read by Marshall in Washington on February 2, 1819, committed the court to protect the chartered rights of private corporations. It focused on the sanctity of private property and on the corporation charter as a contract. Marshall exempted from the purview of the contract clause many of the civil laws states had enacted. But he ruled that grants of franchises to corporations were contracts to which both parties had given assent and which created binding obligations for both. In the charter of Dartmouth College the crown had created a corporation of trustees who had been assigned the property rights of the donor or the donors in exchange for the promise that the donated funds would be applied in perpetuity to the objects specified by the donor. The crown had yielded its prerogative to bestow the same franchise to another corporate body, and the trustees now held in stewardship all the rights mentioned in the charter. The fact that the students, the ultimate beneficiaries of the charity, were perpetually changing did not exempt the present case from the general rule. Marshall reminded his colleagues and his listeners that the great majority of eleemosynary corporations were incorporated in the name of trustees. He could see no reason why such eleemosynary corporations should be exempted from the protection of the contract clause.[13]

Both Justices Washington and Story in their separate opinions supported Marshall's findings. Story, however, went beyond Marshall in affirming the contractual nature of grants and in including the private property of public corporations as well as incorporeal donations under the protection of the contract clause. Even if the crown had not received a valuable consideration in exchange for the charter, said Story, the crown had nonetheless made a gift of property that had been duly accepted by the recipient. Such a gift could not then be revoked by the crown. A completed donation involved a contract "as much as if it had been founded on the most valuable consideration."

At Dartmouth, Story continued, this reasoning did not apply anyway. With his gift of the property of Moor's Charity School and his surrender of the right to maintain and manage it, Dr. Wheelock had, in fact, given a valuable consideration. He also had agreed to serve as president of the college, and the trustees had obliged themselves to act without compensation. The crown had promised not to revoke or alter the charter and not to change the administration of the college without the Corporation's consent. "In every view of the case," Story emphasized, "a valuable consideration did exist, as to the founder, the trustees, and the benefactors."

Story argued similarly on the subject of public corporations. The trustees, he said, could enjoy their franchises even if the Court had found Dartmouth College to be a public corporation. A legislature could not, "at its will take away the private property of [a public] corporation, or change the uses of its private funds, acquired under the public faith," because civil corporations were established by a compact based on public faith, and such compact was "subject only to judicial inquiry, construction and abrogation . . . The only authority remaining to the government," Story concluded, "is judicial, to ascertain the validity of the grant, to enforce its proper uses, to suppress frauds, and, if the uses are charitable, to secure their regular administration, through the means of equitable tribunals, in cases where there would otherwise be a failure of justice."

Finally, Story stated that a franchise was not less valuable than property and should be equally protected by the contract clause. "All incorporeal hereditaments, whether they be immunities, dignities, offices or franchises, or other rights, are deemed valuable in law."[14] Story went out of his way to invoke constitutional protection for any donation given to a college, regardless of whether the college was a private or a public corporation. The trustees could not have asked for more.

Marshall, though not Story, paid relatively little attention to the arguments on the nature of visitatorial power advanced by the attorneys for the trustees, Jeremiah Mason, Jeremiah Smith, and Daniel Webster. The three lawyers used English cases to show that where visitatorial power was rightfully applied, it precluded legislative and judicial interference. But this argument did not fit the conditions in the colonies and states. The New Hampshire legislators, as had the Connecticut, Pennsylvania, Virginia, Tennessee, and New York legislators before them, contemplated the alteration or revocation of a college charter. Whatever prerogatives visitors might have claimed under such a charter would also have been threatened. Visitors, on the other hand, were not empowered to alter, amend, or revoke a charter. The question of charter alteration or revocation, then, did not pertain to the rights of visitors, but to the competencies of courts and legislatures. Whether or not English eleemosynary corporations had visitors as well as trustees, whether or not the crown exercised visitatorial or general jurisdiction over civil corporations were irrelevant distinctions in America. References to the English law of charitable corporations could not decide whether in their general supervisory functions over corporations American legislatures had taken on the powers of crown or Parliament. Marshall preferred to forge a defense for private property and corporation charters from native materials.

Not only could English case law not solve the question of whether Dartmouth College was a civil or an eleemosynary corporation, but there was little help to be gained from a study of the charter. That document named Eleazar Wheelock as the founder, but it did not clarify who donated the first funds to the college. By authorizing the trustees to grant degrees and to institute additional faculties, the charter placed Dartmouth on a level with an English university and gave it the character of a civil corporation. The trustees, nonetheless, administered charities and viewed themselves as an eleemosynary corporation. Marshall decided in their favor by deliberately shunning the references to English law, the rights of visitors, and the charter's description of the founder or founders. Instead he spoke of property rights protected by a contract.

The court's decision also took note of the Revolution's impact on the legal standing of American colleges and supported the trustees' contention that the colleges, like all other corporations, had not been affected in their legal rights. It rejected the university lawyers' claim that with the Revolution the plenary and absolute power of Parliament had passed to the American state legislatures and was limited only by express provisions in the state constitutions. The United States Attorney General, William Wirt, argued that the Revolution had destroyed the Dartmouth charter of 1769. As a consequence, the legal estate of the college had passed from the trustees to the holders of the equitable estate, the people of New Hampshire. Jeremiah Mason professed amazement and shock: "But whatever be the extent of this undefined and arbitrary power of the British Parliament, I trust it will not be contended that it has descended to our legislature." The unrestrained exercise of parliamentary power had provoked the Revolution and brought about independence. If American legislatures had inherited the power to create corporations, it was the power of the crown limited by the courts. That power, Mason added, would not allow the New Hampshire legislature to pass the acts in question. His colleague Jeremiah Smith put the matter very plainly: "Precedents drawn from the English parliament in troublesome times, or any other assembly of legislators or judges in such times, are about as good authority here, at this day, as the decisions in the reign of Richard the second, where the judges were capitally condemned for the judgments they gave. The condemnations and the judgments were pretty much alike."[15]

Justices Story and Marshall gave short shrift to the defense argument that the power of Parliament had descended upon state legislatures. Story simply declared it to be a recognized common law principle "that the division of an empire works no forfeiture of previously-vested rights of property." This maxim, he said, was "equally consonant with the common sense of mankind and the maxims of eternal justice." The defense objection could be "safely dismissed without further comment." The Chief Justice admitted that "the transcendent power of parliament" had devolved on the people of New Hampshire, but that it was nonetheless "too clear to require the support of argument, that all contracts and rights respecting property, remained unchanged by the revolution."[16] In short, college charters prevailed against the edicts of hostile assemblies.

## A Postscript

The Supreme Court's 1819 decision brought to an end the series of inconclusive confrontations between legislatures and college corporations. What Thomas Clap had maintained, what the trustees of the College of Philadelphia and what the governors of Liberty Hall and Davidson academies had asked, had now become accepted legal doctrine. For a corporation charter to be altered, the corporation had to agree to the changes or else be convicted of wrongdoing by due process in a duly constituted court of law. No longer could a legislature unilaterally interfere in college affairs in disregard of the rights and privileges guaranted by charter. There might still be disputes over the meaning and implications of charter provisions, and a legislature might reserve to itself in the charter powers of interference or charter alteration. But no longer could legislators on their own determination and without recourse to reserve powers alter, ignore, or abolish a charter. That issue was now settled.

The Dartmouth case recognized the rights of nonpublic college corporations to legal protection equal to that accorded to private business corporations. It recognized that colleges, as a means for development, were as important as business corporations. To Willard Hurst's statement that "the substance of what business wanted from law was the provision for ordinary use of an organization through which entrepreneurs could better mobilize and release economic energy," we can now add that this applied to college founders as well.[17] As a result, the distinctions of status between education and business began to grow dim. Traditional prerogatives of social rank, an inheritance from a European feudal past, were less likely to be reaffirmed through education. A passion for economic expansion and development motivated both business and education and placed private venture capitalism next to government as the custodian of the public weal. Higher education found its place in both the private and the public spheres.

By 1820 higher education's two-pronged advance had become visible in the governments of the forty-four institutions then in operation. Nine of these dated back to the colonial past; the post-colonial foundations were divided approximately evenly between public and private institutions.[18] The variety of their charter provisions prohibits hard and fast definitions. The governing boards of the public institutions frequently included ex officio state legislators or officials; their trustees or visitors might be appointed or confirmed by the legislature; the colleges themselves often bore the name of their state. But not all of these schools were publicly endowed and constituted as public corporations in Story's meaning of the term. The variety in the governmental arrangements of the private colleges was greater yet, but this was only a beginning. The decades following the Dartmouth decision were to witness an unprecedented increase in the number of private colleges, and they established the private college as one of the country's most characteristic and unique institutions.[19]

One more point needs to be added concerning the impact of the Dartmouth decision on the place and function of higher education in American life. The decision neither lessened the significance of public colleges and universities nor did it necessarily undercut the exercise of public authority over higher education. The colleges were free to become or remain private institutions. By protecting their chartered rights, it added immeasurably to their stability and to their ability to survive and flourish in the new nation. By safeguarding chartered college government, it answered clearly the question of who governs a college.

But in doing so the court did not move the colleges beyond the reach of governmental authority. With a view toward the future, Justice Story stated that if any legislature wanted to enact legislation "which takes away any powers or franchises vested by its charter in a private corporation, or its corporate officers, or which restrains or controls the legitimate exercise of them, or transfers them to other persons, without its assent . . . such an authority . . . must be reserved in the grant."[20] While governments were barred from ex post facto legislation of this kind, they could continue to rely on reserve power clauses contained in corporate charters. Such clauses were neither Justice Story's innovation nor introduced into college charters only after 1819. We find them in the 1783 and 1787 Pennsylvania charters for Dickinson and Franklin colleges where they permitted charter alterations by the state legislature. In the 1817 charter of Allegheny College the same legislature reserved the right to remove president and trustees. In Massachusetts the 1793 charter of Williams and the 1794 charter of Bowdoin authorized the legislature to grant additional powers or alter, limit, annul, or restrain the powers granted in the charter. Similar provisions can be found in the charters of Ohio and Kentucky colleges.[21]

After 1819 such powers became a normal part of college incorporation. They made possible the simultaneous development of public and private institutions of higher education, each independent within the sphere delineated in their charter or legislative enactment, and each yet subject to responsible public oversight. The Dartmouth College decision was the stimulus for American higher education as we have known it since 1819.

# APPENDIX A

The Fifty-Two Degree-Granting Institutions of Higher Learning Chartered between 1636 and 1820. (An asterisk indicates that by 1820 there was no report of the institution's existence as a college; "n.a." indicates that information is not available.)

| Charter date | Name changes (with year of change) | Colony or state | Year of opening | Year of first B.A. | Affiliation |
|---|---|---|---|---|---|
| | "School or college" (1636) | Mass. Bay | 1638 | 1642 | Colony; Congregational |
| 5 / 31 / 1650 | Harvard College (1639) | | | | |
| | Harvard University (1780) | | | | |
| 2 / 8 / 1693 | College of William and Mary | Va. | 1694 | 1753(?) | Colony; Anglican |
| 10 / 9 / 1701 | "A collegiate school" | Conn. | 1702 | 1702 | Colony; Congregational-Presbyterian |
| 5 / 9 / 1745 | Yale College (1718) | | | | |
| | Yale University (1887) | | | | |
| 10 / 22 / 1746 | College of New Jersey | N.J. | 1747 | | Colony; Presbyterian |
| 9 / 14 / 1748 | | | | 1748 | |
| | Princeton University (1896) | | | | |

244

APPENDIX A

| Charter date | Name changes (with year of change) | Colony or state | Year of opening | Year of first B.A. | Affiliation |
|---|---|---|---|---|---|
| 10 / 31 / 1754 | King's College<br><br>Columbia College (1784)<br><br>Columbia University (1912) | N.Y. | 1754 | 1758 | Colony; Anglican |
| 5 / 14 / 1755 | The Academy and Charitable School in the Province of Pennsylvania (1753)<br><br>The College, Academy, and Charitable School of Philadelphia<br><br>The University of the State of Pennsylvania (1779)<br><br>The University of Pennsylvania (1791) | Pa. | 1755 | 1757 | City; Colony; Anglican; Presbyterian State |
| 10 / 24 / 1765 | Latin School at Warren (1764)<br><br>College or University in the Colony of Rhode Island and Providence Plantations<br><br>Brown University (1804) | R.I. | 1765 | 1769 | Colony; Baptist |
| 11 / 10 / 1766<br>3 / 20 / 1770 | Queen's College<br><br>Rutgers College (1825)<br><br>Rutgers College, The State University of New Jersey (1917)<br><br>Rutgers University, The State University of New Jersey (1946)<br><br>Rutgers, The State University (1956) | N.J. | 1771 | 1774 | Dutch Reformed |

| Charter date | Name changes (with year of change) | Colony or state | Year of opening | Year of first B.A. | Affiliation |
|---|---|---|---|---|---|
| | Moor's Indian Charity School (1755) | Conn. | | | |
| 12 / 13 / 1769 | Dartmouth College | N.H. | 1769 | 1771 | Colony; Congregational |
| | Kent County School (1723) | Md. | | | |
| 4 / ? / 1782 | Washington College | | 1782 | 1783 | State; Episcopal |
| | Augusta Academy (1749) | Va. | | | |
| | Liberty Hall (1776) | | | | |
| 10 / ? / 1782 | Liberty Hall Academy | | 1782 | 1785 | Presbyterian |
| | College of Washington (1796) | | | | |
| | Washington Academy (1798) | | | | |
| | Washington College (1813) | | | | |
| | Washington and Lee University (1871) | | | | |
| | Prince Edward Academy (1775) | Va. | | | |
| | Hampden-Sydney Academy (1776) | | | | |
| 5 / ? / 1783 | Hampden-Sydney College | | 1783 | 1786 | Presbyterian |
| 6 / 24 / 1783 | Transylvania Seminary | Va. | 1789 | 1802 | State; Presbyterian |
| | Transylvania University (1799) | Ky. | | | |
| | Kentucky University (1865) | | | | |
| | Transylvania University (1908) | | | | |
| | Transylvania College (1915) | | | | |
| | Transylvania University (1969) | | | | |

## APPENDIX A

| Charter date | Name changes (with year of change) | Colony or state | Year of opening | Year of first B.A. | Affiliation |
|---|---|---|---|---|---|
| | Carlisle Grammar School (1773) | Pa. | | | |
| 9 / 9 / 1783 | Dickinson College | | 1784 | 1787 | Presbyterian |
| | King William's School (1696) | Md. | | | State; Episcopal |
| 11 / ? / 1784 | St. John's College | | 1789 | 1793 | |
| 1 / 27 / 1785 | University of Georgia | Ga. | 1801 | 1804 | State |
| | Winnsborough School (1777) | S.C. | | | Presbyterian |
| 3 / 19 / 1785 | *Mount Sion College [functioned as elementary school by 1790s] | | 1785 | 1787 | |
| | Academy of Robert Smith (1785) | S.C. | | | |
| 3 / 19 / 1785 | College of Charleston | | 1789 | | State |
| 12 / 20 / 1791 | College of Charleston | | | 1794 | Independent |
| | Salem School and Seminary (1768) | S.C. | | | |
| 3 / 19 / 1785 | *College of Cambridge | | ? | n.a. | Presbyterian |
| 3 / 10 / 1787 | Franklin College | Pa. | 1787 | | German Reformed; German Lutheran |
| | Franklin Academy (1807) | | | | |
| | Franklin College (1837) | | | | |
| | Franklin and Marshall College (1853) | | | 1853 | |
| 12 / 11 / 1789 | University of North Carolina | N.C. | 1795 | 1798 | State |

APPENDIX A

| Charter date | Name changes (with year of change) | Colony or state | Year of opening | Year of first B.A. | Affiliation |
|---|---|---|---|---|---|
| 11 / 3 / 1791 | University of Vermont | Vt. | 1799 | 1804 | State |
| 6 / 22 / 1793 | Williamstown Free School (1791)<br>Williams College | Mass. | 1793 | 1795 | State: Congregational |
| 6 / 24 / 1794 | Bowdoin College | Mass.<br>Me. | 1802 | 1806 | State; Congregational |
| 9 / 3 / 1794 | Academy of Hezekiah Balch (1785)<br>Greeneville College<br>Tusculum College (1913) | Tenn. | 1805 | 1808 | Presbyterian |
| 9 / 10 / 1794<br><br>10 / 26 / 1807 | Academy of Samuel Carrick<br>Blount College<br>East Tennessee College [College suspended from 1808 to 1820]<br>East Tennessee University (1840)<br>University of Tennessee, Knoxville (1879) | Tenn. | 1804<br>1820 | 1806<br>1825 | Presbyterian<br>State |
| 12 / 26 / 1794 | Cokesbury Academy (1787)<br>*Cokesbury College [Suspended as college in 1795; authorized to be dissolved, 1 / 15 / 1799] | Md. | 1794 | n.a. | Methodist |

| Charter date | Name changes (with year of change) | Colony or state | Year of opening | Year of first B.A. | Affiliation |
|---|---|---|---|---|---|
| | Schenectady Academy (1785) | N.Y. | | | Presbyterian, Reformed, and others |
| | Academy of the Town of Schenectady (1793) | | | | |
| 2 / 25 / 1795 | Union College | | 1795 | 1797 | |
| 3 / 29 / 1806 | Union College | | | | |
| | Union University (1873) | | | | |
| | Martin's Academy (1780) | Tenn. | | | Presbyterian |
| 7 / 8 / 1795 | Washington College | | 1795 | 1796 | |
| | Washington College Academy (1953) | | | | |
| 12 / 19 / 1795 | *College of Beaufort | S.C. | n.a. | n.a. | ? |
| 12 / 16 / 1797 | *Alexandria College | S.C. | n.a. | n.a. | Presbyterian |
| | Addison County Grammar School (1797) | Vt. | | | |
| 11 / 1 / 1800 | Middlebury College | | 1800 | 1802 | Congregational |
| 12 / 19 / 1801 | South Carolina College | S.C. | 1805 | 1806 | State |
| | University of South Carolina (1865) | | | | |
| | College of South Carolina (1878) | | | | |
| | South Carolina College of Agriculture and Mechanical Arts (1880) | | | | |
| | South Carolina College (1882) | | | | |
| | University of South Carolina (1887) | | | | |
| | South Carolina College (1890) | | | | |
| | University of South Carolina (1906) | | | | |

APPENDIX A

| Charter date | Name changes (with year of change) | Colony or state | Year of opening | Year of first B.A. | Affiliation |
|---|---|---|---|---|---|
| 1 / 9 / 1802 | American Western University | N.W. Terr. | n.a. | n.a. | Territory |
| 2 / 18 / 1804 | Ohio University | Ohio | 1808 | 1815 | State |
| | Canonsburg Academy (1794) | Pa. | | | Presbyterian |
| 1 / 15 / 1802 | Jefferson College | | 1802 | 1802 | |
| | Washington and Jefferson College (1865) | | | | |
| 1 / 7 / 1804 | *Baltimore College [Remained an academy and merged with University of Maryland in 1830] | Md. | 1804 | n.a. | Civic |
| | St. Mary's Seminary (1791) | Md. | | | |
| | St. Mary's Academy (1799) | | | | |
| 1 / 19 / 1805 | St. Mary's | | 1805 | 1806 | Sulpician |
| | St. Mary's Seminary and University (1969) | | | | |
| 4 / 19 / 1805 | University of Orleans and College of New Orleans [University abolished in 1821; college in 1826] | La. | n.a. ? | n.a. ? | Territory |
| | Washington Academy (1787) | Pa. | | | Presbyterian |
| 3 / 28 / 1806 | Washington College | | 1806 | 1809 | |
| | Washington and Jefferson College (1865) | | | | |

# APPENDIX A

| Charter date | Name changes (with year of change) | Colony or state | Year of opening | Year of first B.A. | Affiliation |
|---|---|---|---|---|---|
| | Davidson Academy (1785) | Tenn. | | | Presbyterian |
| | Davidson College (1803) [Repealed 1805] | | | | |
| 9 / 11 / 1806 | Cumberland College [Closed 1816-1823] | | 1806 | n.a. | State |
| | University of Nashville (1826) | | | | |
| | State Normal College (1875) | | | | |
| | Peabody Normal College (1889) | | | | |
| | George Peabody College for Teachers (1909) | | | | |
| | Medical Chirurgical Faculty of the State of Maryland (1798) | Md. | | | Professional |
| 1 / 20 / 1808 | The College of Medicine of Maryland | | 1807 | n.a. | |
| 12 / 29 / 1812 | University of Maryland | | | 1859 | |
| 2 / 17 / 1809 | Miami University | Ohio | 1818 | 1826 | State |
| | Hamilton-Oneida Academy (1793) | N.Y. | | | Presbyterian |
| 5 / 26 / 1812 | Hamilton College | | 1812 | 1814 | |
| | Georgetown Academy (1791) | D.C. | | | Catholic |
| 3 / 1 / 1815 | College of Georgetown | | 1815 | 1817 | |
| | Georgetown College (1844) | | | | |
| | Goergetown University (1851) | | | | |

APPENDIX A

| Charter date | Name changes (with year of change) | Colony or state | Year of opening | Year of first B.A. | Affiliation |
|---|---|---|---|---|---|
| | Albemarle Academy (1803) | Va. | | | |
| 2 / 14 / 1816 | Central College | | n.a. | n.a. | State |
| 1 / 25 / 1819 | University of Virginia | | 1825 | 1849 | State |
| 3 / 24 / 1817 | Allegheny College | Pa. | 1816 | 1821 | State; Congregational |
| 2 / 10 / 1818 | Asbury College [Closed in 1830s] | Md. | 1818 | n.a. | Methodist |
| 1 / 21 / 1819 | Centre College | Ky. | 1820 | 1824 | Presbyterian |
| | Cincinnati University (1807) [Never opened] | Ohio | n.a. | n.a. | Civic |
| | Medical College of Ohio 1819 | | 1819 | | Professional |
| 1 / 22 / 1819 | Cincinnati College | | 1819 | 1821 | Civic |
| | University of Cincinnati (1870) [Merged with Medical College of Ohio in 1896 and with Cincinnati College in 1897] | | | | |
| | Worthington Academy | Ohio | 1808 | n.a. | Episcopal |
| 2 / 8 / 1819 | *Worthington College | | ? | n.a. | |
| | Pittsburgh Academy (1787) | Pa. | | | |
| 2 / 18 / 1819 | Western University of Pennsylvania | | 1819 | 1823 | Presbyterian |
| | University of Pittsburgh (1908) | | | | |

## APPENDIX A

| Charter date | Name changes (with year of change) | Colony or state | Year of opening | Year of first B.A. | Affiliation |
|---|---|---|---|---|---|
| | Maine Literary and Theological Institution (1813) | Mass. | 1818 | | Baptist |
| 6 / 19 / 1820 | Maine Literary and Theological Institution | Me. | | 1822 | State; Baptist |
| | Waterville College (1821) | | | | |
| | Colby University (1867) | | | | |
| | Colby College (1899) | | | | |

# APPENDIX B

Number of Earned First Degrees Awarded by American Colleges
and Universities, 1642-1820

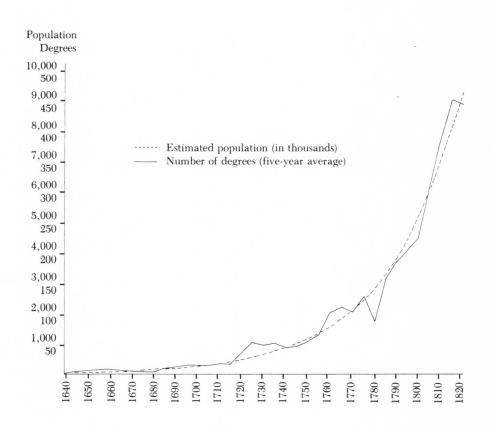

Population
Degrees

Estimated population (in thousands)
Number of degrees (five-year average)

# NOTES

## I. Introduction

1. The 1643 quotation is from "New England's First Fruits," reprinted in Samuel Eliot Morison, *The Founding of Harvard College* (Cambridge, Mass.: Harvard University Press, 1935), p. 432; the phrase from the charter of William and Mary is to be found in Edgar W. Knight, ed., *A Documentary History of Education in the South before 1860* (Chapel Hill, N.C.: The University of North Carolina Press, 1949), I, 401; the quote from the charter of the Collegiate School is in Franklin Bowditch Dexter, ed., *Documentary History of Yale University* (New Haven, Conn.: Yale University Press, 1916), p. 21.

2. On the medieval unity see Herbert Grundmann, "*Sacerdotium — Regnum — Studium:* Zur Wertung der Wissenschaft im 13. Jahrhundert," *Archiv für Kulturgeschichte*, 34 (1952), 5-21; on the Reformation universities consult Stephen d'Irsay, *Histoire des universités françaises et étrangères des origines à nos jours*, vol. I: *Moyen âge et Renaissance* (Paris: A. Picard, 1933), pp. 315-316.

3. The origins of the University of Paris are discussed in Hastings Rashdall, *The Universities of Europe in the Middle Ages*, ed. F. M. Powicke and A. B. Emden (London: Oxford University Press, 1936), I, 298-320, and in John P. Davis, *Corporations* (New York: Capricorn Books, 1961), I, 264.

4. On the German universities see Friedrich von Bezold, "Die ältesten deutschen Universitäten in ihrem Verhältnis zum Staat," in *Aus Mittelalter und Renaissance* (Munich: R. Oldenbourg, 1918), pp. 220-245; Herbert Grundmann, *Vom Ursprung der Universität im Mittelalter*, Berichte über die Verhandlungen der Sächsischen Akademie der Wissenschaften zu Leipzig, Philologisch-Historische Klasse, vol. 103, no. 2 (Berlin: Akademie Verlag, 1957); Georg Kaufmann, *Die Geschichte der Deutschen Universitäten* (Stuttgart, 1896), II, 80-81; and Friedrich Paulsen, *The German Universities: Their Character and Historical Development* (New York, 1895), pp. 21-22, 45.

5. Edward H. Reisner, "The Origin of Lay University Boards of Control in the United States," *Columbia University Quarterly*, 23 (1931), 63-69.

6. See Martin Luther, "To the Christian Nobility of the German Nation," in *Luther's Works*, ed. Helmut T. Lehmann (Philadelphia: Fortress Press, 1966), XLIV, 200-207.

7. The acts referred to are the 1533 Act for Restraint of Appeals (24 Henry VIII, chap. 12), the 1534 Act for the Submission of the Clergy (25 Henry VIII, chap. 19) and the Act of Visitation (25 Henry VIII, chap. 21), also of 1534. The royal incorporation of the universities is enacted in 13 Eliz., chap. 29; see also James Williams, *The Law of the Universities* (London: Butterworth, 1910), pp. 1-54 passim, and 83.

## 1. A Provincial School in the Wilderness

1. Nathaniel B. Shurtleff, ed., *Records of the Governor and Company of the Massachusetts Bay in New England* (Boston, 1853), I, 183. Whenever appropriate, spelling in quoted passages has been modernized.

2. See "The Constitutional Rights and Privileges of Harvard College," in *The Writings and Speeches of Daniel Webster*, ed. James W. McIntyre (Boston: Little, Brown, 1903), XV, 88-89.

3. See Samuel Eliot Morison, *The Founding of Harvard College* (Cambridge, Mass.: Harvard University Press, 1935), p. 169n.

4. Margery Somers Foster, *"Out of Smalle Beginnings . . .": An Economic History of Harvard College in the Puritan Period* (1636-1712) (Cambridge, Mass.: Harvard University Press, 1962), pp. 86-88; *Publications of the Colonial Society of Massachusetts* (hereafter abbreviated *PCSM*), 15 (1925), 21, 172.

5. Shurtleff, ed., *Records*, I, 217; John Maynard Hoffmann, "Commonwealth College: The Governance of Harvard in the Puritan Period" (Ph. D. diss., Harvard University, 1972), pp. 1-36 passim.

6. But see the different view of Morison in *The Founding*, pp. 193n2, 144.

7. See Morison, *The Founding*, pp. 199, 208, 235, 241-262, 325-326.

8. On the definition of a quasi-corporation see John P. Davis, *Corporations* (New York: Capricorn Books, 1961), I, 19.

9. Cf. Walter Friedensburg, *Geschichte der Universität Wittenberg* (Halle: Niemeyer, 1917), p. 28.

10. The act of September 27, 1642, is given in Shurtleff, ed., *Records*, II, 30, in *PCSM*, 15 (1925), 173-174, and in Josiah Quincy, *The History of Harvard University* (Boston, 1860), I, 48; see also Morison, *The Founding*, pp. 325-326.

11. See William S. Holdsworth, *A History of English Law*, 2nd ed. (London: Methuen, 1937), IV, 399, 477-478, and Austin W. Scott, *The Law of Trusts*, 2nd ed. (Boston: Little, Brown, 1956), IV, 2553. The Statute of Charitable Uses is conveniently reprinted in Gareth Jones, *History of the Law of Charity*, 1532-1827 (London: Cambridge University Press, 1969), pp. 224-228.

12. *New England's First Fruits* (London, 1643), reprinted in Morison, *The Founding*, pp. 419-447.

13. Samuel Eliot Morison, *Three Centuries of Harvard*, 1636-1936 (Cambridge, Mass.: Harvard University Press, 1936), p. 35; also in Morison's *Harvard College in the Seventeenth Century* (hereafter abbreviated *HCSC*) (Cambridge, Mass.: Harvard University Press, 1936), I, 70.

14. *PCSM*, 15 (1925), 35, and Morison, *The Founding*, p. 261.

15. See John Langdon Sibley, *Biographical Sketches of Graduates of Harvard University*, vol. I: 1642-1658 (Cambridge, Mass., 1873).

16. *PCSM*, 15 (1925), 36, 177.

17. For a different view as it applies to Harvard, see the letter of A. C. Goodell to the Rev. J. Henry Thayer, June 29, 1883, available in Harvard University Archives.

18. Shurtleff, ed., *Records*, III, 207-208.

19. Andrew M. Davis, "Corporations in the Days of the Colony," *PCSM*, 1 (1894), 195; also see *Rumford v. Wood*, 13 Mass. (1816), 198.

20. Morison, *HCSC*, I, 5.

21. For reprints of the charter see *PCSM*, 31 (1935), 3-6, and Morison, *HCSC*, I, 5-8.

22. On trusteeship of the Overseers cf. Hoffmann, "Commonwealth College," p. 650.

23. *The Case of Sutton's Hospital*, 10 Co. Rep. (1612), 31a; see also Roscoe Pound, "Visitatorial Jurisdiction over Corporations in Equity," *Harvard Law Review*, 49 (January 1936), 371.

24. Morison, *HCSC*, I, 12-13.

25. Hoffmann, "Commonwealth College," pp. 658-659.

26. See Andrew M. Davis, "Corporations," *PCSM*, 1 (1894), 199.

27. Ibid., I, 209; Morison, *HCSC*, I, 4-5; Alexander Brody, *The American State and Higher Education* (Washington, D.C.: American Council on Education, 1935), pp. 15-17; Julius Goebel, Jr., "King's Law and Local Custom in Seventeenth-Century New England," *Columbia Law Review*, 31 (March 1931), 429; and Simeon Eben Baldwin, "History of the Law of Private Corporations in the Colonies and States," in *Select Essays in Anglo-American Legal History*, ed. Committee of the Association of American Law Schools (Boston: Little, Brown, 1909), III, 241.

28. Hoffmann, "Commonwealth College," p. 684. The statutes in question are 39 Elizabeth, chap. 5 (1597), and 21 Jac., chap. 1(1625).

29. 10 Co. Rep. (1612), 33b, and *Landewibrevye College Case*, 3 Dyer (1568), 267a.

30. *Att.-Gen. v. Corporation of Newcastle*, 5 Beav. (1798), 307; see also Hoffmann, "Commonwealth College," p. 698.

31. See Simeon E. Baldwin, *Modern Political Institutions* (Boston, 1898), pp. 174-175.

## 2. Harvard College: The New World's Oldest Corporation

1. Samuel Eliot Morison, *Harvard College in the Seventeenth Century* (Cambridge, Mass.: Harvard University Press, 1936), I, 9.

2. *PCSM*, 15 (1925), cliv-clix; and Morison, *HCSC*, I, 13-23.

3. Morison, *HCSC*, II, 569-570; also Nathaniel B. Shurtleff, ed., *Records of the Governor and Company of the Massachusetts Bay in New England* (Boston, 1853), IV, part I, 178-180.

4. Samuel Eliot Morison, *The Founding of Harvard College* (Cambridge, Mass.: Harvard University Press, 1935), pp. 448-451.

5. Morison, *HCSC*, II, 570-573, 575.

6. Ibid., I, 304-310.

7. Ibid., I, 320; the appendix of 1657 is printed in *HCSC*, I, 11-12.

8. Ibid., II, 389-399; Albert Matthews, "The Harvard College Charter of 1672," *PCSM*, 21 (April 1919), 363-402; and Shurtleff, ed., *Records*, IV, part II, 535-537.

9. Morison, *HCSC*, II, 401-408, 415-418, 436-445.

10. Ibid., II, 472-490; *PCSM*, 15 (1925), xxxix.

11. Morison, *HCSC*, II, 489-494, 654-656; and see George H. Williams, *Wilderness and Paradise in Christian Thought* (New York: Harper, 1962), pp. 152-153.

12. The English law concerning visitation was stated in *The Case of Sutton's Hospital*, 10. Co. Rep. (1612), 31a; and *Philips v. Bury*, 2 T.R. (1693), 352, 353.

13. See the charter in Josiah Quincy, *The History of Harvard University* (Boston, 1860), I, 597-599.

14. *PCSM*, 15 (1925), xliii-xlvii; Morison, *HCSC*, II, 512; *Calendar of State Papers, Colonial Series: America and West Indies*, 1696-1697 (London: H. M. Stationery Office, 1906), p. 495.

15. Morison, *HCSC*, II, 513-515, 517; for text of 1697 charter see ibid., II, 656-659. See also the Corporation memorial to the General Court of June 9, 1698, in Quincy, *History of Harvard*, I, 497-498.

16. Quotations from the 1699 charter draft are in Quincy, *History of Harvard*, I, 602-607; see also Morison, *HCSC*, II, 525.

17. Morison, *HCSC*, II, 529, and Quincy, *History of Harvard*, I, 607-610.

18. Morison, *HCSC*, II, 526, 527.

19. For the text of the temporary settlement see ibid., II, 659-660.

20. See Mather's letter to Dudley, January 20, 1708, in *Collections of the Massachusetts Historical Society for the Year 1794*, III (Boston, 1810), 126-128.

21. Printed in Morison, *HCSC*, II, 660-661.

22. Samuel Eliot Morison, *Three Centuries of Harvard, 1636-1936* (Cambridge, Mass.: Harvard University Press, 1936), p. 60; Kathryn M. Moore, "Old Saints and Young Sinners: A Study of Student Discipline at Harvard College, 1635-1724" (Ph.D. diss., Unversity of Wisconsin-Madison, 1972).

23. John L. Sibley, "John Leverett," in *Biographical Sketches of Graduates of Harvard University* (Cambridge, Mass., 1885), III, 180-198; Arthur D. Kaledin, "The Mind of John Leverett" (Ph.D. diss., Harvard University, 1965); and Bernard Bailyn, *The New England Merchants in the Seventeenth Century* (Cambridge, Mass.: Harvard University Press, 1955), p. 139.

24. In *PCSM*, 16 (1925), 441, 442; 49 (1975), 276; John Leverett's Diary, typescript, p. 168, by permission of Harvard University Archives; Clifford K. Shipton, *Sibley's Harvard Graduates* (Boston: Massachusetts Historical Society, 1937), V, 92.

25. In *PCSM*, 16 (1925), 442, and Leverett's Diary, pp. 170, 172-173.

26. Leverett's Diary, pp. 175-178, and Overseer's Record, I, 12-14, by permission of Harvard University Archives.

27. Mather to Shute, October 31, 1718, in Quincy, *History of Harvard*, I, 523-524.

28. A convenient summary of the affair is provided in the minutes of "A

Meeting of the Overseers of Harvard College held at the Council Chamber in Boston on Friday, October 31, 1718," typescript, document no. 23, file on tutor controversy of 1720, Harvard University Archives.

29. Quincy, *History of Harvard*, I, 307, 546, and Albert Matthews, ed., "Draught of a Royal Charter for Harvard College, 1723," *PCSM*, 25 (January 1924), 390-400. I believe Matthews is correct when he dates the draft charter some time between February 5 and April 23, 1723.

## 3. The College of William and Mary

1. In Edgar W. Knight, ed., *A Documentary History of Education in the South before 1860* (Chapel Hill, N.C.: University of North Carolina Press, 1949), I, 372, 667.

2. On the College of William and Mary see Herbert B. Adams, *The College of William and Mary*, U.S. Bureau of Education, Circular of Information No. 1, 1887 (Washington, D.C., 1887); for background on the English schools see Joan Simon, *Education and Society in Tudor England* (Cambridge, Eng.: University Press, 1966); Kenneth Charlton, *Education in Renaissance England* (London: Routledge and K. Paul, 1965); and the older, now outdated, study by Arthur F. Leach, *English Schools at the Reformation*, 1546-1548 (London, 1896).

3. Knight, ed., *Documentary History*, I, 377-380.

4. "Blair to Nicholson, Dec. 3, 1691," in "Papers Relating to the Administration of Governor Nicholson and to the Founding of William and Mary College," *Virginia Magazine of History and Biography* (hereafter abbreviated *VMHB*), 7 (1899-1900), 160-163; for the position of vice-chancellor in government of English colleges see Mark H. Curtis, *Oxford and Cambridge in Transition*, 1558-1642 (Oxford: Clarendon Press, 1959), pp. 41-45.

5. "Blair to Nicholson," *VMHB*, 7 (1899-1900), 161

6. The most adequate biography of Blair is Parke Rouse, Jr., *James Blair of Virginia* (Chapel Hill, N.C.: University of North Carolina Press, 1971); other useful accounts are G. MacLaren Brydon, "James Blair, Commissary," *Historical Magazine of the Protestant Episcopal Church*, 14 (June 1945), 85-118; and Daniel E. Motley, "Life of Commissary James Blair, Founder of William and Mary College," *Johns Hopkins University Studies in Historical and Political Science*, 19 (October 1901), 451-503.

7. G. D. Henderson, *The Founding of Marischal College Aberdeen* (Aberdeen: University Press, 1947), p. 34; on the college see also Robert S. Rait, *The Universities of Aberdeen: A History* (Aberdeen, 1895); and on the Scottish universities see Hastings Rashdall, *The Universities of Europe in the Middle Ages*, ed. F. M. Powicke and A. B. Emden, new ed. (London: Oxford University Press, 1936), II, 320-321; and Henry Malden, *On the Origin of Universities and Academical Degrees* (London, 1835), pp. 144-147.

8. Alexander Morgan, ed., *University of Edinburgh Charters, Statutes, and Acts of the Town Council and the Senatus*, 1583-1858 (Edinburgh: Oliver and Boyd, 1937); Alexander Grant, *The Story of the University of Edinburgh*, 2 vols. (London, 1884); and Alexander Law, *Education in Edinburgh in the Eigh-*

teenth Century (London: University of London Press, 1965); the quotation is from D. B. Horn, *A Short History of the University of Edinburgh* 1556–1889 (Edinburgh: University Press, 1967), p. 9.

9. The charter is reprinted in Knight, ed., *Documentary History*, I, 400-439.

10. For the 1728 English version of the statutes as printed in 1736 in Williamsburg see the *Bulletin of the College of William and Mary*, 7 (April 1914), 7-21. The Latin and English text of the 1758 edition is contained in Knight, ed., *Documentary History*, I, 500-528. Another English copy of the 1758 version is reprinted in the *William and Mary College Quarterly* (hereafter abbreviated *WMQ*), 16 (April 1908): 239-256.

11. See "The Transfer of the College of William and Mary in Virginia," reprinted in *The History of the College of William and Mary* (Richmond, Va.: J. Randolph, 1874), pp. 17-33; also Rouse, *James Blair*, p. 214.

12. Cf. for a discussion of the problems of outlying provinces John Clive and Bernard Bailyn, "England's Cultural Provinces: Scotland and America," *WMQ*, 3rd ser., 11 (April 1954): 200-213.

13. Scholars have debated at some length the relative influence of Scottish and English examples on the College of William and Mary. Lyon G. Tyler, "Early Courses and Professors at William and Mary College," *WMQ*, 1st ser., 14 (October 1905): 71-83; Courtlandt Canby, "A Note on the Influence of Oxford upon William and Mary College in the Eighteenth Century," *WMQ*, 2nd ser., 21 (July 1941): 243-247; and Richard Hofstadter and Walter P. Metzger, *The Development of Academic Freedom in the United States* (New York: Columbia University Press, 1955), p. 131, n. 30, have tended to play down Scottish influences. On the other side, A. Bailey Cutts, "The Educational Influence of Aberdeen in Seventeenth Century Virginia," *WMQ*, 2nd ser., 15 (July 1935): 229-249; George S. Pryde, *The Scottish Universities and the Colleges of Colonial America* (Glasgow: Jackson, 1957), pp. 15-16; and Douglas Sloan, *The Scottish Enlightenment and the American College Ideal* (New York: Teachers College Press, 1971), p. 21n, have upheld—and correctly, I believe—the Scottish derivation of college government in Virginia from Edinburgh through Blair. Tyler's description of the William and Mary college government as "thoroughly English" is simply wrong. He fell into this error when he equated a curriculum imported from England with English-style academic government and overlooked that there is no necessary relationship between curriculum and government. Canby and Hofstadter derived their observations on the clash between Oxford ideals and American realities from the struggle for control of the college that erupted after 1755. That strife, however, did not dominate the early years of the college.

## 4. Connecticut's Collegiate School

1. From the charter of the Collegiate School, printed in Franklin B. Dexter, ed., *Documentary History of Yale University* (New Haven, Conn.: Yale University Press, 1916), p. 21.

2. For my account of the history of Yale College in the years under discussion I have relied heavily on Richard Warch, *School of the Prophets: Yale College*, 1701–1740 (New Haven, Conn.: Yale University Press, 1973); see also Brooks M. Kelly, *Yale: A History* (New Haven, Conn.: Yale University Press, 1974).

3. Mather's communications with the Connecticut ministers are quoted from Dexter, ed., *Documentary History*, pp. 6-9.

4. The respective statutes were 39 Eliz. chap. 5, 21 Jac. chap. 1, and 43 Eliz. chap. 4; the "Statute of Charitable Uses" is reprinted in full in Gareth Jones, *History of the Law of Charity*, 1532–1827 (London: Cambridge University Press, 1969), p. 224-228.

5. Bulkley's letter of September 27, 1701, is printed in Dexter, ed., *Documentary History*, pp. 9-11.

6. For Kimberley and Eliot see Dexter, ed., *Documentary History*, pp. 11-15.

7. *Calvin's Case*, 7 Coke Rep. (1608), 1; for summaries of the case see St. George L. Sioussat, "The English Statutes in Maryland," *Johns Hopkins University Studies in Historical and Political Science*, 21 (1903), 482, and Joseph H. Smith, *Appeals to the Privy Council from the American Plantations* (New York: Columbia University Press, 1950), pp. 467-469.

8. See Joseph S. Davis, *Essays in the Earlier History of American Corporations* (Cambridge, Mass.: Harvard University Press, 1917), I, 62. For *Hill v. Boston* see 122 Mass. (1877), 349.

9. On trusts see Austin W. Scott, *The Law of Trusts*, 2nd ed. (Boston: Little, Brown, 1956), I, 5; IV, 2551-2553.

10. In Dexter, ed., *Documentary History*, p. 14.

11. On the privilege of parliamentary representation of colleges see James Williams, *The Law of the Universities* (London: Butterworth & Co., 1910), pp. 83, 146, 148.

12. See draft and final charter in Dexter, ed., *Documentary History*, pp. 16-19, 20-23.

13. On Fitch's gift see ibid., pp. 19-20.

14. On partnership see Theophilus Parsons, *A Treatise on the Law of Partnership* (Boston, 1867), pp. 218-220, and Edward H. Warren, *Corporate Advantages without Incorporation* (New York: Voorhis & Co., 1929), p. 22.

15. Dexter, ed., *Documentary History*, pp. 21-22.

16. Ibid., pp. 84-88.

17. For background on Connecticut's legal system see Thomas Day, *A Concise Historical Account of the Judiciary of Connecticut* (Hartford, 1817), p. 17.

18. Dexter, ed., *Documentary History*, pp. 247-248.

19. Ibid., pp. 248-250.

20. See Forrest Morgan, ed., *Connecticut as Colony and as State* (Hartford, Conn.: The Publishing Society of Connecticut, 1904), I, 495-497.

21. Dexter, ed., *Documentary History*, pp. 275-276; also in *PCSM*, 6 (1904), 207-209.

22. Cf. Ralph H. Gabriel, *Religion and Learning at Yale: The Church of*

*Christ in the College and University,* 1757–1957 (New Haven, Conn.: Yale University Press, 1958), p. 4, and Warch, *School of the Prophets,* pp. 54-58.

23. The charter is reprinted in Edward C. Elliott and M. M. Chambers, eds., *Charters and Basic Laws of Selected American Universities and Colleges* (New York: The Carnegie Foundation for the Advancement of Teaching, 1934), pp. 587-593.

## 5. The Triumph of External Government

1. *PCSM,* 16 (1925), 434-435.

2. For tutors Sever, Stevens, and Robie see Clifford K. Shipton, *Sibley's Harvard Graduates* (Boston: Massachusetts Historical Society, 1937), V, 90-96, 239-243, 450-455.

3. *PSCM,* 16 (1925), 436-439; John Leverett's Diary, Harvard University Archives, pp. 153, 158-159.

4. Documents on Tutor Controversy, no. 3, Harvard University Archives.

5. *PCSM,* 16 (1925), 445, 449; Memorial of Flynt, Sever, and Robie, May 30, 1720, Documents on Tutor Controversy, no. 6.

6. Quincy, *History,* I, 542, 543-544, 557-558.

7. Documents on Tutor Controversy, nos. 16 and 18; Quincy, *History,* I, 265-268.

8. *PCSM,* 16 (1925), 460-461, 464; Quincy, *History,* I, 289-291.

9. Quincy, *History,* I, 293-295; *PCSM,* 16 (1925), 465-466.

10. Quincy, *History,* I, 297-298; *PCSM,* 16 (1925), 468, 473.

11. Quincy, *History,* I, 299-303; *Journal of the House of Representatives of Massachusetts,* IV (1923), 25, 37, 58.

12. Quincy, *History,* I, 303-305; *House Journal,* IV (1923), 58, 71-72; Nathaniel B. Shurtleff, ed., *Records of the Governor and Company of the Massachusetts Bay in New England* (Boston, 1853), III, 207-208.

13. Quincy, *History,* I, 305-307, 311; *PCSM,* 16 (1925), 474, 478-480, 483, 486; *House Journal,* IV (1923), 116-117, 147, 196, 207, 215; V (1923), 67; Documents on Tutor Controversy, no. 19; Overseers Record, I (1701–1743), 41, by permission of Harvard University Archives.

14. Quincy, *History,* I, 312-313; *PCSM,* 16 (1925), 486-487; *House Journal,* V (1923), 95-96, 111, 113; Documents on Tutor Controversy, no. 20; Overseers Record, I, 48, 53, by permission of Harvard University Archives.

15. Quincy, *History,* I, 546-556; *PSCM,* 16 (1925), 489-500.

16. See George Dexter, ed., "Tutor Sever's Argument," *Publications of the Massachusetts Historical Society,* 16 (February 1878): 50-67.

17. Quincy, *History,* I, 317-320; *PCSM,* 16 (1925), 503; *House Journal,* V (1923), 152.

18. Quincy, *History,* I, chs. 26 and 27, passim; *PCSM,* 16 (1925), 511, 517, 523-525; cf. John M. Hoffmann, "Commonwealth College: The Governance of Harvard in the Puritan Period," (Ph.D. diss., Harvard University, 1972), p. 604.

19. For a good account of the Two Penny Act and the Parsons' Cause that followed see Richard L. Morton, *Colonial Virginia* (Chapel Hill, N.C.: Univer-

sity of North Carolina Press, 1960), II, 751-819; see also Hamilton J. Eckenrode, *Separation of Church and State in Virginia* (Richmond, Va.: Superintendent of Public Printing, 1910), pp. 20-30.

20. Dawson to the Bishop of London, Feb. 25, 1756, in William S. Perry, ed., *Historical Collections Relating to the American Colonial Church* (Hartford, Conn., 1870), I, 446-448, and in Fulham Papers, Lambeth Palace Library, American Colonial Section, XIII, 220-221. [Identification by volume and page according to William W. Manross, ed., *The Fulham Papers . . . Calendar and Indexes* (Oxford: Clarendon Press, 1965).]

21. Colonial Williamsburg, Survey Report 1099, Reel M-357, Lambeth Palace Library, p. 99.

22. See "Proceedings of the Virginia Committee of Correspondence," *VMHB*, 10 (April 1903): 355.

23. H. L. Ganter, ed., "Documents Relating to the Early History of the College of William and Mary," *WMQ*, 2nd ser., 20 (1940), 537-541, and Fulham Papers, XIII, 227-235.

24. Perry, ed., *Historical Collections*, I, 456-457, and Fulham Papers, XIII, 240-241.

25. Ganter, ed., "Documents," pp. 541-544, and Fulham Papers, XIII, 242-243.

26. "Minutes of the College Faculty, 1758," *WMQ*, 2nd ser., 1 (January 1921): 24-26.

27. "Journal of the Meetings of the President and Masters of William and Mary College," *WMQ*, 1st ser., 4 (July 1895): 45; William and Mary College Papers, folders 12 and 55, in Swem Library, College of William and Mary; Fulham Papers, XIV, 119-126; see also Morton, *Colonial Virginia*, II, 776.

28. Perry, ed., *Historical Collections*, I, 463-470; Fulham Papers, XIII, 288-293.

29. Morton, *Colonial Virginia*, II, 770; Perry, ed., *Historical Collections*, I, 472, 473; Fulham Papers, XIV, 1-2, 13-24, 281-298.

30. Fulham Papers, XIII, 284-287; Morton, *Colonial Virginia*, II, 779-780; "Journal," *WMQ*, 1st ser., 3 (October 1894): 130, 131; 3 (January 1895): 196.

31 Perry, ed., *Historical Collections*, I, 518; Fulham Papers, XIV, 51-72, 85-90, 119-126.

32. Perry, ed., *Historical Collections*, I, 523; Fulham Papers, XIV, 95-102.

33. Fulham Papers, XIV, 91-92; Perry, ed., *Historical Collections*, I, 523.

34. Fulham Papers, XIV, 113-126.

35. Perry, ed., *Historical Collections*, I, 528-529; Fulham Papers, XIV, 127-134, 137-140.

36. "Journal," *WMQ*, 1st ser., 5 (1896–1897), 83-89, 188-189; Fulham Papers, XIV, 153-156, 147-152.

37. "Journal," ibid., 5 (1897), 224-229; Fulham Papers, XIV, 157-160.

38. Fulham Papers, XIV, 161-196, 199-202; Perry, ed., *Historical Collections*, I, 530-532; "Minutes of the Visitors," *WMQ*, 1st ser., 27 (April 1919): 239-240; "Journal," ibid., 13 (October 1904): 150-154.

39. See Robert P. Thomson, "The Reform of the College of William and

Mary, 1763–1780," *Proceedings of the American Philosophical Society*, 115 (June 1971): 196.

## II. Introduction

1. On the Great Awakening and its impact on education see Lawrence A. Cremin, *American Education: The Colonial Experience*, 1607–1783 (New York: Harper and Row, 1970), ch. 10; Douglas Sloan, ed., *The Great Awakening and American Education: A Documentary History* (New York: Teachers College Press, 1973); William W. Sweet, *Revivalism in America: Its Origin, Growth, and Decline* (New York: C. Scribner's Sons, 1944); and Alan Heimert and Perry Miller, eds., *The Great Awakening: Documents Illustrating the Crisis and Its Consequences* (Indianapolis, Ind.: Bobbs-Merrill, 1967).

2. "Order in Council," reprinted in U.S. Bureau of Education, *Circular of Information*, no. 2, 1892 (Washington, D.C., 1893), pp. 77-79.

3. On Harvard during this period see Samuel Eliot Morison, *Three Centuries of Harvard*, 1636–1936 (Cambridge, Mass.: Harvard University Press, 1936), pp. 53-100.

4. The Yale story of these years is best told by Louis L. Tucker, *Puritan Protagonist: President Thomas Clap of Yale College* (Chapel Hill, N.C.: University of North Carolina Press, 1962), pp. 144-231.

5. For the College of New Jersey consult Thomas J. Wertenbaker, *Princeton, 1746–1896* (Princeton, N.J.: Princeton University Press, 1946), pp. 3-46, and part I of Howard Miller, *The Revolutionary College: American Presbyterian Higher Education 1707–1837* (New York: New York University Press, 1976).

6. The early history of King's College is best presented by David C. Humphrey in *From King's College to Columbia*, 1746–1800 (New York: Columbia University Press, 1976); a brief summary may be found in John H. Van Amringe, "King's College and Columbia College," in *A History of Columbia University, 1754–1904* (New York: Columbia University Press, 1904), pp. 1-41.

7. I have described this development in "From Religion to Politics: Debates and Confrontations over American College Governance in the Mid-Eighteenth Century," *Harvard Educational Review*, 46 (August 1976): 397-424.

## 6. Yale College and the Awakening

1. Richard Warch, *School of the Prophets: Yale College, 1701–1740* (New Haven, Conn.: Yale University Press, 1973), p. 310.

2. For narratives of the events in Connecticut, New Haven, and the college see Benjamin Trumbull, *A Complete History of Connecticut* (New Haven, Conn., 1818), II, 160-175; Brooks M. Kelley, *Yale: A History* (New Haven, Conn.: Yale University Press, 1974), pp. 49-72; and Louis Leonard Tucker, *Puritan Protagonist: President Thomas Clap of Yale College* (Chapel Hill, N.C.: University of North Carolina Press, 1962), pp. 123-141.

3. In Stephen Nissenbaum, ed., *The Great Awakening at Yale College*

(Belmont, Calif.: Wadsworth Publishing Company, 1972), p. 59.

4. Nissenbaum, ed., *The Great Awakening*, pp. 136-139.

5. See Franklin B. Dexter, ed., *Biographical Sketches of the Graduates of Yale College with Annals of the College History* (New York, 1885), I, 662, 663, and Dexter, ed., *Documentary History of Yale University* (New Haven, Conn.: Yale University Press, 1916) , pp. 356-358, 363.

6. See Richard Warch, "The Shepherd's Tent: Education and Enthusiasm in the Great Awakening," *American Quarterly*, 30 (Summer 1978): 177-198.

7. For a brief narrative and relevant documents on the Shepherd's Tent see Nissenbaum, ed., *The Great Awakening*, pp. 179-187.

8. Richard Hofstadter and Wilson Smith, eds., *American Higher Education: A Documentary History* (Chicago: University of Chicago Press, 1961), I, 62-64; Dexter, ed., *Documentary History*, pp. 369-370.

9. Hofstadter and Smith, eds., *American Higher Education*, I, 66-74; see also Richard Hofstadter and Walter Metzger, *The Development of Academic Freedom in the United States* (New York: Columbia University Press, 1955), pp. 161-163.

10. Nissenbaum, ed., *The Great Awakening*, pp. 227, 239.

11. Ibid., p. 239; Hofstadter and Smith, eds., *American Higher Education*, I, 81-82.

12. Nissenbaum, ed., *The Great Awakening*, p. 240.

13. Dexter, ed., *Documentary History*, pp. 370-372.

14. Trumbull, *A Complete History*, II, 182-183; Nissenbaum, ed., *The Great Awakening*, pp. 246-250.

15. On Pierpont see Clifford K. Shipton, *Sibley's Harvard Graduates* (Boston: Massachusetts Historical Society, 1937), VI, 98-100; Trumbull, *A Complete History*, II, 183.

16. For the events of 1723 and 1728 see Dexter, ed., *Documentary History*, pp. 247-250, 275-276; Clap's account of drafting charter and laws is contained in his "Annals of Yale College in New Haven," 1747 ms. in Yale University Archives.

17. For the 1701 charter of Yale see Franklin B. Dexter, ed., *Documentary History*, pp. 20-23; the 1745 charter is printed in Edward C. Elliott and M. M. Chambers, eds., *Charters and Basic Laws of Selected American Universities and Colleges* (New York: The Carnegie Foundation for the Advancement of Teaching, 1934), pp. 588-593.

18. For the defection of Cutler and Johnson see Warch, *School of the Prophets*, pp. 96-117. I have described the Harvard tutor rebellion in chapter 5.

19. The laws are printed in Dexter, *Biographical Sketches*, II, 2-18.

20. See Tucker, *Puritan Protagonist*, pp. 166-183.

21. Herbert and Carol Schneider, eds., *Samuel Johnson, President of King's College: His Career and Writings* (New York: Columbia University Press, 1929), I, 178-182.

22. Thomas Clap, *The Religious Constitution of Colleges* (New London, Conn., 1754).

23. For this and subsequent developments see Ralph Henry Gabriel,

*Religion and Learning at Yale: The Church of Christ in the College and University,* 1757–1957 (New Haven, Conn.: Yale University Press, 1958), pp. 1-29, and Tucker, *Puritan Protagonist,* pp. 183-200.

24. Tucker, *Puritan Protagonist,* p. 199.

25. Benjamin Gale, *The Present State of the Colony of Connecticut Considered* (New London, Conn., 1775), pp. 7, 9-11. See also Dexter, ed., *Biographical Sketches,* II, 357, and Thomas Clap, *A Brief History* (New Haven, Conn., 1775), p. 9.

26. [Thomas Clap], *The Answer of the Friend in the West* (New Haven, Conn., 1775), pp. 8, 9; Benjamin Gale, *A Reply to a Pamphlet entitled, The Answer of the Friend in the West* (New London, Conn., 1775).

27. In *Patrick's Case,* Raym., Sir T. (1664), 101, the Court of King's Bench had recognized a college as a lay corporation.

28. Gale, *A Reply,* p. 41; on Gale see also George C. Groce, Jr., "Benjamin Gale," *New England Quarterly,* 10 (December 1937): 697-716.

29. Ms. copy of trustee memorial in *Connecticut Archives* (Hartford, Connecticut State Library Archives), I, 338a, 338b.

30. Gale, *A Calm and Full Vindication of a Letter Wrote to a Member of the Lower House of the Assembly* (New Haven, Conn., 1759), pp. 28-30; Gale, *A Letter to a Member of the Lower House* (New Haven, Conn., 1759), pp. 17-18.

31. *Philips v. Bury,* 2 T.R. (1693), 352; *The Case of Sutton's Hospital,* 10 Co. Rep. (1612), 31a.

32. Samuel Eliot Morison, *Three Centuries of Harvard,* 1636–1936 (Cambridge, Mass.: Harvard University Press, 1936), pp. 101-102, 118; "Alison to Stiles," in Franklin B. Dexter, ed., *Extracts from the Itineraries and Other Miscellanies of Ezra Stiles, D.D., L.L.D.,* 1755–1794 (New Haven, Conn.: Yale University Press, 1916), p. 423; Neda M. Westlake, intro., *Minutes of the Trustees of the College, Academy and Charitable Schools, University of Pennsylvania,* Vol. I: 1749 *to* 1768 (Wilmington, Del.: Scholarly Resources, Inc., 1974), pp. 147, 201, 239.

33. Corporation Meeting, July 21, 1761, ms. in *Connecticut Archives,* 1st ser., I, 340a-c, in Connecticut State Library Archives; Thomas Fuller et al., "Letter to the Assembly," Oct. 6, 1761, ms. in Yale University Archives, Yale University Library.

34. Dexter, ed., *Itineraries,* pp. 58, 507, 585; Records of Yale Corporation, November 30, 1762, ms. in Yale University Archives, Yale University Library.

35. Edward Dorr et al., Memorial of March 10, 1763, ms. copy in *Connecticut Archives,* "Colleges and Schools," 1st ser., II, 66a-h; and Ebenezer Devotion et al., Memorial of April, 1763, ms. copy in *Connecticut Archives,* "Colleges and Schools," 1st ser., II, 67a-b, both in Connecticut State Library Archives and Yale University Archives, Yale University Library.

## 7. College Founding in the Middle Colonies

1. For information on the middle colony Presbyterians see Archibald Alexander, *Biographical Sketches of the Founder and Principal Alumni of the Log*

*College* (Princeton, N.J., 1845); Leonard Trinterud, *The Forming of an American Tradition* (Philadelphia: Westminster Press, 1949), pp. 53-108; Elijah R. Craven, "The Log College of Neshaminy and Princeton University," *Journal of the Presbyterian Historical Society*, 1 (June 1902): 308-314; and Thomas J. Wertenbaker, *Princeton, 1746-1896* (Princeton, N.J.: Princeton University Press, 1946), pp. 1-15; on the Presbyterian academies see Douglas Sloan, *The Scottish Enlightenment and the American College Ideal* (New York: Teachers College Press, 1971), pp. 36-102.

2. See Thomas C. Pears, Jr. and Guy S. Klett, comps., "Documentary History of William Tennent and the Log College," *Journal of the Presbyterian Historical Society*, 28 (September 1950): 190, 191.

3. See Leonard W. Labaree, ed., *The Papers of Benjamin Franklin* (New Haven, Conn.: Yale University Press, 1960), II, 392.

4. Cf. John Maclean, *History of the College of New Jersey, 1746-1854* (New York: Arno Press, 1969), I, 24-31, and George H. Ryden, "The Newark Academy of Delaware in Colonial Days," *Pennsylvania History*, 2 (October 1935): 208. Quotations are from a letter of the Philadelphia synod to President Clap, May 30, 1746, reprinted in *Records of the Presbyterian Church in the United States of America* (New York: Arno Press, 1969), pp. 186-189.

5. *Records*, pp. 167, 168.

6. An account and documents of the Cleaveland affair may be found in Stephen Nissenbaum, ed., *The Great Awakening at Yale College* (Belmont, Calif.: Wadsworth Publishing Company, 1972), pp. 219-250, and in Richard Hofstadter and Wilson Smith, eds., *American Higher Education: A Documentary History* (Chicago: The University of Chicago Press, 1961), I, 74-82.

7. See Wertenbaker, *Princeton*, pp. 19-20, 21.

8. Both the 1746 and the 1748 charters are reprinted in Wertenbaker, *Princeton*, pp. 396-404.

9. Cf. Wertenbaker, *Princeton*, pp. 25-27, and Maclean, *History*, I, 70-113; see also Jonathan Edwards's account of the charter negotiations in *The Works of President Edwards* (New York, 1830), I, 266-268, 275.

10. Cf. Wertenbaker, *Princeton*, pp. 30-35; Maclean, *History*, I, 147-154; Varnum L. Collins, *Princeton* (New York: Oxford University Press, 1914), pp. 19-20; and George W. Pilcher, ed., *The Reverend Samuel Davies Abroad: The Diary of a Journey to England and Scotland, 1753-1755* (Urbana, Ill.: University of Illinois Press, 1967); see also Alison B. Olson, "The Founding of Princeton University: Religion and Politics in Eighteenth-Century New Jersey," *New Jersey History*, 87 (Autumn 1969): 133-150.

11. See Edward P. Cheyney, *History of the University of Pennsylvania, 1740-1940* (Philadelphia: University of Pennsylvania Press, 1940).

12. Leonard W. Labaree, ed., *Franklin Papers*, III, 385-388, 397-429.

13. Labaree, ed., *Franklin Papers*, III, 399, 400, 462; IV, 34-37.

14. Neda M. Westlake, intro., *Minutes of the Trustees of the College, Academy and Charitable Schools, University of Pennsylvania*, Vol. I: 1749 to 1768 (Wilmington, Del.: Scholarly Resources, Inc., 1974), p. 5; Labaree, ed., *Franklin Papers*, III, 467.

15. Labaree, ed., *Franklin Papers*, III, 404; IV, 36.

16. Ibid., IV, 108.

17. John Bigelow, ed., *The Works of Benjamin Franklin* (New York: G. P. Putnam's Sons, 1904), XII, 75; Westlake, intro., *Minutes*, p. 7 ¼; Labaree, ed., *Franklin Papers*, III, 415.

18. Westlake, intro., *Minutes*, pp. 23, 33, 34; Labaree, ed., *Franklin Papers*, V, 7-11; IV, 38.

19. William Smith, *A General Idea of the College of Mirania*, ed. Edward M. Griffin (1753; New York: Johnson Reprint Corporation, 1969), pp. 10, 67, 71, 75; Labaree, ed., *Franklin Papers*, IV, 467-470, 475.

20. Smith, *A General Idea*, pp. 11, 14-16, 26-27, 34, 36, 41, 49, 59, 66, 68, 86.

21. Westlake, intro., *Minutes*, 40, 45-50; Horace W. Smith, *Life and Correspondence of the Rev. William Smith, D. D.* (New York: Arno Press, 1972), I, 106.

22. Labaree, ed., *Franklin Papers*, V, 193, 331; Smith, *Life and Correspondence*, I, 143; Westlake, intro., *Minutes*, p. 53.

23. Labaree, ed., *Franklin Papers*, VI, 28-37, 103-108.

24. Cf. Bruce R. Lively, "William Smith, The College and Academy of Philadelphia, and Pennsylvania Politics, 1753-1758," *Historical Magazine of the Protestant Episcopal Church*, 38 (September 1969): 237-258; Westlake, intro., *Minutes*, pp. 68, 70-72, 91, 97.

25. Smith, *Life and Correspondence*, I, 143; the two pamphlets of Smith are *A Brief State of the Province of Pennsylvania*, and *A Brief View of the Conduct of Pennsylvania* (both 1755); Labaree, ed., *Franklin Papers*, VII, 12; VIII, 416.

26. Westlake, intro., *Minutes*, pp. 260-262.

27. See Pennsylvanicus in *The Pennsylvania Journal and Weekly Advertiser* of September 28, November 30, 1758, and January 25, February 8, and March 1 and 15, 1759; Westlake, intro., *Minutes*, p. 99; see also Cheyney, *History*, pp. 104-125.

## 8. A College for New York

1. Lewis Morris to Secretary of the Society for the Propagation of the Gospel, June 1704, in SPG Papers, Series A, vol. 2, no. 171, microfilm; *Colonial Laws of New York* (Albany, 1894), III, 607-616; Johnson to Cadwallader Colden, April 15, 1747, in *Collections of the New York Historical Society*, LII (1919), 374-375; SPG Letters and Papers, Series B, vol. 15, no. 51.

2. *The New York Evening Post*, no. 130 (May 18, 1747).

3. *Colonial Laws*, III, 679-688, 731-732; William Livingston, *Some Serious Thoughts on the Design of Erecting a College in the Province of New York* (New York, 1749), pp. 1-7.

4. Livingston, *Some Serious Thoughts*, p. 3; Herbert and Carol Schneider, eds., *Samuel Johnson, President of King's College: His Career and Writings* (New York: Columbia University Press, 1929), I, 135.

5. *Colonial Laws*, III, 842-844.

6. Hugh Hastings, ed., *Ecclesiastical Records: State of New York* (Albany, N.Y.: J. B. Lyon, State Printer, 1905), V, 3220; [William Smith], *Some Thoughts on Education* (New York, 1752), pp. 9, 17; *New York Mercury* (November 6, 1752).

7. See Milton M. Klein, ed., *The Independent Reflector* (Cambridge, Mass.: Harvard University Press, 1963).

8. The letter is reprinted in Klein, ed., *Reflector*, pp. 36-37.

9. Klein, ed., *Reflector*, p. 202.

10. Klein, ed., *Reflector*, pp. 174, 182, 185, 192, 195, 213, 214.

11. Klein, ed., *Reflector*, pp. 197, 200, 204.

12. William Smith, *A General Idea of the College of Mirania*, ed. Edward M. Griffin (1753; New York: Johnson Reprint Corporation, 1969), pp. 10, 67, 71.

13. In *New York Mercury* (April 30, July 9 and 23, 1753); Klein, ed., *Reflector*, pp. 201-203.

14. Smith, *General Idea*, pp. 41, 59.

15. Ibid., pp. 66, 86.

16. Cf. Bernard Bailyn, *The Origins of American Politics* (New York: Knopf, 1968), p. 114; *Colonial Laws*, III, 899, 930-939; Schneider and Schneider, eds., *Samuel Johnson*, IV, 4-6.

17. Schneider and Schneider, eds., *Samuel Johnson*, I, 173-174; IV, 5, 7-8, 8-9.

18. Hastings, ed., *Ecclesiastical Records*, V, 3478; *Journal of the General Assembly* (New York, 1766), II, 399-402.

19. Hastings, ed., *Ecclesiastical Records*, V, 3479-3483.

20. Schneider and Schneider, eds., *Samuel Johnson*, IV, 13-14, 243-244; "Advertisement," in John B. Pine, ed., *Charters, Acts of the Legislature, Official Documents and Records*, rev. ed. (New York: Printed for the College, 1920), pp. 32-33.

21. Pine, ed., *Charters*, p. 34.

22. Schneider and Schneider, eds., *Samuel Johnson*, IV, 21; Ellis, *The New England Mind*, pp. 236-240.

23. Hastings, ed., *Ecclesiastical Records*, V, 3501, 3505.

24. Schneider and Schneider, eds., *Samuel Johnson*, IV, 19, 22.

25. The college charter is printed in Hastings, ed. *Ecclesiastical Records*, V, 3508-3514.

26. Cf. Milton Klein, "The American Whig: William Livingston of New York" (Ph.D. diss., Columbia University, 1954), p. 412; Schneider and Schneider, eds., *Samuel Johnson*, IV, 24-25; *Journal of the General Assembly*, II, 404, 422; and Petition of the Freemen of New York, no. 1, ms. in Butler Library, Columbia University, Special Collections.

27. The bill is printed in *Journal of the General Assembly*, II, 412-419.

28. *New York Mercury* (October 20 and November 17, 1755); Schneider and Schneider, eds., *Samuel Johnson*, IV, 28-29, 191-207; Society for the Propagation of the Gospel, Minutes of March 21, 1755, ms. extract in Special Collections, Butler Library.

29. Schneider and Schneider, eds., *Samuel Johnson*, IV, 36-38, 213-214;

*Colonial Laws*, IV, 160-162; see also ms. report of Committee to Consider Ways and Means, June 2, 1755, Butler Library.

30. On the Dutch Reformed college see Nelson R. Burr, *Education in New Jersey, 1630–1871* (Princeton, N.J.: Princeton University Press, 1942), pp. 19-21; William H. S. Demarest, *A History of Rutgers College* (New Brunswick, N.J.: Rutgers College, 1924), pp. 23-50; and Richard P. McCormick, *Rutgers: A Bicentennial History* (New Brunswick, N.J.: Rutgers University Press, 1966), pp. 1-8; Hastings, ed., *Ecclesiastical Records*, V, 3542-3545, 3554-3556, 3574-3576; Pine, ed., *Charters*, pp. 26-27.

31. Hastings, ed., *Ecclesiastical Records*, V, 3576-3577, 3605, 3611-3613. Frelinghuysen's statement was pseudonymously published as David Marin Ben Jesse, *A Remark on the Disputes and Contentions in this Province* (New York, 1755); on the authenticity of the authorship see Beverly McAnear, "American Imprints Concerning King's College," *Papers of the Bibliographical Society of America*, 44 (1950), 327, n. 53.

32. Cf. George P. Schmidt, *Princeton and Rutgers: The Two Colonial Colleges of New Jersey* (Princeton, N.J.: Van Nostrand, 1964). Since the 1766 charter seems to have been lost, all quotations from the charter are from *Charter of a College to be Erected in New Jersey* (New York, 1770).

33. The controversies surrounding negotiations over an American classis and college may be followed in Hastings, ed., *Ecclesiastical Records*, VI, passim; see also the narratives in Demarest, *A History*, and McCormick, *Rutgers*.

34. Hastings, ed., *Ecclesiastical Records*, VI, 4085-4086, 4102-4103, 4120-4124, 4140-4144; Demarest, *A History*, pp. 75-100.

# 9. Autocracy in Connecticut and Pluralism in Rhode Island

1. The story of the May 15 meeting is told by Clap in "Annals of Yale College in New Haven," 1766 ms., Yale University Archives; this is also printed as *The Annals or History of Yale College* (New Haven, Conn., 1766). Other reports are in Benjamin Trumbull, *A Complete History of Connecticut* (New Haven, Conn., 1818), II, 327-333; Franklin B. Dexter, ed., *Biographical Sketches of the Graduates of Yale College with Annals of the College History* (New York, 1885), II, 780-781; and, in greatest detail, in Louis L. Tucker, *Puritan Protagonist: President Thomas Clap of Yale College* (Chapel Hill, N.C.: University of North Carolina Press, 1962), pp. 224-231; also see mss. in *Connecticut Archives*, Colleges and Schools, 1st ser., II, 67b, Connecticut State Library, Hartford.

2. Stephen White, *Civil Rulers Gods by Office, and the Duties of Such Considered and Enforced* (New London, Conn., 1763), p. 32.

3. [Thomas Clap], *The Answer of the Friend in the West* (New Haven, Conn., 1755), p. 16.

4. *The Case of Sutton's Hospital*, 10 Co. Rep. (1612), 33a; Thomas Wood, *An Institute of the Laws of England* (London, 1720).

5. "The Answer of President and Fellows," ms. copies in the Beinecke Rare Book and Manuscript Library, Yale University, and *Connecticut Archives*, Col-

leges and Schools, 1st ser., II, 71a-w, Connecticut State Library Archives. In the *Connecticut Archives* copy is inserted between the words "to give this Assembly" and "an account of" the crossed-out phrase "or perhaps to any one of them." The copy in the Beinecke Library reads: "And we shall always be ready to give to this assembly or to any of them an account . . ." Apparently Clap wanted to make sure that any inquiry into the college be viewed as an extraordinary matter requiring the attention of both houses and not to be delegated to a committee.

6. The material in this and subsequent paragraphs is based on a comparison of the manuscripts of the 1747 and 1766 editions of Clap's "Annals of Yale College in New Haven" and the published *Annals or History of Yale College* in 1766.

7. Thomas Clap, *The Religious Constitution of Colleges* (New London, Conn., 1754), pp. 7, 9.

8. [Clap], *The Answer*, pp. 15, 16.

9. Thomas Clap, *A Brief History* (New Haven, Conn., 1755), p. 9.

10. Clap, *The Annals*, pp. 2, 3. Clap's "discovery" of the year 1700 as the founding date occurred sometime between the appearance of *The Religious Constitution of Colleges* in 1754 and the publication of *The Answer to the Friend in the West* in 1755, and not as he prepared himself for the 1763 confrontation with the Assembly, as had been assumed by Franklin B. Dexter in "The Founding of Yale College," *Papers of the New Haven Colony Historical Society*, III (1882), 22, and by Simeon E. Baldwin in "The Ecclesiastical Constitution of Yale College," ibid., III (1882), 421. Still, it remains a puzzle why in the original manuscript of the 1757 Annals, Clap still (or again?) listed 1701 as the founding date, unless this was simply the result of copying the first part of the 1747 manuscript and neglecting to change the date. Further support for 1754/1755 comes from the fact that Clap's antagonist, Benjamin Gale, entered the public debate over the relationship of Yale to the General Court in 1755, and in that year the Court ceased to grant its annual subsidy. These events apparently persuaded Clap to rewrite the early history of the Collegiate School.

11. "Answer of President and Fellows," *Connecticut Archives*, 71 g, h, s; Edward Dorr et al., Memorial of March 10, 1763, ms. in ibid., 66f, in Connecticut State Library Archives; Edward Stillingfleet, "The Case of Visitation of Colleges in the House of Lords, in Exeter College Case," *Works* (London, 1710), III, 877, 879.

12. "Answer of President and Fellows," *Connecticut Archives*, 71 r, m. n, in Connecticut State Library Archives.

13. Benjamin Gale, *A Letter to a Member of the Lower House* (New Haven, Conn., 1759), pp. 17-18, and *A Calm and Full Vindication of a Letter Wrote to a Member of the Lower House of the Assembly* (New Haven, Conn., 1759), p. 29; "Answer of President and Fellows," *Connecticut Archives*, 71, t, u, in Connecticut State Library Archives.

14. See Joseph S. Davis, *Essays in the Earlier History of American Corporations* (Cambridge, Mass.: Harvard University Press, 1917), I, 5, n.1; St. George L. Sioussat, "The English Statutes in Maryland," *Johns Hopkins University*

*Studies in Historical and Political Science*, 21 (1903), 482; and Joseph H. Smith, *Appeals to the Privy Council from the American Plantations* (New York: Columbia University Press, 1950), pp. 467-476.

15. Clap, *The Annals*, pp. 76-77; Trumbull, *A Complete History*, II, 333; and Dexter, ed., *Biographical Sketches*, 780-781.

16. See Tucker, *Puritan Protagonist*, pp. 232-270; Richard Hofstadter and Walter P. Metzger, *The Development of Academic Freedom in the United States* (New York: Columbia University Press, 1955), pp. 175-176.

17. Clap, "Letter on the Right of Appeal of Students in College," February 2, 1764, ms. in Yale University Archives.

18. Clap, "Some Observations Relating to the Government of Yale College," 1764, ms. in Yale University Archives.

19. The *Annals* were printed in 1766 in New Haven; the Yale University Archives also have the ms. of the 1766 edition; Anon., *A Letter to an Honourable Gentleman* (New Haven, Conn., 1766).

20. See Dexter, ed., *Biographical Sketches*, III, 167; Tucker, *Puritan Protagonist*, p. 257; and Dexter, ed., *Extracts from the Itineraries and Other Miscellanies of Ezra Stiles, D.D., L.L.D.*, 1755–1794 (New Haven, Conn.: Yale University Press, 1916), pp. 62, 455-457, 589.

21. *Public Records of the Colony of Connecticut from May 1762 to October 1767* (Hartford, Conn., 1881), pp. 513-514; Dexter, ed., *Itineraries*, pp. 458, 492.

22. Edward C. Elliott and M. M. Chambers, eds., *Charters and Basic Laws of Selected American Universities and Colleges* (New York: The Carnegie Foundation for the Advancement of Teaching, 1934), p. 589, n. 3.

23. Dexter, ed., *Itineraries*, p. 105.

24. On Stiles's concern with Christian union see his *A Discourse on the Christian Union* (Boston, 1761), and Carl Bridenbaugh's discussion in *Mitre and Sceptre: Transatlantic Faiths, Ideas, Personalities, and Politics 1689–1775* (New York: Oxford University Press, 1962), pp. 3-22.

25. For the founding of the College of Rhode Island see Walter C. Bronson, *The History of Brown University, 1764–1914* (Providence, R.I., 1914), pp. 1-14, and Reuben A. Guild, *Early History of Brown University, including the Life, Times, and Correspondence of President Manning, 1756–1791*(Providence, R.I., 1897), pp. 7-45.

26. For Stiles's views and activities in Rhode Island see Edmund S. Morgan, *The Gentle Puritan: A Life of Ezra Stiles, 1727–1795* (Chapel Hill, N.C.: The University of North Carolina Press, 1962), pp. 196-209, and Dexter, ed., *Itineraries*, pp. 24-25, 583-584.

27. Both the 1763 draft charter and the 1764 charter are reprinted in Reuben A. Guild, *Life, Times, and Correspondence of James Manning* (Boston, 1864), pp. 465-481; the 1764 charter is also printed in Bronson, *The History*, pp. 493-499. On the charter negotiations see Bronson, *The History*, pp. 13-33, Guild, *Early History*, pp. 510-534, and Morgan, *The Gentle Puritan*, pp. 204-206. The various versions of the Stiles charter are discussed also in Bronson, *The History*, pp. 493-499. Manning's remark is given in Bronson, *The History*, p. 24. On William Ellery see Edward T. Channing, "Life of William Ellery," in

Jared Sparks, ed., *The Library of American Biography* (New York, 1835), VI, 85-159.

28. Franklin B. Dexter, ed., *The Literary Diary of Ezra Stiles* (New York: Charles Scribner's Sons, 1901), I, 22, 39.

29. See Stiles's statistics in Dexter, ed., *Literary Diary*, I, 278, and *Itineraries*, p. 13.

30. For the text of the charter and additional comments and analysis see my "The Charter for a Proposed College in Newport, Rhode Island: A Chapter in the History of Eighteenth Century Higher Education in America," *Newport History*, 49 (Spring 1976): 25-49.

31. General Assembly of Governor and Company, South Kingstown, February 26–March 2, 1770, microfilm, Early State Records.

32. The text of the remonstrance is reprinted in Guild, *Early History*, pp. 133-134; for the political situation in which the Newport college project was defeated see David Lovejoy, *Rhode Island Politics and the American Revolution, 1760-1776* (Providence, R.I.: Brown University Press, 1958), pp. 147-153.

## 10. The American Provincial College

1. Franklin B. Dexter, ed., *The Literary Diary of Ezra Stiles* (New York: Charles Scribner's Sons, 1901), I, 45-46.

2. For an account of Wheelock's work in Lebanon see Leon Burr Richardson, *History of Dartmouth College* (Hanover, N.H.: Dartmouth College Publications, 1932), I, 1-90, and James Dow McCallum, *Eleazar Wheelock: Founder of Dartmouth College* (Hanover, N.H.: Dartmouth College Publications, 1939), pp. 74-166.

3. On the Indian students see David C. Humphrey, "King's College in the City of New York, 1754-1776" (Ph.D. diss., Northwestern University, 1968), pp. 267-275, Richardson, *Dartmouth College*, I, 49-90, and McCallum *Wheelock*, pp. 120-123.

4. McCallum, *Wheelock*, p. 132.

5. Franklin B. Dexter, ed., *Extracts from the Itineraries and other Miscellanies of Ezra Stiles, D.D., L.L.D., 1755-1794, with a Selection from his Correspondence* (New Haven: Yale University Press, 1916), pp. 471-472.

6. McCallum, *Wheelock*, p. 170.

7. Reuben Aldridge Guild, *Early History of Brown University, including the Life, Times, and Correspondence of President Manning, 1756-1791* (Providence, R.I.: Snow and Farnham, 1896), p. 178.

8. The charter is reprinted in Frederick Chase, *A History of Dartmouth College*, ed. John K. Lord (Cambridge, England: John Wilson and Son, 1891), I, 639-649.

9. Material in this and the preceding paragraph is based on McCallum, *Wheelock*, pp. 173-175, 193, Richardson, *Dartmouth College*, I, 112-117, 144, 211-217, and Chase, *A History*, I, 277, 353, 365, 548-549.

10. Nathaniel Bouton, *The Fathers of the New Hampshire Ministry* (Concord, N.H., 1848), pp. 36-37, and Bouton, "A Discourse [on the History of

Education in New Hampshire]," *Collections of the New-Hampshire Historical Society*, IV (1834), 18; see also ibid., IX (1889), 36-39.

11. Allen D. Candler, ed., *The Colonial Records of the State of Georgia* (Atlanta, Ga.: C. P. Byrd, State Printer, 1907), IX, 260.

12. George Whitefield, *Works* (London, 1771), III, 481.

13. Ibid., III, 475, 476. See also Mollie C. Davis, "Whitefield's Attempt to Establish a College in Georgia," *Georgia Historical Quarterly*, 55 (Winter 1971): 459-470, and Robert L. McCaul, "Whitefield's Bethesda College Project and Other Attempts to Found Colonial Colleges," ibid., 44 (September 1960): 263-277, (December 1960), 381-398.

14. The charter of Queen's College is reprinted in Walter Clark, ed., *The State Records of North Carolina* (Goldsboro, N.C.: P. M. Hale, 1906), XXV, 519d-519f.

15. In William L. Saunders, ed., *The Colonial Records of North Carolina* (Raleigh, N.C., 1890), VIII, 526.

16. For the English reaction see ibid., IX, 248-250, 284-285. See also Marshall D. Haywood, "The Story of Queen's College or Liberty Hall in the Province of North Carolina," *The North Carolina Booklet*, II (January 1912): 169-175.

17. See Colyer Meriwether, *History of Higher Education in South Carolina*, U.S. Bureau of Education, Circular of Information No. 3, 1888 (Washington, D.C., 1888).

18. For a history and the text of the 1770 education bill see J. H. Easterby, ed., "The South Carolina Education Bill of 1770," *South Carolina Historical and Genealogical Magazine*, 48 (April 1947): 95-111.

19. On the college agitation in western Massachusetts see Henry Lefavour, "The Proposed College in Hampshire County in 1762," *Proceedings of the Massachusetts Historical Society*, 66 (1942), 53-79; Leverett W. Spring, *A History of Williams College* (Boston: Houghton Mifflin, 1917), pp. 43-44; and William S. Tyler, *History of Amherst College During its First Half-Century, 1821–1871* (Springfield, Mass., 1873), pp. 13, 144. Ephraim Williams's will is reprinted in Calvin Dufree, *A History of Williams College* (Boston, 1860), pp. 405-409.

20. For a copy of the proposed charter see Lefavour, "The Proposed College," pp. 75-77.

21. Ms. bill for incorporating Queen's College, Massachusetts State Archives.

22. Ms. letter of Israel Williams to William Smith, [1762?], Massachusetts Historical Society.

23. Lefavour, "The Proposed College" pp. 60-63; *Journals of the House of Representatives of Massachusetts*, 38, part 2 (1762), 212, 239, 246, 261, 276, 297; Josiah Quincy, *The History of Harvard University* (Boston, 1860), II, 106-107.

24. The remonstrance is reprinted in Benjamin Peirce, *A History of Harvard University* (Cambridge, Mass., 1833), pp. 114-124, and Quincy, *The History*, II, 464-475.

25. See Lefavour, "The Proposed College," pp. 65-66, 68; *Journals of the House*, pp. 308, 311; "Circular Address from the Overseers," in Quincy, *The*

History, II, 475-478; letter of J. Mayhew to Thomas Hollis in Francis Blackburne, *Memoirs of Thomas Hollis* (London, 1780), pp. 159-160.

26. Amherst's involvement is told in John C. Long, *Lord Jeffery Amherst: A Soldier of the King* (New York: Macmillan, 1933), pp. 167-176; the petition is reprinted in Lefavour, "The Proposed College," pp. 77-79.

27. For enrollment statistics see Milton H. Thomas, *Columbia University: Officers and Alumni, 1754-1857* (New York: Columbia University Press, 1936), and Herbert and Carol Schneider, eds., *Samuel Johnson: President of King's College, His Career and Writings* (New York: Columbia University Press, 1929), IV, 243-262.

28. See David C. Humphrey, *From King's College to Columbia, 1746-1800* (New York: Columbia University Press, 1976), pp. 126-138, and Schneider and Schneider, eds., *Samuel Johnson*, IV, 46-113.

29. Ms. draft, Governors to George III, October 12, 1771, Rare Book and Manuscript Library, Butler Library, Columbia University.

30. Minutes of the Governors, book no. 1, September 30, 1771, October 12, 1772, August 4, 1774, pp. 13, 38-40, 68-69, Rare Book and Manuscript Library, Butler Library, Columbia University.

31. Myles Cooper, Report to Governors, October 12, 1772, Rare Book and Manuscript Library, Butler Library, Columbia University.

32. William Tryon to Earl of Dartmouth, February 17, 1775, and Cadwallader Colden to Governor Tryon, August 22, 1774, in *Colonial Papers: America and West Indies*, vol. 185, fo. 55, copy in Columbiana Collection, Columbia University Libraries; see also E. B. O'Callaghan, ed., *Documents Relative to the Colonial History of the State of New York* (Albany, N.Y., 1857), VIII, 486.

33. Copy of Charter of the American University, ms. 129, Columbiana Collection, Columbia University Libraries.

34. On the eclecticism of European and American academic traditions of government see Humphrey, *From King's College to Columbia*, pp. 146-148.

35. Schneider and Schneider, eds., *Samuel Johnson*, IV, 260-261.

## III. Introduction

1. Trustee Minutes, ms. copy, p. 52, Brown University Archives.

2. Cf. Howard H. Peckham, "Collegia Ante Bellum: Attitudes of College Professors and Students Toward the American Revolution," *Pennsylvania Magazine of History and Biography*, 95 (January 1971): 50-72.

3. 4 Wheaton (1819), 517.

## 11. War and Revolution

1. Assembly Committee statement of July 10, 1777; ms. in Stiles Papers, Beinecke Library, Yale University.

2. Letter of Richard Peters, October 17, 1763, in William Stevens Perry, ed., *Historical Collections of the American Colonial Church*, Vol. II: *Pennsylvania* (Hartford, Conn., 1871), p. 391; Neda M. Westlake, intro., *Minutes of*

*the Trustees of the College, Academy and Charitable School, University of Pennsylvania*, Vol. I: *1749 to 1769* (Wilmington, Del.: Scholarly Resources, Inc., 1974), pp. 258-259.

3. Alison in Franklin B. Dexter, ed., *Extracts from the Itineraries and other Miscellanies of Ezra Stiles, D.D., L.L.D., 1775-1794, with a Selection from his Correspondence* (New Haven, Conn.: Yale University Press, 1916), p. 428.

4. "Journal of President and Masters," Nov. 29, 1776, in *WMQ*, 1st ser., 15(October 1906): 140-142.

5. For an extract of the 1779 statute see the *Virginia Gazette*, December 18, 1779, and Edgar W. Knight, ed., *A Documentary History of Education in the South before 1860* (Chapel Hill, N.C.: University of North Carolina Press, 1949), I, 546-548.

6. Benjamin Peirce, *A History of Harvard University* (Cambridge, Mass., 1883), pp. 164-167.

7. Overseers Records I, April 26, 1737–July 30, 1738, Harvard University Archives.

8. Josiah Quincy, *The History of Harvard University* (Boston, 1860), II, 29-34, 461-462; Overseers Records I, October 21, 1741–April 1, 1742, Harvard University Archives.

9. Nathan Prince, *The Constitution and Government of Harvard College*, p. 15.

10. Quincy, *The History*, II, 161-174; on the Kneeland affair see College Records, III, 21-23, by permission of Harvard University Archives.

11. See Charles J. Hoadley, ed., *The Public Records of the Colony of Connecticut* (Hartford, Conn., 1885 and 1887), XIII, 104, 261, 396, 622; XIV, 36, 63, 323; [Ebenezer Baldwin], *A Letter to an Honourable Gentleman of the Council-Board for the Colony of Connecticut* (New Haven, Conn., 1776); and Committee Report, January 1774, ms. in *Connecticut Archives*, Colleges and Schools, 1st ser., II, 114a-c, Connecticut State Library Archives.

12. Kelley, *Yale: A History*, pp. 98-99; Franklin B. Dexter, ed., *The Literary Diary of Ezra Stiles* (New York: Charles Scribners Sons, 1901), II, 230.

13. *Connecticut Courant*, April 16, June 4, August 13, and September 3, 1771.

14. "Heads of Conference Proposed by Committee of Corporation," July 9, 1777, and "Answer of the Committee of Assembly," July 10, 1777, with "Heads of Conference Proposed by Committee of Assembly," ms. in Stiles Papers, section 17, 1777–1792, Beinecke Library, Yale University.

15. "Final Answer of the Corporation and Plan Proposed by Corporation Committee," February 11, 1778, ms in Stiles Papers, section 17, 1777–1782, Beinecke Library, Yale University.

16. Dexter, ed., *Literary Diary*, II, 214, 229.

17. See Franklin B. Dexter, *Biographical Sketches of the Graduates of Yale College with Annals of the College History* (New York: Henry Holt and Co., 1903), III, 168, and Kelley, *Yale*, pp. 81-83.

18. See the documents in Quincy, *The History*, II, 497-499.

19. Morison, *Three Centuries*, pp. 90, 104-105, 117-118, 133, 138; Seymour

M. Lipset and David Riesman, *Education and Politics at Harvard* (New York: McGraw-Hill, 1975), pp. 35-39; and Thomas S. Harding, *College Literary Societies: Their Contribution to Higher Education in the United States, 1815-1876* (New York: Pageant Press International, 1971), p. 22.

20. Westlake, intro., *Trustee Minutes*, I, 147; II, 61, 63.

21. Wertenbaker, *Princeton*, pp. 80-117.

22. McCormick, *Rutgers*, pp. 13-17.

23. See Demarest, *A History*, pp. 155-156, and Hugh Hastings, ed., *Ecclesiastical Records of the State of New York* (Albany, N.Y.: J. B. Lyon, State Printer, 1905), VI, 4322-4323.

24. Samuel H. Fisher, *The Litchfield Law School, 1775-1833* (New Haven, Conn.: Yale University Press, 1933).

25. See Knight, ed., *Documentary History*, II, 94-134; Richard H. Gaines, "Richmond's First Academy," *Collections of the Virginia Historical Society*, new series, XI (1892), 167-175; and John G. Roberts, "An Exchange of Letters between Jefferson and Quesnay de Beaurepaire," *Virginia Magazine of History and Biography*, 50 (April 1942): 139.

26. Benjamin Rush in Frederick Rudolph, ed., *Essays on Education in the Early Republic* (Cambridge, Mass.: Harvard University Press, 1965), p. 17, and see "Letter to Richard Price," in Lyman H. Butterfield, ed., *Letters of Benjamin Rush* (Princeton, N.J.: Princeton University Press, 1951), I, 388-389; also *The American Museum*, 1 (January 1787): 9-10; and 4 (November 1788): 442-444.

27. See David W. Robson, "Pennsylvania's 'Lost' National University: Johann Forster's Plan," *The Pennsylvania Magazine of History and Biography*, 102 (July 1978): 364-374.

28. Knight, ed., *Documentary History*, II, 13-14, and David Madsen, *The National University: Enduring Dream of the USA* (Detroit, Mich.: Wayne State University Press, 1966), pp. 15-24.

## 12. The Birth of the American University

1. A more detailed presentation of the material in this and the following chapter may be found in my "The American Revolution and the American University," *Perspectives in American History*, 10 (1976), 279-354.

2. On the two colonial medical schools see Genevieve Miller, "Medical Schools in the Colonies," *Ciba Symposia*, 8 (January 1947): 522-532, and Byron Stookey, "America's Two Colonial Medical Schools," *Bulletin of the New York Academy of Medicine*, 40 (April 1964): 269-284; a useful account of medical instruction may be found in Edward P. Cheney, *History of the University of Pennsylvania, 1740-1940* (Philadelphia: University of Pennsylvania Press, 1940), pp. 96-104, and in David C. Humphrey, "King's College in the City of New York, 1754-1776" (Ph.D. diss., Northwestern University, 1968), pp. 554-612.

3. John Morgan, *A Discourse upon the Institution of Medical Schools in America* (Philadelphia, 1765), p. 2.

4. Samuel Clossy, Peter Middleton, John Jones, James Smith, and Samuel Bard, "Petition to the Governors of King's College," August 4, 1767, ms. in Rare

Book and Manuscript Library, Columbia University Libraries.

5. Morgan, *A Discourse*, pp. 17-18, 35.

6. Clossy et al., "Petition to the Governors," *supra*, n. 6.

7. For admission and graduation requirements in Philadelphia see Miller, "Medical Schools," and Stookey, "America's Two Colonial Medical Schools."

8. Morgan, *A Discourse*, p. 37.

9. See Byron Stookey, *A History of Colonial Medical Education in the Province of New York* (Springfield, Ill: Thomas, 1962), pp. 41, 75; the degree statistics are based on Frederick C. Waite, "Medical Degrees Conferred in the American Colonies and in the United States in the Eighteenth Century," *Annals of Medical History*, new series, 9 (July 1937): 314-320.

10. Ezra Stiles, *Plan of a University: A Proposal Addressed to the Corporation of Yale College, 3 December 1777* (New Haven: The Fellows of Pierson College, 1953).

11. See letters in the *Virginia Gazette* (Rind, December 30, 1773; Purdie and Dixon, May 12, 1774, and Purdie, November 22, 1776).

12. *Virginia Gazette* (Purdie and Dixon, May 12, 1774, and Rind, May 19, 1774).

13. *Virginia Gazette* (Dixon, April 4, 1777).

14. The Jefferson quote may be found in the "Notes on Virginia," in Adrienne Koch and William Peden, eds., *The Life and Selected Writings of Thomas Jefferson* (New York: Random House, Modern Library, 1944), p. 267; for an extract of the 1779 statute see *Virginia Gazette* (Dixon, December 18, 1779), or Edgar W. Knight, ed., *A Documentary History of Education in the South Before 1860* (Chapel Hill, N.C.: University of North Carolina Press, 1949), I, 546-548.

15. See "Statutes of the College in 1792," *William and Mary College Quarterly Historical Magazine*, 20 (1911), 52-59; letter of James Madison to Ezra Stiles, August 1, 1780, in Franklin B. Dexter, ed., *The Literary Diary of Ezra Stiles* (New York: Charles Scribner's Sons, 1901), II, 446-449; and Julian P. Boyd, ed., *The Papers of Thomas Jefferson* (Princeton, N.J.: Princeton University Press, 1950), II, 535-543; also see Boyd, "The Murder of George Wythe," *WMQ*, 3rd ser., 12 (October 1955): 513-518; and Lyon Gardiner Tyler, "The First Chair of Law and Police," *William and Mary College Quarterly Historical Magazine*, 4 (1896), 264-265.

16. See Cheyney, *History*, p. 135.

17. See Samuel Eliot Morison, *Three Centuries of Harvard*, 1636-1936 (Cambridge, Mass.: Harvard University Press, 1936), pp. 167-171.

18. See Daniel J. Pratt, ed., "Annals of Public Education in the State of New York," *Proceedings of the Twelfth Anniversary of the University Convocation* (Albany, N.Y., 1875), pp. 226-230.

19. William Douglass, *A Summary, Historical and Political, of the Planting, Progressive Improvements, and Present State of the British Settlements in North America* (Boston, 1755), pp. 256-257.

20. "Autobiography of Thomas Jefferson," in Koch and Peden, eds., *Life and Selected Writings*, pp. 49-50, and Boyd, ed., *Papers*, II, 246-249, 526-543.

21. On the history of Washington College see Gilbert W. Mead and Charles B. Clark, "Washington College," in *The Eastern Shore of Maryland and Virginia*, ed. Charles B. Clark (New York: Lewis Historical Publishing Co., 1950), II, 723-741, and L. Wethered Barroll, "Washington College, 1783," *Maryland Historical Magazine*, 6 (June 1911): 164-179.

22. The Washington College charter is printed in *Laws of the State of Maryland*, 1782, ch. 8.

23. See Horace Wemyss Smith, *Life and Correspondence of the Rev. William Smith* (Philadelphia, 1880), II, 88, and *Votes and Proceedings of the House of Delegates*, November Session, 1784, pp. 15-18, 22, 69-70, and November Session 1785, pp. 7-8.

24. *Laws of the State of Maryland*, 1784, chs. 7, 37; Tench Francis Tilghman, "The Founding of St. John's College, 1784-1789," *Maryland Historical Magazine*, 44 (June 1949): 75-92; and George H. Callcott, *A History of the University of Maryland* (Baltimore: Maryland Historical Society, 1966), p. 14.

25. See Hugh Hastings, ed., *Ecclestiastical Records of the State of New York* (Albany, N.Y.: J. B. Lyon, State Printer, 1905), VI, 4312-4331; Pratt, ed., "Annals of Public Education," pp. 197-203; and Sidney Sherwood, *The University of the State of New York*, United States Bureau of Education, Circular of Information No. 3, 1900 (Washington, D.C.: Government Printing Office, 1900), p. 50. A charge that the legislature altered the King's College charter without the consent of the governors in violation of the 1777 state constitution and the principle later upheld in the Dartmouth College case was brought by John B. Pine, ed., *Charters, Acts of the Legislature, Official Documents and Records*, rev. ed. (New York: Printed for the College, 1920), p. 37, n. 1.

26. *New York Session Laws* 1784, 7th Session, ch. 51 (May 1, 1784).

27. Pratt, ed., "Annals of Public Education," pp. 209-254, and *New York Session Laws 1784*, 8th Session, chap. 15 (November 26, 1784); see also Frank C. Abbott, *Government Policy and Higher Education: A Study of the Regents of the University of the State of New York*, 1784-1949 (Ithaca, N.Y.: Cornell University Press, 1958), p. 12.

28. Minutes of the Regents, February 15, 1787, typescript in Columbia University Libraries, pp. 55-58; also in Pratt, "Annals of Public Education," pp. 252-253.

29. *New York Session Laws* 1787, chap. 82 (April 13, 1787).

30. Sidney Sherwood, in *The University of the State of New York*, on pp. 57-99, points — mistakenly, I believe — to a certain parallelism between New York's enactments and French proposals for educational centralization, without adducing evidence for causal influences. The autonomy of the colleges under the regent system certainly contrasts sharply with French ideas of administrative centralization. See also John B. Pine, "The Origin of the University of the State of New York," *Columbia University Quarterly*, 11 (March 1909): 155-162, and Abbott, *Government Policy*, pp. 13-17.

31. Allen D. Candler, *The Colonial Records of the State of Georgia* (Atlanta, Ga.: C. P. Byrd, State Printer, 1911), XIX, part II, 300-301, and E. Merton Coulter, ed., "Abraham Baldwin's Speech to the University of Georgia

Trustees," *Georgia Historical Quarterly*, 10 (December 1926): 332. On the Yale graduates see Franklin B. Dexter, ed., *Biographical Sketches of the Graduates of Yale College* (New York, 1896), II, 116-119, 690-691, and III, 432-434; on Baldwin see Dexter, ed., *Literary Diary*, III, 8-9, and Henry C. White, *Abraham Baldwin* (Athens, Ga.: The McGregor Company, 1926), pp. 33-39, 153-163.

32. Candler, ed., *Colonial Records*, XIX, part II, 363-371; Robert Preston Brooks, *The University of Georgia under Sixteen Administrations 1785-1955* (Athens, Ga.: University of Georgia Press, 1956), pp. 11-13; and E. Merton Coulter, *College Life in the Old South* (Athens, Ga.: University of Georgia Press, 1951), pp. 1-13.

33. See Rush's letters to John Montgomery, October 15, 1782, and November 15, 1783, in Lyman H. Butterfield, ed., *Letters of Benjamin Rush* (Princeton, N.J.: Princeton University Press, 1951), I, 290-291, 314, and Frederick Rudolph, ed., *Essays on Education in the Early Republic* (Cambridge, Mass.: Harvard University Press, 1965), pp. 1-23.

34. Rudolph, ed., *Essays*, p. 5.

35. For an account of the dispute see Leon Burr Richardson, *History of Dartmouth College* (Hanover: Dartmouth College Publications, 1932), I, 177-184, and Robert D. Benedict, *Charter History of the University of Vermont* (Burlington, Vt., 1892), pp. 17-18.

36. *Vermont State Papers*, V (Brattleboro, Vt., 1939), 25-27; VIII (Montpelier, Vt., 1952), 18.

37. Ms. Vermont State Papers, XXI, 321 (in Pavilion Office Building, Montpelier, Vt.) and *Vermont State Papers*, XIV, (Montpelier, Vt., 1966), 41.

38. Cf. John S. Whitehead, *The Separation of College and State: Columbia, Dartmouth, Harvard, and Yale, 1776-1876* (New Haven: Yale University Press, 1973), p. 34.

39. *Vermont State Papers*, VIII (Montpelier, Vt., 1952), 180-181.

40. Ms. Vermont State Papers, XXIV, 17, and *Records of the Governor and Council of the State of Vermont* (Montpelier, Vt., 1875), III, 107-108.

41. Ms. Vermont State Papers, XXIV, 18.

42. *Vermont State Papers*, IV (Bellows Falls, 1932), 38.

43. Ibid., III, part 3, p. 313, and *Journal of the Proceedings of the General Assembly: 1787* (Windsor, Vt., 1787), p. 45.

## 13. The People versus the Colleges

1. Parnassus Letter No. 3, February 18, 1783, in *Connecticut Courant and Intelligencer*.

2. Parnassus Letter No. 2, February 11, 1783, ibid.

3. See Samuel Whittelsey Dana, *Yale College Subject to the General Assembly* (New Haven, 1784); and Petition to General Assembly, April 20, 1784, in Trumbull Papers, vol. XXIII, no. 239, Connecticut State Library Archives.

4. Yale College Register, I, part 2, in *Yale College Records*, p. 290, typescript in Yale University Archives, Yale University Library.

5. Franklin B. Dexter, ed., *The Literary Diary of Ezra Stiles* (New York: Charles Scribners Sons, 1901), III, 455-456.

6. *Resolves and Private Laws of the State of Connecticut, 1789-1836* (Hartford, Conn., 1837), I, 477-478; *Yale College Records*, I, 289-299; Dexter, ed., *Literary Diary*, III, 457.

7. Ms. Minutes of the Trustees, vol. II, pp. 124, 128, 129, 148, University of Pennsylvania Archives.

8. *Minutes of the General Assembly of Pennsylvania* (September 9, 1799), p. 121.

9. Ibid. (October 2, 1779), pp. 143-145. For a detailed account of the issues raised in 1779 see Ann Gordon, "The College of Philadelphia, 1749–1799: Impact of an Institution" (Ph.D. dissertation, University of Wisconsin-Madison, 1975), pp. 251-285.

10. *Minutes of the General Assembly* (October 2, 1779) pp. 145-146.

11. Ibid. (November 22 to 25, 1779), pp. 167-171, and ms. Minutes of Trustees, II, 156-157.

12. The dissent is printed in *Minutes of the General Assembly* (November 27, 1779), p. 172.

13. The Declaratory Act of 1764 may be found in Neda M. Westlake, intro., *Minutes of the Trustees of the College, Academy and Charitable School, University of Pennsylvania*, Vol. I: *1749 to 1768* (Wilmington, Del.: Scholarly Resources, Inc., 1974), pp. 262-263; the act of 1779 in *Acts of the General Assembly of the Commonwealth of Pennsylvania* (Philadelphia, 1782), I, 250-256.

14. *Acts of the General Assembly*, I, 250-256.

15. *Pennsylvania Archives*, 3rd series, X (Harrisburg, 1896), 781.

16. Ms. memorial of Robert Morris et al., July 16, 1784, Archives of the University of Pennsylvania.

17. *Journal of the Second Session of the Council of Censors* (August 27, 1784), p. 131.

18. Ibid., p. 131.

19. Ibid., pp. 130, 132.

20. The description of the hearing is taken from notes by Charles Pettit deposited in the Joseph Reed papers, courtesy of The New-York Historical Society, New York City. The committee of the whole report may be found in *Minutes of the General Assembly* (September 21, 1784), p. 343.

21. William Smith, *An Address to the General Assembly of Pennsylvania, in the Case of the Violated Charter of the College, etc. of Philadelphia* (Philadelphia, 1788), pp. 5, 6, 21.

22. *Laws of the Commonwealth of Pennsylvania*, 1789, chap. 12, pp. 16-20.

23. *Acts of the General Assembly* (Philadelphia, 1791), ch. 78, pp. 160-163.

24. "An Old Soldier," Baltimore *Maryland Gazette* (April 1, 1785).

25. *Maryland Session Laws*, 1796; Minutes of the Visitors of St. John's College, November 29, 1796, pp. 115-116, St. John's College Archives, Maryland Hall of Records.

26. *Maryland Session Laws*, 1798, chap. 107, and *Maryland Session Laws*,

1805, chap. 85.

27. See Norman K. Risjord, *Chesapeake Politics* 1781-1800 (New York: Columbia University Press, 1978), pp. 214-215.

28. Samuel Knox, "An Essay on the Best Systems of Liberal Education, Adapted to the Genius of the Government of the United States," in Frederick Rudolph, ed., *Essays on Education in the Early Republic* (Cambridge, Mass.: Harvard University Press, 1965), pp. 275-276, 285.

29. *Virginia Gazette* (Purdie, November 22, 1776).

30. "The Autobiography of Thomas Jefferson," in *The Life and Selected Writings of Thomas Jefferson*, ed. Adrienne Koch and William Peden (New York: Random House, Modern Library, 1944), p. 50.

31. Julian P. Boyd, ed., *The Papers of Thomas Jefferson* (Princeton, N.J.: Princeton University Press, 1950), II, 535-543.

32. Smith to Jefferson, March and April 19, 1779, in Boyd, ed., *Papers*, II, 246-249, 252-255. The quotation is from p. 247.

33. Jefferson to Joseph Priestley, 1800, in Edgar W. Knight, ed., *A Documentary History of Education in the South Before* 1860 (Chapel Hill: University of North Carolina Press, 1952), III, 42.

34. See Josiah Quincy, *The History of Harvard University* (Boston, 1860), II, 174-176, 507-509.

35. See Oscar and Mary Handlin, eds., *The Popular Sources of Political Authority: Documents on the Massachusetts Constitution of* 1780 (Cambridge, Mass.: Harvard University Press, 1966), pp. 483, 699.

36. Petition of January 31, 1781, in Harvard Corporation Records, by permission of the Harvard University Archives; John S. Whitehead, *The Separation of College and State: Columbia, Dartmouth, Harvard, and Yale*, 1776-1876 (New Haven, Conn.: Yale University Press, 1973), pp. 16-18.

37. Knight, ed., *Documentary History*, III, 1-5.

38. Walter Clark, ed., *The State Records of North Carolina* (Goldsboro, N.C.: Nash Brothers, 1906), XXV, 21-24.

39. R.D.W. Connor, *North Carolina: Rebuilding an Ancient Commonwealth*, 1584-1925 (Chicago: The American Historical Society, 1929), I, 386; Kemp P. Battle, *History of the University of North Carolina* (Raleigh, N.C.: Edwards and Broughton Company, 1907), I, 12; and William Earle Drake, *Higher Education in North Carolina before* 1860 (New York: Carlton Press, 1964), p. 96.

40. R. D. W. Connor, ed., *A Documentary History of the University of North Carolina*, 1776-1799 (Chapel Hill, N.C.: University of North Carolina Press, 1953), I, 87-88, 218, and Knight, ed., *Documentary History*, III, 15-16.

41. Battle, *History*, I, 17, 137.

42. See the *Acts of the 4th General Assembly of the State of New Jersey* (Trenton, N.J., 1780), pp. 62-63, and the *Acts of the 5th General Assembly* (1781), pp. 77-78.

43. Reuben A. Guild, *Early History of Brown University* (Providence, R.I., 1897), pp. 336, 381, and Walter C. Bronson, *The History of Brown University* (Providence, R.I., 1914), pp. 81-82.

## 14. The Private Colleges

1. The standard work on the American denominational frontier college is Donald G. Tewksbury, *The Founding of American Colleges and Universities Before the Civil War* (New York: Teachers College, Columbia, 1932). For a critique see Natalie A. Naylor, "The Ante-Bellum College Movement: A Reappraisal of Tewksbury's Founding of American Colleges and Universities," *History of Education Quarterly*, 13 (1973), 261-274. The concept of the "booster college" was introduced by Daniel J. Boorstin in *The Americans: The National Experience* (New York: Random House, 1965), pp. 152-161.

2. See *above*, chap. 8, n. 34.

3. Quoted in Richard Hofstadter and Wilson Smith, eds., *American Higher Education: A Documentary History* (Chicago: University of Chicago Press, 1961), I, 379.

4. An excellent discussion of the social role played by the Presbyterian clergymen may be found in Howard Miller, *The Revolutionary College: American Presbyterian Higher Education 1707-1837* (New York: New York University Press, 1976).

5. See Donald Robert Come, "The Influence of Princeton on Higher Education in the South before 1825," *WMQ*, 3rd series, 2 (October 1945): 359-396.

6. Henry Ruffner, "Early History of Washington College, now Washington and Lee University," *Washington and Lee University Historical Papers*, no. 1 (1890), 1-40; see also the concluding remarks in Appendix A, "The Problem of Origins," of Ollinger Crenshaw's typescript of "General Lee's College," Archives of Washington and Lee University.

7. See *above*, chap. 13, n. 33.

8. Alfred J. Morrison, *The College of Hampden-Sydney: Calendar of Board Minutes 1776-1876* (Richmond, Va.: Hermitage Press, 1912), p. 17.

9. On the history of the academy and college see Morrison, *The College of Hampden-Sydney* and his *College of Hampden-Sydney Dictionary of Biography 1776-1825* (Hampden Sydney, Va., 1921); also see Leonard Wesley Topping, "A History of Hampden-Sydney College in Virginia, 1771–1883" (M.A. thesis, Union Theological Seminary, Richmond, Va., 1950).

10. William W. Hening, ed., *The Statutes at Large of Virginia* (Richmond, Va., 1823), XI, 272-275.

11. See Walter W. Jennings, *Transylvania: Pioneer University of the West* (New York: Pageant Press, 1955); Robert and Johanna Peter, *Transylvania University: Its Origin, Rise, Decline, and Fall*, Filson Club Publications no. 11 (Louisville, Ky., 1896); and Niels H. Sonne, *Liberal Kentucky, 1780–1828* (Lexington, Ky.: University of Kentucky Press, 1968), pp. 46-77.

12. See the charter in Hening, ed., *Statutes*, XI, 282-287.

13. Quoted in Jennings, *Transylvania*, p. 10. For the debate in the *Kentucky Gazette* see ibid., pp. 9-10, and Sonne, *Liberal Kentucky*, pp. 48-50.

14. William Littell, ed., *The Statute Law of Kentucky* (Frankfort, Ky., 1809), I, 345-346; see also Sonne, *Liberal Kentucky*, pp. 33-39, 55-64, and Jen-

nings, *Transylvania*, pp. 20-29.

15. Sonne, *Liberal Kentucky*, pp. 64-66; Jennings, *Transylvania*, pp. 33-35; and Littell, ed., *Statute Law*, II, 107-109, 234-236, 240-246.

16. See William H. Whitsitt, *Life and Times of Judge Caleb Wallace*, Filson Club Publications no. 4 (Louisville, Ky., 1888), pp. 127-135.

17. Minutes of the synod of Kentucky, II, 122-123, quoted in Walter A. Groves, "A School of the Prophets at Danville," *Filson Club Historical Quarterly*, 27 (1953), 233-234. For the history of Centre College see also James H. Hewlett, "Centre College of Kentucky, 1819-1830," ibid., 18 (July 1944): 173-191, and Norman L. Snider, "Centre College and the Presbyterians: Corporation and Partnership," *The Register of the Kentucky Historical Society*, 67 (April 1969): 103-118.

18. *Acts Passed at the First Session of the 27th General Assembly for the Commonwealth of Kentucky* (Frankfort, Ky., 1819), pp. 618-621.

19. Ibid., pp. 737-739.

20. M. Carey and J. Bioren, eds., *Laws of the Commonwealth of Pennsylvania* (Philadelphia, Pa., 1803), II, 413-418.

21. Lyman H. Butterfield, ed., *The Letters of Benjamin Rush* (Princeton, N.J.: Princeton University Press, 1951), I, 319, 322.

22. Miller, *The Revolutionary College*, pp. 135-137.

23. Butterfield, ed., *Letters*, I, 294-295, 296.

24. Ibid., I, 298.

25. John Bioren, ed., *Laws of Pennsylvania*, 1700-1810 (Philadelphia, 1813), II, 377; Saul Sack, "The State and Higher Education," *Pennsylvania History*, 26 (July 1959): 242.

26. *Acts Passed at the First Session of the First General Assembly of the Territory of the United States of America South of the River Ohio* (Knoxville, 1794), chap. 18, pp. 89-91; chap. 19, pp. 91-93; *Acts Passed at the Second Session* (Knoxville, 1795), chap. 8, pp. 21-23.

27. On the respective colleges see *General Catalogue of Greeneville and Tusculum College, Tusculum, Tennessee*, 1794-1901 (Knoxville, Tenn.: Ogden Bros., 1901); Allen E. Ragan, *A History of Tusculum College, 1794–1944* (Bristol, Tenn.: Tusculum Sesquicentennial Committee, 1945), p. 23; Moses White, *Early History of the University of Tennessee* (Knoxville, Tenn., 1879), p. 14; Edward T. Sanford, *Blount College and the University of Tennessee* (Knoxville, Tenn., 1894), p. 21; Stanley J. Folmsbee, "Blount College and East Tennessee College, 1794-1840: The First Predecessors of the University of Tennessee," *East Tennessee Historical Society's Publications*, XVII (1945), 22-50; Howard E. Carr, *Washington College: A Study of an Attempt to Provide Higher Education in Eastern Tennessee* (Knoxville, Tenn.: S. B. Newman, 1935), pp. 7, 13; and Isabella Foster, "Washington College and Washington College Academy," *Tennessee Historical Quarterly*, 30 (Fall 1971): 251.

28. Lucius S. Merriam, *Higher Education in Tennessee*, United States Bureau of Education, Circular of Information, No. 5, 1893 (Washington, D.C., 1893), p. 23.

29. *Acts of Tennessee*, 1806, chap. 7, pp. 44-47, and *Acts of Tennessee*, 1807, chap. 64, pp. 108-111.

30. *Acts of Tennessee*, 1807, chap. 78, pp. 127-130.

31. *Acts of Tennessee*, 1809, chap. 32, pp. 48-49.

32. Merriam, *Higher Education in Tennessee*, p. 24, and Henry C. Witherington, *A History of State Higher Education in Tennessee* (Chicago, Ill.: University of Chicago Libraries, 1931), p. 18.

33. *Acts of Tennessee*, 1817, chap. 32, pp. 37-38.

34. C. Harve Geiger, *The Program of Higher Education of the Presbyterian Church in the United States of America* (Cedar Rapids, Iowa: Laurance Press, 1940), pp. 33-37; see also W. F. Hamilton, et al., *History of the Presbytery of Washington* (Philadelphia, 1889), p. 29.

35. See Joseph Smith, *History of Jefferson College* (Pittsburgh, 1857), and Helen T. W. Coleman, *Banners in the Wilderness: Early Years of Washington and Jefferson College* (Pittsburgh, Pa.: University of Pittsburgh Press, 1956).

36. For the charters of the two colleges see Coleman, *Banners*, pp. 206-214.

37. Microfilm of Minutes of Board of Trustees, Washington and Jefferson College, vol. 1, September 26 and October 25, 1815; also Minutes of the Trustees of Canonsburg Academy, October 25, 1815.

38. Microfilm of Minutes of Board of Trustees, Washington and Jefferson College, vol. 1, April 30, 1817; typewritten minutes of Jefferson College, December 29, 1817, p. 101.

39. On the early history of Allegheny College see Ernest A. Smith, *Allegheny: A Century of Education 1815-1915* (Meadville, Pa.: The Allegheny College History Company, 1916), and Saul Sack, *History of Higher Education in Pennsylvania* (Harrisburg, Pa.: Pennsylvania Historical and Museum Commission, 1963), I, 74-79. For the charter see *Acts of the General Assembly of the Commonwealth of Pennsylvania* (Harrisburg, Pa., 1817), pp. 236-241.

40. Margaret A. Hunter, *Education in Pennsylvania Promoted by the Presbyterian Church 1726-1877* (Philadelphia, Pa., 1937), p. 151.

41. For a history of what later became the University of Pittsburgh see Agnes Lynch Starrett, *Through One Hundred and Fifty Years* (Pittsburgh, Pa.: University of Pittsburgh Press, 1937), pp. 1-69.

42. Thomas Cooper, ed., *The Statutes at Large of South Carolina* (Columbia, S.C., 1839), IV, 674-678.

43. George Howe, *History of the Presbyterian Church in South Carolina* (Columbia, S.C., 1870), pp. 504, 506-507.

44. Cooper, ed., *Statutes*, V, 223-224; VIII, 198-199.

45. Howe, *History*, p. 604.

46. Butterfield, ed., *Letters*, I, 364, 366, 368.

47. Ibid., I, 423.

48. See the charter in James T. Mitchell and Henry Flanders, eds., *The Statutes at Large of Pennsylvania* (Harrisburg, Pa., 1906), XII, 391-398; for a history of the college see Joseph H. Dubbs, *History of Franklin and Marshall College* (Lancaster, Pa.: Franklin and Marshall College Alumni Association, 1903), and Frederic S. Klein, *Since 1787: The Franklin and Marshall College Story* (Lancaster, Pa.: Franklin and Marshall College, 1968).

49. For histories of Cokesbury College see George W. Archer, *An Authentic History of Cokesbury College* (Bel Air, Md., 1894), and William Hamilton,

"Some Account of Cokesbury College," *Methodist Quarterly Review*, 41 (April 1859): 173-187; the charter is printed in *Maryland Laws of* 1794, chap. 26, and the act granting permission to dissolve the college in *Maryland Laws of* 1798, chap. 60.

50. On Asbury College see Bernard C. Steiner, *History of Education in Maryland*, United States Bureau of Education, Circular of Information, No. 2, 1894 (Washington, D.C., 1894), pp. 247-254, and Leo Joseph McCormick, *Church-State Relationships in Education in Maryland* (Washington, D.C.: Catholic University of America Press, 1942), pp. 65-72; the college charter is printed in *Laws of Maryland, December Session* 1817, chap. 144, pp. 151-155.

51. Thomas O'Brien Hanley, ed., *The John Carroll Papers* (Notre Dame, Ind.: University of Notre Dame Press, 1976), I, 78.

52. Ibid., I, 158.

53. See the 1789 "Proposals to Establish an Academy at George Town," in John Tracy Ellis, ed., *Documents of American Catholic History* (Milwaukee, Wis.: Bruce Publishing Company, 1956), pp. 171-173.

54. See the charter in John M. Daley, *Georgetown University: Origin and Early Years* (Washington, D.C.: Georgetown University Press, 1957), p. 190. For an evaluation of Bishop Carroll's educational endeavors, see Philip Gleason, "The Main Sheet Anchor: John Carroll and Catholic Higher Education," *The Review of Politics*, 38 (October 1976): 576-613.

55. Hanley, ed., *The John Carroll Papers*, I, 457; on the Sulpicians see Charles G. Herbermann, *The Sulpicians in the United States (New York: The Encyclopedia Press*, 1916), ch. 5, and Joseph W. Ruane, *The Beginnings, of the Society of St. Sulpice in the United States* (1791–1829), Catholic University of America Studies in American Church History, vol. XXII (Washington, D.C., 1935), chs. 3, 5.

56. Hanley, ed., *The John Carroll Papers*, II, 313, 382, 461, and Daley, *Georgetown University*, pp. 90, 105-106.

57. Ruane, *The Beginnings*, pp. 95-121.

58. *Laws of Maryland, November Session*, 1804, chap. 71. On the history of St. Mary's College see Steiner, *History of Education in Maryland*, pp. 272-276, and McCormick, *Church-State Relationships*, pp. 120-126.

59. Ruane, *The Beginnings*, pp. 135, 211-213.

60. *Laws of Maryland*, 1803, chap. 74.

61. *Memorial of the Trustees of the University of Maryland and the Trustees of Baltimore College to the Legislature of Maryland* (Baltimore, 1830), p. 5; Steiner, *History of Education in Maryland*, pp. 245-246; and McCormick, *State-Church Relationships*, pp. 126-128.

62. For background see William Frederick Norwood, *Medical Education in the United States before the Civil War* (Philadelphia, Pa.: University of Pennsylvania Press, 1944), pp. 223-241; Eugene F. Cordell, *The Medical Annals of Maryland*, 1799–1899 (Baltimore, Md.: Press of Williams and Wilkins Company, 1903), pp. 11-63; and *Historical Sketch of the University of Maryland School of Medicine*, 1807–1890 (Baltimore, 1891), pp. 1-55.

63. *Maryland Session Laws* 1798, chap. 105.

64. *Laws of Maryland, November Session* 1807, chap. 53; Cordell, *Historical Sketch*, p. 6; and Ruane, *The Beginnings*, pp. 134.136.

65. Norwood, *Medical Education*, p. 430. On the question of bestowing the first medical degrees, Norwood, p. 228, accepts 1810 as the correct date, though Cordell's list of graduates in *Historical Sketch*, pp. 161-208, cites names beginning with the year 1812.

66. George H. Callcott, *A History of the University of Maryland* (Baltimore: Maryland Historical Society, 1966), p. 29.

67. *Laws of Maryland, November Session* 1812, chap. 159, pp. 173-179.

68. For other views on the relationship of faculty and college after 1812, see Cordell, *Medical Annals*, p. 63, and *Historical Sketch*, p. 29; also Norwood, *Medical Education*, pp. 228-229.

69. Callcott, *A History*, pp. 28-46.

## 15. State Colleges and Universities

1. In Adrienne Koch and William Peden, eds., *The Life and Selected Writings of Thomas Jefferson* (New York: Random House, Modern Library, 1944), p. 633.

2. On the University of North Carolina see Edgar W. Knight, ed., *A Documentary History of Education in the South before* 1860 (Chapel Hill, N.C.: University of North Carolina Press, 1952), III, 1-5; R. D. W. Connor, *North Carolina: Rebuilding an Ancient Commonwealth*, 1584–1925 (Chicago: The American Historical Society, 1929), p. 386; Kemp P. Battle, *History of the University of North Carolina* (Raleigh, N.C.: Edwards and Broughton, 1907), I, 12; William E. Drake, *Higher Education in North Carolina before* 1860 (New York: Carlton Press, 1964), p. 96; Walter Clark, ed., *The State Records of North Carolina* (Goldsboro, N.C.: M. P. Hale, 1906), pp. 21-24; and *Laws of North Carolina*, 1789, ch. 21, p. 16.

3. See R. D. W. Connor, ed., *A Documentary History of the University of North Carolina*, 1776–1799 (Chapel Hill: University of North Carolina Press, 1963), I, 388, 389; II, 42, 71, 79.

4. Records of the Proceedings of the Board of Trustees, 1799–1810, September 16, 1799, p. 23; the manuscript is in the Frances Carrick Thomas Library, Transylvania College, Lexington, Ky.

5. Ibid., pp. 214-215, 299.

6. The sermon is excerpted at length in Niels Henry Sonne, *Liberal Kentucky*, 1780–1828 (Lexington, Ky.: University of Kentucky Press, 1968), pp. 119-124. The quote is from p. 122.

7. See the letters of "Civis" in the *Kentucky Gazette*, May 1, 8, 15, 29; June 5 and 12, 1815.

8. Transylvania Trustee Proceedings, July 5, 1815, p. 181.

9. Ibid., July 22, 1815, pp. 184-187.

10. Ibid., November 11, 1815, p. 205, and March 22, 1816, p. 232.

11. State of Kentucky, *Journal of the House*, 1815–1816, pp. 200-202.

12. Sonne, *Liberal Kentucky*, p. 152.

13. *Journal of the House,* 1815–1816, p. 203.

14. Ibid., p. 216.

15. *Senate Journal,* 1817–1818, p. 13.

16. John D. Wright, *Transylvania: Tutor to the West* (Lexington, Ky.: Transylvania College, 1975), pp. 58-59.

17. *Acts of the General Assembly* (Frankfort, Ky., 1818), ch. 294, pp. 554-555.

18. Cf. Sonne, *Liberal Kentucky,* p. 158.

19. On the early history of the University of Georgia see the documents in Allen D. Candler, ed., *The Colonial Records of the State of Georgia* (Atlanta, Ga.: C. P. Byrd, 1911), XIX, part II, 363-371; E. Merton Coulter, *College Life in the Old South* (Athens, Ga.: University of Georgia Press, 1951), pp. 1-13, "Franklin College as a Name for the University of Georgia," and "The Birth of a University, a Town, and a County," *Georgia Historical Quarterly,* 34 (September 1950): 189-194, and 46 (June 1962): 113-150; O. Burton Adams, "Yale Influence on the Formation of the University of Georgia," ibid., 51 (June 1967): 175-185.

20. Coulter, *College Life,* pp. 18-42, 74, 196-197.

21. Elmer D. Johnson and Kathleen L. Sloan, eds., *South Carolina: A Documentary Profile of the Palmetto State* (Columbia, S.C.: University of South Carolina Press, 1971), pp. 198-199, 234-236; Thomas Cooper, ed., *Statutes at Large of South Carolina* (Columbia, S.C., 1839), V, 198-200.

22. J. H. Easterby, *A History of the College of Charleston Founded* 1770 (Charleston, S.C., 1935), pp. 1-62, 286-289.

23. Daniel W. Hollis, *The University of South Carolina, Vol.* 1: *South Carolina College* (Columbia, S.C.: University of South Carolina Press, 1951), pp. 5, 14, 18, 21, 24; John H. Wolfe, *Jeffersonian Democracy in South Carolina* (Chapel Hill, N.C.: University of North Carolina Press, 1940), pp. 171-173; for the charter see Cooper, ed., *Statutes at Large,* V, 403-405, 494.

24. Hollis, *The University,* I, 34.

25. The charter of university and college is printed in Edwin Whitfield Fay, *The History of Education in Louisiana,* United States Bureau of Education Circular of Information No. 1, 1898 (Washington, D.C., 1898), pp. 27-30.

26. *Early History of the University of Virginia, as Contained in the Letters of Thomas Jefferson and Joseph C. Cabell* (Richmond, Va., 1856), pp. 379, 384-393.

27. The report was submitted in December 1816 and is reprinted in Knight, ed., *Documentary History,* III, 129-136.

28. See Jefferson's bill in *Early History,* pp. 413-427.

29. *Early History,* pp. 400-404.

30. Ibid., pp. 430-432.

31. Ibid., pp. 432-447.

32. The charter is reprinted ibid., pp. 447-450.

33. Ibid., p. 339.

34. Koch and Peden, eds., *Life,* p. 726.

35. Richard J. Purcell, *Connecticut in Transition: 1775–1818,* new ed.

(Middletown, Conn.: Wesleyan University Press, 1963), pp. 62-63, and M. Louise Greene, *The Development of Religious Liberty in Connecticut* (Boston: Houghton Mifflin, 1905), pp. 379-380.

36. For the sections of the 1780 constitution referring to Harvard, see Benjamin Peirce, *A History of Harvard University* (Cambridge, Mass., 1833), appendix, pp. 72-73.

37. Ms. Harvard Corporation Records, January 31, 1781, by permission of Harvard University Archives; see also Samuel E. Morison, *Three Centuries of Harvard*, 1636–1936(Cambridge, Mass.: Harvard University Press, 1936), pp. 158-160.

38. Morison, *Three Centuries*, pp. 185-191, 212. The act is reprinted in Peirce, *A History*, appendix, pp. 73-76.

39. Harvard Corporation Records, V, 69, 85; by permission of Harvard University Archives; also Josiah Quincy, *The History of Harvard University* (Boston, 1860), II, 302-303.

40. Quincy, *The History*, II, 304.

41. *Boston Patriot and Daily Chronicler* (July 13, September 8, October 2 and 26, and December 7, 1819).

42. See the trustee petition of 1792 in Calvin Durfee, *A History of Williams College* (Boston, 1860), pp. 61-64.

43. The charter is printed in *The General Laws of Massachusetts* (Boston, 1823), I, 427-429; for legislative grants to the college see documents nos. 41, 5974, 6032, and 6253 in the Massachusetts State Archives. Also see Durfee, *A History*, pp. 82, 100-101, and Leverett W. Spring, *A History of Williams College* (Boston: Houghton Mifflin, 1917), pp. 42-93.

44. Spring, *A History*, pp. 94-99, Calvin Durfee, *Williams Biographical Annals*, (New York, 1871), and Noah Webster, *Collection of Papers on Political, Literary, and Moral Subjects* (New York, 1843), p. 227.

45. William S. Tyler, *History of Amherst College During Its First Half Century*, 1821–1871 (Springfield, Mass., 1873), pp. 54-55, and Webster, *Collection*, p. 244.

46. The petition of president and trustees for removal, the remonstrance of the town of Williamstown, and the committee report on the removal are reprinted in Calvin Durfee, *A History*, pp. 411-429; ms. copies of these documents are in the Massachusetts State Archives, documents nos. 6570, 6570/1, and 6570/2.

47. The announcement of February 7, 1788, is kept in the Bowdoin College Archives, as are most of the other petitions and bills. The petitions of 1788 may also be found in the Massachusetts State Archives, document no. 1134, as may the bill of March 2, 1791, no. 3561, and the committee report of June 20, 1794, no. 1922.

48. The Bowdoin charter is printed in *Acts and Laws of the Commonwealth of Massachusetts*, 1794, chap. 12 (Boston, 1896), pp. 41-47; see also Louis C. Hatch, *The History of Bowdoin College* (Portland, Me.: Loring, Short, & Harmon, 1927), pp. 21, 243.

49. See ms. records in Bowdoin College Archives and Massachusetts State

Archives, as well as Hatch, *The History*, p. 41.

50. Franklin B. Hough, ed., *Constitutional Provisions Relating to Education, Literature, and Science*, United States Bureau of Education Circular of Information No. 7, 1875 (Washington, D.C., 1875), p. 46.

51. Ibid., p. 45.

52. Ms. no. 6302/4, Massachusetts State Archives; Trustee Papers, May 17, 1820, in Bowdoin College Records.

53. *Special Laws of the State of Maine*, 1820–1821, chap. 79 (Augusta, Me., 1874), pp. 87-88.

54. Charles P. Chipman, *The Formative Period in Colby's History* (Waterville, Me., 1870), pp. 7-8, 11-15, 16-21, and Ernest C. Marriner, *The History of Colby College* (Waterville, Me.: Colby College Press, 1963), pp. 603-604, 604-606, 607-611.

55. Chapman, *Formative Period*, p. 23, and Marriner, *The History*, pp. 20, 617-620, 621-622.

56. *Laws of the State of Maine*, 1820, chap. 11 (Portland, Me., 1820), pp. 9-10; Marriner, *The History*, p. 621.

57. Marriner, *The History*, p. 47, and Edwin Carey Whittemore, *Colby College, 1820–1925* (Waterville, Me.: Trustees of Colby College, 1927), p. 29.

## 16. Novus Ordo Collegiorum

1. See James Willard Hurst, *Law and the Conditions of Freedom in the Nineteenth-Century United States* (Madison, Wis.: University of Wisconsin Press, 1956), pp. 3-32.

2. The two Bracken cases were heard in the Court of Appeals in the November term of 1790 and in the October term of 1797; the first is printed in 3 Call, 573-599, the second in 1 Call, 161-164.

3. Marshall's argument, together with an introduction by the editors, is printed also in Charles T. Cullen and Herbert A. Johnson, eds., *The Papers of John Marshall* (Chapel Hill, N.C.: University of North Carolina Press, 1977), II, 67-81; see also Florian Bartosic, "With John Marshall from William and Mary to Dartmouth College," *William and Mary Law Review*, 7 (1966), 259-266.

4. *Bracken v. College of William and Mary*, 3 Call (1790), 590.

5. *Laws of North Carolina*, 1799, p. 1, and ibid., 1800, p. 3.

6. Ibid., 1805, p. 2; ibid., 1804, pp. 3-4, and ibid., 1805, pp. 12-13. See also Blackwell P. Robinson, *The History of Escheats* (Chapel Hill, N.C.: University of North Carolina Press, 1955).

7. *Trustees of the University of North Carolina v. Foy and Bishop*, 5 N.C. (1805), 78-79, 86.

8. James M. Hutcheson, "Virginia's 'Dartmouth College Case'," *Virginia Magazine of History and Biography*, 51 (April, 1943): 134-140.

9. Hening, ed., *The Statutes at Large of Virginia*, n.s. (Richmond, Va., 1835), II, 44-45.

10. The excerpts are from the Board of Trustees Minutes, Washington and Lee University, January 1793–March 2, 1803, pp. 167, 171, and from the

"Reasons why the Trustees will not submit to the Act of 1796," mss. in The University Library, Washington and Lee University, Lexington, Va.

11. See the exchange of letters between the trustees of Liberty Hall and of Hampden-Sydney, November 16 and December 22, 1797, mss. in The University Library, Washington and Lee University; see also Ollinger Crenshaw, *General Lee's College: The Rise and Growth of Washington and Lee University* (New York: Random House, 1969), pp. 30, 38.

12. *Acts of Tennessee*, 1803, chap. 72, pp. 124-126.

13. *Acts of Tennessee*, 1805, chap. 51, pp. 51-52; see also A. W. Putnam, *History of Middle Tennessee* (Nashville, 1859), pp. 647-648.

14. Lucius S. Merriam, *Higher Education in Tennessee*, U.S. Bureau of Education, Circular of Information No. 5, 1893 (Washington, D.C., 1893), p. 23.

15. *Acts of Tennessee*, 1806, chap. 7, pp. 44-47.

16. Alfred B. Street, *The Council of Revision of the State of New York* (Albany, 1859), p. 345.

17. Julian I. Lindsay, *Tradition Looks Forward: The University of Vermont, A History,* 1791–1904 (Burlington, Vt.: The University of Vermont, 1954), p. 11; *Records of Governor and Council*, III, 386, 391; ms. Vermont State Papers, XXIV, 138, in the Pavilion Office Building, Montpelier, Vt.; *Journal of the Proceedings of the General Assembly of the State of Vermont*, 1791 (Windsor, Vt.), pp. 17-22, and *Acts and Laws passed by the Legislature of the State of Vermont, October Session*, 1791, pp. 28-31.

18. *Vermont State Papers* (Brattleboro, Vt., 1939), V, 423-424.

19. *Records of the Governor and Council*, IV, 266-267, 279; *Acts and Laws, October Session* 1800, pp. 36-40; Lindsay, *Tradition Looks Forward*, pp. 50-59; and W. Storrs Lee, *Father Went to College: The Story of Middlebury* (New York: Wilson-Erickson, Inc., 1936), pp. 1-29.

20. Samuel Williams, *The Natural and Civil History of Vermont*, 2nd ed., (Burlington, Vt., 1809), II, 382, 383.

21. From the unpublished autobiography of Asa Burton, quoted in Lindsay, *Tradition Looks Forward*, pp. 78-79.

22. I owe much insight into the community college aspects of Middlebury College to the unpublished work of David Stameshkin on the history of Middlebury College.

23. *Acts and Laws*, 1810, pp. 117-120.

24. University of Vermont, Trustee Minutes (January 3, 1811), I, 144; ms. in University of Vermont Archives.

25. Daniel Sanders to John Kirkland, September 3, 1811, ms. from Daniel Clark Sanders Papers, University of Vermont Archives.

26. *Journal of the General Assembly of the State of Vermont*, 1817 (Rutland), pp. 184-185.

27. Ibid., p. 175.

28. Ibid., p. 53, and Treasurer's Report of Middlebury College, October 23, 1819, in ms. Vermont State Papers, LXVII, 44.

29. Ms. Trustee Minutes, I, 66-67, 95-96 (August 17, 1814, and October 17, 1817), in Old Chapel Archives, Middlebury College.

30. See ms. Trustee Minutes, I, 122 (August 19, 1819).

31. In ms. Vermont State Papers (October 19, 1820), LV, 13.

32. Cf. Merle Curti and Roderick Nash, *Philanthropy in the Shaping of American Higher Education* (New Brunswick, N.J.: Rutgers University Press, 1965), pp. 44-45.

33. Sidney Sherwood, *The University of the State of New York*, United States Bureau of Education Circular of Information No. 3, 1900 (Washington, D.C., 1900), p. 109.

34. See draft of the charter in Andrew V. V. Raymond, *Union University* (New York: Lewis Publishing Company, 1907), I, 9-10.

35. For the early history of Union College see Samuel B. Fortenbaugh, Jr., *In Order to Form a More Perfect Union: An Inquiry into the Origins of a College* (Schenectady, N.Y.: Union College Press, 1978); Raymond, *Union University*; Franklin B. Hough, *Historical and Statistical Record of the University of the State of New York* (Albany, N.Y., 1885), pp. 133-159; and Codman Hislop, "The Ghost College that Came to Life," *American Heritage*, 3 (Spring 1952): 29-31.

36. See Hough, *Historical and Statistical Record*, pp. 147, 148, and Fortenbaugh, *In Order to Form a More Perfect Union*, pp. 42, 59.

37. For charter and related documents see Raymond, *Union University*, I, 518-520, 524.

38. Quoted in Fortenbaugh, *In Order to Form a More Perfect Union*, p. 104.

39. Franklin B. Hough, *Historical Sketch of Union College* (Washington, D.C., 1876), p. 11.

40. Reprinted in Raymond, *Union University*, I, 520-521, 528-531.

41. Cf. Codman Hislop, *Eliphalet Nott* (Middletown, Conn.: Wesleyan University Press, 1971), pp. 83-91, 153-163.

42. For academy and college charter see *Documentary History of Hamilton College* (Clinton, N.Y.: The College, 1922), pp. 66-69, 106-111; the quotation is from p. 20. For background consult Walter Pilkington, *Hamilton College 1812–1962* (Clinton, N.Y.: Hamilton College, 1962), pp. 1-97.

43. William P. Cutler and Julia P. Cutler, eds., *Life, Journals, and Correspondence of Rev. Manasseh Cutler* (Cincinnati, Ohio, 1888), pp. 22-31.

44. In William E. Peters, *Legal History of the Ohio University* (Cincinnati, Ohio: Press of the Western Methodist Book Concern, 1910), pp. 92-99.

45. Ibid., pp. 99-109; also *Acts of the State of Ohio*, 1803–1804, II, 193-206.

46. See Thomas N. Hoover, *The History of Ohio University* (Athens, Ohio: Ohio University Press, 1954), pp. 99-100.

47. *Acts of the State of Ohio*, I, 66, and VII, 184-192; and see Walter Havighurst, *The Miami Years*, 1809–1969 (New York: Putnam, 1969), pp. 1-61, and James H. Rodabaugh, "History of Miami University from its Origin to 1885" (Ph.d. diss., Ohio State University, 1937), pp. 1-76.

48. Havighurst, *The Miami Years*, p. 46.

49. Rodabaugh, "History of Miami University," p. 66.

50. *Acts of the State of Ohio*, V, 64-68; Raymond Walters, *Historical*

*Sketch of the University of Cincinnati* (Cincinnati, Ohio: Mountel Press, 1940), p. 13.

51. *Acts of the State of Ohio*, XVII, 46-50; see also Reginald McGrane, *The University of Cincinnati* (New York: Harper & Row, 1963), pp. 1-13.

52. *Acts of the State of Ohio*, XVII, 154-160; see also Harvey W. Felter, *History of the Eclectic Medical Institute Cincinnati, Ohio, 1845–1902* (Cincinnati, Ohio, 1902), pp. 8-10.

## 17. Dartmouth College: The Supreme Court Speaks

1. In *The Separation of College and State* (New Haven, Conn.: Yale University Press, 1973), p. 87, John Whitehead argues that the importance of the Dartmouth College case did not lie in its legal implications as a factor in the story of the separation of college and state, but in the Dartmouth trustees' willingness to renounce the university movement generated by the Revolution and to cast aspersions on the virtue of civil government. This argument plays down or ignores the precedents of college-state conflicts that turned on the chartered rights of Yale, Columbia, the College of Philadelphia, and colleges in Virginia and Tennessee. A more comprehensive view, going beyond Whitehead's study of Columbia, Dartmouth, Harvard, and Yale, will, I believe, restore the emphasis on the legal implications of the Dartmouth case for college-state relations.

2. Wheaton (1819), 632-635.

3. *The Case of Sutton's Hospital*, 10 Co. Rep. (1612), 33a.

4. See Leon B. Richardson, *History of Dartmouth College* (Hanover, N.H.: Dartmouth College Publications, 1932), I, 287.

5. [John Wheelock], *Sketches of the History of Dartmouth College and Moor's Charity School* (1815), pp. 86-87.

6. [Elijah Parish], *A Candid, Analytical Review of the Sketches of the History of Dartmouth College* (1815), pp. 26-27.

7. On Plumer see Francis N. Stites, *Private Interest and Public Gain: The Dartmouth College Case, 1819* (Amherst, Mass.: University of Massachusetts Press, 1972), p. 24; Plumer's message to the legislature of June 6, 1816, is excerpted in Theodore R. Crane, ed., *The Colleges and the Public, 1787–1862* (New York: Teachers College, Columbia University, 1963), pp. 64-66.

8. For the report of the legislative committee see *New Hampshire Journal of the Senate* (Concord, N.H., 1816), pp. 104-107.

9. In Andrew A. Lipscomb, ed., *The Writings of Thomas Jefferson*, Monticello edition (Washington, D.C., 1904), XV, 46-47.

10. *Laws of New Hampshire, 1811–1820* (Concord, N.H., 1920), VIII, 505-508.

11. The trustee proposal is contained in an 8-page printed memorial addressed *To the Honorable the Senate and House of Representatives of the State of New Hampshire in General Court convened*, and signed by Thomas W. Thompson, Elijah Paine, and Asa M'Farland on June 19, 1816.

12. Trustee proposal, see n. 11, above.

13. 4 Wheaton (1819), 654-666; the quotation is on pp. 643-644.

14. Ibid., pp. 684, 690, 694, 695, 698, 699.

15. Timothy Farrar, *Report of the Case of the Trustees of Dartmouth College against William H. Woodward* (Portsmouth, N.H., 1819), pp. 294, 49, 153.

16. 4 Wheaton ( 1819), 651-652.

17. James Willard Hurst, *Law and the Conditions of Freedom in the Nineteenth Century United States* (Madison, Wis.: University of Wisconsin Press, 1956), p. 17.

18. Appendix A shows that of the forty-four institutions in nominal or actual operation in 1820, sixteen may be counted as "public" and nineteen as "private." The remaining nine are the colonial foundations.

19. See the tables in Donald G. Tewksbury, *The Founding of American Colleges and Universities Before the Civil War* (New York: Teachers College, Columbia University, 1932), pp. 16, 28.

20. 4 Wheaton (1819), 712.

21. Reserve clauses are contained in the 1802 charter of the American Western University, the 1809 charter of Miami University, and the 1819 charters of Cincinnati College and Worthington College. In Kentucky the 1819 charters of Centre College, Southern College, the College of Urania, and Western College carry similar clauses.

# INDEX

Academy of Sciences and the Fine Arts, Richmond, Va., 157–158
Academy of the Town of Schenectady. *See* Union College
Adams, John, 206
Addison County Grammar School. *See* Middlebury College
Albemarle Academy, 210
Alden, Timothy, 198–199
Alexander, James, 105
Alexandria College, 199
Alison, Francis, 78, 83, 86, 93, 149
Allegheny College, 198–199, 242
Allen, Ira, 223
Allen, William, 93
American Philosophical Society, 184
American University in the Province of New York, 139–141, 160, 165, 166, 169, 234
American Western University. *See* Ohio University
Amherst, Jeffrey, 137
Amherst College, 137
Andover Academy, 215
Appleton, Nathaniel, 49
Archbishop of Canterbury, 95, 108, 132, 149
Armstrong, John, 195–196
Asbury College, 201, 205
Atwater, Jeremiah, 224
Augusta Academy. *See* Liberty Hall Academy, Virginia
Ayliffe, John, 76

Backus, Azel, 228

Balch, Hezekiah, 196
Baldwin, Abraham, 154, 169–170
Baltimore College, 203, 205
Bancker, Gerard, 167
Barclay, Henry, 103, 104, 107
Beaurepaire, Quesnay de, 157–158
Belcher, Jonathan, 64, 86, 87
Bellomont, Earl of. *See* Coote, Richard
Benson, Egbert, 167
Berkeley, George, 74, 98
Berkeley, William, 29–30, 31
Bernard, Francis, 135–137
Bickerstaff, Timothy, 152
Bishop of London, 2, 29, 30, 34
Blair, James, 30–36, 94
Blount, William, 196
Blount College, 196, 197
Blythe, James, 207–208
Booster colleges, 189
Botecourt, Norborne Berkeley Baron de, 60
Bowdoin College, 213, 215–217, 242
Bracken, John, 149, 219–220
Bracken v. College of William and Mary, 219–220
Brainerd, David, 67
Bronson, Nathan, 169
Brown, John, 209
Browne, Joseph, 20
Buckingham, Thomas, 43
Buckminster, Joseph, 152
Bulkley, Gershom, 39
Bull, William, 133
Burr, Aaron, 82, 83, 85, 86, 87

Burton, Asa, 224

Cabell, Joseph C., 212
Caldwell, Joseph, 207
Calvin's Case, 39
Cambridge University, 3, 6, 9, 31, 34,
  36, 163, 176, 233
Camm, John, 55, 56, 57, 58, 59, 60, 61,
  149, 164
Carrick's Academy. *See* Blount College
Carroll, John, 201–203
Case of Sutton's Hospital, 12, 14, 78,
  115, 234
Central College, 211
Centre College, 194
Chambers, John, 105
Charterhouse Case. *See* Case of Sutton's
  Hospital
Chauncey, Charles, 13, 19
Cincinnati College, 229–230
Cincinnati University. *See* Cincinnati
  College
Clap, Thomas, 47, 98, 100, 104, 151,
  169, 174, 175, 179, 182, 241; career at
  Yale, 64, 66–81, 114–122; on re-
  ligious constitution of colleges, 74–75;
  relations with Pennsylvania Presbyter-
  ians, 83–84; struggle with Samuel
  Johnson, 103; on visitation, 115–116;
  on right of appeal, 117–118, 120–121
Cleaveland, John and Ebenezer, 68–70,
  80
Clinton, George, 167, 227
Clinton College. *See* Union College
Cokesbury College, 201, 205
Colby College, 217–218
Colden, Cadwallader, 90, 97, 139
Coleman, Benjamin, 49
College in Georgia (1764), 132
College in New Hampshire (1758), 132
College of Cambridge, South Carolina,
  199
College of Charleston, 209
College of Hampden-Sydney, 185, 192,
  222
College of Medicine of Maryland. *See*
  University of Maryland, second
College of New Jersey, 90, 97, 108, 111,
  132, 143, 185, 188, 199, 207, 209, 228,
  230; and Great Awakening, 64; found-
  ing of, 82–88; student societies at,

156; as source of Presbyterian college
  foundations, 191
College of New Orleans, 210
College of Newport, 125–127
College of Philadelphia, 63, 143, 156, 171,
  183, 221, 232, 241; founding of, 64–65;
  88–96; medical instruction in, 160–162;
  and Revolution, 176–183. *See also*
  University of Pennsylvania; University
  of the State of Pennsylvania
College of Rhode Island, 123–127, 130,
  131, 156, 188
College of South Carolina, 133–134
College of Urania, 194
College of Washington. *See* Liberty
  Hall Academy, Virginia
College of William and Mary, 48, 94,
  134, 159, 234; founding and charter of,
  1, 2, 29–37; and Two-Penny Act,
  55, 57, 60, 156; dispute between mas-
  ters and visitors, 55–61, 149, 163–164;
  and professional education, 163–164;
  and Thomas Jefferson, 184–185, 210.
  *See also* Bracken v. College of William
  and Mary
Collegiate School of Connecticut. *See*
  Yale College
Collins, John, 17
Collinson, Peter, 95
Columbia College, 167, 168–169, 222,
  232. *See also* King's College
Common law of England, 13, 14, 15,
  22, 39–40, 44
Connecticut Wits, 155
Continental Congress, 131
Cook, William, 51
Cooper, Myles, 129, 138–141, 165, 166,
  169
Coote, Richard, 23, 24
Cumberland College, 197, 222
Cutler, Manasseh, 228
Cutler, Timothy, 28, 45, 54, 72, 73,
  97, 104, 150

Daggett, Naphtali, 75, 121, 152, 155
Dana, James, 121
Danforth, Samuel, 9–10, 20
Dartmouth College, 128–131, 148,
  171–173, 214, 223, 232–243
Dartmouth College Case, 146, 206,
  232–243

Davenport, James, 66
Davenport, John, 45
Davidson Academy, 197, 222, 232, 241
Davies, Samuel, 87
Davis, Henry, 224
Dawson, Thomas, 55, 56, 57
Degrees, academic, 9–10, 21, 35,
    161–162
DeLancey, James, 105
Demographic diversity and change, 21,
    24, 25–26, 28, 63, 113
Devotion, Ebenezer, 80
Devotion, John, 122, 129
Dexter, Franklin Bowditch, 120
Dickinson, John, 195
Dickinson, Jonathan, 82, 83, 85, 86
Dickinson College, 171, 194–196, 198,
    242
Dinwiddie, Robert, 55, 56
Dixon, John, 149, 164
Douglass, William, 165
Duane, James, 167
Du Bourg, Father Louis Guillaume
    Valentin, 202
Dudley, Joseph, 11, 25, 26, 27, 28
Dudley, Paul, 26, 27, 28, 50
Dunster, Henry, 7, 9, 10, 11, 12, 13,
    17–19
Dwight, Timothy, 152, 155, 223, 224

East Tennessee College, 197
Eaton, Nathaniel, 6, 7
Eaton, Samuel, 17
Eliot, Jared, 77
Eliot, John, 39, 40, 41
Elizabeth I, 3
Ellery, William, 124–127
English grammar schools, 5, 6, 30, 35
Ewing, James, 195
Exeter College, 76

Fauquier, Francis, 55, 57, 58, 59
Federal university. See National
    university
Finley, Robert, 209
Fitch, James, 43
Flynt, Henry, 49, 50
Fontaine, James M., 59
Forster, Johann Reinhold, 158
Francis, Tench, 93
Franklin, Benjamin, 89, 90–93, 95,

158, 179, 200
Franklin, William, 112
Franklin College, Athens. See
    University of Georgia
Franklin College, Pennsylvania, 200–201,
    241
Frelinghuysen, Frederick, 156
Frelinghuysen, Theodore, 110–111, 190

Gale, Benjamin, 76–78, 119, 120, 122,
    174
Garrard, James, 193
George II, 46
Georgetown College, 202
Gordon, Thomas, 169
Gould, James, 157
Graham, Richard, 56–57
Great Awakening, 63–65, 82, 86, 88,
    97, 112, 128
Greeneville College, 196, 197
Greenwood, Isaac, 150
Gymnasium illustre or academicum, 5,
    9, 32, 159, 234

Hall, Lyman, 169
Hamilton, James, 91
Hamilton, John, 84, 86
Hamilton College, 212, 215, 228
Hamilton-Oneida Academy. See
    Hamilton College
Hampden-Sydney Academy, Tennessee,
    197
Hampden-Sydney Academy, Virginia. See
    College of Hampden-Sydney
Hardy, Sir Charles, 109
Harris, Charles W., 207
Harvard, John, 5, 6, 8
Harvard College, 36, 40, 78, 150–151,
    155–156, 215, 216, 224, 225; founding
    of, 1, 2, 5–10; charter of 1650, 10–
    16, 19; other charters and charter con-
    flicts, 19, 20–25, 25–28; two-board
    system of, 48, 150; tutor rebellion,
    49–55, 72; and Great Awakening, 63,
    64, 68; riot of 1766, 79, 155; and
    Queen's College, Massachusetts, 134–
    137; and medical education, 165, 186–
    187; as state institution, 185–187, 212–
    214. See also Dunster, Henry; Pier-
    pont, Ebenezer; Sever, Nicholas;
    Greenwood, Isaac

Havighurst, Walter, 229
Heister, Joseph, 200
Henry VIII, 3
Hoar, Leonard, 13, 19, 20
Holland, Edward, 105
Holley, Horace, 194, 208
Hollis professorships, 52, 54, 94, 150, 160, 213, 224
Holt, Chief Justice Lord, 78
Horrocks, James, 57, 58, 59, 60
Hubard, James, 56
Hurst, J. Willard, 219, 241

Ingersoll, Jared, 114

James I, 3
Jefferson, Thomas, 145, 192, 206, 209; at the College of William and Mary, 149, 164, 184–185; and Academy of Sciences and the Fine Arts, 157; on comprehensive school system, 165–166, 170, 171; and University of Virginia, 210–212; and Dartmouth College Case, 235, 236
Jefferson College, 191, 198
Johnson, Josiah, 60
Johnson, Samuel, 72, 73, 91, 97, 98, 99; at Yale College, 44; dispute with Thomas Clap, 73–74; views on toleration, 102; as president of King's College, 103–109, 138
Johnson, Sir William, 129
Johnson, William Samuel, 105, 114
Jones, Emmanuel, 56, 149, 164

Kent County School. See Washington College, Maryland
Kentucky Academy, 193
Ker, David, 207
Kimberley, Eleazar, 39, 40
King William's School. See St. John's College
King's College, Aberdeen, 32
King's College, New York, 63, 65, 132, 134; founding of, 97–110; charter of 107–108; missionary efforts of, 129, 138; as foundation for American university, 137–141, 165, 234; medical instruction at, 138, 161–162, 165; as cornerstone of state university system, 167–169
Kirkland, John Thornton, 213, 225

Kirkland, Samuel, 228
Kneeland, William, 151
Knox, John, 229
Knox, Samuel, 184

Legal education, 144, 157
Leverett, John, 25, 26, 27, 28, 46, 49–54
Lewis, John, 152
Liberty Hall Academy, North Carolina. See Queen's College, North Carolina
Liberty Hall Academy, Virginia, 191, 221–222, 232, 241
Lindsley, Philip, 190
Litchfield Law School, 157
Livingston, James, 99
Livingston, John H., 157
Livingston, Peter Van Burgh, 84
Livingston, William, 98, 99, 125, 169; author of Independent Reflector essays, 100–103; relationship with Samuel Johnson, 103–104; opposed to King's College, 104–105, 106–107; author of provincial college bill, 108–109. See also Toleration
Log college, 82, 85, 86
Luther, Martin, 3

Madison, James (1749–1812), 149
Madison, James (1750/51–1836), 212
Maine College. See Bowdoin College
Maine Literary and Theological College. See Colby College
Maine Literary and Theological Institution. See Colby College
Manning, James, 123, 124, 130
Marischal College, Aberdeen, 32, 41
Marshall, John, 146, 220, 233, 234, 237, 238, 239–240
Martin Academy. See Washington College, Tennessee
Mason, Jeremiah, 239, 240
Massachusetts General Court: as visitor of Harvard College, 12, 18, 19, 20, 22, 78; as judicial forum for questions concerning Harvard College, 27. See also Harvard College
Mather, Cotton, 27, 28
Mather, Increase, 20–25, 28, 38, 50
Mather, Samuel, 9, 10, 45
McCaule, Thomas Harris, 199

McClurg, 164
McKean, Thomas, 200
Medical Chirurgical Faculty of the State of Maryland. *See* University of Maryland, second
Medical education, 144, 156, 159, 160–165, 203–204, 217, 230
Meigs, Josiah, 209
Miami University, 229
Middlebury College, 212, 215, 223–226, 228
Mifflin, Thomas, 200
Montgomery, John, 195
Moor, Joshua, 129
Moor's Indian Charity School, 129–131 238
Morgan, John, 160–161
Morris, Lewis, 84
Morris, Richard, 167
Mt. Sion College, 199
Muhlenberg, Peter, 200
Myles, Samuel, 150

National university, 158
New Light Presbyterianism, 63, 66, 67, 76, 82–88, 97, 111, 149. *See also* Old Light Presbyterianism
Nichols, Wilson C., 211
Nicholson, Francis, 31, 32
Nicoll, Benjamin, 99
Nott, Eliphalet, 227–228
Noyes, Joseph, 66, 75, 77

Oakes, Urian, 17, 20
Ohio University, 228–229, 230
Old Light Presbyterianism, 67, 70, 71, 76, 82–88, 93. *See also* New Light Presbyterianism
Owen, Gronow, 57
Oxford University, 3, 6, 9, 31, 34, 36, 76, 163, 176, 233

Parish, Elijah, 235
Parnassus letters, 175
Partnership, 42–45, 70
Pemberton, Ebenezer, 82, 83
Pendleton, Edmund, 220
Penn, Richard, 89, 93
Penn, Thomas, 89, 93
Pennsylvanicus, 95
Peters, Richard, 95, 148

Phips, Sir William, 21
Pierpont, Ebenezer, 26, 27, 50, 70
Pierson, John, 83
Plumer, William, 235–236
Presbyterian colleges, 145–146, 190–199
Preston, William, 56
Prince, Nathan, 54, 150
Princeton. *See* College of New Jersey
Private colleges, 113, 189–205
Professorships, 94, 160. *See also* Hollis professorships
Provincial College of New York. *See* Livingston, William
Provincial colleges, 128–141, 143, 191; Harvard, 5, 15–16, 28; Yale, 67, 72, 174; College of New Jersey, 87, 111; Dickinson College, 195, 196

Quasi-corporation, 7, 15, 39, 40, 42–45, 70
Queen's College, Massachusetts, 135–137
Queen's College, New Jersey, 110–113, 143, 156, 157, 188, 189, 227
Queen's College, North Carolina, 133
Quincy, Josiah, 150

Reed, Joseph, 177, 179
Reeve, Tapping, 157
Reformation pattern of college government, 2–4, 15, 21, 25, 33, 36, 37, 54
Reformed Medical College of Ohio. *See* Worthington College
Regius professorships, 153
Richardson, John, 20
Ritzema, John, 110, 112
Robie, Thomas, 49, 50, 51, 52
Robinson, Thomas, 56, 57
Robinson, William, 57
Rogers, John, 20
Romeyn, Dirck, 227
Rowe, Jacob, 57
Ruggles, Benjamin, 77
Rush, Benjamin, 145, 158, 170–171, 195–196, 200

St. John's College, 167, 183, 201
St. Mary's College and Seminary, 202–203
Sanders, Daniel Clarke, 223–226
Saybrook Platform, 47, 75, 76
Scott, John Morin, 100, 167

Scottish universities, 32, 34, 36, 94
Seabury, Samuel, 102
Secker, Thomas, 132, 138
Sever, Nicholas, 26, 27, 49–54, 150
Sewall, Joseph, 51, 54
Sewall, Samuel, 51, 54
Shepard, Thomas, 20
Shepherd's Tent, 67, 68, 83
Sherlock, Thomas, 55, 56, 57
Shute, Samuel, 26, 27, 28, 51
Slack, Elijah, 230
Slaughter, Gabriel, 208
Smith, Jeremiah, 239, 240
Smith, John Blair, 227
Smith, Robert, 209
Smith, Samuel Stanhope, 185, 192
Smith, William (1697–1769), 84, 105,
    107, 110
Smith, William (1727–1803), 106; rela-
    tions with Franklin, 92–95; influence
    on King's College, 99, 100, 102–103; in
    Maryland, 166, 167, 183; defends his
    college before the Assembly, 178–182
Smith, William, Jr. (1728–1793), 100, 135
Smith, William Peartree, 84, 100
Society for the Propagation of the Gospel,
    97, 109, 129, 172, 223
South Carolina College, 209–210
Southern College of Kentucky, 194
Stamp Act, 133, 137
Statute of Charitable Uses of 1601, 8,
    39, 40–41
Stevens, Joseph, 49, 51
Stiles, Ezra, 79, 122, 128, 129, 145,
    170, 179, 209; at Newport, 123–127;
    as president of Yale, 154, 162–163,
    175–176
Stillingfleet, Edward, 76
Story, Joseph, 238–239, 240, 242
Strong, Nehemiah, 152, 175
Student societies, 155, 156
Syng, Philip, 89

Taylor, John (1751–1801), 156
Taylor, John (1753–1824), 220
Tennent, Gilbert, 66, 82–83, 87, 88
Tennent, William, Sr., 82, 83
Terrick, Richard, 59, 60
Theological education, 156–157, 160
Theological Seminary of the Dutch
    Reformed Church, 157

Toleration, 23, 24, 39, 100–101, 128, 140;
    equal toleration, 65, 102, 201, 224;
    toleration with preferment, 65, 103,
    111, 125, 143, 144, 150, 191, 195, 224
Toulmin, Harry, 193
Transylvania Seminary, 192–193
Transylvania University, 193–194,
    207–208
Trinity Church, 99, 103, 104, 105, 107.
    See also King's College
Trinity College, Connecticut, 212
Trinity College, Dublin, 36, 41, 139,
    234
Trumbull, Benjamin, 119–120
Trumbull, John, 155
Trustees of Dartmouth College v. Wood-
    ward. See Dartmouth College Case
Trustees of the University of North
    Carolina v. Foy and Bishop, 220–221
Trusteeship, 8, 12–13, 19, 41
Tryon, William, 133, 139
Tusculum College. See Greeneville College
Two-Penny Act. See College of William
    and Mary

Union College, 212, 215, 226–228
University of Aberdeen, 32, 99
University of Bologna, 9
University of Cincinnati. See Cincinnati
    College
University of Cologne, 2
University of Edinburgh, 32, 34, 41, 161
University of Erfurt, 2
University of Georgia, 169–170, 209
University of Halle, 158
University of Heidelberg, 2
University of Leyden, 161
University of Maryland, first, 166–167,
    184; second, 203–204
University of Nashville, 190. See also
    Cumberland College
University of New Orleans. See College
    of New Orleans
University of North Carolina, 187–188,
    207, 220–221
University of Paris, 2, 9
University of Pennsylvania, 171, 182–183.
    See also University of the State of
    Pennsylvania
University of Pittsburgh, 199
University of Prague, 2

University of the State of New York, 168–169
University of the State of Pennsylvania, 164, 179, 182, 195. *See also* University of Pennsylvania
University of Vermont, 171–173, 212, 215, 223–226
University of Vienna, 2
University of Virginia, 185, 210–212. *See also* College of William and Mary
University representation in legislatures, 3, 33–34, 41

Visitors, function of college, 12, 22, 41, 78, 115, 239

Waddel, Moses, 209
Wadsworth, Benjamin, 54
Ware, Henry, 213
Washington, Bushrod, 238
Washington, George, 221
Washington Academy. *See* Liberty Hall Academy, Virginia
Washington College, Connecticut. *See* Trinity College
Washington College, Maryland, 166–167, 183–184, 201
Washington College, Pennsylvania, 191, 198
Washington College, Tennessee, 196, 197
Waterville College. *See* Colby College
Webster, Daniel, 239
Webster, Noah, 155
Welles, Noah, 100
Welsh, James, 207
Welsteed, William, 51, 52, 54
Wentworth, Benning, 132
Wentworth, John, 129, 130
Western College of Kentucky, 194
Western University of Pennsylvania, 198–199
Wheelock, Eleazar, 128–131, 228, 232, 238, 239
Wheelock, John, 171–173, 223, 235, 236

White, John, 50
White, Stephen, 80, 114
Whitefield, George, 66, 68, 88, 90, 128, 132
Whitman, Samuel, 45
Whittelsey, Chauncey, 79, 103, 106, 107, 121
Wigglesworth, Edward, 51, 52, 54, 68
Willard, Samuel, 25
William and Mary, 1, 39
Williams, Elisha, 46–47, 70
Williams, Ephraim, 135, 214
Williams, Israel, 135–137
Williams, Samuel, 224
Williams College, 137, 212, 213, 214–215, 216, 242
Winthrop, John, 10
Wirt, William, 240
Witherspoon, John, 156
Wollstonecraft, Mary, 207
Wood, Thomas, 115
Woodbridge, Timothy, 43, 46
Woodward, Bezalell, 172
Worthington College, 230
Wright, James, 132
Wythe, George, 164

Yale, Elihu, 45, 74
Yale College, 1, 2, 28, 36, 63, 90, 221, 223, 224, 225, 232; founding of, 38–42; as trust, 40–41; charters of, 42–43, 45–47, 70–72, 116; site controversy, 43–45; and the Awakening, 64, 66–70; laws of 1745, 72; and college church, 72–75; and Clap-Gale controversy, 75–81; confrontation of 1763, 114–119; Clap's defeat, 119–122; conflicts of the 1770s, 1780, and 1790s, 151–154, 174–176, 212; student societies at, 155–156; professional education at, 162–163; influence on University of Georgia, 169–170. *See also* Clap, Thomas; Stiles, Ezra